Praise for *Tudor*

"Deeply researched but vibrantly accessible." —*Wall Street Journal*

"This fresh take on the Tudor dynasty is history at its best . . . an engaging and well-sourced account, sprinkled with provocative anecdotes that will appeal to both scholars and general readers. . . . This compelling tale is driven by three-dimensional people and relationships, and de Lisle does a fantastic job of making them feel lived and dramatic." —*Publishers Weekly*, starred

"Six centuries after they began, the Tudors are still England's most famous family. Their story is told in full in Leanda de Lisle's *Tudor*, a wonderfully fluent portrait of five generations that connects the often overlooked fifteenth-century Tudors with the more famous stuff. In bridging this divide, de Lisle brings an entirely fresh feel to the Tudor story, reminding us of the one thing the monarchs themselves wanted us to forget: the sheer improbability of their royal rule."
—*The Times* (London)

"A reliable and amply researched guide." —*Kirkus Reviews*

"De Lisle's masterful command of the facts—great and small—provides a complete and entertaining overview." —*The Guardian*

"Leanda de Lisle has the gift of reminding us that history is the story of real people; real men, real women, full of rage and ambition and lust and hope and love. The Tudors are already our most vivid dynasty, by quite a long chalk, but these pages render them more vivid still. This was an age when the game was worth the candle, when a chance remark could result in a crown or the axe. Wonderful, passionate, dangerous, fascinating stuff. I couldn't put it down."
—Julian Fellowes, creator of *Downton Abbey*

"Enjoyable, well-written . . . De Lisle examines the key events and characters that make the Tudor story interesting. . . . This is a very well-done popular history ideal for general readers." —*Booklist*

"Leanda de Lisle reveals such hidden depths in the vivid history of England's most famous dynasty." —*The American Conservative*

"Europe has produced no family saga that could match the Tudors. Rarely has that story been so well told as here." —*The Mail*

"Leanda de Lisle's accomplished survey of the 'Renaissance romance and gothic horror' of the Tudor era provides a vibrant reappraisal of this turbulent family saga . . . she introduces a different perspective. Avoiding sensationalism, she is meticulous in her use of sources. Her account confirms the Tudors as one of history's great success stories, even though their reigns were marked by bloodshed, religious upheaval and the fearful prospect of a disputed succession."
—*The Spectator*

"Absorbing. . . . In de Lisle's hands, this is a deeply human tale, a family tree come to vivid life, rather than a narrative of politics and power structures." —*The Sunday Telegraph*

"[De Lisle's] crisp, uninterfering style lets the story tell itself. Almost every page is vivid with the well-noted detail." —*The Telegraph*

"*Tudor* is a gripping account of a family riven by passionate jealousies, murderous ambitions, and crippling tragedies. Leanda de Lisle is a master storyteller, and this is her greatest work yet. Immersive and exhaustively researched, Tudor is a triumph."
—Amanda Foreman, author of *Georgiana: Duchess of Devonshire*

TUDOR

TUDOR

Passion. Manipulation. Murder.
The Story of England's
Most Notorious Royal Family

LEANDA
DE LISLE

PUBLICAFFAIRS

New York

In memory of Eric Ives

First published in Great Britain in 2013 by Chatto & Windus.
Hardcover published in 2013 in the United States by PublicAffairs™,
a Member of the Perseus Books Group
Paperback published in 2015 by PublicAffairs

PublicAffairs books are available at special discounts for bulk purchases in the U.S. by corporations,
institutions, and other organizations. For more information, please contact the Special Markets
Department at the Perseus Books Group, 2300 Chestnut Street, Suite 200, Philadelphia, PA 19103,
call (800) 810–4145, ext. 5000, or e-mail special.markets@perseusbooks.com.

Typeset in Arno Pro by Palimpsest Book Production Limited,
Falkirk, Stirlingshire

Library of Congress Control Number: 201394541
ISBN 978-1-61039-363-8 (HC)
ISBN 978-1-61039-364-5 (EB)
ISBN 978-1-61039-545-8 (PB)

10 9 8 7 6 5 4 3 2 1

Contents

Part One
THE COMING OF THE TUDORS:
A MOTHER'S LOVE

Part Two

INHERITANCE:
THE LEGACY OF ARTHUR

Part Three

SETTING SUN:
THE TUDOR QUEENS

List of Illustrations

8: Copy of *The Whitehall Mural*, George Vertue, 1737, after Hans Holbein the Younger, 1537. (Royal Collection Trust/© Her Majesty Queen Elizabeth II 2013).

9: The Family of Henry VIII – Henry, Jane Seymour, Mary, Elizabeth and Edward – British school, *c*.1545 (Royal Collection Trust/© Her Majesty Queen Elizabeth II 2013).

10a: Catherine of Aragon, unknown artist, *c*.1520 (By permission of the Archbishop of Canterbury and the Church Commissioners).

10b: Ring with a portrait of Anne Boleyn (© The Chequers Trust).

10c: Jane Seymour, Hans Holbein, 1536–7 (Kunsthistorisches Museum, Vienna).

10d: Anne of Cleves, Bartel Bruyen the Elder (The President and Fellows of St. John's College, Oxford).

10e: Portrait of a lady, perhaps Katherine Howard, Hans Holbein the Younger, *c*.1540 (Royal Collection Trust/© Her Majesty Queen Elizabeth II 2013).

10f: Catherine Parr, attributed to Master John, *c*.1545 (© National Portrait Gallery, London).

11a: Mary I, Master John, 1544 (© National Portrait Gallery, London).

11b: Elizabeth I when a Princess, attributed to William Scrots, *c*.1546 (Royal Collection Trust/© Her Majesty Queen Elizabeth II 2013).

11c: Edward VI as a Child, Hans Holkein the Younger, probably 1538 (© NGA Images, Washington, D.C.).

12a: Edward VI, attributed to William Scrots, before 1547 (Royal Collection Trust/© Her Majesty Queen Elizabeth II 2013).

12b: The Execution of Lady Jane Grey, Paul Delaroche, 1833 (© National Gallery, London).

12c: Mary I, Anthonis Mor, 1554 (© Madrid, Museo Nacional del Prado).

13a: Queen Elizabeth I, 'The Rainbow Portrait', Isaac Oliver, *c*.1600 (Hatfield House, Hertfordshire, UK/The Bridgeman Art Library).

13b: Portrait miniature of Lady Katherine Seymour, née Grey, holding her infant son, attributed to Lievine Teerlink, *c*.1562 (© Belvoir Castle, Leicestershire, UK/The Bridgeman Art Library).

14a: The Somerley portrait, originally identified as Lady Jane Grey, perhaps Margaret Douglas, *c*. 1530s (Used by permission, Somerley Estate, and J. Stephan Edwards).

14b: Tomb of Margaret Douglas, with kneeling images of her four children, Westminster Abbey, 1578 (Werner Forman Archive/The Bridgeman Art Library).

15a: Mary, Queen of Scots, Nicholas Hilliard, 1579 (Royal Collection Trust/© Her Majesty Queen Elizabeth II 2013).

15b: Henry Stuart, Lord Darnley, and his brother Charles Stuart, Earl of Lennox, Hans Eworth, 1563 (Royal Collection Trust/© Her Majesty Queen Elizabeth II 2013).

15c: James VI of Scotland, aged twenty, Falkland Palace (© National Trust for Scotland Images).

15d: Lady Arbella Stuart aged 23 months, anon, 1577 (© National Trust Images/John Hammond).

16: Genealogical chart tracing the Tudor roots of Mary, Queen of Scots, and her son James VI of Scotland and I of England *c*.1603 (Parham Park, Nr Pulborough, West Sussex, UK/Photo © Mark Fiennes/The Bridgeman Art Library).

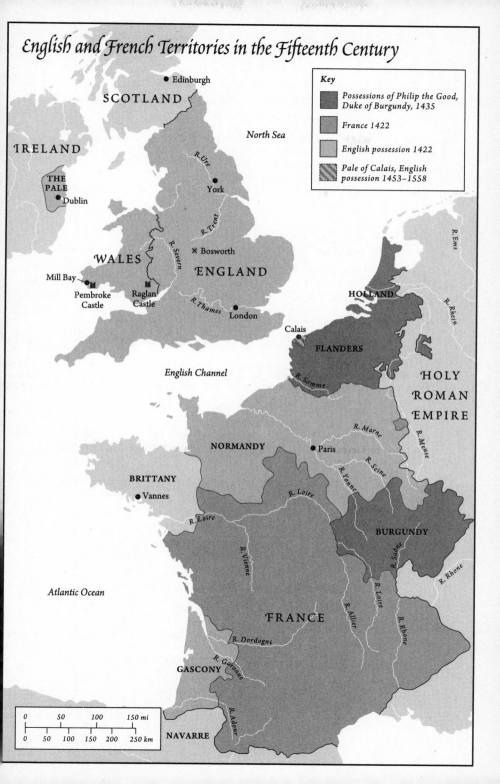

English and French Territories in the Fifteenth Century

Key

- Possessions of Philip the Good, Duke of Burgundy, 1435
- France 1422
- English possession 1422
- Pale of Calais, English possession 1453–1558

SCOTLAND

Edinburgh

North Sea

IRELAND

THE PALE

Dublin

R. Ure

York

R. Trent

WALES

R. Severn

× Bosworth

ENGLAND

Mill Bay

Pembroke Castle

Raglan Castle

R. Thames

London

HOLLAND

R. Ems

R. Rhein

Calais

FLANDERS

R. Somme

English Channel

HOLY ROMAN EMPIRE

R. Marne

NORMANDY

Paris

R. Meuse

BRITTANY

Vannes

R. Seine

R. Yonne

R. Loire

R. Loire

BURGUNDY

Atlantic Ocean

R. Vienne

R. Saône

R. Rhône

FRANCE

R. Loire

R. Allier

R. Rhône

R. Dordogne

GASCONY

R. Garonne

0   50   100   150 mi

0   50   100   150   200   250 km

R. Adour

NAVARRE

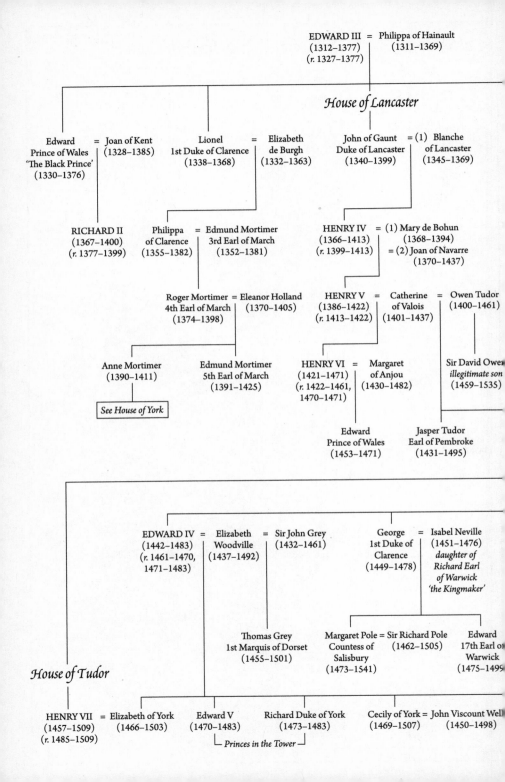

The Past: The Houses of Lancaster and York

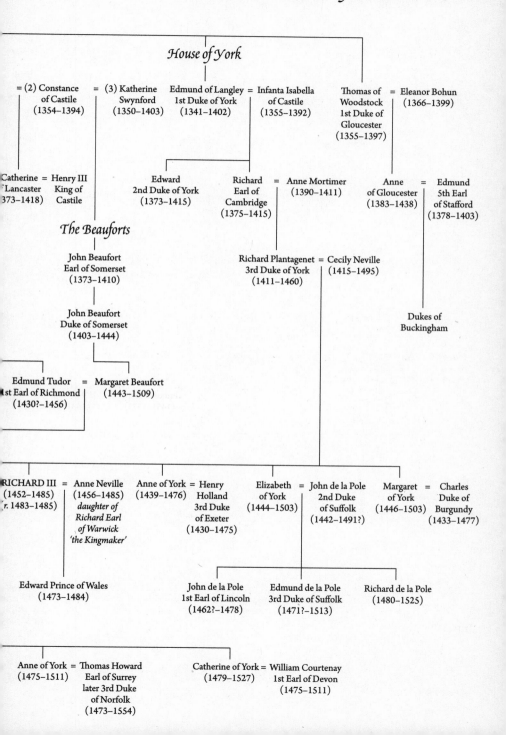

House of York

= (2) Constance
of Castile
(1354–1394)

= (3) Katherine
Swynford
(1350–1403)

Edmund of Langley
1st Duke of York
(1341–1402)

= Infanta Isabella
of Castile
(1355–1392)

Thomas of
Woodstock
1st Duke of
Gloucester
(1355–1397)

= Eleanor Bohun
(1366–1399)

Catherine
Lancaster
1373–1418)

= Henry III
King of
Castile

Edward
2nd Duke of York
(1373–1415)

Richard
Earl of
Cambridge
(1375–1415)

= Anne Mortimer
(1390–1411)

Anne
of Gloucester
(1383–1438)

= Edmund
5th Earl
of Stafford
(1378–1403)

The Beauforts

John Beaufort
Earl of Somerset
(1373–1410)

Richard Plantagenet
3rd Duke of York
(1411–1460)

= Cecily Neville
(1415–1495)

John Beaufort
Duke of Somerset
(1403–1444)

Dukes of
Buckingham

Edmund Tudor
1st Earl of Richmond
(1430?–1456)

= Margaret Beaufort
(1443–1509)

RICHARD III
(1452–1485)
r. 1483–1485)

= Anne Neville
(1456–1485)
*daughter of
Richard Earl
of Warwick
'the Kingmaker'*

Anne of York
(1439–1476)

= Henry
Holland
3rd Duke
of Exeter
(1430–1475)

Elizabeth
of York
(1444–1503)

= John de la Pole
2nd Duke
of Suffolk
(1442–1491?)

Margaret
of York
(1446–1503)

= Charles
Duke of
Burgundy
(1433–1477)

Edward Prince of Wales
(1473–1484)

John de la Pole
1st Earl of Lincoln
(1462?–1478)

Edmund de la Pole
3rd Duke of Suffolk
(1471?–1513)

Richard de la Pole
(1480–1525)

Anne of York
(1475–1511)

= Thomas Howard
Earl of Surrey
later 3rd Duke
of Norfolk
(1473–1554)

Catherine of York
(1479–1527)

= William Courtenay
1st Earl of Devon
(1475–1511)

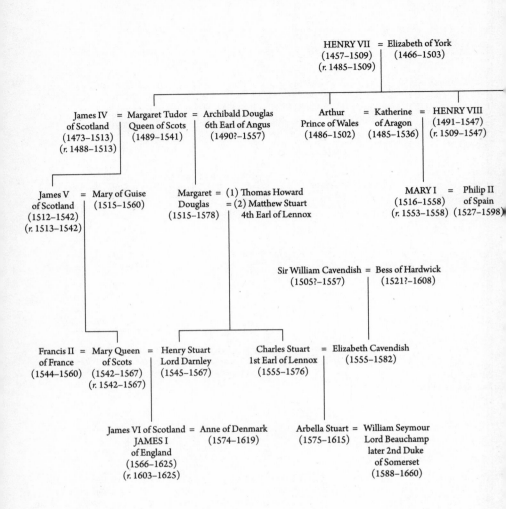

HENRY VII = Elizabeth of York
(1457–1509) | (1466–1503)
(r. 1485–1509)

James IV = Margaret Tudor = Archibald Douglas
of Scotland | Queen of Scots | 6th Earl of Angus
(1473–1513) | (1489–1541) | (1490?–1557)
(r. 1488–1513)

Arthur = Katherine = HENRY VIII
Prince of Wales | of Aragon | (1491–1547)
(1486–1502) | (1485–1536) | (r. 1509–1547)

James V = Mary of Guise
of Scotland | (1515–1560)
(1512–1542)
(r. 1513–1542)

Margaret = (1) Thomas Howard
Douglas = (2) Matthew Stuart
(1515–1578)   4th Earl of Lennox

MARY I = Philip II
(1516–1558) | of Spain
(r. 1553–1558) | (1527–1598)

Sir William Cavendish = Bess of Hardwick
(1505?–1557) | (1521?–1608)

Francis II = Mary Queen = Henry Stuart
of France | of Scots | Lord Darnley
(1544–1560) | (1542–1567) | (1545–1567)
            (r. 1542–1567)

Charles Stuart = Elizabeth Cavendish
1st Earl of Lennox | (1555–1582)
(1555–1576)

James VI of Scotland = Anne of Denmark
JAMES I | (1574–1619)
of England
(1566–1625)
(r. 1603–1625)

Arbella Stuart = William Seymour
(1575–1615) | Lord Beauchamp
later 2nd Duke
of Somerset
(1588–1660)

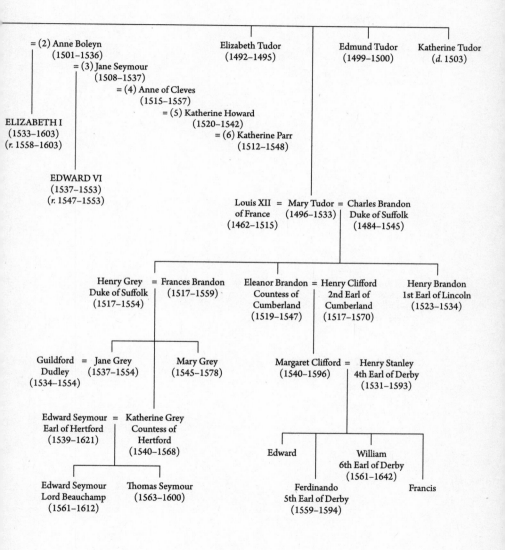

= (2) Anne Boleyn
(1501–1536)

= (3) Jane Seymour
(1508–1537)

= (4) Anne of Cleves
(1515–1557)

= (5) Katherine Howard
(1520–1542)

= (6) Katherine Parr
(1512–1548)

Elizabeth Tudor
(1492–1495)

Edmund Tudor
(1499–1500)

Katherine Tudor
(d. 1503)

ELIZABETH I
(1533–1603)
(r. 1558–1603)

EDWARD VI
(1537–1553)
(r. 1547–1553)

Louis XII = Mary Tudor = Charles Brandon
of France   (1496–1533)   Duke of Suffolk
(1462–1515)   (1484–1545)

Henry Grey = Frances Brandon
Duke of Suffolk   (1517–1559)
(1517–1554)

Eleanor Brandon = Henry Clifford
Countess of   2nd Earl of
Cumberland   Cumberland
(1519–1547)   (1517–1570)

Henry Brandon
1st Earl of Lincoln
(1523–1534)

Guildford = Jane Grey
Dudley   (1537–1554)
(1534–1554)

Mary Grey
(1545–1578)

Margaret Clifford = Henry Stanley
(1540–1596)   4th Earl of Derby
                    (1531–1593)

Edward Seymour = Katherine Grey
Earl of Hertford   Countess of
(1539–1621)   Hertford
                   (1540–1568)

Edward

William
6th Earl of Derby
(1561–1642)

Edward Seymour
Lord Beauchamp
(1561–1612)

Thomas Seymour
(1563–1600)

Ferdinando
5th Earl of Derby
(1559–1594)

Francis

Introduction

For God's sake, let us sit upon the ground
And tell sad stories of the death of kings;
How some have been deposed; some slain in war,
Some haunted by the ghosts they have deposed.

WILLIAM SHAKESPEARE,
RICHARD II ACT 3, SCENE 2

In fifteenth-century France it was believed that the English bore the mark of Cain for their habit of killing their kings.[1] Before the slaughter of Richard III in 1485, when the Tudor crown was won on the battlefield of Bosworth, a series of English kings had been deposed and then died or disappeared in mysterious circumstances that century. The overthrow of the first of these, Richard II, in 1399, had brought a long-standing element of instability to the monarchy.

At that time, the paternal ancestors of the Tudors were modest land-owners in north Wales – and even this status was lost the following year. In 1400 they joined a Welsh rebellion against Richard II's heir, the usurper Henry IV, first king of the House of Lancaster. The family was ruined after the rebellion was crushed, but eventually a child of the youngest son left Wales with his son to seek a better life in England. It was this man, Owen Tudor, who was to give the Tudor dynasty its name.

Looking back, Owen's life is that of a modern-day hero: a common man who lived against convention, often thumbed his nose at authority, and died, bravely, with a joke on his lips. Owen, however, is lost to the family story in histories of the Tudors that so often begin at Bosworth in 1485. So is the remarkable life of Owen's daughter-in-law, Lady Margaret Beaufort, whose descent from the House of Lancaster provided the basis for her son Henry Tudor's royal claim. Indeed his reign, as Henry VII, rarely merits more than a chapter or two before these Tudor histories propel us towards Henry VIII and the 'divorce' from Katherine of Aragon. Written by the children of the Reformation, the Reformation has become where the story of the 'real' Tudors begins; but the Tudors were the children of an earlier period, and their preoccupations and myths were rooted in that past.

The famous mystery of the disappearance of the princes in the Tower in 1483, which turned Henry Tudor from a helpless exile into Richard III's rival overnight, becomes less mysterious when it is considered in the light of the culture and beliefs of the fifteenth century; the life of Margaret Beaufort also emerges in a more sympathetic light once we have recalibrated our perspective, and the actions of Henry VIII and his children can likewise be much better understood. England was not predominantly Protestant until very late in the Tudor period, and habits of thought were still shaped by England's long, and recent, Catholic past. Similarly, while the Tudors are often recalled in terms of a historical enmity with Spain, this too is history written with hindsight: the Armada did not take place until a generation after Elizabeth became queen. It was memories of the Hundred Years War with France that remained strong, and although the war that began with Edward III laying claim to the French throne had ended in 1453, over thirty years before Bosworth, it was to have a lasting impact on England's political character.

The English had not needed French land, as the country was underpopulated after the Black Death. Successive English kings had been obliged to persuade their subjects to come into partnership with them to help achieve their ambitions for the French throne. The result was that in England military service was offered, not assumed, and royal revenue was a matter of negotiation, not of taxation imposed on the realm. English kings were, in practical terms, dependent on obedience freely given, and that had to be earned. They had certain duties, such as ensuring peace, prosperity, harmony and justice (if a crown was taken from an expected heir or an incumbent monarch, the perceived ability to restore harmony within the kingdom was particularly important) and kings were also supposed to maintain, or even increase, their landed inheritance. England's empire in France had reached its zenith under Henry IV's son, Henry V, and his son Henry VI was crowned as a boy King of France as well as England. But then he lost the empire he had inherited. The humiliation of the final defeat at French hands in 1453 was not something England had recovered from even a century later, which is why the Tudors were devastated by the loss of Calais. It was the last remnant of a once great empire.

In England the loss of France in 1453 was followed by eighteen years of sporadic but violent struggle as the rival royal House of York fought for supremacy over Henry VI and the House of Lancaster. This was the period into which the first Tudor king, Henry VII, was born. It was still remembered in the reign of his grandson with horror as a time when 'the nobles as well as the common people were into two parts divided, to the destruction of many a man, and to the great ruin and decay of this region'.[2] It was the promise of peace, and the healing of old wounds, that was the *raison d'être* of the Tudor dynasty. The Pope himself praised Henry's marriage to Elizabeth of York in 1486 as marking the conciliation of the royal houses. This was symbolised in the union rose of red (for Henry VII and Lancaster) and white (for York). Although Henry VII denied he owed any of his royal right to his marriage and faced further opposition from within the House of York, the union rose became an immensely popular image with artists and poets in the sixteenth century.

The key importance of the royal lines of Lancaster and York that stretched back long before Henry VII, and which had nothing to do with his non-royal Tudor ancestors, has inspired the recent assertion that the Tudor kings and queens did not see themselves as Tudors at all, but as individual monarchs sprung from the ancient royal house, and that the use of terms such as 'the Tudor age' only creates a false separation from a hypothetical Middle Ages.[3] This is an important reminder that the Tudors did not exist in a time bubble, yet it is not the full story. It was well understood in 1603 that the Stuarts were a break from the family which had preceded them, and if Henry VII and his descendants did not see themselves exactly as a dynasty – a term not then used to describe an English royal line – they had a palpable sense of family.[4] It is there in Henry VII's tomb in the Lady Chapel at Westminster Abbey, where he lies with his mother, his wife and three crowned Tudor grandchildren; it is also there in the Holbein mural commissioned by Henry VIII of the king with his parents and his son's late mother. The Tudors believed they were building on the past to create something different – and better – even if they differed on how.

The struggle of Henry VII and his heirs to secure the line of succession, and the hopes, loves and losses of the claimants – which dominated and shaped the history of the Tudor family and their times – are the focus of this book. The universal appeal of the Tudors also lies in the family stories: of a mother's love for her son, of the husband who kills his wives, of siblings who betray one another, of reckless love affairs, of rival cousins, of an old spinster whose heirs hope to hurry her to her end. 'I am Richard II,' as the last of the Tudors joked bitterly, 'know ye not that?'[5]

Part One

THE COMING OF THE TUDORS: A MOTHER'S LOVE

Henry Tudor, son of Edmund Tudor, son of Owen Tudor, who of his ambitious and insatiable covertise encroaches and usurps upon him the name and title of royal estate of this Realm of England whereunto he has no manner, interest, right, title or colour, as every man well knows.

RICHARD III PROCLAMATION, 23 JUNE 1485

1

AN ORDINARY MAN

ON 8 FEBRUARY 1437 A ROYAL FUNERAL PROCESSION WOUND through the streets of London. At its heart was a hearse pulled by horses and bearing a queen's coffin. It was draped with red cloth of gold stitched with golden flowers. On top lay her effigy carved in wood and dressed in a mantle of purple satin.[1] The head, resting on a velvet cushion, bore a crown of silver gilt, while the face was painted to look as the lovely Catherine of Valois had in life, the eyes blue and the lips red. Real light-brown hair was dressed above delicately carved ears, and the arms, crossing the body, embraced a sceptre, the insignia of her royal rank.

At Westminster the coffin was carried into the abbey under a canopy of black velvet hung with bells that tinkled as it moved.[2] Following a requiem Mass, Catherine was buried in the Lady Chapel, so called because it was dedicated to the Virgin Mary. Her tomb had been built close to that of her first husband, Henry V, the great victor of Agincourt. His successes would be remembered in song and tales of chivalric romance for generations. In 1420, as conqueror of France, he had been recognised as heir to Catherine's father, the French king Charles VI, with their marriage sealing the treaty and the union of the crowns. But though it proved happy, their marriage was as short-lived as the peace. Catherine of Valois had been Queen of England for only eighteen months when Henry V died on campaign in France, leaving her a widow aged twenty, with their son, Henry VI, a mere eight months old.

As Catherine's coffin was lowered into the ground, Henry V's tomb effigy, with its silver head and armoured with silver plates, glinted in the candlelight.[3] There was nothing in this scene, however, to suggest Catherine had left behind a grieving widower, and if her second husband witnessed her funeral it was only as a face in the crowd.

It is not certain when, or how, the queen had met the modest Welsh squire Owen Tudor. What information we have suggests he had found a position in Catherine's household as a chamber servant in about 1427.[4] The widowed queen was then twenty-six, and her son, aged six, was considered old enough to be raised by men in the masculine business of rule. Since she was no longer required full time at court a new household was being set up for her.

Owen's grandfather had been ruined after taking part in a Welsh rebellion against Henry V's father, Henry IV, in 1400, and he was seeking a new life in England. Owen's Welsh name, Owain ap Maredudd ap Tudur, meant 'Owen son of Meredith son of Tudor', but that was too much of a mouthful for the English so he had become simply Owen Tudor. If the attempts to anglicise it had gone differently we might have had a dynasty of Merediths – not that it had seemed very likely that Owen would spawn a dynasty at all. He was, however, about to marry very well indeed.

Catherine was lonely, and resentful that the council Henry V had appointed to rule during his son's minority had forbidden her from remarrying. She was expected to wait at least until Henry VI had reached his majority and could approve a match. This was backed with an Act of Parliament that threatened to confiscate the lands of any great man who ignored the injunction.[5] It never occurred to anyone that Catherine might instead marry a mere chamber servant. Later some wondered if Catherine chose to marry Owen specifically because he was 'a poor man' who posed no threat to the king or his nobles, and so the council 'might not reasonably take vengeance on his life'.[6] But Owen also appealed to Catherine in a more straightforward way. Although the early Tudor historian Polydore Vergil claimed Owen was 'adorned with wonderful gifts of body and mind', we hear little about his mind from anyone else.[7] Other reports point exclusively to his physical attractions. One account describes how the queen fell in love with Owen after coming upon him swimming naked[8]. But the most repeated story, and the one most likely to have some basis in fact, describes how Owen came to her attention in dramatic fashion during a party in her household[9]. There was music playing, and her servants were dancing. While Catherine watched, Owen performed a leap which span out of control, and he fell straight into her lap. As an Elizabethan poet asked, 'Who would not judge it fortune's greatest grace, Since he must fall, to fall in such a place?'[10] It was not long before Catherine and her handsome chamber servant were married and, according to a rather disapproving sixteenth-century account, when they made love she would scream in ecstasy.

Catherine and Owen had their first child, a boy called Edmund, in about 1430.[11] A second son, named Jasper, soon followed and within seven years the couple are reputed to have had four children. This could not easily have been hidden from the council. As a seventeenth-century historian observed, 'it is not to be supposed the court could be hoodwinked in four great bellies'.[12] Indeed, since no doubt was ever expressed that the children were legitimate, it is likely they knew of the marriage before Edmund was born. But the council had decided the marriage should remain outside the public domain until Henry VI was old enough to decide what to do about it. Meanwhile, if the marriage was accepted as fact, it was not welcomed.

Female virtue was closely associated with the ability to control powerful sexual urges (women being more prone to lust than men).[13] That a Queen of England had 'proved unable to control her carnal passions', and with 'no man of birth neither of livelihood', was deeply shocking.[14] Catherine tried to defend herself by insisting that although Owen's Welsh family did not speak any language she knew, they were 'the goodliest dumb creatures that ever she saw'.[15] Appearance as well as behaviour mattered during the fifteenth century, and she was convinced Owen's handsome family must be of noble origin.[16] But as Sir John Wynn of Gwydir observed acidly, 'Queen Catherine being a French woman' failed to understand that there were considered to be racial differences between the English and the Welsh, and that Owen's 'kindred and country were objected to . . . as most vile and barbarous'.[17]

The couple had lived quietly near London, away from the disapproving eyes of the court, until 1436. Catherine, 'long vexed', as she complained, with a 'grievous malady', had then retired to Bermondsey Abbey, Southwark, where she died on 3 January 1437.[18] Henry VI, a precocious but prim adolescent of fifteen, now had to be told in short order that his mother was dead, that she had married a commoner, and that he had four half-siblings bearing the strange name of 'Tudor'. Owen was understandably nervous about how he might react. For a commoner to have married a Queen of England was unprecedented. It was possibly also punishable by imprisonment or worse, and fleeing back to north Wales seemed his best option. The children, Owen could be sure, would be well looked after. Whatever the shame of their Tudor name, they were the king's half-brothers and sisters.

Owen packed all his best goods: gilt cups, chalices, enamelled salts, silver ewers, candlesticks and flagons, many of them gifts from the queen, and some of them breaking in his frantic hurry to leave for his homeland.[19] But as Owen rode west the king's messenger was already in pursuit. With Owen's baggage slowing his horses, the messenger caught up with him at Daventry in Northamptonshire, where Owen was handed a summons to the royal palace in Westminster. Owen demanded he be first given a written promise of free passage, guaranteeing he could leave London afterwards. Only when he received it did he turn his horses around.

The borough of Westminster was the heart of political and legal business in England, and had for centuries been distinct from the rest of London, with its focus on trade. Dominated by the royal palace and its neighbouring abbey, it had a resident population of around 3,000 and lay under the jurisdiction of the abbot, rather than London's mayor. The neighbouring areas were, however, beginning to grow together both socially and economically. It was not untypical to live in London and be rowed daily to Westminster for work. One clerk recalled later how he used to spend his days hunched over parchment in Westminster and his nights taking out girls, drinking and kissing, before being rowed home alone (and deeply frustrated) to the Strand.[20] Owen had good friends here, and one warned him the council had been stoking the young king's anger. Again Owen's instinct was to make a bolt for it, this time for the sanctuary of Westminster Abbey.

Anyone could claim sanctuary from the authorities in a church, and at Westminster sanctuary also covered a large area behind the abbey's precinct wall. Here Owen could hide out amongst a hive of criminals, men fleeing their creditors, and the packed stalls of shopkeepers selling unregulated goods. After several days he was still 'eschewing to come out thereof', despite the fact that 'divers persons stirred him of friendship and fellowship to have come out'.[21] Owen could even have been amongst the crowd that watched Catherine's funeral in February and afterwards seen her effigy, displayed standing in a niche like those of female saints, five feet four inches tall, dressed in royal robes over a red painted shift[22]. Eventually, however, Owen was persuaded that he was only making matters worse for himself and so he left for the palace, pushing his way through the throngs of poor awaiting alms from the monks at the abbey gates, and down the muddy street.

Inside the neighbouring Palace of Westminster Owen found himself in the enormous space of the Great Hall with the splendid hammer-beam roof commissioned by Richard II. It had been completed only after Richard had resigned the throne in 1399, accused by his cousin and heir, Henry Bolingbroke, of leaving the realm 'in point to be undone for default of governance and undoing of the good laws'.[23] He had never got to see it, while Bolingbroke had celebrated his coronation feast here as Henry IV: the king who had destroyed Owen's family after the great Welsh rebellion of the following year. It was strange that it was to Henry IV's grandson, Henry VI, that Owen was, awkwardly, stepfather.

Henry VI's councillors were awaiting Owen in a chamber situated along the east wall of the hall. Now that the king had reached his majority they acted as his principal advisers. As Owen stood before them he argued 'that he had nothing done that should give the king occasion or matter of offence or displeasure against him'.[24] From their perspective, however, he had broken a strict social code in marrying so far above his rank. It was only because Owen had his promise of safe conduct that he was permitted to return to Wales. There he was soon arrested on a trumped-up charge of failing to keep to the rules under which the promise had been issued: a neat riposte to his gall in having asked for it.

From having been the husband of a queen, Owen found himself a common prisoner at Newgate in London. The 300-year-old gates that formed the prison had recently been restored and rebuilt. Owen could drink fresh water from newly laid pipes and eat in an airy central hall.[25] There were terrible dungeons where prisoners were kept chained to the walls, but Owen was allowed a servant, access to his own chaplain, and he was locked in some of the better rooms. These all had privies and chimneys, while those in the turrets also had access to the roof and fresh air. Nevertheless Owen resented his loss of freedom, and the prison food at Newgate was not only disgusting, but like all prisoners he was obliged to buy it at the inflated prices set by the prison staff.[26]

By early February 1438 Owen had had enough and planned to break out of Newgate, along with his chaplain and his servant. They attacked the guard who fought hard to prevent the escape, knowing he would be fined for losing Owen. But the escapees fought harder, and after they had fled it took weeks for the council to track Owen down and capture him. He was imprisoned once again, this time in Windsor, and accused of 'hurting foul his keeper' at Newgate. Had Owen angered a different king that might have been the end of him, but Henry VI proved merciful and the following year Owen was pardoned. His charm and loyalty stood him in good stead thereafter, and by 1444 Henry VI was even referring to him as 'our well beloved squire'.

Owen's and Catherine's children, meanwhile, had been taken into the king's protection and were being educated at Barking Abbey. The sixteenth-century chronicler Edward Hall claims that the youngest two, Owen and Catherine, would subsequently join the church with Owen becoming a monk at Westminster Abbey and Katherine Tudor a nun, possibly at Barking.[27] The elder two sons, Edmund and Jasper, had, however, been groomed for life at court, where they had arrived as early as 1442 when Edmund was about twelve. They found their half-brother the king, aged twenty, a tall, slender, baby-faced neurotic.[28] He had inherited the crowns of France and England before he was even a year old and had never known a superior or equal. Unsurprisingly he was profoundly conscious of his regal dignity, and as such he was determined there would be no further unsanctioned marriages within his family. He personally protected Edmund and Jasper from sexual temptation, keeping 'careful watch through hidden windows of his chamber, lest any foolish impertinence of woman coming into the house should grow to a head'.[29] By 1453, when they were in their early twenties, Henry VI had even come to regard them as potentially useful allies. That winter, he created Edmund Earl of Richmond, and Jasper Earl of Pembroke, giving them precedence over all other magnates, excepting dukes.[30] He also had a bride of royal blood in mind for Edmund: his cousin, Margaret Beaufort.[31] It was to be a marriage with consequences their father Owen could never have imagined.

2

A CHILD BRIDE

HENRY VI'S COUSIN, MARGARET BEAUFORT, WAS NINE YEARS OLD when her mother received a royal summons to bring her to London, and wait on the king's command. Her father, John Beaufort, Duke of Somerset, had died when she was an infant.[1] She had been his only child but she nevertheless enjoyed the warmth of a large family of half-brothers and sisters as well as step-siblings. She would always remain devoted to her extended family, and it was a much-loved girl that was about to take her first steps on the national stage.[2]

Courtiers who came to London regularly all had their usual haunts. Some stayed at taverns in Westminster, while many of the great lords had their own 'inns': sprawling buildings built around courts in which they could also house their followers. Margaret's mother had a tower house called Le Ryall on the site of what is now the College of Arms in the City of London. It was here that mother and daughter awaited the royal summons.[3]

Margaret was aware she had been invited to court because the king 'did make means for Edmund [Tudor], his [half] brother' to marry her. It would be some years, however, before she could understand the full background to his decision. Margaret Beaufort was, like the king, descended from John of Gaunt, the father of Henry IV and founder of the House of Lancaster.[4] The significant difference was that the Beaufort line was of illegitimate descent, having sprung from

Gaunt's relationship with his mistress, Katherine Swynford, and so they had no right to the throne.[5] Nevertheless a marriage to Margaret Beaufort meant Edmund Tudor would gain the power that came with wealth. Margaret was a great heiress, with a Beaufort inheritance estimated at £1,000 a year.[6] Still more significantly, the Franco-Welsh Edmund could have children of English royal blood and this would bolster the House of Lancaster, which was badly needed.

Henry VI as yet had no children while his cousin and heir, the wiry, dark-haired Richard Plantagenet, Duke of York, was already the father of several sons. The House of York thus represented the future and that posed a possible threat to the king. As the last Tudor, Queen Elizabeth I, would observe: 'more men worship the rising than the setting sun'.

There was just one small difficulty for the king's plans. Margaret had been promised, aged six, to the son of a leading councillor.[7] Happily, such youthful betrothals only became binding when a girl was twelve, and Margaret had been invited to court to repudiate hers in a public ceremony.

Margaret's summons arrived during the period of feasting enjoyed in the run-up to Ash Wednesday and she was at court by 14 February.[8] The royal household was divided into two main areas: below stairs, concerned with practical daily necessities such as food and drink, under the Lord Steward, and, secondly, the king's apartment or chamber, under the Lord Chamberlain, whose department staged public ceremonies and provided the king's private service. There was meaning as well as practical consequences in who could, and who could not, approach the monarch. 'What is the belly or where is the womb of this great public body of England but that and there where the king is himself, his court and his council?' declared one bishop of the period.[9] For some there was the enormous importance of being able to counsel the sacred representative of God. But for Margaret even seeing the king would feel like a blessing, and Henry VI made a significant impression on the young girl.

Now aged thirty-one, Henry VI was pious and scholarly, with an elegance and otherworldliness that only added to his regal presence. Henry would greet visiting envoys standing by his throne, dressed in wonderful rich robes that fell to the ground. Beauty and bounty reflected the divine, with the king having 'a prerogative in his array above all others, whereby his dignity is worshipped'.[10] Henry's queen, the twenty-two-year-old Margaret of Anjou, 'a most handsome woman, though somewhat dark', set the high standards for the ladies of the court with her jewellery and fine clothes.[11] Margaret Beaufort would be provided with a hundred marks for silks and velvets in order that she too might meet them.[12]

Looking back in her old age Margaret remembered a different scenario to that with which, in reality, she was presented as a powerless girl of nine. She convinced herself she had been offered a choice between her two possible grooms. 'Doubtful in her mind what she were best to do', she recalled turning for advice to an 'old gentlewoman whom she much loved and trusted'. The woman suggested she pray to St Nicholas, the patron saint of unmarried girls.[13] Margaret duly prayed to him that night, and while she was half asleep St Nicholas had appeared to her, 'arrayed like a bishop'. He named Edmund Tudor as the better choice and that, she later believed, was why she chose him the next day.[14] It helped reassure her, as well as others, that the marriage and everything that followed was God's plan – and that it was one in which she had a dynamic role.[15]

In March the king granted the Tudor brothers Margaret's wardship, clearing the way for Edmund to marry her when she reached the age of twelve. The following month, with Margaret still at court for the Garter ceremony, the remarkable news was announced that, after eight years of disappointment, the queen was pregnant. A son and heir for the king was a cause for national rejoicing. But it was quickly overshadowed by events in France, with repercussions that would directly affect the newly betrothed Margaret and Edmund and change the course of their future.

What became known as the Hundred Years War had begun when Henry VI's great-great-grandfather, Edward III, had laid claim to the French throne. The rules of inheritance concerning the English and French crowns were not straightforward. Ideally they followed the rules of male primogeniture, but if there was no legitimate son it was uncertain whether a king's daughter could transmit her rights to a son, or whether the crown had to pass entirely through the male line. Edward III had decided to claim the French crown through his mother, the daughter of the last king of the Capetian dynasty.[16] The French nobility asserted against this that under ancient 'Salic' law no right to the throne could pass through a woman, and had instead backed the House of Valois.

Henry V's victories against the Valois led to the Treaty of Troyes in 1420, under the terms of which Henry VI had inherited the French crown of his maternal grandfather, Charles VI. Many French accepted his rule, either because they acknowledged the historic claims of the English kings to France, or because it brought them a greater measure of political stability. But others, most of whom lived south of the river Loire, saw the treaty as a betrayal of the rights of Charles VI's son the dauphin. These two French nations had since been pitted against each other in a series of military confrontations, which ended in July 1453 in a final defeat for Henry VI at Castillon, on the Dordogne river. An English-ruled French nation, which had once extended across the whole of northern France, as well as Gascony, was reduced to a small area around Calais known as the Pale. The humiliation was terrible and Henry VI fell into a state of mental collapse.

The king at first suffered a sudden 'frenzy', after which he could neither move, nor speak. His 'wit and reason withdrawn', he had to be spoon-fed to keep him alive. These symptoms indicate a severe form of depression, but it has also been suggested that he was suffering from catatonic schizophrenia, or even porphyria. It is possible he had inherited a disposition to mental illness through his mother.[17] Her father, Charles VI, had suffered periods of madness for the last thirty years of his life, and believed for a time that he was made of glass. When Henry VI's son was born in October, Henry was incapable even of acknowledging him.[18] In this desperate situation his cousin, Richard Plantagenet, Duke of York, was made Protector, a role that encompassed the protection of the physical person of the monarch, as well as of the realm. It proved to be a role he was reluctant to give up as the king's faculties returned.

The Duke of York had long claimed to stand for good government in opposition to the king's preferred councillors – and he did not want to see them back. On 22 May 1455, nine days before Margaret Beaufort's crucial twelfth birthday, thousands of York's retainers attacked the king and his accompanying force in the streets of St Albans, twenty-two miles north of London. The local abbot saw one man fall 'with his brains dashed out, there another with a broken arm, a third with a throat cut and a fourth with a pierced chest'.[19] The killing ended with the king grazed by an arrow, and surrounded by the bodies of his noble servants and knights. The period which the nineteenth-century novelist Sir Walter Scott romantically but inaccurately termed the 'Wars of the Roses' had begun.[20]

The simple five-petal design of the heraldic rose was inspired by the wild dog rose that grows in English hedgerows. As a symbol it had a long association with the Virgin Mary, who is sometimes called the 'Mystical Rose of Heaven'. But although the king's grandfather, Henry IV, had once used red roses to decorate his pavilion at a joust, their use as a Lancastrian royal badge was not widespread before the advent of the Tudors.[21] Equally, the white rose had yet to be associated strongly with the House of York.[22] Lancastrian supporters sometimes even boasted white-rose badges.[23] Whatever the origin of the term Wars of the Roses, however, the coming succession of battles between royal cousins would prove to be bloody and real enough.

When Margaret turned twelve it was decided she should marry Edmund Tudor without delay, before the Duke of York could intervene. While it was usual for young brides to stay with their parents or guardians until they were physically mature – in their mid-teens, at least – Margaret would not be returned home after her wedding. Instead she discovered she was also to leave England with Edmund. He was under orders to consolidate royal power in the unsettled regions of north and south Wales and he had to consummate their marriage for it to be irrevocably valid. If she became pregnant it would also guarantee he received the income from her estates.

The belief that children were more 'mature' then than they are today is misplaced. In physical terms they were far less so. This placed Margaret in great danger at childbirth. Nevertheless, by late August of the following year she was three months pregnant. Little good it did Edmund Tudor, captured that same month by a supporter of the Duke of York. Although released from Carmarthen Castle only a few weeks later, his health had suffered and he proved insufficiently strong to fight off the plague that was sweeping the town. The Welsh poet Llywelyn Fychan, lamenting the death of his four daughters killed by plague a century earlier, noted pustules like 'brittle coal fragments' scattered over their bodies.[24] There had been regular epidemics over the previous decade, but Margaret was still appalled by her husband's death on 1 November.[25] For the rest of her life she would keep books describing the best means of protection from the disease.

Having given Edmund a hurried burial in front of the high altar at the Greyfriars in Carmarthen, Margaret now had to consider what to do next.[26] Thirteen years old, pregnant and alone in a remote region of Wales, she would surely have liked to return home. But icy rains could turn the roads to mud in hours and with her baby due in less than two months, she was in no state to travel to her mother in the Midlands. Instead, as soon as she was able, Margaret began making her way to Pembroke Castle, held by her brother-in-law and guardian, Jasper Tudor. Margaret was terrified that the plague which had killed Edmund would follow her.[27] Happily it did not. She found safety within the castle's massive walls, where Jasper joined her as soon as he had permission to leave the king's side.

In January, when Margaret's pregnancy entered its last weeks, she withdrew into a tower room overlooking the river. This was the traditional period of confinement, in which the expectant mother rested before her labour. When it came the pain was terrifying. As her later friend and confessor John Fisher, the Bishop of Rochester, recalled, Margaret was never 'a woman of great stature' and 'she was so much smaller at that stage'. The birth of her son on 28 January 1457 left her immature body so damaged that she would never be able to bear another child. He was given a Lancastrian rather than a Tudor name, the same name as her cousin the king: Henry.[28]

Just over a month after Margaret had delivered her baby Jasper travelled with her to meet Humphrey Stafford, Duke of Buckingham, in Gwent. It was less than two years since the Battle of St Albans and already a second marriage was to be arranged for her. Buckingham had a reputation for having an ungovernable temper. Famously he had tried to stab the French rebel leader Joan of Arc during an interrogation in 1431. But he was the only man in England whose power matched that of the Duke of York, and his second son, Henry Stafford, was free to marry. An agreement between Jasper and Buckingham was soon thrashed out. Although the Staffords were not descendants of the Lancastrian house, they were of royal blood, as descendants of John of Gaunt's youngest brother Thomas of Woodstock.[29] Margaret's marriage to Stafford, sealed when her son was a year old in January 1458, thus had a political dimension, yet it was also to prove happy.

Sir Henry Stafford became devoted to his young wife. A friend later recalled that Margaret was 'of singular easiness to be spoken unto'. She was the kind of woman who never forgot a kindness, or a service done for her. She was intellectually curious, read extensively, and worked hard at managing her estates, which she did with great efficiency. She found she had an excellent 'holding memory' for those things, 'of weight and substance wherein she might profit', as well as great deter-mination. Her friend later observed that she would not let a positive opportunity pass her by, 'for any pain or labour'.[30]

Margaret's wealth ensured that the family were able to live on the grandest scale, and as the fifteenth-century *Noble Babees Noble Book* reminded children, magnificence was a matter of noble duty. Fine clothes and great feasts were not a matter of personal indulgence but intended to advertise the degree to which a noble was willing to help their 'dependers', the families that looked to them for protection and advancement. Indeed nobles were expected to recall Christ's example of self-sacrifice. Margaret loved to entertain lavishly, but however many dishes she served at her table she always ate and drank moderately. She also liked 'to be joyous' and 'to hear those tales that were honest to make her merry', but after joking for a while, she would have a reading from the life of Christ, and then move the conversation on to more serious and spiritual matters.[31] As Margaret got older and more pious, she would even occasionally wear haircloth beneath her rich clothes, as a reminder of Christ's suffering for men and of her duties.

For Margaret, as for many other members of the nobility, Christ was often physically present in her house. It was usual to hear Mass daily, as she did in her private chapels, and in Catholic belief, at the moment of consecration the bread and wine is trans-formed into the actual body and blood of Christ – the miracle known as transubstantiation. If Christ's presence felt immediate, the Devil unfortunately also seemed close at hand. It was said the Devil had once been a high-ranking angel, but when God revealed that His son, Christ, was to be born a man, the Devil in his pride could not tolerate having a mere human raised above him. He had rebelled against God and now sought to destroy all peace and harmony.[32] People had a visceral fear of the violence the Devil sought by exploiting mens' weaknesses. Yet such conflict was coming to England soon enough.

After the bloodshed at St Albans in 1455 Henry VI had worked hard to reconcile his quarrelling subjects. It was the desire for vengeance that meant in the end he failed. As one chronicler recorded, 'there was evermore a grouch and wrath had by the heirs of them that were slain'.[33] It sapped the will of the supporters of the king's chosen councillors, and of their Yorkist enemies, to keep the peace. This in turn affected all those 'dependers' who were expected to offer service in battle for their masters if called on to do so. The century of war with France meant all boys were trained from childhood to fight 'up and down the streets clashing on their shields with blunted swords or stout staves', and even the girls were expert archers.[34] An army could be raised quickly.

The blue-eyed three-year-old Henry Tudor lost his step-grandfather, the Duke of Buckingham, at the Battle of Northampton in July 1460; over the following months the killing would continue to sweep around him like a tornado, spiralling with all the peculiar viciousness of a family vendetta.

3

A PRISONER, HONOURABLY BROUGHT UP

A PAPER CROWN CLUNG, FLUTTERING, ON ONE OF A ROW OF HEADS impaled on the southern gate to the City of York. Until September 1460 the fighting had been about whom Henry VI should have as his councillors, but then the Duke of York had claimed the throne, arguing he had the senior descent in the female line from Edward III, making his ancestor, Roger Mortimer, Richard II's rightful heir, and the House of Lancaster usurpers.[1] It was an unpopular move, soon abandoned, and now God had given his judgement on it. The duke was dead, killed at the Battle of Wakefield on 30 December. 'York could look upon York' the Lancastrians jeered as they spiked his head high on the gate, the paper crown mocking his former ambitions. Next to it was the head of one of his younger sons, aged seventeen, and that of his brother-in-law. Soon there would be a fresh settling of scores.

Only weeks later, in the first days of February 1461, Jasper and Owen Tudor's Lancastrian army confronted the late duke's eldest son and heir, Edward of York, at Mortimer's Cross, Herefordshire. Blond, handsome, and standing at six feet three, Edward of York was only nineteen and he lacked the experience of the Tudor commanders. But no one had ever seen anything like the strange dawn that greeted them on that icy morning. Blinking in the breaking light the rival armies saw three suns appear in the sky. The phenomenon, known as a parhelion, is caused by light shining through ice crystals in the atmosphere. Edward, a natural leader, seized the opportunity to tell his frightened troops that the triple stars represented God the Father, the Son and the Holy Ghost which were shining a blessing on their enterprise. With his army's morale renewed, 'freshly and manly he took the field upon his enemy, and put them at flight, and slew three thousand'.[2]

Few other details of the battle survive, but we know that Jasper escaped and was on the road when he learned, to his horror, that his father, Owen Tudor, was captured. Owen lived not far from Jasper at Pembroke Castle, and he had also remained close to Henry VI, who had give him the plum post of Keeper of the Parks of north Wales, 'in consideration of his good services' the previous year.[3] Even in his old age, Owen was prepared to fight in his stepson King Henry's cause – but it would be for the last time. Edward had ordered that Owen be executed along with eight other Lancastrian commanders. In Hereford, where he was taken, Owen still assumed he would be ransomed when a Yorkist solider grabbed the collar of his red doublet and ripped it off to expose his neck. Facing the rough wooden log that served as the block, and now realising his fate, he recalled with mordant wit how 'The head that shall lie on the stock was wont to lie on Queen Katherine's lap.' At the fall of the axe the extraordinary life that began with a stumble at a dance was ended.

Owen Tudor's head was placed on the top step of the market cross where a woman 'combed his hair and washed away the blood off his face', before she placed candles around him.[4] No one has yet suggested who she was. The watching crowd thought she was mad, as she carefully lit over a hundred small flames. She was surely, however, the grief-stricken mother of Owen's illegitimate son, David, who was almost two. Even as an old man in his fifties, it seems Owen had had the power to attract a woman's love.[5]

The four-year-old Henry Tudor would have understood his grandfather's fate only as an absence. Owen had been a familiar face at

Pembroke, yet he was nowhere to be seen when Henry was brought with his mother and stepfather to the castle in May. It was here Margaret Beaufort had come looking for protection from Jasper before Henry was born. But Jasper too was absent: he was on the run. In the three months since Mortimer's Cross, Edward of York had reasserted his father's claim to the throne, denounced Henry VI as a false king, and been proclaimed Edward IV in London on 4 March. For twenty-five days there were two kings in England, a situation ended on 29 March with a decisive battle at Towton in Yorkshire. It was one that left Henry's family, and much of England, traumatised.

Margaret Beaufort's husband, Sir Henry Stafford, and her step-father, Lord Welles, had been arrayed with the Lancastrian forces while Henry VI spent the day in prayer nearby. It was Palm Sunday, a spring day. But the wild flowers in the fields and hedgerows were bitten by unseasonable cold and the sky was low and dark. The two armies, the largest England had ever seen – amounting to perhaps more than 30,000 out of a population of three million – faced a fight to the death.[6] When the banners of two kings were unfurled it invoked 'guerre mortelle', the most ruthless form of armed combat in the Middle Ages, with no quarter given for the supporters of a false king.

As the men began to put on their armour there were flurries of snow. By 10 a.m a snowstorm was blowing straight into the faces of the Lancastrian forces. The Yorkists advanced on foot into the whiteout. Blind, and with the wind against them, the arrows fired by the Lancastrian archers fell short. The Yorkists collected them and returned them: thousands of arrows a minute poured into the Lancastrian ranks, leaving them with no choice but to engage their enemy. As the armies hammered at each other the sheer weight of numbers on the Lancastrian side forced the Yorkists back, but with Edward IV and his cousin germane, 'that noble knight and flower of manhood', Richard Neville, Earl of Warwick, leading from the front the Yorkists gave ground only slowly.

For hour upon hour the Lancastrians and Yorkists battled on.

When the heaps of dead made it impossible for the men to engage, short truces were arranged so the corpses could be heaved out of the way to allow the fighting to continue. In late afternoon the Duke of Norfolk had brought reinforcement for the Yorkists and as daylight faded the Lancastrian ranks at last gave way. Bridges over the nearby rivers had broken under the weight of fleeing men. Some fell into the freezing water, drowning in their heavy armour. Others who had cast off their helmets to help them breathe as they ran became easy targets for the Yorkists who smashed their skulls in a frenzy of bloodlust.[7] A last stand was made to the north at the little town of Tadcaster. Then it was over, save for the executions of those survivors who had not managed to escape. The bodies, scattered over an area of at least six miles by four, included that of Margaret's stepfather Lord Welles, the only father she had ever known.

Relieved that Stafford had survived, Margaret spent time with her mother in the first terrible weeks of grieving for Lord Welles. Meanwhile, Henry VI had fled into exile in Scotland with his queen and their son. Most surviving supporters of the House of Lancaster now judged it prudent to acknowledge the authority of King Edward. Jasper was an exception, but he would soon follow his half-brother into exile. Pembroke Castle was left garrisoned with sufficient food, men and arms to withstand a long siege, however, and there Margaret Beaufort now awaited King Edward's next move, anxious to see what he intended for her son, the 'false' King Henry's nephew.

Over the summer Margaret ensured that something of Henry's normal life continued.[8] Henry would later honour Owen Tudor's son David with wealth and knighthoods, and since the boy lived nearby and was close in age, he was, perhaps, a playmate.[9] Henry was also old enough to learn to read and it was a mother's task to teach their young children. One of the favourite images of the Middle Ages was that of St Anne, the mother of the Virgin, teaching her daughter to read. Margaret had a variation on this image in the Book of Hours she inherited from her own mother, with St Anne and the Virgin teaching Christ to read. The most popular books of the period, they were divided into eight sections, imitating a monk's 'Office' or cycle of daily devotions. Those of aristocrats were illuminated with pictures that had a special significance for them, and people added whatever religious stories or prayers they fancied.[10] Margaret would note major events in her life, including, later, the outcome of battles.

The aftershocks of Towton were already being felt in Wales. King Edward had given one of his principal supporters, William, Lord Herbert, the task of seizing Jasper Tudor's estates, and on 30 September Herbert arrived at the twin-towered gates of Pembroke Castle with a large force.[11] The governor Jasper had placed in charge succumbed to the promise of a pardon and the castle was surrendered without a fight.[12] Margaret was then simply informed of Edward's intentions for her son Henry: she was to hand him over to Herbert as his ward. King Edward hoped that, in due course, he could co-opt Henry Tudor to the Yorkist cause, and had intimated to Herbert that if Henry proved loyal, he could in time inherit his father Edmund Tudor's lands and his title, as Earl of Richmond. With this in mind Herbert had invested over £1,000 in securing the wardship and planned to marry Henry to his daughter, Maud. Margaret had to accept this willingly if she was ever to see her son again, and there was no struggle, therefore, when the unhappy mother said her goodbyes to her child in February 1462, just after his fifth birthday.

Henry had travelled often between the family properties in the Midlands and Pembroke Castle.[13] He was used to being on the road, sitting on a horse with a servant holding him securely, a train of men and carts stretching far behind. This time he was without his familiar servants or family and taken to a new destination: Raglan Castle in the south-east of Wales. The adventure of leaving home had begun all too soon, and it would be many years before he saw his mother again.

When Raglan Castle was approached from the village, a hexagonal sandstone tower came into view before the rest of the fortress loomed over the slight rise on the hill. The castle was entered through a new gatehouse, leading to a large cobbled courtyard framed by a 'hundred rooms filled with festive fare'.[14] It was here, Henry later recalled, that he was to spend his childhood, 'kept as prisoner, but honourably brought up'. The vast hall where he ate his meals was thirteen metres high, with beams of Irish oak and a gallery where music was played. The family chapel, where he prayed, was equally impressive, twelve metres long, with brilliant yellow decorative tiles. Outside, orchards, fishponds and deer parks gave way on the horizon to the dramatic Welsh wilderness and the harsh peaks of the mountains.

At first Henry spent time under the care of Herbert's wife, along with her own small children, but by the age of seven he was living in the main household. This amounted to as many as 200 people. Of these, Herbert's wife might have a few female companions to wait on her, but since the menial servants lived and slept communally, most were single men. There were many high-born servants too, as it was common for the sons of the elite to spend part of their youth in the noble household of family friends or patrons. They were expected to serve meals, help their master dress, hone their manners and learn that good service earned the ear of the one served. Even young children were expected to press for family advantage while in a household such as this.[15]

Unusually, Henry's entire education was to take place at Raglan, but he was given the best that Herbert could supply. Henry was taught grammar by graduates of Oxford University, and guidance in the practical skills of a knight, learning horsemanship, archery and how to fight with a wooden sword. He would have to wait until his teens before he began training with a real weapon. The long sword, which weighed about four pounds and was up to forty-three inches long, was a two-handed weapon that required considerable strength as well as skill to wield, as did the popular battleaxe. Amongst his playmates was another of Herbert's wards, an older boy called Henry Percy, whose father, the Earl of Northumberland, had been killed at Towton in the Lancastrian cause. He too would have to earn his earldom back by proving his loyalty to Edward IV.

Although Henry did not see his mother, she was permitted to write to him. It was her duty and wish to seek for him to be restored to his rights as Earl of Richmond. To this end she encouraged him to offer good service to Herbert, while at court she did her best to curry favour with the new king. Here Margaret had to adapt to a very changed culture. Where Henry VI had enjoyed, above all, decorous religious display, Edward IV promoted a chivalric aesthetic. Margaret remembered seeing her first Garter ceremony aged nine, when the Lancastrian queen, Margaret of Anjou, had appeared in new blood-red robes. The Order, founded by Edward III, had as its inspiration the knights of the legendary King Arthur's Round Table. For Henry VI the emphasis had been on the religious ritual of the ceremonial; for Edward IV it was on courtly military display. There were other differences too: Henry VI's quiet scholarship and austerity was replaced with the energy of a young warrior who revelled in the pursuit of pleasure. A foreign visitor judged Edward 'a very young and handsome prince, amongst the handsomest people in the world', and thought that 'Never had a man taken as much pleasure from women, feasts, banquets and hunting.' Edward IV appeared affable, and 'so genial in his greeting that if he saw a newcomer bewildered by his appearance and royal magnificence, he would give him courage to speak by laying a hand upon his shoulder'.[16] Beneath this bonhomie there lay a brutal nature, but allies had to be won to keep the peace and Edward IV was not only charming, when he wished, he was also a talented propagandist.

Yorkist claims to be the senior royal house were being promoted in handwritten and painted pedigrees that were circulated at court. Each was richly decorated with Edward's badges, symbols that were also seen widely on liveries, banners, and carved in stone on royal palaces. In an age used to visual messages even the illiterate could read their meanings.[17] The famous badge of the Sun in Splendour recalled the three suns at Mortimer's Cross, while adapting the sun badge of Richard II. It reminded those who saw it that God had blessed Edward in battle, with the implicit suggestion that this was because they were the true heirs to Richard II. Sometimes the Sun in Splendour was combined with another badge – that of the famous white rose. This was believed to have been the badge of Edward's ancestor, Roger Mortimer – the man who was supposedly Richard II's 'true' heir, before his right was 'usurped' by Henry IV.[18]

As the years passed and Henry Tudor grew up, Lancastrian fortunes went from bad to worse. Henry VI left Scotland and was hiding out in the north of England when he was captured in 1465. A German merchant described him being led 'through Cheapside to the Tower, on a small horse, a straw hat on his head, and a rope tied round his body, and each side so that he might be held'.[19] A king was expected to look like a king, and the humiliation of Henry VI was a deliberate attempt to undermine his sacred status as an anointed monarch. 'No one, either young or old', the merchant recorded, 'dared . . do him honour, either kneeling or otherwise, for fear of his life'.[20] But as Shakespeare's Richard II boasts, 'Not all the water in the rough rude sea/Can wash the balm off from an anointed king.' Henry VI remained a potential focus of opposition while he lived. When Henry IV had faced unrest in January 1400, he announced that Richard II had 'died' in prison, and it was suggested he had starved himself. A mysterious and sudden death, similarly from grief or shame, was the likely fate of Henry VI. He remained alive only because there was little point in killing him while his son, Prince Edward of Lancaster, was safe with his mother, Margaret of Anjou, in eastern France. If anything happened to the boy, however, the deposed king would not survive for very long.

Against this background of Lancastrian despair, Margaret Beaufort was fortunate that her efforts to ingratiate herself were given an unexpected boost by King Edward's choice of bride. Edward had made the extraordinary decision to marry the widow of a Lancastrian knight.[21] According to the chronicles, he had come across the beautiful Elizabeth Woodville by chance at a forest roadside, and immediately fell in love with her. While it is sometimes difficult to see from a picture of this period why a particular woman was judged beautiful, this is not the case with Elizabeth Woodville, with her high cheekbones and cupid-bow mouth. But the reality of the king's love affair with her was in some contrast to the romantic fiction. Edward knew her from court, where he had hoped to claim her as a mistress. When that failed (it was said she had held him off with a dagger) he married her, becoming the first English king to marry a commoner. Elizabeth Woodville's relatives all now expected to marry into noble families. Amongst them, her sister Katherine was married to Margaret's nephew by marriage, the eleven-year-old Henry, Duke of Buckingham. This had a transformative effect on Margaret's ability to attract the king's favour, and in 1567, having not seen her son for six years, she enjoyed a full week with Henry at Raglan.[22]

Margaret found Henry Tudor had grown into a lean, intelligent ten-year-old, above average height for his age, with a slight cast to his blue eyes. Margaret was grateful to see that peace – even a Yorkist peace – was keeping her son safe. The following year Margaret entertained King Edward at her husband's hunting lodge near Guildford. She bought a pewter dinner service in London for the occasion, and served a vast array of delicacies: half a great conger eel, thirteen lampreys and several hundred oysters were washed down with five barrels of ale.[23] As Edward's minstrels played for the company, Margaret could feel well satisfied. Dressed in a new gown of velvet and fine wool, she was sitting on one side of the king under a purple cloth of estate, a symbol of authority, while her husband sat on the other side. For Margaret and her son, the future seemed hopeful.

4

THE WHEEL OF FORTUNE

FROM HIS VANTAGE POINT THE TWELVE-YEAR-OLD HENRY TUDOR could see William Herbert manoeuvre his forces into their battle positions. For Henry, witnessing the coming battle of Edgecote Moor, six miles north-east of Banbury, was to be part of his training in war. Herbert had gathered 'the extremity of all his power' and his men were 'the best in Wales'.[1] A great feast had been given at Raglan before they headed out to face the enemy, which happily was not a Lancastrian army. The rebel leader was a traitor from within the House of York: Edward IV's ambitious and brilliant cousin, Richard Neville, Earl of Warwick. At dawn on 26 July 1469, Warwick's forces were still on their way to join his allies in the field, and Herbert intended to defeat them before Warwick arrived. He looked forward to his Tudor ward learning from his victory.

The chink of armour and the noise of clanking weaponry swelled into a roar as the rebels swept forward with battle cries. The impact drove Herbert back across the river, but he put up a determined defence. His co-commander's Welsh archers were only a few miles away and at last the news came that the archers were coming, and fast.[2] Then, suddenly, the advance guard of Warwick's army appeared, their red coats stitched with his distinctive badge of the ragged staff, sewn in silver.[3] Warwick's name alone was enough to send a bolt of terror through Herbert's forces. The fear that Warwick could not be far behind shattered morale and sent Herbert's army into flight. At least 2,000 Welshmen were slaughtered. Warwick also wanted prisoners, however, and he ordered his men on the hunt for those he considered to be of value. Henry's first training in war proved to be the taste of mortal fear, as he too fled, with one man to guide him.

As soon as the news of the battle reached Margaret Beaufort in Surrey, she sent eight of her best men across country to discover her son's fate. When at last they sent word back, there was horror as well as relief. Henry was with Herbert's brother-in-law at Weobley Castle near Hereford, but Herbert had been captured and executed.[4] Henry's guardian had been a dominant figure in his life and, when Margaret's servants rode on to Weobley, she sent money for Henry to be spent on bows and arrows, 'for his disports': a distraction from the trauma he had been through.[5] It would be over a year, however, before Margaret would see her son, as the political situation remained highly unstable.

The origins of Warwick's betrayal of his cousin dated back to the king's controversial marriage to Elizabeth Woodville. Warwick, fourteen years older than Edward, and used to having his counsel heeded, had been in the middle of negotiating a match between Edward and a French princess. There was growing tension in Europe between Louis XI of France on the one side and the Dukes of Burgundy and Brittany on the other, as Louis attempted to exert his authority over their independent duchies. The marriage and associated foreign policy would have meant an alliance with Louis, but it had had to be dropped after Edward revealed he had married his English bride. It then emerged that Edward favoured a Burgundian alliance. This was confirmed when his sister, Margaret of York, married Charles the Bold, Duke of Burgundy, in February 1468.

Warwick's resentment of the king's growing independence only reached boiling point, however, when Edward blocked a marriage between Warwick's daughter, Isabel Neville, and the elder of the king's two brothers, George, Duke of Clarence.[6] When Warwick rebelled he had hoped to make Clarence king, but it was only after he had formed an alliance with the Lancastrian queen, Margaret of Anjou, in October 1470, that he was able to find sufficient support to drive Edward into exile in Burgundy. Warwick's sobriquet – 'the Kingmaker' – was well earned with the ailing Henry VI promptly released from the Tower and readapted as king. Prince Edward of Lancaster was promised in marriage to Warwick's second daughter, Anne Neville, and Henry Tudor was free to leave Weobley. Jasper Tudor, newly returned from exile in France, escorted the boy from Hereford to his mother in London that same month.

Henry had not seen Jasper since he was four years old, but Jasper's exploits had been infamous in the Herbert household and at Weobley.[7] Stories abounded describing Jasper's raids into Wales, where he moved through the countryside like a will-o'-the-wisp, holding sessions and assizes in the name of Henry VI, reminding everyone who the true king was, before vanishing with his men. Jasper had nearly been caught in 1468 when the Lancastrian outpost of Harlech fell to Herbert's troops, but he had escaped dressed as a peasant carrying a bundle of pea-straw on his back, before sailing for Brittany, more by his own skill, it was said, than that of his sailors.[8] The ride to London with Henry marked the beginning of a close friendship between the dashing Jasper Tudor and his young nephew, and for the next fifteen years they would rarely be apart for long.

On reaching London, Henry found himself in a city like no other. Over 40,000 people lived here, and its tall houses with their overhanging roofs seemed to block out the light and heighten the senses. Shops, cottages and taverns crowded on to the streets. Stalls glittered with goldsmiths' work and the flash of silks, while the air was thick with the smells of beer, hot meat pies and cheese flans. Priests and monks were a ubiquitous sight, dressed in distinctive clothes and with the crown of their heads shaved, or tonsured. Well educated, they were an obvious choice for the rich to employ as their secretaries and administrators, and those in London tended to be the more ambitious members of clergy, attracted to the capital, as others were, for the opportunities it offered.[9] Here and there you came across the great houses of the powerful, and gardens too. One offered a particularly striking sight: the Grocers Company had uprooted the white roses they had planted as a display of loyalty to Edward IV and had replaced them with red roses.[10]

Happily reunited with his mother, Henry Tudor and his family travelled by barge to the Palace of Westminster on 27 October. King Henry VI was back in his rightful place, but for Margaret Beaufort, who had known him in better days, it was shocking to see how five years of imprisonment and mental illness had taken its toll. Henry VI had never completely recovered his health after 1453 when he had had to be spoon-fed to keep him alive. The additional strain of his recent years in the Tower had left him strangely passive: 'simple', was how he was described. There was an awkward moment when the frail king saw the self-possessed young Henry Tudor and made a bizarre pronouncement: 'This truly is he unto whom both we and our adversaries must yield, and give over the domain.'[11] The words suggest a torch being passed from one king to another. But it is most unlikely Henry VI would have intended any such prophecy. His seventeen-year-old son, Prince Edward of Lancaster, would shortly be on his way to England from France with his mother the queen. There was no reason to believe he would not, one day, inherit his father's throne. It may be that the king had confused Henry Tudor with the son he had not seen for five years.

From London, Henry Tudor rode on to his mother's Surrey house at Woking on the river Wye. It was a lovely manor with gardens lined with fruit trees, and beneath them the clear waters of a winding river. Margaret at last had an opportunity to lavish him with the love and attention she had been unable to give him as a little boy, but their time together was not to last. By 11 November King Edward was sailing home from Burgundy to fight for his crown with an army subsidised by his brother-in-law, Charles the Bold. Henry said his goodbyes, and having packed in his baggage his mother's gift of a fine new horse blanket, he set off to rejoin Jasper. Together they would travel onward to south Wales to raise an army in the same region from which Herbert had drawn his men.

Meanwhile, as Warwick scrambled to get another army ready in England to face Edward immediately, the Yorkist king took London. Henry VI was returned to the Tower, 'as a man amazed and utterly dulled with troubles and adversity'.[12] No wonder contemporaries were obsessed with the image of the wheel of fortune, which raised men up one day, only to hurtle them down the next. It seemed to some that the world had 'turned right queasy'.

On 13 April 1471, with Henry VI locked in the Tower, the Yorkist cousins Warwick and Edward assembled their rival armies at Barnet in Hertfordshire. Margaret Beaufort's husband, Stafford, had decided the family should hedge their bets on the outcome. While the fourteen-year-old Henry Tudor stayed with Jasper in the west, Stafford was preparing to fight alongside Edward IV's forces. He feared he would not survive – this was to be '*guerre mortelle*', and Stafford remembered well the horrors of Towton a decade earlier. On the eve of the battle, he wrote his will, naming his 'most entirely beloved wife' as his executor and asking simply that his body be 'buried where it shall best please God that I die'.[13]

As the first confused reports on the outcome of the battle reached Margaret, it emerged that the two sides had fought almost blind in thick fog early in the morning of the 14th. In the confusion Lancastrian archers had fired into the ranks of their own side, and with survivors crying 'Treason! Treason!' they had soon lost the battle. According to one account Warwick had fought on until overwhelmed, 'beating down and killing the enemy far from his own forces' until he was 'thrust through and slain'.[14] Another described how he 'leapt on horseback and fled to a wood', hoping to escape to fight another day, but that a Yorkist soldier 'came upon him, and killed him, and despoiled him naked'.[15] Battlefield commanders usually tried to escape, but trapped in that wood the Kingmaker knew better than to be taken alive and suffer a post-battle execution such as he had delivered to Henry's former guardian, William Herbert. He had fought to the death.

There was still no news of Stafford, and as Margaret sent her men on to Barnet to discover whether her husband was alive, the survivors from both armies were trickling into London. Many were terribly injured. Their armour had protected the trunks of their bodies, but they had been cut below the hips and on their faces. Often they had lost their noses, and these unlucky souls retreated into the houses of friends to escape the merciless stares of the public.[16] Stafford proved to be amongst the injured. Unable to march on with Edward IV to the west, he was to be spared the denouement. The Tudor army expected to join Margaret of Anjou's forces for this final battle, but Edward IV cut off her army at Tewkesbury in Gloucestershire. Her seventeen-year-old son, Prince Edward of Lancaster, was killed there 'in plain battle' on 4 May 1471.[17]

Two and a half weeks later Edward IV was riding through the streets of London in a victory parade with Margaret of Anjou seated in a chariot like a royal prisoner from the days of ancient Rome. He intended now to destroy the remnants of the Lancastrian royal house. In the Tower Margaret of Anjou was not permitted to see her husband, and would never see him again. Henry VI was murdered on the night of 21 May 1471, between eleven and twelve o'clock.[18] The Yorkists put it about that he had taken the news of his son's death 'to so great despite, ire and indignation that of pure displeasure and melancholy he died'. Few can have believed it. There was, however, as yet no tradition in England of killing queens. Margaret of Anjou would be ransomed and eventually returned to France. There she died in 1482, so poor that Louis XI decided her dogs were the only things she owned worth keeping.[19]

With the legitimate line of the House of Lancaster extinct, one Yorkist noted that 'no one from that stock remained who could now claim the crown'.[20] Nevertheless, Edward IV was not going to take any chances with Henry Tudor remaining a possible focus of old Lancastrian loyalties. An insight into Edward IV's intentions is given by the fact that the man he ordered to lead the pursuit of Henry and Jasper Tudor was the same man who had carried out the execution of Owen Tudor on his orders in 1461.[21] Jasper had become an expert escape artist, however, and as he fled with Henry into north Wales he turned the tables on their pursuer, capturing him instead. When the man pleaded for his life, Jasper retorted 'he should have as much favour as he showed to Owen, his father' and so 'caused his head to be smitten off'.[22] As one Frenchman summarised it: 'the lords in England killed their enemies, then later the children of their enemies gained their revenge'.[23]

Louis XI had backed the Lancastrian cause since Edward went into alliance with the Burgundians, and when Jasper and Henry at last reached the port of Tenby they set sail for France. The weather was stormy, however, and, blown off course, the Tudors landed instead at the independent duchy of Brittany. Happily the duke, Frances II, who was the son of Catherine of Valois' sister Jeanne, welcomed his cousins 'as though they had been his brothers'. Jasper and Henry were safe for the time being, but how long would this last? Whatever the displays of friendship from Duke Francis, they were now pawns in Brittany's efforts to remain independent of France. King Edward would offer Duke Francis men and money in exchange for returning them to England, and there was no reason to believe he would resist the king's bribes for ever, even if the Tudors were cousins.

It was late September before Margaret Beaufort learned of Henry's and Jasper's safe escape. It was good news in bad times. Margaret had watched her husband sicken from the injuries he had received at Barnet five months earlier. Married to Sir Henry Stafford aged fourteen – the same age her son now was – she had grown up with him and, each year, they had celebrated their wedding anniversary as a mark of their love. They would not do so again. Stafford died on 4 October 1471.

The grieving Margaret retreated to her mother's house in the City, Le Ryall, to consider what to do next.[24] It seemed to Margaret that the only way to secure her son's life in the long term was to obtain a pardon from Edward IV, but regaining his trust was a formidable task. The quickest route would be to marry someone close to Edward. As a mere woman it would be assumed her loyalties were those of her husband, or, at the very least, that he could control her.

Still only twenty-eight, extremely rich and with a royal descent that would add lustre to any noble house, Margaret soon attracted the attention of the new Steward of the King's Household, Thomas, Lord Stanley. Eight years older than Margaret and a regular member of Edward's council, he had useful links to the queen's family, the Woodvilles.[25] He was also independently powerful, the leading nobleman of the north-west and a man of considerable cunning. He had avoided committing his retainers to any of the major battles of the past thirteen years.[26] Margaret married him in June 1472, just eight months after Stafford's death. She feared she could not afford to be sentimental if her son was ever to return to his homeland.

5

ENTER RICHARD III

MARGARET BEAUFORT AND THOMAS, LORD STANLEY WERE AN effective partnership. At Lathom Castle in Lincolnshire Margaret assisted her husband in local arbitration awards. At court she helped him manage the below-stairs household concerned with mundane daily necessities such as providing food, drink, lighting and fuel, and which was part of his role as steward. He, in turn, ensured she took part in ceremonial occasions, even attending the christening of Edward IV's children. Over the years their mutual respect and affection grew. Stanley liked to give her expensive fabrics and gowns in rich greens and elegant striped black damasks.[1] She, in turn, would buy Stanley valuable books, such as the one with special prayers to protect him in battle and from plague, the deaths that had taken her previous husbands. But the chief purpose of the marriage for Margaret was that it opened up the possibility of the king's favour for her son. Progress towards the pardon she longed for proved agonisingly slow, however.

It cannot have helped Margaret's cause that the gentle, mad, Henry VI had come back to haunt King Edward in the guise of a popular saint. Edward IV had promulgated a belief that the defunct House of Lancaster had been cursed by their usurpation of Richard II, and that was why they were no more. But the dead king had come to be venerated, with rich and poor alike judging him to have been an innocent whose troubles gave him some insight into the difficulties of their own lives. Miracles were reported at the site of his modest grave in Chertsey Abbey, Surrey. A peasant claimed that Henry VI had even deigned to help him when he had a bean trapped in his ear, which popped out after he had prayed to the late king. People scribbled prayers to Henry VI in their Books of Hours, and painted images of him in their churches, while Edward tried, and failed, to put a halt to the growing cult.

Edward's court was often an uncomfortable place for Margaret in other respects too. Once described as 'the most splendid court . . . in all Christendom', it was growing decadent.[2] The strikingly handsome, young King Edward was now fat, and it was later claimed he not only ate vast amounts, he also liked to 'take an emetic for the delight of gorging his stomach once more'. The same (hostile) source claims Edward showed similar incontinence when it came to sex, acquiring mistresses, married and unmarried, with 'no discrimination'.[3] Certainly there were mistresses, and vicious quarrels broke out between courtiers (sometimes over women), while Edward's murderous streak took its toll within the royal family.

In 1475, Henry Holland, Duke of Exeter, a descendant of Henry IV's sister, 'fell' off an English ship in the Channel and drowned, reputedly on the king's orders.[4] The following year Edward IV almost succeeded in persuading Francis, Duke of Brittany, to return Henry Tudor to him, pretending he hoped to arrange a royal marriage for him. It was only because a Breton friend managed to convince Duke Francis that Henry still needed his protection, and remained a useful pawn, that his life was saved. The most shocking event came in 1478, when the king ordered the death of his own brother, George, Duke of Clarence, who had married Warwick the Kingmaker's elder daughter. Later immortalised by Shakespeare as 'false, fleeting, perjur'd Clarence', the silver-tongued duke had reconciled with Edward before the Battle of Barnet, but the brothers had begun quarrelling again. After a farcical trial for treason Clarence was executed in the Tower. The hard-drinking

king may have thought the method a kindly one – he had Clarence drowned in a vat of Malmsey wine.[5]

It was a further four years, and Henry Tudor had already turned twenty-five, before Margaret's determined efforts to appease Edward at last achieved a draft pardon for her son.[6] Whether it would ever be signed was another matter. His stepfather, Stanley, later claimed that Edward IV had grown genuinely interested in arranging a marriage for Henry with one of his daughters. But there is no contemporary evidence for this. On the contrary, Edward offered Duke Francis of Brittany 4,000 archers in exchange for Henry and Jasper Tudor that same year.

Henry's future remained very uncertain therefore, when, on 9 April 1483, the king died, aged only forty. He had suffered regular bouts of 'an ague', and his carousing had also taken its toll. In this weakened state he had succumbed to a cold he caught when out fishing.[7] Margaret Beaufort's efforts to cultivate the House of York would have to begin anew. But after the frustrations of the previous dozen years it was possible a genuine opportunity to help her son might appear and Margaret was determined that, if it did, she would seize it, whatever quarter it came from.

The day after the king's death, Stanley and Edward IV's other councillors acknowledged his twelve-year-old elder son as Edward V. The new king was at Ludlow with his maternal uncle, Anthony Woodville, Lord Rivers, when he received the news and learned he would be crowned on 4 May. Since Edward V was a minor, some had expected a Protector would rule England in the king's name until he reached his majority. The immediate coronation meant that Edward V would instead rule alone, with the guidance of a council. His mother's Woodville relatives, with whom he lived, were likely to be highly influential in deciding who those councillors were, a fact that was immediately resented by the Woodville family's enemies.

Happily for the Woodvilles, the leading choice for Protector, Edward IV's surviving brother Richard, Duke of Gloucester, accepted the decision to crown Edward instead. A pious man who had always been loyal to the late king, he swore an oath of loyalty to his nephew promptly at York, where he was based. He also agreed to meet Edward V on his journey to London and accompany him on his formal entrance into the city. Richard was already expected, therefore, when he arrived at the meeting point at Stony Stratford on 30 April, his horse still sweating from the gallop.[8]

There was no sign in Richard of his brother's decadent style of living. Thirty years old, he was a soldier, about five feet eight, with a wiry build, slender limbs, fine bones and dark features.[9] It was claimed later in the century that his right shoulder was notably higher than his left, and indeed the body of Richard excavated in Leicester in 2012 has severe scoliosis (an S-shaped spine.) The Shakespearean legend of Richard's hump may have originated in this, and certainly it would have reduced his height considerably, but it is worth recording that the sixteenth-century Tudor king Edward VI also had one shoulder higher than another, which was not perceived as a gross deformity.[10]

Riding with Richard and his substantial force of retainers was also the large, imposing figure of Henry Stafford, 2nd Duke of Buckingham. He was a descendant of Thomas Woodstock, the younger brother of John of Gaunt, and the only other adult royal male in the kingdom.[11] Edward V knew his maternal uncle, Lord Rivers, had left to have dinner with Richard and Buckingham at Northampton the night before, and it was surprising to see that he wasn't with them. But an explanation would surely soon be forthcoming.

Richard and Buckingham dismounted and fell to their knees before the golden-haired boy, greeting the twelve-year-old with 'mournful' looks. They expressed profound sorrow at his father's death. But then, to the boy's astonishment, they began to speak angrily of corrupt councillors who had overthrown his father's will, which they said had named Richard as Protector. They accused the same councillors of being responsible for his father's death, in having encouraged him in his vices, and finally they warned the young king that both his life and Richard's were in danger.

Edward V, described by one of his bishops as having 'a ripe understanding, far passing the nature of his youth', insisted vigorously his father had appointed his councillors for him, and that he had complete confidence in them, as well as 'the peers of the realm and the queen'. At this mention of Elizabeth Woodville, Buckingham exploded: 'it was not the business of women but of men to govern kingdoms, and so if he cherished any confidence in her he had better relinquish it'.[12]

Buckingham was said to have resented being married off aged eleven to one of Elizabeth Woodville's low-born sisters, and he made it clear he viewed the Woodvilles as upstarts. He had been one of the first to contact Richard with his concerns about the power they were about to wield – but he was not alone. Another contact had been Edward IV's best friend William, Lord Hastings, who had quarrelled previously with members of the Woodville family. Their letters to Richard have not survived, but it is possible they had suggested to Richard his life was in danger, as he claimed. History had seen Edward IV, Henry VI and Richard II all face dangers at the hands of their adult male heirs. The Woodvilles had reason to see Richard also as a possible threat to Edward V, while Richard had the death of his brother Clarence to consider. If one royal duke was easily disposed of, so might another be. At the very least his standing as a royal duke was threatened by a Woodville monopoly of power. It made sense, therefore, for Richard to take the role of Protector long enough to destroy the Woodvilles and gain the king's trust.

There was shock in London when the news arrived that Richard had seized control of Edward V and that Lord Rivers had been arrested on charges of treason. Richard's action appeared, however, to be directed only against the Woodvilles and people were given no reason to suppose that Edward V's coronation would not go ahead. On 4 May, 400 citizens in mulberry gowns greeted the king on his official entry, and, dressed in blue velvet, he was escorted to the luxury of the Bishop's Palace in St Paul's Churchyard, where he was lodged. Richard, dressed in 'coarse black cloth' as a mark of mourning for his brother, was to stay nearby in Bishopsgate Street.[13]

With Elizabeth Woodville in sanctuary at Westminster Abbey along with her youngest son and five daughters, the situation remained tense, nevertheless. Richard issued a reassuring statement, rescheduling the coronation for Sunday 22 June. Events were, however, taking on a momentum that Richard may not have anticipated before he had seized the king. It was clear that Edward V did not accept that he was being rescued from evil councillors. The Woodvilles now had scores to settle with Richard, and when the king grew up, they would get their opportunity. How safe even was the future of Richard's nine-year-old son? It was also valid to wonder if England might not be better off in the hands of an experienced, adult royal, than a child puppet of the upstart Woodvilles. But if Edward V was to be deposed Richard had first to overawe, or dispose of any diehard Edwardian loyalists.

On 10 June Richard wrote secretly to the City of York, summoning his northern supporters. He warned that the queen and her adherents planned to 'murder and utterly destroy' him and Buckingham, 'the old Royal blood of this realm'.[14] He then called a council meeting to take place at the Tower on Friday the 13th, ostensibly to discuss the coronation. Margaret Beaufort's husband, Lord Stanley, and Edward IV's former intimate, Lord Hastings, were amongst those present. According to a Tudor account, Stanley had slept badly. He told Hastings he had had a nightmare in which they were being gored in the face by a boar and blood was pouring over their shoulders. As everyone knew, Richard's badge was the white boar. Hastings advised him to dismiss his fears.[15] But barely had the meeting begun when it descended into violence. Hastings – who had been completely loyal to Edward – was arrested by Richard's men, taken outside and beheaded on Tower Green. Stanley, who cut his forehead as he ducked under the table, was also arrested, but quickly released.

As a shaken Stanley returned home to Margaret, Richard ordered Elizabeth Woodville to hand over Edward V's little brother, the Duke of York. He claimed the boy was needed to accompany the king for the coronation, which he still insisted was scheduled to go ahead. With the abbey surrounded, Elizabeth Woodville had little choice but to capitulate, and on 16 June the two princes were lodged in the royal apartments at the Tower. This was not imprisonment – at least not officially so. The Tower was a royal palace as well as a fortress, and this was where monarchs traditionally awaited their coronations. But the prospects for Edward V and his younger brother looked increasingly grim. Richard was now courting popularity riding through the capital dressed in regal purple and entertaining significant citizens to dinner.

There was no coronation on Sunday 22 June.[16] Instead on the 25th the young king's uncle, Lord Rivers, and his half-brother Richard Grey (a son of Elizabeth Woodville's first marriage to a Lancastrian knight) were executed. The following day an assembly of lords and other notables, led by Buckingham, presented Richard with a petition urging him to accept the throne. The Bishop of Bath had come forward as a witness to claim that Edward IV had been contracted in marriage to another woman at the time of his marriage to Elizabeth Woodville.[17] Following this bigamous marriage, it was argued that Edward IV had fallen into further sin, 'the order of all politic rule was perverted, the laws of God, and God's Church, and also the laws of nature and of England'.[18]

With the 'truth' revealed about Edward IV's marriage to Elizabeth Woodville his children were dismissed as illegitimate. The next in line was Edward Plantagenet, Earl of Warwick, the eight-year-old son of Richard's elder brother, the executed Duke of Clarence.[19] Here it was argued the boy was excluded from the line of succession by his father's treason, since attainder or 'corruption of blood' deprived any traitor's descendants of the right to inherit property from or through him. With some display of reluctance Richard accepted the petition and was proclaimed Richard III.[20] Edward V's coronation was cancelled indefinitely and his servants dismissed.

The deposed king's doctor, who was amongst the last of his servants to leave his service, reported that Edward V was now 'like a victim prepared for sacrifice . . . because he believed that death was facing him'.[21] The fates of those monarchs deposed previously that century – Richard II and Henry VI – did not bode well for the princes. Nevertheless, the nine-year-old Duke of York remained innocent of the mortal danger they faced. A story related in Burgundy described him as 'very joyous and witty', ready for 'frolics and dance'.[22] It may have been the little duke who persuaded his older brother to play with him in the gardens of the Tower where they were spotted firing bows and arrows. In the streets men wept for them as 'day by day they began to be seen more rarely behind the bars and windows till at length they ceased to appear altogether'.[23]

With the new coronation date set for 6 July no one moved against Richard. The men from the north had answered his summons and thousands were camped on Finsbury Field just outside London.[24] But fear would not be enough to keep Richard on the throne. He needed support from the political elite – amongst them the powerful Lord Stanley, who was invited to an audience with the king on the eve of his coronation, along with his wife, Margaret Beaufort. She was anxious to resolve a financial dispute inherited from her mother. Richard was equally anxious to please the wife of a man who controlled large areas of the north. Tellingly, however, nothing was said of Henry Tudor.

According to a slightly later account, Margaret had approached Buckingham about a pardon for her son, reminding him that his father and grandfathers had fought in the Lancastrian cause. She had known Buckingham for years: her late husband, Sir Henry Stafford, had been his uncle. He had even met Henry Tudor as a small child. She hoped his friendship with Richard would enable him to persuade the king to bring Henry into the fold at last. But if that account is true, her hopes were disappointed and other later claims that Margaret had also hoped to persuade Richard to marry Henry off to one of Edward IV's now illegitimate daughters are nonsensical. Why on earth would Richard have wished to ally them to the remnants of the Lancastrian house, and thereby empower both? There was no advantage to him in that, as Margaret would have known.

Margaret played a leading role at the coronation the following day, as she had in earlier Edwardian ceremonies. Dressed in six yards of scarlet velvet bordered with cloth of gold, she carried the train of Richard's queen, Anne Neville, the widow of Edward of Lancaster, who was crowned alongside her husband.[25] That night Margaret changed for the coronation banquet into blue velvet and crimson cloth of gold, and arrived with six attendants dressed in scarlet cloth. A great feast was produced, with delicacies brought from every corner of England: pheasant dressed with tail feathers trailing, sturgeon with fennel, exotic baked oranges and fritters flavoured with rose and jasmine. The dishes may well have been ordered earlier for the expected coronation of Edward V and, for many who attended, this feast was difficult to stomach. Although Richard had kept most of Edward IV's former servants in their posts, there was tremendous anger over his usurpation of Edward V's throne. Soon Margaret would find there was enough even to turn the powerless exile Henry Tudor into a leader, and revive the moribund Lancastrian cause.

6

THE PRINCES IN THE TOWER

FLUENT IN FRENCH, SLIM AND ABOVE AVERAGE HEIGHT, WITH LONG, wavy brown hair and an animated face, Henry Tudor was regarded at Duke Francis' court as a most 'pleasant and elegant person'.[1] But the twenty-six-year-old had learned to mask his true feelings behind a veneer of charm. Edward IV had hunted him since he was fourteen and for twelve years he had lived with the constant fear that, one day, the feckless Duke Francis would turn him over to his death. Henry was desperate for an opportunity to end his penniless, powerless, exile. It was brought by a fair wind in June 1483, when two English ships, painted vermilion, gold and sky blue, and captained by Elizabeth Woodville's brother, Sir Edward Woodville, arrived off the coast of Brittany.[2] If Henry Tudor had not yet learned of the dramatic events in England, he would soon do so.

The following month further ships from England reached Brittany, standards and streamers flying, carrying Sir Edward Woodville's pursuers, the envoys of the newly crowned Richard III. If their primary orders were to persuade Duke Francis to hand over Sir Edward with his men, Henry and Jasper Tudor were also targets.[3] In this, at least, Richard was to follow his brother's policy. It seemed Henry's best chance of changing his desperate situation was to help the Woodvilles to restore Edward V to the throne, for a pardon and royal favour would surely follow. Henry was already in correspondence with his mother and according to the Elizabethan antiquary, Stow, before long he was in contact with men who were planning to rescue the princes from the Tower. What information we have suggests the rescue attempt was made sometime near the end of July, but something went wrong. The men were caught and executed.

At the time, Richard III was on a royal progress that took him through Windsor, Oxford and Gloucester, before travelling on to Warwick and then York. Progresses were punctuated by pomp and pageantry and intended to boost public support for a king. The petition in June asking Richard to accept the crown had complained that under Edward IV, England had been 'ruled by self will and pleasure, fear and dread . . . all manner of equity and laws despised'.[4] This was Richard's opportunity to demonstrate that he offered a return to good kingship, and he did so in spades. Richard was 'worshipfully received with pageants' and had 'his lords and judges sitting in every place, determining the complaints of poor folk with due punishments of offenders against his laws'.[5] 13,000 livery devices bearing his badge of the white boar were distributed as he passed through the various towns, while behind the scenes he also dealt firmly with opponents of his rule.[6]

On 29 July, Richard III wrote to his chancellor concerning the punishment of the perpetrators of an 'enterprise', possibly the attempt to rescue the princes.[7] In any event it was evident that having them declared illegitimate had not neutralised the danger they posed, any more than Edward IV having Henry VI declared a false king had made him so.[8] According to an early sixteenth-century account it was only four days later, at Gloucester on 2 August, that Richard decided the princes in the Tower had to die.[9] All we know of the princes' fate, however, is that they vanished that summer.[10]

The question of who killed the royal children, if indeed they were murdered, remains one of history's great whodunits.[11] Richard III's personal piety and his qualities as a king have led many to assume he would never have ordered his nephews to be killed. But the opposite may be true. The rule of law, maintaining peace and harmony in reflection of the divine order, was Richard's sacred duty and the vital responsibility of any monarch. It is said that Richard had been in the Tower when Henry VI had met his death on the orders of Edward IV – and it is very possible that someone close to Richard now helped encourage him to believe that the deaths of the princes were also for the greater good.

A short manuscript dating to around 1512, and preserved in the College of Arms, asserts that the princes 'were put to death in the Tower of London by the vise [advice or device] of the Duke of Buckingham.'[12] This is supported by another source, the memoirs of Philippe de Commynes, a valued councillor at Louis XI's court in Richard's reign. He records how Richard 'had his two nephews murdered and made himself king', but later asserts, 'King Richard did not last long; nor did the Duke of Buckingham, who had put the two children to death.'[13] It is unlikely that Buckingham would have taken matters into his own hands. The Lieutenant of the Tower, Richard Brackenbury, answered to the king alone for his royal prisoners, and he remained loyal to Richard until his death. But Buckingham, described by Polydore Vergil as 'a sore and hard-dealing man', had been at Gloucester with Richard.

As Richard's progress now continued on towards Warwick and York, Buckingham headed for his castle at Brecon in mid-Wales. Remarkably, however, Buckingham was soon to display a dramatic change of direction in his loyalties. Vergil indicates that despite the appearance that all was well between Buckingham and Richard, something triggered a change of heart in the duke, and he was soon plotting to betray the king. If Buckingham believed the princes were still alive it is possible he hoped to pose as one of their rescuers. Yet he had no reason to suppose Edward V would reward his loyalty more fulsomely than Richard III. After all, Buckingham was associated with the arrest, and subsequent death, of Edward V's half-brother, Richard Grey. If, on the other hand, he believed the princes were dead – or would soon be so – something else must have brought about this volte-face. The answer surely lies in motives played out so often before and during the Wars of the Roses: ambition and revenge.

As Margaret Beaufort had reminded Buckingham, his family had been Lancastrians until Edward IV had obliterated that royal house. If the princes in the Tower were killed, the House of York would be left vulnerable to a similar fate, with Richard III the last adult male. Killing him would avenge Buckingham's grandfathers, both killed in the Lancastrian cause, and his father, who had died a lingering death from wounds. It could also clear the way for either a 'Lancastrian' restoration under Henry Tudor – or for Buckingham to become king. He was, after all, the senior descendant of Thomas of Woodstock, youngest son of Edward III in the male line, and his mother was a Beaufort (although from a slightly junior line to that of Henry Tudor).

At Brecon, Buckingham drew into his plans a prisoner he had under his care, a former Lancastrian and one of Edward IV's servants: John Morton, Bishop of Ely.[14] A man 'of great resource and daring', Morton understood immediately that Buckingham had little support either from Lancastrians – who preferred the claims of Henry Tudor – or Yorkists, who would not easily forget the role Buckingham had played in making Richard king.[15] But if Buckingham did not have the makings of a king himself, he could certainly be a kingmaker, giving powerful support to Henry Tudor's cause. Buckingham duly made contact with Margaret Beaufort who responded immediately to his approach. Her half-brother John Welles had been declared a rebel against Richard by mid-August and had fled to Brittany, while she was using a Welsh physician to communicate secretly with Elizabeth Woodville in sanctuary at Westminster Abbey.[16]

While Margaret had assumed the princes were alive she had hoped only to see Henry's rights as Earl of Richmond returned to him. But if the princes were dead, then she saw as well as anyone that a

'Lancastrian' restoration was possible and Margaret was determined to grasp this opportunity for her son. It was his best chance for survival. She intended now to change the focus of her communications and negotiate with Elizabeth Woodville for Henry's marriage to Woodville's eldest daughter, Elizabeth of York. Such a marriage would gain Henry Yorkist loyalties in addition to his Lancastrian support, and greatly strengthen his position. This, in turn, would allow Elizabeth Woodville to see her sons avenged. It is, perhaps, sensitivity to the fact that Elizabeth Woodville would only have considered such a marriage if her sons were dead, that explains the later claims emanating from the Tudor camp that Edward IV had once considered such a marriage, or that Margaret had attempted to negotiate such a marriage with Richard III.[17] But it also begs the question: why and how was Elizabeth Woodville convinced that her sons were dead? Edward IV had publicised Henry VI's death by displaying his body. Richard III made no such announcements concerning the princes and they were to be given no funeral or public burial. Indeed the most interesting mystery about the disappearance of the princes is why were they disappeared? Why the divergence from the successful modus operandi of earlier usurpers? That is, kill the deposed monarch, and then claim death resulted from natural causes or emotional breakdown.

Although historians have not yet offered a satisfactory explanation for the princes' disappearance the answer may be a simple one: Richard feared a public burial would see a cult grow up around the princes similar to that which surrounded Henry VI. Richard was highly aware of the tremendous power of this cult, which had a strong following in his home city of York, where a statue of 'Henry the saint' had been built on the choir screen at York Minster.[18] He would not have wanted such religious enthusiasm attached to the dead princes and there was a high risk it could happen. In the princes the religious qualities attached to royalty were combined with the purity and innocence of youth. If there were to be any suggestion of foul play, matters would be still more dangerous for Richard.

In the twelfth century a famous cult had sprung up after an ordinary local boy was murdered near Norwich. An image of this 'little St William' survives today in the village church of Eye in Suffolk, alongside one of Henry VI. The child's death was blamed on local Jews in an early example of the medieval 'blood libel', with claims that his killing was part of a religious ritual. The Jews had since been expelled from England, but the murder of children retained a particular biblical resonance. The annual mystery plays (a series of biblical stories acted out around the time of the feast of Corpus Christi, performed with great extravagance in York) included the story of the slaughter of the innocents by King Herod – a role for which King Richard was the obvious candidate.[19] The disappearance of the princes was, for Richard, a case of least said, soonest mended, for without a grave there could be no focus for a cult, and without a body or items belonging to the dead placed on display, there would be no relics either.

Nevertheless Richard III needed Elizabeth Woodville – and others – to know her sons were dead, since the entire point of their deaths was to forestall plots raised in their name. Believing Buckingham was entirely trustworthy he may have chosen the duke as his messenger. Buckingham was appointed on 28 August to a commission to investigate treason in the London area, and so would have been in the capital soon after. Buckingham's wife, Katherine Woodville, certainly believed Richard was capable of ordering the killing of the children. She would go to considerable lengths to hide her own young sons from Richard after her husband's treason emerged.[20] And if it was Buckingham who gave his sister-in-law Elizabeth Woodville the details of the killings, then no wonder he was said to have been involved, for how could he have known them if he were not?

The stories – or myths – that later emerged concerning the deaths of the princes were horrible. It was claimed variously that they were thrown in the moat, poisoned, or bled to death. In several accounts they were suffocated with their feather bedding. One such told how the Duke of York had hidden under their bed while his elder brother was being stifled, only then to be hauled out to have his throat cut. But the most telling claim was that they were drowned in Malmsey wine, in revenge for the death of their father's brother Clarence. To the fifteenth-century mind there were no coincidences: their universe was ordered, rational, and one thing led to another. Something had caused the princes to suffer so terrible an end, and the Bible offered a possible explanation in the tale of Cain, killer of his brother Abel, who was cursed by God, his heirs wiped out in the great flood.[21]

According to Polydore Vergil, Elizabeth Woodville fainted when she was told her sons were dead. As she came round, 'she wept, she cryed out loud, and with lamentable shrieks made all the house ring, she struck her breast, tore and cut her hair'. She also called for vengeance. Margaret was informed that she was willing to promise her daughter Elizabeth of York to be married to Henry Tudor. She further agreed to invite Edward IV's friends and former servants to support Henry's cause. Margaret Beaufort was now able to send a servant south to raise support for the enterprise amongst Edwardian Yorkists, and anyone else who resented Richard's northern-dominated establishment. Another of her messengers carried letters to Brittany along with large sums of money she had raised in loans from the City. Margaret advised Henry to gather together an army as soon as possible. He was then to sail to Wales to raise Jasper Tudor's former estates, and join forces with Buckingham.[22]

Henry, in Brittany, realised that at last he was a player rather than a pawn, and leapt at the opportunity, 'rejoicing wondrously'. Duke Francis was angry with Richard over piracy against Breton ships, and when Henry convinced him that he had 'an assured hope of obtaining the realm of England' he promised to back Henry with money and men. Back in England plans were laid for risings to take place across the south-east on 18 October. At the same time there was to be a mock attack on London from Kent. This, it was hoped, would keep the king distracted while Buckingham brought forces from Wales to the west of England. It was there that Buckingham was to meet up with Henry and the Breton soldiers Duke Francis had provided. But on 8 October Richard, travelling south from Lincolnshire, already knew something was up, and Buckingham was summoned. Buckingham responded by claiming he had a stomach upset. Richard insisted. Buckingham ignored him.

Rumours of the murders of the princes in the Tower were now spreading like wildfire in London and the Edwardian heartlands of the south.[23] A contemporary Londoner later recalled people were 'so sore against the king for the death of the innocents that as gladly would they have been French, as be under his subjection' – and no Englishman could imagine a fate more horrible than being French.[24] On 10 October violence broke out in Kent. The next day Richard learned that Buckingham was assembling his main force in Wales around Brecon Castle. Raising men proved harder than Buckingham had expected, however. He was an unpopular landlord, and as torrential rain drenched his army over the following ten days the men he had recruited lost heart. By the time Henry set sale for England in late October Buckingham's army was disintegrating. Henry remained ignorant of this as he struggled for his own survival, the storms buffeting his flotilla of around fifteen ships as they sailed towards England. The English joined the Bretons in praying to St Armel, a Breton prince who had killed a dragon, while some of the ships were driven to Normandy, and others back to Brittany. When Henry's ship, and a few others, at last dropped anchor off Plymouth his men were so relieved they would later dedicate shrines to St Armel in England.

A group of soldiers were spotted on shore waving in greeting to the battered fleet, and Henry sent a boat to reconnoitre. The soldiers advised Henry's men to land immediately, explaining they had come from the Duke of Buckingham. Henry chose instead to wait for the other ships in his fleet to arrive. After a lifetime as an observer, with his life often at risk, Henry was a watcher and waiter. And as he waited news reached him that Buckingham had been betrayed by one of his own servants, captured and executed. The southern risings had collapsed and the soldiers on shore were working for Richard III. The king had prepared an ambush for Henry amidst the rolling hills of Devon; but his last rival was already sailing back to Brittany to prepare for invasion another day.

7

THE EXILE

OVER THE EARLY WINTER OF 1483, 400–500 ENGLISH EXILES ARRIVED at the coastal town of Vannes in southern Brittany.[1] Most were in their mid to late twenties – the same generation as Henry. Some were Lancastrians and former supporters of Henry VI, others were former servants of Edward IV, or members of the Woodville family. One such was Elizabeth Woodville's sole surviving son, Thomas Grey, Marquess of Dorset, her eldest son by her first husband, the Lancastrian Sir John Grey of Groby.[2] The town porter was happy to point these new arrivals in Henry's direction. They usually found him sitting with two or three other lords, a lean-looking man, dressed elegantly in black, his narrow, expressive face marked only by a small red mole above the chin.[3]

It was evident Henry was more comfortable speaking French than English – he had grown to manhood in Brittany and was imbued with Breton culture. He had charm, even charisma, and began immediately to build a sense of mission amongst the exiles. At the same time, however, Henry had to come to terms personally with his new role. His childhood quest to regain his rightful place in England as Earl of Richmond was now replaced with a higher goal, and it seemed to Henry that God must be guiding his destiny. If the grandson of a mere Welsh squire was to be a king, it was the only possible explanation. His royal mother believed that St Nicholas had guided her in choosing to marry his Tudor father. Henry also recalled his audience in 1470 with his uncle, Henry VI, when the king had said that the young Henry was someone to whom 'both we and our adversaries must yield, and give over the domain'. At the time the king's words may have seemed like ramblings, but now that Henry VI was judged to be a saint, it was clear they had been a prophecy.

The belief in divine providence gave Henry's long years of suffering in exile meaning and purpose, for they were now revealed as preparation for what was to come: his overthrow of the false King Richard III.[4] Henry had a duty to live up to this sacred task and for that he needed God's help. Later Henry would be remembered as 'someone who daily participated with great piety in religious services'. In Brittany he had developed what would prove to be a lifelong devotion to a saint whose shrine lay in the local cathedral at Vannes: Vincent Ferrer.[5] An early fifteenth-century Dominican missionary, Ferrer's writings are a manual to spiritual self-improvement. They suggest daily declarations on sin, asking for God's help to feel true sorrow for them, and apologising for repeating sins previously confessed to a priest. Henry would also pray regularly to the Virgin Mary, who he described later as his 'continual refuge'. The only records he was to leave in Vannes are those of the offerings he made at High Mass in the cathedral on the Virgin's feast days.[6]

At Christmas 1483, Henry was ready to take the exiles to the heavily fortified Breton city of Rennes. There, in a religious service at the cathedral, the exiles swore their loyalty to Henry and he, in turn, made his solemn vow to marry Elizabeth of York and so to unite the houses of Lancaster and York. Richard's claims that his kingship would bring peace and concord had been badly dented by the October risings and Henry's proposed marriage promised to deliver what Richard had not. Brittany was, however, becoming an increasingly dangerous place for Henry. Duke Francis was growing senile and, by the time the first anniversary of Richard's coronation came round, the king had found an ally in the Breton treasurer, Pierre Landais. A warning from a spy at Richard's court in the summer of 1484 gave Henry the time to gain assurances of protection from France.[7] He then had to plan his escape.

In late September or early October, Jasper Tudor left Vannes with a small group of English nobles, supposedly on a mission to Rennes. On the way he slipped across the border into neighbouring France. A couple of days later Henry followed, also riding with a small retinue, ostensibly to visit a friend at a nearby manor house. Five miles from the town he rode into woodland and changed into the clothes of a serving man. With a guide acting the part of his master, Henry then galloped towards Anjou, stopping only to water his horse. His absence in Vannes was noticed almost immediately, however, and when he crossed the border his pursuers were less than an hour behind him.[8]

Henry had been fortunate in having escaped and also in having gained the backing of the fourteen-year-old French king, Charles VIII, along with the regent, his sister Anne of Beaujeu.[9] But Richard III still had England's resources of wealth and manpower at his disposal, and he was proving in many respects an excellent king. His actions and proclamations stressed that his laws were to be administered impartially, without delay or favour; bail was introduced so the innocent would not suffer while they awaited trial; forced loans to the Crown were being abolished, the fledgling printing industry and book trade were encouraged, and Richard was also showing himself to be a good friend and protector to the church. Nevertheless, despite all the good he did, there was a sense of deep malaise.

The faction that had brought Richard to power had contracted following the executions of his former allies: Edward IV's close friend, Hastings, in June 1483, and Buckingham in October 1483. This had forced him to lean more heavily on his northern support base and the cost of maintaining order in the south only increased his unpopularity there. More troubling still was the absence of God's blessings on the king. When Richard's young son had died in April 1484 it looked like punishment for his usurpation of Edward V. When his grief-stricken queen, Anne Neville, followed their only child to the grave in March

1485, Henry's friends spread rumours that Richard had poisoned her in order to marry Elizabeth of York – and even some of Richard's friends believed he was indeed planning an incestuous union with his niece.

The princess had left the sanctuary of Westminster Abbey with her mother and sisters, after Richard had made a written promise to protect the girls from 'ravishment or defouling contrary to their wills', and not to imprison them.[10] Richard had thereafter treated them well. Elizabeth of York was seen dancing at court at Christmas, dressed to match the queen. This, now, only encouraged the rumours he wished to marry her and he had to issue a public denial that this was the case. Certainly, however, Richard was determined to reconcile the Woodvilles – as Henry discovered to his shock after his men caught Thomas Grey, Marquess of Dorset, en route from Paris to Flanders. It transpired Elizabeth Woodville had sent messages telling Grey that Richard had agreed to pardon him and he was planning to desert Henry's cause. Henry was relieved Grey could not now take Richard information on his invasion plans. But when he later also heard the rumour that Richard III was to marry Elizabeth of York the news 'pinched Henry by the very stomach'. If she were to be married to Richard rather than Henry, it would leave Henry unable to claim he could unite the royal houses.

The Lancastrian exiles reassured Henry, telling him the advantages of marrying a York were exaggerated. They believed he should claim the throne in his own right – as a Lancastrian.[11] That he would now do, and Henry made another crucial decision – his invasion was to take place just a few months later, in August 1485. He didn't want any more surprises.

BOSWORTH

ON 22 JUNE 1485 RICHARD III SUMMONED MILITARY AND CIVILIAN forces in defence of his kingdom. The following day he issued a proclamation. It warned England they faced an invader with an outlandish name, 'one Henry Tudor, son of Edmund Tudor, son of Owen Tudor, who of his ambitious and insatiable covertise encroaches and usurps upon him the name and title of royal estate of this Realm of England whereunto he has no manner, interest, right, title or colour, as every man well knows; for he is descended of bastard blood both of the father side and mother side'.[1] It was plain fact that Margaret Beaufort's family were of bastard descent, and it was through her alone that Henry Tudor had English royal blood. The claim that he was also descended from a bastard on his father's side – and that Owen Tudor was the son of an innkeeper from Conway – is probably untrue. But the Tudor name was a reminder that Henry's father was the result of a scandalous misalliance between a servant and a queen. As a fifteenth-century ballad observed:

> They called him Henry Tudor, in scorn truly,
> And said, in England he should wear no crown.[2]

Henry was always known by his title, Richmond, and had taken to signing himself with a regal R. This may have stood for Richmond, but it could also be read as Rex, the Latin for king, a confusion that was surely deliberate for if Henry were the 'rightful' King of England then he was already king. Henry still needed a convincing narrative to support his claim to the crown, and to find one he imitated Edward IV's plundering of the myths of Geoffrey of Monmouth's twelfth-century 'History of the Kings of Britain'. The most significant of these popular myths concerned the wizard Merlin, King Arthur, and the life of the last British king, Cadwaladr, from whom the House of York claimed descent through the Mortimers.[3] In one of these stories, the fifth-century British king, Vortigan, was building a fortress when he discovered a pool. In it were two sleeping dragons. One was red, the other white. Merlin told the king the red dragon represented the people of Britain, and the white the Saxon invader they would one day fight and defeat.[4] In another, an angel appeared to Cadwaladr, and foretold how a prince of his line would come to defeat the Saxons. Yorkist propaganda created an association between the House of Lancaster and the invaders, and conflated the old myths. The fulfiller of the angel's prophecy to Cadwaladr thus became 'Draco Rubius', the Red Dragon – supposedly Edward IV.[5] Henry reversed this so that he was Draco Rubius and Richard III the outsider – a narrative already proving popular in Wales, where they still spoke a 'British' tongue.

Wales was the one place where the Tudor name had popular resonance, and in its Lancastrian heartlands the Yorkist claims to be the heirs of Cadwaladr had never taken root. The Tudors had maintained their contacts with the Welsh bards who were now churning out prophecies of Henry's eventual triumph, full of references to the myths of Cadwaladr and the Red Dragon. Jasper Tudor had a dragon as his badge and Henry now took as his principal standard the 'Red Dragon Dreadful'. In doing so he took on the mantle of the model hero of popular chivalric romances, the 'fair unknown'. This was a true heir, raised in obscurity only to emerge one day as the rightful king and claim his crown, as King Arthur had. If God had truly chosen this destiny for Henry, his invasion of England was a holy crusade.

In England on the last day of July, the printer William Caxton published his version of Sir Thomas Malory's *Le Morte d'Arthur*, a new reworking of the old myths. It described how King Arthur had once had a dream of a fight in the sky between a dragon and a boar. A philosopher had told him that he was the victorious dragon, while the boar denoted 'some tyrant that tormenteth the people'.[6] On the sunny morning of the following day, Henry's ships embarked from Honfleur at the mouth of the Seine, and sailed on a gentle southerly breeze. His army included about 400 Englishmen and over 800 Scots, the latter recruited from companies brought over to France by a Scottish nobleman long resident there. A further 1,500 were French or Breton. These included experienced soldiers as well as people on the criminal fringe, 'the worst kind which could be found anywhere', one Frenchman recorded.[7] Amongst his commanders Henry had one truly notable figure: John de Vere, Earl of Oxford. Once a great champion of the House of Lancaster, he had escaped a decade of imprisonment at Hammes Castle near Calais to join this latest enterprise in their cause.

After six days at sea the flotilla landed safety at Mill Bay on the Dale peninsula along the rugged coastline of Pembrokeshire. Amongst those waiting on the shore was Owen Tudor's illegitimate son, the twenty-six-year-old David Owen. Henry's grandfather had left much of his wealth to David, who still treasured his father's campaign bed in black velvet and russet satin embroidered with swallows and wolves, as well as the letters that sounded out his name, 'O, N' in gold. He also had a magnificent tapestry that must have belonged to Catherine of Valois, which depicted Henry V along with his brothers and son. David Owen had been serving Henry loyally 'beyond and within the sea', and as the sun began to set Henry now knighted his uncle, along with others who had rallied to his army.[8] Then, with the Red Dragon standard fluttering in the breeze, Henry knelt and recited the psalm, 'Judge me, O Lord, and defend my cause against the unmerciful people.'

Henry intended to strike out through north Pembrokeshire, putting his faith in the pro-Lancastrian western and northern counties of

Wales. To prepare the ground, letters were sent to 'our loving friends and true subjects', describing Richard as a usurper 'of our right'. The crusading element in Henry's invasion was implicit in his expressed trust in the help of 'Almighty God'.[9] Henry also hoped to recruit support in Cheshire, where his stepfather, Lord Stanley, was a powerful landowner. But Richard III had also invested in Stanley's loyalty. Stanley had been on progress with Richard when the risings of October 1483 had broken out, and he had been obliged to help crush them. This had earned King Richard's gratitude and saved Margaret Beaufort's life. The 'mother of the king's great rebel and traitor Henry, Earl of Richmond', condemned in January 1484 for having 'conspired, confederated and committed high treason', was made Stanley's prisoner – and his responsibility.[10] Stanley had since ignored Richard's orders to prevent his wife from contacting her son, but neither side could wholly trust this wily nobleman, who had avoided committing his retainers in any of the bloody battles of the previous twenty years.

Four days after Henry's landing the news reached Richard III at his principal military base at Nottingham Castle. That same day Richard sent summonses to the sheriffs and commissioners of array who mustered men in their localities, as well as to hundreds of individual nobles and gentlemen expected to raise their affinity. Amongst them Lord Stanley and his brother Sir William were instructed to organise north Wales in readiness to confront the invader.[11] A few days later Richard learned that despite his orders Henry was marching unopposed through the region and even gaining recruits. Richard summoned Lord Stanley for an explanation. In an ominous echo of Buckingham's response to such a summons in 1483, Stanley excused himself on grounds of illness. Richard then played an ace. The message was sent that he had Stanley's son, Lord Strange, as his prisoner. The boy was now a hostage to his loyalty in the coming conflict. If he betrayed Richard, his son would be executed. He had to choose: his stepson, or his own child's life?

By 17 August Henry had reached Shrewsbury in the West Midlands.

The city had shut its Welsh Gate against him, signalling to other cities that his was an enemy force. He was hugely relieved when one of Sir William Stanley's messengers arrived and persuaded the mayor to open the gates to Henry's motley foreign army. The messenger had brought letters and cash from Margaret Beaufort and her husband Lord Stanley, but what Henry really needed were men: he had only managed to raise about 500 extra soldiers in Wales. To his Red Dragon standard he now added two further standards: the Cross of St George, patron saint of England, and the Dun Cow, which had local Neville associations.[12] Henry's allies in the region had continued to exploit the rumours that Richard III had murdered his wife, Anne Neville; flying the Dun Cow would help recruit still more effectively amongst her family's affinity.

Sir William Stanley met Henry in person on 19 August, at Stone, seven miles north of Stafford. It was there that he delivered the devastating news that Richard had Lord Stanley's son as hostage. Henry feared he could not now be certain of even Sir William's support. Richard III, heading for Leicester, already had the weight of numbers on his side, as well as his long experience as a military commander. As Henry Tudor's army set off towards Tamworth in the heart of England, he fell back from the main body of his men, with a group of twenty trusted individuals The next day, when Henry caught up he claimed he had got lost. Was Henry, in fact, planning his escape from the battle ahead? Jasper Tudor's name is never mentioned in connection with the Battle of Bosworth. He may have been busy securing a suitable route. Henry had got out of tight spots with Jasper many times before and there was no one he could trust better with such a task.

It was at Atherstone, later that day, that Henry at last met his step-father, Lord Stanley. They shook hands and discussed their battle plans, although it remained to be seen whether they would be carried out. Meanwhile, Richard III had left the ancient city of Leicester that morning, riding with his army though its narrow streets of timber-framed houses 'with great triumph and pomp'.[13] The rich reds and blues of the royal standards, the glint of his crown and the drama of the trumpets provided one of the greatest spectacles the town had ever seen. Although there had been some desertions from Richard's army he gained supporters with this impressive display. From Leicester Richard proceeded 'until he come unto a village called Bosworth', his vanguard arrayed along the brow of the hill so his army could be seen for miles, giving 'a terror of the multitude'.[14] He then made camp for the night.

The next day, the *Great Chronicle of London* recalls, 'in the fields adjoining, both hosts met.'[15] Where exactly these fields were has long been a subject of debate. The earliest sources refer to the battlefield of Redemore, rather than Bosworth. The story became that the battle took place on Ambion Hill near Sutton Cheney, but it is now believed Redemore refers to marshland near the smaller villages of Dadlington and Stoke Golding, just south of Bosworth. Recent archaeology has found more cannonballs here than across all the medieval battlefields of Europe, as well as twenty-two pieces of lead shot from hand-held guns. The personal artefacts found include belt buckles and spurs, but most dramatic of all, dug out of the ground after 500 years – and the item that pinpoints the battle – is a silver gilt badge, an inch and a half across, of a white boar: the insignia of Richard III, worn by his knights.

The ordinary soldier in Richard III's army was used to physical work and most were well fed. They varied in age from around seventeen to their mid-fifties. An Italian visitor to England described them as huge men, with 'hands and arms of iron', their bows 'thicker and longer than those used by other nations, just as their bodies are stronger'. They did not have the fitted plate armour of the knights but wore quilted tunics, which they claimed to prefer, being lighter and more comfortable. Most had helmets, however, and all had bows and arrows, as well as a sword and shield.[16] But for all their strength and training, the English at Bosworth were not professional soldiers of the kind found on the Continent. Henry was fortunate to have brought some of these from France. Nevertheless, he remained badly outnumbered and as Henry looked towards Stanley's force for reassurance he was horrified to see his stepfather placing his men equidistant from the two armies. He sent a message asking Stanley to redeploy his men in the form they had agreed. The reply came that 'the Earl [of Richmond – i.e. Henry] should put his own folks in order'. Understandably 'vexed' and 'appalled' by this response Henry was obliged to 'make a slender vanguard for the smaller number of his people'.[17]

Richard's army had kept the high ground and looking down the hill the king could see Henry Tudor's men circling the marsh. Richard cut a striking figure on the skyline, with his surcoat bearing the royal arms and his battle crown on his helmet. But he was grim-faced. He had slept badly and Mass had been delayed, for 'when his chaplain had one thing ready evermore they wanted another, when they had wine they lacked bread'.[18] There had been no time for breakfast and, like his opponent, he was fearful of betrayal. One sixteenth-century account, only slightly altered by Shakespeare in *Richard III*, records how Richard's ally John, Duke of Norfolk, woke to find a piece of doggerel pinned to his gate. It warned, 'Jack of Norfolk be not too bold/For Dickon thy master is bought and sold.'[19] And who was likely to sell out Richard for Henry's shilling? Clearly the Stanleys could not be relied on, but there was also a question mark over Henry Percy, Earl of Northumberland. The earl had been raised with Henry as another of William Herbert's wards, and after Henry went into exile he had married Maude Herbert, the daughter that had been earmarked for Henry.[20] He had proved loyal to Edward IV, but he had dragged his responsibilities in mustering the northern levies for Richard. Less than a week earlier the loyal citizens of York had still been begging to learn the king's military requirements.

The battle was heralded with an opening shower of arrows. Then, Richard ordered Norfolk to attack and:

They countered together sad and sore
Archers they let sharp arrows fly
They shot guns both fell and far
Bows of yew bended did be,
Springals sped them speedily.[21]

Henry Tudor's general, the Earl of Oxford, had placed his men in a wedge formation that withstood Norfolk's charge. Fierce hand-to-hand fighting followed in which Norfolk fell, either killed outright or captured and executed shortly afterwards. Also likely to have been among those who died at this point was Thomas Longe of Ashwelthorpe, Norfolk, who like many ordinary soldiers had prepared to do battle for his king by writing a will. As he left home he had declared himself 'willing to die as a child of the church, the said day and time, doing forth unto the king's host'.[22]

The advantage of numbers was still with Richard and in the slow hammering of medieval warfare this was important, yet there remained a risk of treachery. Stanley and Northumberland had not yet engaged, but from his viewpoint on the hill Richard now spotted a means of ending the battle quickly, and in his favour. Henry was riding under his standard with only a small number of bodyguards. Richard realised if he could reach and kill Henry the battle would be over, and, characteristically, he decided to seize his opportunity. 'This day I will die as king or win', he told one his commanders.[23]

As Richard's cavalry thundered down the hill, standards streaming, Henry looked up and saw the crowned figure of the king galloping towards him 'like a hungry lion', battleaxe in hand.[24] As Henry dismounted his bodyguards surrounded him, while his professional pikemen and other foot soldiers formed a defensive position in front. When Richard's charge hit, the force of it was so great that a lance pierced through Henry's standard-bearer, Sir William Brandon, and snapped in half. The Dragon standard fell. But Henry's pikemen held their ground, their weapons piercing the charging horses. Richard and a trusted group of men began cutting their way on foot towards Henry. Bills, axes and swords replaced pikes in the hand-to-hand fighting. As the two sides hacked and slashed at each other, however, they became aware of the rumble of more cavalry bearing down on them. Henry's guard was on the point of despair when a glimpse of red coat told them it was Sir William Stanley's 'tall men'. He too had decided to seize the opportunity to bring the battle to a close – by killing Richard. The king's only hope was to escape the field and fight another day.

According to a Burgundian account, Richard's horse foundered in the marsh and fell. Shakespeare has Richard calling out 'A horse! A horse! My kingdom for a horse!' But with the king unable to escape, the sources attest that Richard was determined not to surrender, and shouting 'Treason! Treason! Treason!' he continued to fight his way towards his rival.[25] Henry's guard, Sir John Cheyne, threw himself in front of Richard, but was knocked out of the way as the king cut his way forward. Meanwhile Sir William's men were killing Richard's body-guard. The royal standard-bearer Sir Percival Thirlwall had his legs severed from under him, and one by one the king's men all fell. It was at the marsh of Fen Hole, in a field behind what is now Fen Lane Farm that the badge of the white boar was found. Eventually Richard 'fighting manfully in the middle of his enemies was slain'.[26] The Burgundian chronicler claims it was a Welshman armed with a pike fitted with an axe, known as a halberd, who took King Richard's life.[27] Others joined him in striking the king's body, smashing his skull, 'until the brain came out with blood'.[28] The body of Richard found in Leicester has a massive injury to the skull that would have exposed the brain and is consistent with a blow from a halberd.

As the news of Richard's death spread, Norfolk's men fled the field with Lord Stanley's in pursuit. Northumberland's men, who had never engaged in the battle, simply rode away. Henry Tudor, 'replenished with joy', rode up the nearest hill. With soldiers and nobles gathered around, he thanked God for his victory and them for their aid, 'promising that he would be mindful of their benefits'. The men in turn shouted 'God save King Henry! God save King Henry!' Their cries inspired Sir William Stanley to fetch Richard's battle crown, though it was not caught in a hawthorn bush as myth now has it. The Tudor heraldic device of the hawthorn was an ancient biblical symbol of renewal and would be used by Henry to represent the rebirth of the House of Lancaster and of Cadwaladr. The crown of the last Yorkist king was found amongst the 'spoils of the field' lying scattered on the ground. Sir William placed it on Henry's head saying 'Sir I make you King of England.'[29]

The last Plantagenet king continued to be stripped until, with 'his body despoiled to the skin, and nought being left about him, so much as would cover his privy member', he was tied on to a horse like 'an hog or another vile beast'. In this manner, and with his hair dangling down, Richard was taken to Leicester behind a junior officer of arms called Norrey. Just 'as gloriously as he by the morning departed from that town, so as irreverently he was that afternoon brought into that town', a chronicler recalled.[30] One of the further injuries discovered on the Leicester bones indicates that he was stabbed through the buttocks, into the pelvis, most likely while he was tied to the horse. His corpse, caked in mud and blood, was to be left exposed to public view for two days, then covered from the waist down with a 'black cloth of poor quality'.[31] Notably, his face had been left largely unmarked.

The killings of the Wars of the Roses spared no one's dignity. Descriptions of Richard III's death resemble those of Warwick the Kingmaker: fighting in the midst of his enemies, suggestions of a blocked escape, and a stripped corpse. That Richard's body was beaten and stabbed after death is also not untypical of the period. The excavated bones of the soldiers killed at Towton in 1461 have revealed similar levels of brutality with skulls shattered and limbs smashed in an orgy of violence. Richard was buried without ceremony at the church of the Greyfriars, where excavations in 2012 uncovered his body. Sir William Stanley was given his pick of

Richard's possessions and chose tapestries from the royal tent. Henry made a more personal choice for his mother: Richard's beautifully illuminated Book of Hours. The dead king had adapted an early fifteenth-century prayer to beg Christ 'to free me thy servant King Richard from all the tribulations, grief and anguish in which I am held, and from all the snares of my enemies'.[32] It seemed God had turned His back on Richard. But Henry's position was still far from secure.

In York, the capital of the north, they mourned King Richard, 'piteously slain and murdered to the great heaviness of this city'.[33] In Coventry the City Annals also record with disgust how 'King Richard . . . was shamefully carried to Leicester.'[34] They were obliged to welcome Henry Tudor that night, nevertheless. He stayed at the house of the mayor, who saw to it that Henry received a gift from the city merchants of £100, and that his men had the provisions they demanded. Over a hundred gallons of red wine were consumed during the celebrations of Henry's army, but notably only about four and a half gallons of ale. Henry had been raised with a preference for claret over English beer, as had many of the foreign troops with him. He was a stranger in this country, at the head of an invading army, with no experience even of managing a nobleman's estate, let alone the kingdom he now held.

9

THE ROSE AND THE PASSION

ON THE BANKS OF THE THAMES, VAST WOODEN CRANES UNLOADED merchandise from the arriving ships, while London's streets jostled with people of every rank.[1] One described England's capital as a town of sharp eyes, silver tongues and barely suppressed violence.[2] When the news that Richard III was dead reached London two days after the battle, the mayor feared it could trigger a free-for-all in the settling of scores. He promptly instituted a curfew while a proclamation threatened immediate jail for those who broke it, or committed any other offence. Plans also began to be laid for the official welcome for England's new ruler.

During twenty-five years of turmoil Londoners had become accustomed to preparing a welcome for the victor of the latest struggle, whoever it was. Yet never had a victor been so obscure. A merchant from Danzig, who regularly visited England, learned that he was called 'King Richmond', and was somehow 'related to Harry' VI.[3] Others knew his name was Tudor only because Richard III had described him as the grandchild of one 'Owen Tudor, bastard born'. Obscurity had its advantages, however. The dubious nature of Henry's Lancastrian claim and the help his invasion had enjoyed from the hated French were potentially embarrassing. He did not want such details exposed now the adventures of his youth were over and the hard business of holding on to power had begun.

Henry's mother sent him the appropriate velvets and silks for his official entry into London and when he arrived with his army north of the City at Shoreditch in early September he was richly dressed, as Edward V had been as he entered London two years earlier.[4] As then, too, hundreds of London's official representatives were waiting, splendidly arrayed in scarlet gowns, and others of tawny and the bright purple-red called 'murrey'. The Spanish merchants in the city reported that the strain of Henry's exile was etched on his face, and he looked older than his twenty-eight years. Nevertheless he was judged 'of pleasing countenance and physique'.[5] Henry listened as Latin verses were read celebrating his return to the city he had not seen since he was thirteen. The man who delivered them was French and it is probable he was hand-picked for the task: Henry still didn't like surprises. The waiting officials then gave Henry a bag of gold raised from local taxes and he thanked them before riding on with his army, trumpets blowing, and the spoils of battle displayed. At the great medieval church of St Paul's Henry offered his three standards at the altar: the Cross of St George, the Red Dragon Dreadful, and the Dun Cow. He gave thanks to God and the Virgin for his victory and the great hymn of thanks, the 'Te Deum', was sung:

> To thee all Angels cry aloud:
> > the Heavens, and all the Powers therein.
> To thee Cherubim and Seraphim:
> > continually do cry,
> Holy, Holy, Holy:
> > Lord God of Sabaoth;
> Heaven and earth are full of the Majesty:
> > of thy glory.

Henry's mother, who had only spent weeks with her son since he was five, was reunited joyfully with him while he rested in the house of the Bishop of London.[6] But they were not to stay in the capital for long. The sense of uncertainty and danger following the killing of Richard III was heightened by the sudden outbreak of a new, virulent disease. It struck only two weeks after Henry entered the city, and was probably brought by his army. It came to be known as the 'sweating sickness'. Like the Spanish flu that swept the world in 1918, 'the sweat' could take the life of a healthy adult in a single day. Victims would develop cold shivers, giddiness, headache and severe pains in the neck, shoulders and limbs. Later came heat and sweating, headache, delirium, a rapid pulse and intense thirst. Palpitations and pains in the heart ended in exhaustion and death. The sweat killed the mayor only a month after Henry's arrival, and a week after that the mayor's replacement had also succumbed.[7]

Henry and Margaret left London for her house at Woking where they had last been together before Henry's exile. Henry loved its gardens and orchards but there was little time that September for reflection and relaxation. He had to take practical measures to secure his position and he needed his mother's advice on a kingdom he knew little about. One of Henry's first actions was to grant Margaret the Palace of Coldharbour in London. There she was to take care of Edward Plantagenet, Earl of Warwick, the ten-year-old son of the executed Duke of Clarence. Even before Henry left the Midlands for London, he had ensured that this boy, the last male Plantagenet, was under lock and key in the Tower. Little Edward Plantagenet must have been in fear for his life. Not only had his father died there, drowned in that infamous barrel of Malmsey wine, the fate of the princes in the Tower still remained a mystery, and one it was evident Henry was in no hurry to solve.

It is possible Henry feared that an investigation into the disappearance of the princes would draw attention to the role of his former ally, Buckingham, or someone else close to his cause. What is certain, however, is that like Richard III, Henry had good reasons for wishing to forestall a cult of the princes. It would not have been wise to allow Yorkist royal saints to compete with the memory of Henry VI, whose cult the Tudor king wished to encourage. Any focus on the princes would also inevitably remind people of the continued strength of the Yorkist claim to the throne represented by Edward Plantagenet and Edward IV's daughters. Nothing was to be said of the princes' disappearance, beyond the vague accusation in Parliament later that autumn that Richard III was guilty of 'treasons, homicides and murders in shedding of infants' blood'.[8]

Henry ordered that Edward Plantagenet should be moved from the Tower to Margaret Beaufort's custody, hoping that eventually the boy would be married to a close ally or relative, as his sister would be. Margaret Beaufort was also to care for Henry's future bride, Elizabeth of York. In order to accommodate them in suitably grand style, Margaret began alterations on Coldharbour almost immediately, with some of the best rooms being made ready for the princess. Henry was in no hurry, however, to fulfil his promise to the Yorkists to marry her. He feared being seen as a mere king consort, and intended to be crowned alone to make it clear that he was king in his own right, as his Lancastrian allies had suggested to him in France. Henry had the perfect excuse for the delay: he needed a papal dispensation to marry the princess since she was a kinswoman. This would take months to arrive, and the coronation ceremonies were planned for October.

Margaret was determined her son's coronation would match, or even surpass, the splendour of that of Richard III. The sudden appearance of a mysterious epidemic had not been a good omen and Henry would need to reassure the country that he was God's chosen ruler. Any speculation on the possible meaning or significance of the sweating sickness was therefore banned, and symbols were chosen that would project the appropriate chivalric values. Amongst them, the most significant was the red rose.

If Henry only wished to associate himself more closely with his half-uncle Henry VI, he could have chosen a more favoured Lancastrian device: Henry VI had used variously a spotted panther, an antelope, and ostrich feathers. Henry Tudor preferred the rarely-used red rose because it was a powerful religious symbol, representing Christ's Passion – his suffering on the Cross for the sins of mankind – the five petals of the heraldic rose corresponding to the five wounds on Christ's crucified body.[9] Twenty-four years later, when the dying Henry ordered thousands of Masses to be said for his soul, he asked for a quarter of them to be dedicated to the Five Wounds.[10]

With the coronation preparations well under way, seven yards of scarlet velvet in dragons and red roses were commissioned, as well as four yards of white cloth of gold with a border of red roses for the ornamental covering, or trapping, for horses. A further couple of hundred roses were ordered in fine lace made of pure gold thread, and the arms of Cadwaladr embroidered, while the footmen were to have jackets in the Tudor colours, of white and green: the colours of purity and renewal.[11]

The coronation began, at last, on 28 October with Henry taking formal possession of the Tower. The next day he was processed to Westminster before the London crowds. Heralds, sergeants-at-arms, trumpeters, esquires, the mayor, aldermen, and nobles, preceded the king dressed in their rich liveries, amongst them the seven-year-old Edward Stafford, Duke of Buckingham, whose father had rebelled against Richard III in 1483. Mindful perhaps of the fate of her nephews, the princes in the Tower, the boy's mother, Katherine Woodville, had hidden him from Richard, shaving his head and dressing him as a girl. With £1,000 on his head he had fled across country from Wales to a family friend in Hereford, riding side-saddle behind a servant.[12] Today he rode astride as a boy once more, dressed in crimson velvet, with a saddle to match his clothes. Henry VII would give his mother Buckingham's wardship the following year, so that any future threat he might pose could be contained, along with that of her other charges.[13]

The king rode under a canopy fringed with twenty-eight ounces of gold and silk, carried by four knights on foot. He was bare-headed, his light brown hair reaching his shoulders, a rich belt slung across his chest, and a long gown of purple velvet furred with ermine on his back. Behind Henry was Jasper Tudor, the newly created Duke of Bedford. He was to be married to the young Duke of Buckingham's mother, Katherine Woodville.[14] Alongside Jasper rode another significant figure: John de la Pole, Duke of Suffolk, husband of Elizabeth Plantagenet, a sister of Edward IV and Richard III. It was said that Richard III had named de la Pole's eldest son, the Earl of Lincoln, as his heir, but Henry was inviting the de la Pole family into the fold, to support him as the true king.[15]

On Sunday 30 October Henry was crowned and anointed at Westminster Abbey, its walls hung with the fine wool cloth known as scarlet. Margaret Beaufort's superior right was overlooked. What power she had would be wielded behind the throne, but it would be very real nonetheless. This was as much her moment of triumph as Henry's, and 'when the king her son was crowned in all that great triumph and glory, she wept marvellously'.[16] Her tears were not of joy alone, however. She was as anxious as her son about the future.

In November Henry sought for his rule the necessary approval of Parliament: the high court of the realm. It was duly confirmed that 'the inheritance of the crowns of England and France abide in the most royal person of our sovereign Lord King Henry VII and in the heirs of his body'. But in contrast to his predecessor, Henry's right to the throne was not described or explained – it was simply accepted as the will of God, made evident by his victory at Bosworth: Henry now had to demonstrate his piety.

The previous year Richard III had announced his 'principal intent and fervent desire . . . to see virtue and cleanliness of living to be advanced'.[17] Henry followed his lead. One of his first statutes was to address the sexual conduct of the clergy. He also intended that his chastity would be publicly advertised in a faithful and fruitful marriage. Henry had met Elizabeth of York several times in the privacy of his mother's house, and found the nineteen-year-old was every inch the beauty she was reputed to be: tall, fair-haired, blue-eyed, with perfectly balanced features.[18] It would emerge that she was also sweet-natured, diplomatic and intelligent. In love, as in war, Henry had proved fortunate.

Elizabeth of York, in turn, was being given an opportunity to get to know her husband-to-be, and she found Henry could be good company. In Brittany he had enjoyed gambling, music, dancing, poetry and literature. He was quick to smile, with an exceptionally expressive face, but his years of vulnerability had made him a man anxious to be in control of every detail of his environment. For his physical protection Henry had replaced the personal service the nobility traditionally offered an English king with a security guard in the French model: huge yeomen, dressed in livery embroidered with red roses. To gain the trust of a man as suspicious as Henry, to breach his defences and win his love: that was Elizabeth of York's challenge.

The royal wedding took place on 18 January 1486. Amongst those present was Owen Tudor's son, Sir David Owen, whose loyalty to Henry was not forgotten. He had been made the king's carver, serving him personally at meals, and would attend all important family occasions over the next forty years. In exchange for his future loyalty as commissioner of the peace in Sussex and serving the king in times of war, he would be given valuable property in England, be made a knight banneret, and marry the heiress to Cowdray in Sussex.[19] He proved to be a chip off the old block too, not only leaving a large family but also several illegitimate children, who were evidently still being conceived well into his old age.[20]

Elizabeth and Henry were reassured that their own children would carry no taint of bastardy. Parliament had rescinded the illegitimacy with which Richard III had labelled Edward IV's children, and the Beaufort line of descent from John of Gaunt had also been declared legitimate, with no exclusion from inheriting the crown, as had existed in the past. With the rights of Elizabeth and Henry's future children secured, their marriage also received particular praise from the Pope, as the basis of a conciliation between the houses of York and Lancaster.[21] The first known broadsheets, the predecessor of the newspaper, were mass printed to advertise this Papal blessing for Henry's rule. Unfortunately the peace Henry had supposedly achieved was not yet truly secured. A Ricardian rebellion had broken out in north Yorkshire and although it soon fizzled out Henry feared there would be further unrest.

The potential Yorkist candidate, as Henry's rival, Edward Planatagent, Earl of Warwick, was returned to the Tower, now aged eleven, and there he would stay.[22] More positive steps were taken to win over the north, with Henry arriving in York in April to woo the capital of Richard III's former heartlands. Reconciliation was to be the theme. Henry VII's entry at the city gate was greeted with designs of red and white roses.[23] The Royal Mint had also issued a coin featuring the first example of the so-called 'Tudor rose' – more accurately the union rose – in which the petals of Henry's red rose are depicted surrounding the petals of the white rose of Elizabeth of York. Most significantly the first child of the union was soon promised: Elizabeth was pregnant.[24]

Late that summer King Henry moved his wife to Winchester, the city believed to have once been the capital of Camelot. Caxton's first edition of Sir Thomas Malory's *Le Morte d'Arthur* had revitalised enthusiasm for the Arthurian legends and Henry saw Malory's account as reflecting his own example of the 'fair unknown' who comes from obscurity to claim his crown. In Malory's story the realm had 'stood in great jeopardy a long while, for every lord that was mighty of men made himself strong, and many wished to be king'. But after Arthur performed the miraculous feat of pulling the sword from the stone the violent English barons were obliged to accept him, 'And so anon was the coronation made, and there was he sworn . . . for to be a true king, to stand with true justice thenceforth, all the days of his life.'[25]

A round table, said to have belonged to Arthur, was displayed on a wall of the Great Hall at Winchester. And it was in this city that Henry hoped his heir – the first prince of the Tudor dynasty – would be born.

10

SECURING THE SUCCESSION

The heavily pregnant Elizabeth of York was processed to her Great Chamber at St Swithin's Priory, Winchester.[1] She stepped up a low platform and sat on a chair under the canopy of rich fabric known as a cloth of estate. A line of courtiers honoured her one by one with formal offerings of wine and spices before she retired in a further procession, with her ladies, to an inner chamber for her confinement. She expected to spend three or four weeks there before she delivered her child, but her labour came early. Margaret Beaufort noted the time in her Book of Hours as 'afore one o'clock after midnight' on 20 September 1486 – only eight months after the marriage.[2] Happily the baby was a healthy boy. Henry VII named him Arthur after the legendary hero on whose tomb the prophecy had been written 'Here lies Arthur, king once, and king to be.'[3]

Margaret Beaufort drew up detailed instructions, based on Lancastrian precedent, for future royal confinements and christenings. Henceforth, Elizabeth of York would deliver her children in a room hung with tapestry decorated with gold fleurs-de-lys, and on a bed with a canopy of crimson satin embroidered with crowns of gold, just as the Lancastrian queen Margaret of Anjou had done.[4] It cannot have been easy for Elizabeth to have her mother-in-law involved, as Margaret was, in even the most intimate areas of her life. Margaret's writ included the running of the nursery, and the private rooms of her son and daughter-in-law. She had ordered, for example, that a physician supervise the nurse breastfeeding Elizabeth's baby, and a yeoman test the king's mattress daily, 'leap upon the bed and roll him up and down'.[5] She was, furthermore, always there, her tiny frame an almost inescapable presence. At Woodstock Palace near Oxford, Margaret's rooms were linked to those of the king by a withdrawing chamber, and in the Tower they were next to the king's chamber. Whenever Elizabeth attended important ceremonial occasions Margaret would be at her side, dressed 'in like mantel and surcoat as the queen, with a rich crownall on her head', or identical 'robes of blood-red cloth furred in white squirrel belly'.[6] This was a public advertisement that they held equal rank.

Although Margaret was known officially only as 'My Lady the King's Mother', she was a queen in all but name and continued to maintain enormous influence over Henry. 'I shall be glad to please you as your heart desire it', he once wrote to her, 'I know well that I am as much bounden so to do, as any creature living, for the great, and singular motherly love and affection that it has pleased you, at all times, to bear me.' He could hardly forget that she had risked her life plotting on his behalf in 1483 and 1485 and it was in this spirit that Henry granted Margaret the rights of a 'femme sole'. Usually a woman's land and legal status went to her husband on her marriage, and only as a widow did she become head of a household as a 'femme sole'. Margaret, although married, could own her property and transact business as a widow could, so that she was subject to no one but the king. Henry also continued to value her judgement. Those who served in her household often went on to serve Henry, and she played an important diplomatic role too, entertaining dignitaries at her London palace, Coldharbour.

Margaret's household was second only to the king's in size and largesse. A servant recalled how at Christmas her hall would feed visiting gentlemen from nine in the morning until seven at night, and no poor were turned away, 'if he were of any honesty, but that he might come to the Buttery or the cellar and drink at his leisure'. 'Few kings [were] better' served than Margaret, and the servant remembered that one Christmas, when he was acting as her carver, he had twenty-five knights follow him in ceremonial procession to her table. There she was sat under a cloth of estate alongside her guest, Cecily of York, the most beautiful of Edward IV's daughters, and a regular visitor.[7]

Cecily's marriage to one of Richard III's allies had been dissolved after Bosworth, and Margaret arranged in 1487/88 for the eighteen-year-old to be married instead to her half-brother Richard Welles. Margaret remained devoted to her non-royal relations, but she extended this warmth to Cecily and Elizabeth of York. Cecily grew very fond of her despite being married off to a man twenty years her senior, and she continued to worship in Margaret's households even after she was widowed in 1499. Later, in 1502, when Cecily angered the king by remarrying a lowly esquire, Margaret defended her, and gave the couple shelter until the king had forgiven them.[8] It is in the context of a loving, but sometimes domineering matriarch, that we have to understand Margaret Beaufort's intriguing relationship with her daughter-in-law.

Margaret kept rooms ever ready for Elizabeth of York to visit, and worried over her daughter-in-law's health and well-being. Following Elizabeth's recovery from one spell of sickness, Margaret thanked God that 'the queen and all our sweet children be in good health'.[9] Elizabeth of York surely found her mother-in-law irritating at times, but a Spanish claim that Elizabeth was 'kept in subjection by the mother of the king', and resented this deeply, is inspired, at least in part, by a long literary tradition of conflict between mother and daughter-in-law. Elizabeth of York had the wisdom to learn to accept Margaret for her warmth, as well as her loyalty, and over the years the two women collaborated on charitable projects, as well as in matters concerning the children. When Henry and Elizabeth had their second child on 28 November 1489 – a girl this time – she was named Margaret after 'my lady the king's mother'.[10]

The devoted new grandmother prepared every detail of the princess' christening and gave her a silver and gilt chest filled with gold.[11] In time Margaret Tudor would prove as crucial to the future of the dynasty as Margaret Beaufort was to its founding, but for the time being the political focus remained on her brother, Arthur, as King Henry's heir. The three-year-old had been created Prince of Wales by 1489 and the royal wardrobe sent regular deliveries for Arthur's servants and himself. They included white velvets and damasks, ermine and black lambskin.

Eighteen months after the birth of Margaret Tudor, a brother was born at Greenwich Palace on 28 June 1491 – the future Henry VIII. It was a testament to Elizabeth of York's fertility that in July 1492 a second daughter was born, named Elizabeth. This was the only time Henry allowed one of his children to be given a name with a stronger association to the queen's family than his own; an acknowledgement of his wife's grief following the recent death of her mother. Sadly, baby Elizabeth died aged three. A further daughter, born in 1496 and named Mary, proved more fortunate, and was an outstandingly pretty child. Two more children would die as infants, Edmund, born in 1499, and Katherine in 1503.

As Henry embarked on fathering this family of the union rose, he continued to work to heal the old divisions amongst the elite. His councillors included veteran Lancastrians like Jasper Tudor, but also old servants of Edward IV like Sir William Stanley, now Chamberlain of the Household. Even former Ricardians were allowed to work their way gradually back into favour. Thomas Howard, Earl of Surrey, whose father, the Duke ('Jack') of Norfolk, was killed at Bosworth, became treasurer. Henry, however, remained an enigma for most Englishmen. The *Great Chronicle of London*, compiled in 1512, could still only venture that the king was 'a gentleman being in the parts of Brittany named Henry and son unto the Earl of Richmond', who was 'induced to claim the crown as right' following the death of the princes in the Tower.[12]

Instead of explaining his past in historical terms Henry promoted the providential nature of his reign – that it was the consequence of God's intervention on earth. The story was told of St Nicholas appearing to his nine-year-old mother, advising her to marry Edmund Tudor, and Henry VI foretelling Henry's reign became all the more significant with the growth of Henry VI's cult. Richard III had hoped to expiate his brother's crime in killing the king and gain control of the cult by moving Henry VI's body from Chertsey Abbey to the royal St George's Chapel at Windsor. With Henry's encouragement the tomb had since become a place of pilgrimage to rival the internationally famous shrine of Thomas Becket at Canterbury. He was now campaigning to have his half-uncle beatified.[13] It was Bosworth, however, that had confirmed the providential nature of Henry's reign, and he wrote proudly of 'the crown which it has pleased God to give us with the victory over our enemy at our first field'.[14] The problem for Henry was that if he lost a future battle, his claims to have been chosen by God would be fatally undermined. All that his enemies needed was a new narrative, and their own 'fair unknown' to rally round.

Henry's anxiety about the continued Yorkist threat was evident in his treatment of Elizabeth Woodville. The dowager queen had been a prominent figure at Arthur's christening, yet five months later, in February 1487, her dower lands were passed to Elizabeth of York and she retired to the convent where she would die in 1492. Historians have suggested that she was mourning the loss of her sons, or that Margaret Beaufort saw her as a rival and wanted her out of the way. But Polydore Vergil believed that Henry wanted her out of sight, and that her retirement was linked to the appearance in Ireland, in February 1487, of a boy claiming he was Edward Plantagenet, Earl of Warwick, and the rightful King of England.[15] Although Henry had the real Plantagenet brought out of the Tower and paraded through the streets of London, not everyone was certain which boy was the genuine article.[16] Henry rightly feared the pretender could, therefore, be used as a Yorkist rallying figure to overthrow him. Elizabeth Woodville's presence at court was extremely unhelpful to Henry in this regard: however loyal she might be to her little grandson Arthur, he was a Tudor and she was a reminder of the former glories of the House of York.[17]

It was not long before the shadowy figures behind this conspiracy of the pretender emerged. The first was Edward IV's nephew, John de la Pole, Earl of Lincoln: the eldest of three brothers who would trouble the Tudor dynasty well into the reign of Henry VIII. Richard III was believed to have named Lincoln as his heir, and his aunt, Margaret, Duchess of Burgundy, had raised an army of Swiss and German mercenaries to place at his disposal. Madame la Grande, as the duchess was known in Burgundy, was the widow of Charles the Bold of Burgundy to whom she had been married in 1468.[18] The duchy which now gives its name to a mere province of France was, at the time of her marriage, then a great power, stretching across not only what remains under that name, but also most of north-west France, Belgium and the Netherlands. Charles the Bold had provided his brother-in-law, Edward IV, with part of the army with which he had overthrown the re-established Henry VI in 1471. There was no reason to suppose that this 'renewed' Lancastrian dynasty, the Tudors, could not be similarly overthrown.

In April 1487 Lincoln sailed with his army from Burgundy to Ireland to join the pretender. His grandfather had been Lord Lieutenant of the country and he had no shortage of friends awaiting him there. Henry, by contrast, angered the most powerful figure in Ireland, Gerald Fitzgerald, Earl of Kildare, by refusing to confirm his role as deputy Lord Lieutenant. As soon as Lincoln landed in Ireland he was welcomed with open arms by Kildare. He promptly recognised the pretender as the 'real' Edward Plantagenet and on 24 May the boy was crowned in Dublin as 'Edward VI', with a gold circlet taken from a statue of the Virgin Mary. The following month, with Kildare's backing, Lincoln launched the first, and last, Irish invasion of England with 'Edward VI' at its head.

According to Tudor accounts the pretender's real name was Lambert Simnel, the son of an artisan in Oxford who had been groomed for his role by a local priest.[19] Lincoln, who had property near Oxford, is assumed to have paid for the necessary education. In public, however, he and the other commanders had to treat the child as their 'king'. Disembarking at Furness in Lancashire, the rebels moved rapidly eastwards, crossing the Pennines into Wensleydale, gathering recruits under the banner of Edward VI, before pressing south. They included a core of Yorkists, their new English recruits, 4,000 Irishmen and the 1,500 German mercenaries, known as *Landsknecht*, who had been provided by Margaret of Burgundy. These latter were a fearsome sight. Their brightly coloured clothes were taken from fallen opponents, and since they didn't always fit properly, they slashed and tied them; while their hats were similarly decorated with bright and gaudy feathers. It inspired fashionable dress at many of the courts of Europe – minus the bloodstains of the fallen enemies that befouled the mercenaries' costumes and added to the terror of the spectacle of their advance.

The scale of Lincoln's army was similar to Henry's invasion force in 1485, and the fragility of the Tudor king's grip on the throne was evident in London where rumours of a rebel victory saw people take to the streets on behalf of 'Edward VI'. Henry was well prepared for the confrontation, however. He had prayed at the famous English shrine to the Virgin at Walsingham, and as he awaited news of the rebel advance in the Midlands, he had twice the rebel numbers at his command. They included 'a great host of the Earl of Derby's folks' – his stepfather Thomas Stanley's men. When the news came Henry bid farewell to 'our dearest wife and . . . our dearest mother' and headed north from Kenilworth Castle in Warwickshire with Jasper Tudor to face the rebels.

The armies met on a hillside near the village of East Stoke in Nottinghamshire. 'Both sides fought with the bitterest energy,' Polydore Vergil records, 'the Germans, so practised in warfare, were in the forefront of the battle and yielded little to the English ... but the Irish, though they fought most spiritedly, were nevertheless (in the tradition of their country) unprotected by body armour and [they] suffered heavy casualties, their slaughter striking no little terror into the other combatants.' As the Irish fell in their hundreds Lincoln was killed, and 'the lad' Simnel, whom the 'rebels called King Edward', was captured.[20]

Margaret Beaufort greeted news of her son's victory with a cele-bratory note in her Book of Hours. A prayer, copied in, also fervently beseeched 'Almighty God' for his favour in sustaining 'our King Henry to govern the realm and increase in glory'.[21] Henry, she knew, still faced the major problem of how to re-engage Yorkist loyalties. He began work on this immediately with a northern progress through the Yorkist heartlands and the announcement of his wife's imminent coronation. It took place that November and was preceded by the first river pageant ever to take place on the eve of a queen's coronation.[22] It proved a splendid occasion. Crowds cheered the tall and lovely Elizabeth of York as she was rowed in a great barge decorated with tapestries followed by other barges filled with the nobility. Yet even here violence lurked close to the surface. The procession to Westminster Abbey, where she was crowned that Sunday, degenerated into a bloody farce as the crowds fought furiously over the ray cloth laid for her to walk on from Westminster Hall. There was a tradition that once a coronation procession had passed, people could keep whatever they grabbed of the cloth, but the free-for-all got so frenzied that 'in the [queen's] presence certain persons were slain'.[23]

The banquet that night proved more decorous with Margaret

Beaufort and the king watching the festivities through a latticed window. Twenty-three dishes were served for the first course and twenty-nine for the second, from pheasant and perch to a 'castle of jelly wisely made'. The ten-year-old Lambert Simnel was soon to be found working in the royal kitchens turning the spit for occasions such as this. Henry believed humiliation would be more effective than death in erasing the aura of kingship in Simnel who, whatever his orgins, had been anointed with Holy Chrism – and it worked. Simnel was eventually promoted to trainer of the king's hawks, surviving well into the next century.[24] Yet the successful conclusion to the conspiracy, and Elizabeth of York's magnificent coronation, had done little to make Henry more secure.

There is a story that Lincoln and the other rebel commanders at East Stoke had been buried with green willow staves plunged into their hearts, to prevent them rising up once more to trouble the living.[25] There were no stakes, however, for the vanished brothers of Elizabeth of York. Not only were their bodies lost, but the fate of their souls had also seemingly been abandoned. Research for this book has uncovered no references to public prayers or Masses being said for the dead princes.[26] Henry may not have wanted chantries – which were endowments that paid for Masses for the souls of loved ones – since the churches where they were established could have become a centre for the kind of cult that he wanted to avoid. But their absence would have struck people as very strange.

Praying for the dead was a crucial part of medieval religion. In December 1485, when Henry issued a special charter refounding his favourite religious order, the ascetic Observant Friars at Greenwich, he noted that offering Masses for the dead was 'the greatest work of piety and mercy, for through it souls would be purged'.[27] It was unthinkable not to help the souls of your loved ones pass from purgatory to heaven with prayers and Masses. On the other hand, it was akin to a curse to say a requiem for a living person – you were effectively praying for their death. The obvious question posed by the lack of prayers for the princes was, were they still alive? And, as Vergil recalled, only four years later there appeared as if 'raised from the dead one of the sons of King Edward . . . a youth by the name of Richard'.[28] It was to have a devastating effect on Henry as a man, and as a king.

11

THE LOST PRINCE

ACCORDING TO THE TALE THAT REACHED THE ENGLISH COURT, THE assassin sent in 1483 to murder the ten-year-old Richard, Duke of York could not bring himself to kill 'so little a child'. Instead he had helped the boy to flee the Tower to Europe, telling him never to reveal his identity. Remembered as 'joyful and witty', Richard was recognised only when he appeared in Ireland in 1491 as an attractive eighteen-year-old with a lazy eye, working in the cloth business. Three marks on his body were said to confirm his identity, although the detective work done for Henry concluded that the man modelling his master's silks was, in fact, born in Tournai, Burgundy. There he was known as 'little Peter the orphan', in Dutch 'Pierrekin Wezebecque', a name anglicised to Perkin Warbeck. The silks he modelled were as princely as he got.

There is no account of how Elizabeth Woodville, in her convent, reacted to the news of her son 'Richard' supposedly being alive. We do know, however, that Henry had been treating her well: by 1490 she was receiving an annuity to compensate for the lands she had lost to her daughter, and even after Perkin appeared, the king gave a Christmas gift of fifty marks to 'our most dear Queen Elizabeth mother to our own dear wife'.[1] Yet when she died in July 1492 she was buried 'privily . . . without any solemn dirge done for her obit', indeed 'nothing was done solemnly for her' except the provision of a hearse, 'such as they use for common people'. It has been suggested that this may reflect her dying wishes to be buried 'without pomp', but while Henry V had eschewed any 'damnable superfluities' for his funeral, and Henry VII would seek to avoid undue 'pomp' at his, they still expected, and got, amongst the most stately funerals of the Middle Ages.[2] Elizabeth Woodville most emphatically had not, and this caused negative comment at the time. Henry remained anxious not to encourage nostalgia for the past glories of the House of York.

In common with Lambert Simnel, Perkin had a powerful foreign backer – in his case Charles VIII of France, and it was to France that Perkin travelled from Ireland under his new name of Richard, Duke of York. Charles had been irritated by Henry's support for the independence of Brittany and now hoped to overthrow the king he had backed against Richard III in 1485. Henry, who believed in using maximum aggression against any perceived threat, promptly laid siege to Boulogne with an army of 15,000 men. Owen Tudor's son, Sir David Owen, was made a knight bannaret for his courage in the field and the siege was successfully concluded with a treaty in which Henry gave up his support for the independence of Brittany, while Henry achieved the two things he most wanted: a pension to pay for his future security, and Perkin's expulsion from France.

Unhappily for Henry, Perkin was still free and he fled on to Burgundy where Edward IV's sister Margaret, Duchess of Burgundy, greeted him as her long-lost nephew. The two opposing Margarets in Henry's life – his devoted mother and the duchess – had met in 1480 during the duchess' last visit to King Edward's court.[3] Tall, like Edward IV, the duchess towered over Margaret Beaufort, who later sniffed about the huge hands the women of Burgundy seemed to have. She also had a formidable presence, with a stiff-backed carriage, a reserved manner, unsmiling, grey eyes, and 'an air of intelligence and will'. The firm belief that women were prisoners of their emotions saw the duchess' motives in backing Perkin ascribed in England to a hysterical desire to avenge Richard III. Polydore Vergil wrote of her 'insatiable hatred' for Henry, and the chronicler Edward Hall of her 'frantic mood' as she worked 'to suck his blood and compass his destruction'. In fact, the duchess acted solely in the interests of Burgundy and worked closely with her step-family.

On the death of the duchess' beloved stepdaughter Marie in 1482, the Duchy of Burgundy had been inherited by Marie's son, Philip the Fair. The old duchess had since worked closely with Philip's father, Maximilian von Hapsburg, who became Holy Roman Emperor in 1493, and was to be regent of Burgundy until Philip was sixteen in 1494. The family were concerned by Henry's rapprochement with their French enemy. But they also had possible ambitions to take England from Henry, just as he had taken it from Richard III. Maximilian was descended from John of Gaunt in a legitimate blood-line, and once Perkin had been used to oust Henry, Maximilian commented icily, 'he would dispose of this duke *ad libitum suum*' – that is, as he saw fit.[4]

Henry might have solved the Perkin problem by proving Perkin was not who he claimed to be. But he had left it rather late to start looking for the bodies of the princes in the Tower. Rather than risk finding at least one body missing, Henry hit upon a means of advertising the death of the little Richard, Duke of York, without mentioning the princes at all. He would bestow the boy's title on his second son.[5]

Henry's decision must have been a painful one for Elizabeth of York, who had loved her brother. Even nineteen years after he had disappeared she was still giving gifts to his old nurse.[6] But dutifully she joined the celebrations when her three-year-old son, 'Lord Harry, Duke of York', was invested with her brother's title in November 1494. It was an occasion the future Henry VIII would never forget. There were three days of tournaments and banquets, with Lord Harry dressed for his parade in a miniature suit of armour, while his five-year-old sister, the princess Margaret, awarded the prizes after the tournaments.

But their father was aware there were traitors at the feasts. An

English conspirator 'turned' by Henry's spies in Burgundy had revealed a plan to assassinate him before an invasion was launched.[7] Henry's children were to be disinherited – or killed – in favour of 'Richard, Duke of York'. And at least one traitor was very close to the Tudor family: Henry's step-uncle, Sir William Stanley.[8] Henry had lavished his favour on Sir William since his forces had won the battle of Bosworth for the king in 1485, and he was reputedly the richest commoner in England. Yet Sir William was reported as having said that if Richard, Duke of York, were alive he would never stand against him. Over the next few weeks Henry watched and waited.

The Christmas celebrations were as lavishly celebrated as ever. The previous year Sir William had spent Twelfth Night with the royal family at Westminster. The entertainments had included 'St George' and a beautiful maiden leading a fire-spitting dragon through the hall, before the singing and dancing began with a procession of twelve masked men and women. As the music played the men danced and leapt so that spangles of gold fell from their costumes and scattered over the floor, while the ladies, moving as one in their long dresses, seemed to be gliding. Afterwards there were wines, ales and fine food spread over a tablecloth that glittered and sparkled in the candlelight. The entertainment went on until dawn.[9] On 7 January 1495, however, the new day brought Sir William's downfall. A spy was prompted to 'reveal' all to Henry, who ordered Sir William's arrest.

Sir William believed his offence – merely saying that he would not stand against Richard, Duke of York – was small enough to earn the king's forgiveness. But, Vergil recorded, 'Henry feared such leniency to be dangerous to himself – others would be encouraged by William's avoidance of punishment and would undertake similar acts of folly'. The man who had saved Henry's life at Bosworth was executed in February 1495. Henry's last acknowledgment of the red coats of Sir William's men riding to his rescue at Bosworth was the £10 he gave to the executioner to make the death as quick and painless as possible. Betrayal by such a man had made the threat of assassination more frightening and Henry withdrew to his chambers as his suspicions bred. It was yet one more example of treachery by a king's close kin and friends: Edward IV by his brother Clarence, Edward V by his uncle Richard III, Richard III by his ally the Duke of Buckingham.

Determined to survive, Henry's desire to control his kingdom now intensified. The nobility were sidelined in favour of officials from lowly origins who owed him everything, and he did not create many new nobles from their ranks. There had been fifty-five nobles at his accession, but by the time of his death there were only forty-two.[10] Rather than ruling with the elite, as Kings of England always had, Henry kept them in fear. He imposed fines for offences, real and imagined, and obliged them to sign bonds for their good behaviour. Henry asked to be paid back only a little each year – so long as they retained his favour. Otherwise they would be ruined. Henry was ruling at the edge of the law, pushing his private rights to preserve his public position, and as the money rolled in the royal accounts were annotated minutely in Henry's own hand. But the more powerful he became the less regal he appeared. In Burgundy, Perkin, by contrast, resembled the young Henry of 1485, the 'fair unknown', awaiting his opportunity.

Perkin had his own court in exile, and by July 1495 he was ready to take 'his' throne, setting sail from Burgundy with fourteen ships and an invasion force of 6,000 men.[11] Perkin had assumed all the charm expected of a prince, but he had none of the battle training. When he reached Deal in Kent his advance guard of 163 were slaughtered on the shore and Perkin ran away with his army, sailing on to Ireland and then Scotland, where at last he found refuge at the court of the twenty-two-year-old James IV. The Scottish king was happy at least to pretend that he believed Perkin was Richard – annoying Kings of England was a pleasurable and traditional pastime for Scottish monarchs.[12] He had Perkin married to a beautiful young lady of the court, Lady Catherine Gordon, and agreed to take part in an invasion of England.

Perkin prepared a manifesto, which he hoped would prompt

spontaneous uprisings in his favour as soon as the invasion began. It described Henry as the son of 'Owen Tudor of low birth in the country of Wales', a usurper, who had cruelly raised taxes, stopped valuable trade with Burgundy, undermined God's order by replacing the nobility with commoners, and persecuted them with his financial bonds.[13] Perkin promised to end this wickedness and return to the 'good governance' of his 'father' Edward IV. From the perspective of his host, King James, if Perkin ended up on the throne all well and good: James was more interested, however, in the benefits of a popular strike against Scotland's hated neighbour, and large-scale pillaging. As soon as the invasion began James IV and his Scots 'laid waste the fields, pillaged and then burnt the houses and villages. The men who resisted he cruelly killed.'[14] This destroyed any chance of the northern English rising for Perkin and he retreated, aghast, back to Scotland to consider his next move.

Once again Henry intended to deal with the threat to his rule aggressively. He levied huge taxes to fund a massive retaliatory assault on Scotland; but then something unexpected happened. Far from the threat of Scottish invasion the impoverished inhabitants of Cornwall, resentful of the taxes, rebelled against Henry. They swept eastwards and had reached Blackheath, only two and a half miles from the royal palace at Greenwich, before Henry at last defeated them on 17 June 1497. The rebel leader 'Lord Audley was drawn from Newgate to the Tower Hill in a coat of his own arms, painted upon paper reversed and all to torn'.[15] Other rebels were sold into slavery, their lands confiscated, or huge fines imposed, and the west still seethed with resentment when, on 3 September, two Italian ambassadors were granted an audience with Henry at Woodstock in Oxfordshire.

Henry had a reputation in Europe as a king who had acquired huge riches and the Italians were anxious to meet him. They were escorted deep into the palace, through ever more richly decorated rooms, until they reached 'a small hall' hung with the tapestries sewn with thread made of pure gold, known as Arras. At the far end stood the king, his hand resting on a gilded chair. Henry was wearing a black cap pinned with 'a large diamond and a most beautiful pearl'. A violet cloak, lined with cloth of gold, fell to the ground, and around his neck he wore a collar with four rows of precious stones and pearls. Standing alongside him was Prince Arthur. A month from his eleventh birthday, Arthur was tall for his age, and of 'singular beauty and grace'. He chatted fluently to the ambassadors in Latin, confirming the view held in diplomatic circles that he was 'a most distinguished' future son-in-law for Ferdinand and Isabella of Spain – Henry had signed a treaty of friendship with the Spanish monarchs which was to be sealed with a marriage between Arthur and their daughter, Katherine of Aragon. Henry too was judged 'gracious' and 'grave', and they admired his clear and exquisite French.[16]

Following a private meeting with Henry after dinner the ambassadors were invited to meet the queen. They found Elizabeth of York in another small room looking most 'handsome', in her stiff cloth of gold. It was best to stand in these royal fabrics, which were made with gold beaten into long strips and wound around a silk core before being woven, sometimes with green, red or white, to give it a particular colour. If you sat, the metal bent, which could leave deep creases. Elizabeth of York was beside her small, energetic mother-in-law, and her boisterous second son, the six-year-old Harry, Duke of York.[17] A terracotta figure of a laughing, red-haired boy dressed in a jacket of green cloth of gold, is believed to be of the future Henry VIII at around this time. The cheeks are round and pink, the narrow eyes look away from the viewer, and the teeth flash white. The Italians were informed that there was famine in the rebel heartlands of the west, a sign 'that the king is under the protection of God eternal'.[18] His sons also advertised the security of succession and Henry seemed to them calm and confident, which was exactly the image he wished to project.

It was a front. Henry was anxiously waiting to see what Perkin would do next and the answer was not long coming. Only four days later Perkin landed at Whitesand Bay in Cornwall. Within weeks he had raised 8,000 men under his standard, which depicted a boy emerging from a tomb, and Exeter was put under siege.[19] But when the king's superior forces moved south, Perkin's lack of military training was again evident. He tried to flee the country, but was soon captured with his wife. Henry treated Lady Catherine Gordon as a victim of Perkin's duplicity, and she was found an honourable place in the queen's household. Once again Elizabeth of York's feelings were not considered, and for a time she was obliged to see the man who had posed as her dead brother at court, where he was expected to admit repeatedly his humble origins in Tournai.[20]

Rumours continued to circulate that Perkin was a Plantagenet, and as they did so his situation became increasingly grim. A deliberately engineered 'escape' attempt saw him sent to the misery and humiliation of the stocks, and then to a dungeon in the Tower. With Perkin placed out of sight, and mind, Henry had a glamorous official history of his own life and accession read at court.[21] Entitled 'The Twelve Triumphs of Henry VII', the story mimicked the myth of the Labours of Hercules, and described how God had helped Henry survive the machinations of the Duchess of Burgundy, who was cast as Juno, Hercules' relentless enemy.[22]

Perkin was to appear at court once more. When a Burgundian bishop requested an interview with him in August 1498, Henry agreed to bring him out of the Tower, and suggested that the Spanish ambassador also see him. Henry hoped to reassure Ferdinand and Isabella that Perkin no longer posed any threat. Perkin was duly brought from the Tower where, the Spanish ambassador was assured, 'he sees neither sun nor moon'. He appeared frail, and 'so much changed' the ambassador judged that he did not have long to live.[23] Henry asked Perkin why he had pretended to be Richard, Duke of York. Perkin dutifully blamed Margaret, Duchess of Burgundy. A previously unnoticed detail in the Great Wardrobe Accounts reveals Henry was so happy with Perkin's performance that in November he rewarded him with a smart new doublet of black damask as well as new shirts and hose to wear in the Tower.[24] However, an incident just a few months later left the Spanish still doubtful the Tudor dynasty had a long-term future.

Shut away in the Tower, along with Perkin, was the genuine last male heir of the House of York: Edward Plantagenet, Earl of Warwick, who after a few brief months in the care of Margaret Beaufort had been imprisoned in 1486 aged eleven, following the first stirring of Yorkist dissent. In February 1499 a new impostor claiming to be Edward Plantagenet was caught. He was soon hanged, but the Spanish were now aware that there was a royal prisoner in the Tower who remained a possible focus for future anti-Tudor feeling. The Spanish sent Henry a message implying strongly that if Arthur's marriage to Katherine of Aragon was to go ahead, Edward Plantagenet's life was a luxury Henry could not afford. Henry was devastated by this threat. King Ferdinand and Queen Isabella had reconquered Granada, expelled the Muslim invaders, and taken a united Spain to the front rank of European powers. Arthur's marriage to their daughter would announce to the world that the Tudors were fit to be embraced by the great monarchies of Europe. Yet Henry shrank from the price now demanded of him. In March he was so troubled that a visitor thought he aged twenty years in a month.

Henry had regular, even daily 'private conversations' with his Franciscan confessors, and still sent expensive gifts to the cathedral in Vannes where St Vincent Ferrer, the messenger of penance, was buried.[25] He was genuinely torn between the requirements of the confessional, with its demand for an honest examination of conscience, and the brutal necessities of rule. As he struggled with his decision Henry heard a sermon every day that Lent, 'and continued for the rest of the day at his devotions'.[26] Eventually, he convinced himself that he would be justified in testing Edward Plantagenet's loyalty, and that if his prisoner proved willing to commit treason, then executing him would be an honest decision, and not plain murder.

Henry chose Perkin to act as his agent provocateur. The new black damask suit Perkin wore had inspired his hope of the king's favour, and this was reinforced when Perkin was transferred to comfortable rooms beneath those of Edward Plantagenet. Perkin duly made contact and the royal prisoner did not prove difficult to fool. Modern forensic psychologists observe that those imprisoned as children remain childlike into adulthood.[27] This was very evident with this long-term inmate of the Tower. Aged twenty-four he was querulous and so under-educated it was said he didn't even know the difference between a chicken and a goose.

In the summer of 1499 Perkin convinced his naive victim that he had a plan that would free them both and place one of them on the throne. Edward Plantagenet listened, rarely making any comment, but in failing to call a halt to the plans he had committed treason. On 3 August the 'conspiracy' was betrayed to the king. Perkin was tried and, after a final confession that he was no Plantagenet, hanged at Tyburn as a common criminal on 23 November. Whatever his hopes of favour had been, he embraced his death 'quietly'. The following Thursday afternoon the bewildered Edward was escorted to Tower Hill, and there the last male Plantagenet was beheaded. The Spanish ambassador crowed: 'there does not remain a drop of doubtful royal blood; the only royal blood being the true blood of the king, the queen and, above all, of the Prince of Wales'.[28] The marriage between Katherine of Aragon and Prince Arthur could now go ahead: a marriage which the bride later commented unhappily was 'made in blood'.[29]

Henry had Edward Plantagenet buried in a family vault alongside his maternal grandfather, Warwick the Kingmaker.[30] But nothing could disguise the brutality of his action. Even the Tudor apologist Polydore Vergil recorded how 'The entire population mourned the death' of the last son of the House of York; 'Why indeed the unhappy boy should have been committed to prison, not for any fault of his own, but only because of his family's offences, why he was retained so long in prison and what, lastly, the worthy youth could have done in prison which could merit his death – all these things could obviously not be comprehended by many'.[31] Vergil went on, however, to supply the answer: 'Earl Edward had to perish in this fashion in order that there should be no surviving male heir to his family'.[32] The House of York was now as defunct as that of Lancaster.

12

PUNISHMENT

'THIS DAY', MARGARET BEAUFORT WROTE, 'I DID BRING YOU INTO this world my good and gracious prince, king and only beloved son.' It was 1501, forty-four years since she had given birth to Henry at Pembroke Castle, and he was losing his most trusted councillors to old age, amongst them his uncle Jasper. Margaret Beaufort was in constant pain from arthritis, while Henry, only thirteen years younger and aged by a hard life, was also suffering physical decline. He complained to his 'beloved lady and mother', 'my sight is nothing so perfect as it has been, and I know well it will impair daily'.[1] Others noticed that his teeth were 'few, poor and blackish' and that he suffered recurring throat infections. In May, when Henry became seriously ill at a royal hunting lodge in Essex, courtiers began to discuss the succession.

Henry's eldest son, Arthur, aged fourteen, was the apple of his father's eye, studious and reserved. As Prince of Wales he already had his own carefully vetted council and household based at Ludlow Castle. His younger brother, the ten-year-old Harry, Duke of York, still luxuriating in the care of his mother and grandmother, was a livelier, more easy-going child. The previous year he had teased the famous scholar Desiderius Erasmus when he came to dinner, sending a note down the table challenging him to match the poetry the young courtier Thomas More had brought as a gift. The great man was sent into a spin of anxiety, yet he also saw in the boy 'a certain dignity, combined with singular courtesy'. They were sons Henry VII could be proud of, and the king 'was full of paternal affection, careful of their education, aspiring to their high advancement, regular to see that they should not want of any due honour and respect'.[2] Nevertheless, an official at Calais reported that, as the king lay ill, his young sons were not mentioned as possible candidates for the throne.

After the instability of the recent past, an adult was preferred as the next king, and 'many divers and great personages' put forward the claims of Edward Stafford, Duke of Buckingham and Edmund de la Pole, Duke of Suffolk. The first of these was the son of the duke who had turned against Richard III and rebelled in 1483. Buckingham had attended Henry VII's coronation procession as a boy, riding on a horse with a red velvet saddle. Now, he was a large athletic twenty-three-year old, and in Calais it was said he was 'a noble man and would be a royal ruler'.[3] He would be long remembered by poets who called him 'the beautiful swan', after the heraldic device of his Bohun ancestors, and as a prince descended from John of Gaunt's brother, Thomas of Woodstock.[4] The other candidate, Edmund de la Pole, Duke of Suffolk, had been younger brother of the late Earl of Lincoln, who had led the Irish invasion against Henry with the boy pretender Lambert Simnel in 1487. Suffolk had worked hard to prove his loyalty since then, but Henry could never quite trust him.

To outsiders Henry's self-control gave the impression of 'most quiet spirit', but beneath the surface his suspicious mind was ever at work. Henry had taken advantage of Buckingham's minority to nibble away at the duke's vast estates, and since then had deprived him of important office. Suffolk, perceived as the greater threat, was kept still more tightly bound, laden with humiliating debts, while being deprived of honours and income. It was fortunate that Henry had recovered his health by August 1501 when Suffolk finally lost patience and left England to claim the sobriquet of 'the White Rose'. It was also a relief to Henry that Arthur's long-planned marriage to Katherine of Aragon was poised to take place.

The king sent orders to every gentleman of substance in England, asking them to prepare to attend on the Spanish princess when she arrived. Margaret Beaufort recorded the great day, 2 October, in her Book of Hours, when, after a difficult sea voyage, 'my lady princess landed' at Plymouth harbour. The English greeted a pretty fifteen-year-old with almond-shaped eyes and red auburn hair. She had been named after her great-grandmother, Katherine of Lancaster, the daughter of John of Gaunt, and if she did not as yet speak any English, this did nothing to dampen public enthusiasm for the marriage. A Spanish attendant wrote home, observing merrily that she 'could not have been received with greater rejoicings if she had been the Saviour of the world'.[5]

Katherine had arrived from the light and heat of Spain as the chill of an English autumn set in. Nevertheless she found there was much for her to admire in her new homeland. The land produced excellent beef, lamb and venison, its waters plentiful fish, seabirds and young swan, and they nurtured a tall, fair, good-looking race. The English were judged 'pious' by an Italian visitor and he noted they put their money where their hearts were, with 'Their riches . . . displayed in the churches treasurers', the buildings well maintained, with painted walls, exquisite stained-glass windows, and masterpieces of carved oak. Often this included a magnificent rood screen. These structures were solid to waist height with open arches above, and across the top a beam that supported the 'rood'. Here were displayed the figures of Christ on the Cross along with his mother, the Virgin Mary, and his friend, St John.[6] They were used to divide the central section of the church between the area where the priest conducted Mass to the east, and where the congregation stood to the west.

In contrast to today, the priest said Mass in Latin facing away from the congregation, who would pray or read privately on the other side of the rood screen. Many attended Mass daily, and the Italian visitor described women 'carrying long rosaries in their hands', reciting the Creed, the Our Father and the Hail Mary in Latin, and also reading prayers in English (or being read to by a friend) 'in a low voice after the manner of churchmen'. For Katherine, whose mother had fought to defend Christian Spain by expelling the Muslim invaders, this was pleasing to watch.

Yet if the church was part of the rhythm of daily life, the English were also interested in ideas. Unity on discipline under the Pope was not matched by unanimity of thought in the late medieval church. There were as many as nine identifiable 'schools', and debates could be fierce. These often took place across dinner tables, for the English loved entertaining. Europeans were astonished by the freedom given to women in this regard: they could come and go to see their friends without their menfolk, and there was a high degree of physical familiarity. Erasmus described it as a 'world of kisses' where your hostess would greet you lip to lip and girls expected to dance while held in a man's arms. With all this warmth and passion around her, the teenage Katherine of Aragon, who was by nature romantic, was surely all the more keen to meet her prince, and when she reached Hampshire she was assured she would do so soon. First, however, she had to meet his father.

It was the afternoon and Katherine was resting when King Henry arrived. Her ladies insisted she was on siesta, but Henry, ever controlling, was determined to ensure she was all he had hoped for his son. Katherine took this in good part, greeting him with 'great joy and gladness'. She seemed to Henry the perfect princess: attractive, collected and gracious. An hour later Katherine was introduced to Arthur. Only just fifteen, he was formal and self-deprecating, of above average height though slightly built, very like his father as a boy. He greeted her in perfect Latin, before she returned the compliment. He 'had never felt so much joy in his life', he wrote to her parents, as when he saw her 'sweet face'.[7] Then they parted, to meet again at their wedding.

It was Friday 12 November by the time Katherine reached London, and prepared for her formal entry into the capital. The city walls were judged very 'handsome' and foreign visitors were struck in particular by the magnificence of the Tower, and 'a convenient and beautiful bridge over the Thames, of many marble arches, which has on it many shops built of stone, and mansions, and even a church of considerable size'.[8]

The women of the Tudor family watched the procession together from a high room, 'not in very open sight'. Margaret Beaufort, married from the age of twelve and never by choice, had used her power as the king's mother to take a vow of celibacy and insist on an amicable separation from her husband, something that was, given his lack of say in the matter, probably unique.[9] She now wanted to focus on her charitable and educative works and was about to embark on translations of religious works in French, achievements that would be followed by later royal women.[10] Alongside her stood Elizabeth of York. The queen had grown plump with the years, but happier. The tension evident in the early days of her marriage, when her husband was so sensitive about their relative status, was gone: Henry had come to love her deeply and her influence on her husband had grown to match that of her mother-in-law.[11] The queen's daughters were also watching: Margaret Tudor, a tomboyish child of almost twelve, was dressed in cloth of gold, while the pretty golden-haired Mary, aged five, was in red velvet, a favourite colour.

Londoners had prepared pageants celebrating Henry's Lancastrian descent from John of Gaunt – the common ancestor of Arthur and Katherine – and the ten-year-old Henry, Duke of York, accompanied his new sister-in-law as the crowds cheered their welcome. He was huge for his age, with a casual artlessness that was quite in contrast to his father's and brother's formality. Later that week he would be seen ripping off his gown to dance freely in his jacket, full of energy and life. Margaret Beaufort had a particularly soft spot for him and had even asked the king's permission for her northern tenants to swear their lives as retainers to 'my Lord of York, your sweet fair son'.[12] But it was the fifteen-year-old Katherine of Aragon who was the centre of attention. Dressed in 'rich apparel' and riding on a mule, she wore 'a little hat fashioned like a cardinal's of a pretty braid' pinned on her long hair.[13] A witness commented that she 'thrilled the hearts of everyone', having 'all those qualities that make for beauty in a very charming young girl'.[14]

Katherine spent her wedding eve with her future mother-in-law and the other women of the family at Baynard's Castle.[15] A programme of building had transformed the fortress into a pleasure palace which stretched between two massive octagonal towers and was crowned by French-inspired turrets. Katherine enjoyed a convivial evening of 'good conversation, dancing and disportes' with the English ladies dressed in the latest French fashions.[16] The following day St Paul's was packed with people for the wedding ceremony. The walls of the cathedral were dressed with tapestries and gold plate, as well as holy relics hanging in their exquisite cases of precious metals and stones.[17] Platforms, covered with red cloth and tacked with gilded nails, had been built at head height so that the bride and groom could be seen above the crowded congregation. Amongst them was Owen Tudor's bastard son, Sir David Owen, who had his memories too of the marriage of Henry VII and Elizabeth of York.[18] Holding hands, Katherine and Arthur turned this way and that on the raised walkways to show themselves: Katherine dressed in white satin, her veil bordered with a broad band of pearls, gold thread and precious stones, and Arthur dressed alike, also in bejewelled white.[19]

There are no contemporary descriptions of Katherine and Arthur in the immediate aftermath to the wedding. It was later claimed that on the first morning Arthur had called for ale to quench his thirst after spending a night 'in the midst of Spain'. Katherine remembered only that they were exhausted by the entertainments. A week of further celebrations followed, culminating in a final party at Richmond Palace, which was in the process of being rebuilt on the ancient royal manor of Sheen. It was to become Henry VII's favourite residence, and the first phase of his project had just been completed. There were courtyards with fountains, light-filled galleries overlooking knot gardens decorated with the royal heraldic beasts, and new, private interior rooms for the royal family. Henry had decided to divide the abovestairs chamber into a personal and a ceremonial area. The former was now called the Privy Chamber, and it was here he found the privacy he longed for, with access granted to only a handful of people, and with a small and humble staff of its own.[20]

The newly-weds left court after Christmas for the principality of Wales, and with the couple installed at Ludlow Castle the stage was left bare for the next royal wedding – the proxy marriage of Arthur's sister, Margaret Tudor, to James IV of Scotland. Henry hoped his eldest daughter's marriage would end the centuries-long feud between the neighbouring kingdoms. The wedding followed a peace treaty signed on 24 January 1502, with the ceremony taking place at Elizabeth of York's great chamber at Richmond. About ninety people were present, but the groom remained in Scotland with his proxy taking his place. Margaret Tudor, at twelve, was the same age her grandmother had been when she was married to Edmund Tudor. Margaret Beaufort had not forgotten her experience of that early marriage, and was determined her granddaughter would not have sex with her husband before she was physically mature. Henry VII admitted to the Spanish ambassador that his mother had joined forces with the queen to insist the girl remain in England for a time, fearful that if they sent her north too soon, 'the King of Scotland would not wait [to consummate the marriage] but injure her and endanger her health'.[21] It would be eighteen months before Margaret Tudor would be sent to James in Scotland. But when the ceremony ended she was considered Queen of Scots, and after the men left, mother and daughter dined as queens and equals.

More days of celebration followed with the rising stars of the court performing at the wedding joust. Charles Brandon, the son of the standard-bearer killed at Henry's side at Bosworth, was one such, and an outstanding athlete. Another was the Duke of Buckingham, whose costume at the wedding was reputed to have cost £1,500: more than all the pageants put together. As a show of strength at the end of the joust, he shattered three spears into the ground. It was an impressive display, but the danger his royal blood posed to Henry's children was fading. The weddings announced they were becoming adults – or so it was hoped. But that spring was to bring tragedy.

Arthur was unwell at Shrovetide in February, and a contemporary observed that his illness 'grew and increased upon his body' until by Easter it had 'overcome the pure and friendful blood'. He died on 2 April, less than five months after his wedding day. Henry VII and Elizabeth of York were at Greenwich Palace when the devastating news arrived. This beautiful brick courtyard house with a river frontage articulated by huge bay windows had been designed by the queen: it was a palace filled with light, but it would now always be associated for them with the darkest of days.[22] Henry's councillors asked his confessor to deliver the news to the king. The humble Franciscan friar knew Henry's inner life better than most, and where he might find solace. On Tuesday morning the priest appeared at the king's chamber door, in his Order's modest habit of undyed wool. He ordered everyone to leave. When they had, he addressed the king in Latin: 'If we receive good from the hand of God, should we not also tolerate the bad?' It was then that he 'showed his Grace that his dearest son was departed to God'.

Henry, who had fought so long to protect his family, had lost his first and favourite child. He had hoped Arthur would be the prince he had aspired to be when he had landed at Mill Bay in 1485 under the banner of the Red Dragon. Distraught, Henry asked for his wife, 'saying that he and his queen would take the painful sorrows together'. Elizabeth of York came immediately. Henry's loyal wife reminded him how 'my Lady his mother' had him as her only child, 'and that by God his Grace had ever preserved him, and brought him where he was.

Over that, how God had left him yet a fair prince, two fair princesses.' They were, she promised, still young enough to have more children. Only when Elizabeth of York had returned to her own room did she allow her grief expression.

The queen was used to hiding her feelings – over her vanished brothers and her mother dying far from the court – but now her emotions overwhelmed her. A witness recorded the 'natural and motherly remembrance of that great loss smote her so sorrowful to the heart' that the king, in turn, had to be called to comfort her. In 'true and faithful love' he did his best to reassure her that 'he would for his part thank God for his [remaining] son and would she would do likewise.'[23] What Elizabeth of York did instead was to try and give her husband another boy. Ten months later, in the Tower where her brothers, the princes, had vanished, the queen went into premature labour. She delivered a girl whom she named Katherine – perhaps a compliment to Arthur's widow, perhaps in memory of Catherine of Valois. The king had the best doctors attending them both, but the queen caught an infection. She died nine days later on her thirty-seventh birthday. Her daughter died the following week.

Henry went into seclusion after his wife's death, 'her departing', noted one contemporary, 'as heavy and dolorous to the king's highness as has been seen or heard of'.[24] Elizabeth of York had been his constant companion for eighteen years, through many trials and after his long period of exile. She had learned from her mother, who had a difficult and wayward husband in Edward IV, how to keep her dignity and remain patient. She had played her role as a wife and a queen to perfection, winning the long-closed heart of Henry Tudor.

An image in a religious book written in French during this period, and which is said to have belonged to Henry, depicts him wearing his royal robes, while behind him are two girls playing music by a roaring fire next to a black-draped table bed. A boy, perhaps their brother, appears to be weeping, his head folded in his arms on the black cloth. It has been suggested they are the surviving Tudor children.[25] Henry VII's physical and mental health would never be the same following his wife's death, and his dynasty looked suddenly more fragile than ever. The death of Arthur and his mother had echoes of the deaths of Richard III's heir and his wife, in 1484 and 1485. It seemed a judgement.[26]

The security Henry thought he had gained with the executions of Perkin Warbeck and Edward Plantagenet, Earl of Warwick, had proved illusory. The new Tudor heir, Henry, Duke of York, aged eleven, was younger even than Edward V had been when he disappeared in 1483. The future of the dynasty depended on Henry VII retaining control over his leading subjects and living long enough for his remaining son to reach adulthood.

13

DEATH AND JUDGEMENT

'It is quite wonderful', the Spanish ambassador noted, 'how much the king likes the Prince of Wales.'[1] The company of Henry VII's good-looking, energetic, surviving son was the breath of life to him. The boy was already bigger than his father but another Spaniard noted Henry was as protective of him as if he had been a young girl.[2] Perhaps more so; in June 1503, just a few months after the death of Elizabeth of York, he was ready to bid farewell to his elder daughter, Margaret, Queen of Scots, and escort her on the first leg of her journey north to her new homeland.

An impatient and gregarious thirteen-year-old who enjoyed archery, music, dancing and cards, Queen Margaret would need all her high spirits and optimism now she was to leave those she loved. Scotland was notoriously violent and it was considered a rare thing for a Scottish king to die of natural causes.[3] The husband she had not yet seen, James IV, wore an iron belt as penance for his unwitting role in the death of his own father, James III, killed by rebels whose cause he had been supporting.

Near Stamford in Lincolnshire Queen Margaret and her father reached her grandmother's house, Collyweston, where the formal court farewell was to take place. Four great bay windows with stained glass depicting the Beaufort arms had been added to the palace especially for this visit. The chapel had been freshly painted too, with new images of angels, the Virgin and the Trinity, and several outstanding singers were brought in to bolster the already impressive chapel choir.[4]

Margaret Beaufort entertained the whole court 'right royally' for a fortnight and when the dances and the feasts were over, the family gathered in the hall. Queen Margaret entered, richly dressed, to make her formal farewells, before she rode boldly out of the main gate with a vast cavalcade towards Grantham and a new life. She had one close family member with her – Sir David Owen, the illegitimate son of Owen Tudor who had been sent by her father as her carver, a highly honoured role, and one he would carry out at her wedding feast, wearing his chain of office.

The marriage was already being celebrated in Scotland as the union of the Scottish thistle and the English rose when Queen Margaret met James IV on 3 August at Dalkeith Castle, Midlothian. She heard James' arrival before she saw him, as he clattered into the courtyard with sixty horsemen. He was a popular king of Scotland. A lover of women and the arts, of hunting and jousting, James was said to be 'of noble stature, neither tall nor short, and as handsome in complexion as a man may be'. He appeared in her rooms dressed in the costume of a hunstman from a chivalric romance, with a jacket of crimson and gold, and a lyre on his back instead of a bow. This fulfilled the tradition of chivalric romances whereby a royal groom would happen to come across his foreign bride, often while out hunting, and they would fall in love at first sight. Margaret's reaction was, however, one of disconcertion. He was thirty years of age, with long hair like her father, but also an enormous red beard. In Scotland it was thought 'to suit him very well'.[5] Margaret, barely past puberty, was less enamoured by it, and although she said nothing in public, on her wedding night she made her feelings plain. He dutifully shaved it off the next day.

James would always treat his young wife with warmth, his future dalliances notwithstanding. But Queen Margaret missed her family badly, and in a letter to her father not long after her arrival she admitted 'I would I were with your grace now, and many times more'.[6] Henry, on his part, must have doubted that he would ever see his eldest daughter again. His health was increasingly poor, and he had already begun work on his tomb in the Lady Chapel at Westminster Abbey where his wife lay. The grandeur of his plans suggests that he hoped it would become a resting place for his successors, a rival to the magnificent mausoleum of the French kings at Saint-Denis. It would also define his reign.

Central to this was Henry's intention to have the body of his half-uncle Henry VI moved from Windsor and re-interred in the heart of the Lady Chapel. Henry was lobbying hard in Rome for official recognition that his half-uncle was a saint, and as soon as this was achieved Henry planned a new tomb in the Lady Chapel where the saint's bones would attract international as well as English pilgrims, and serve as a reminder that Henry VI had foretold Henry's reign. There was also to be a reminder of how the prophecy came to pass. Henry planned to build a life-size, golden image of himself, on his knees, returning to God and the Virgin the actual circlet that he had been crowned with on the battlefield of Bosworth. It was to be placed in the royal shrine of the founding English royal saint, Edward the Confessor.[7]

The chapel was covered with royal and religious symbols – the Beaufort portcullis, the French lily, and everywhere the red rose. They were painted not only on the chapel walls, but were also embroidered on the priests' golden vestments.[8] It is striking, however, that Henry's Tudor antecedents were barely acknowledged. The body of Henry's father, Edmund Tudor, remained buried at the Franciscan priory in Carmarthen, where Henry now paid for a tomb of purbeck marble, and a chantry so Masses might be said for his soul. Equally, Owen Tudor remained buried at the Hereford Greyfriars, to which Jasper had bequeathed his best cloth of gold gown for vestments, and where Sir David Owen would pay for a tomb.[9] In dynastic terms, it was only those of royal blood who mattered. Henry had been unable to prove Tudor descent from the last British king, Cadwaladr, and had lost enthusiasm for the myth of the return of a prince from that line.

For Henry the legend of 'the once and future king' had died with his Arthur.[10]

Amongst the notable things that Henry did further commission for his tomb was a medallion of Vincent Ferrer, the messenger of penance to whom he had been devoted since his time in exile. His continued need to purge himself of his sins saw him suffer periodic spasms of conscience over the ruthless manner in which he found it necessary to rule. He admitted ruefully to his mother that he appointed churchmen rather because they could do 'us and our realm acceptable service' than for any spiritual qualities. In recompense, however, he promoted her devout and brilliant confessor, John Fisher, 'for the great and singular good that I know and see in him'. In August 1504 he also issued a proclamation stating that anyone 'who can reasonably and truly claim' they had been wrongfully indebted to the king, their property rights violated, or received any other wrong at the hands of the Crown, could submit a complaint in writing anytime in the following two years. Yet he still persisted in his old ways.

By September 1504 Henry had employed a new hard man: the lawyer Edmund Dudley, whose task it was to keep the elite 'in danger at his pleasure . . . bound to his grace for great sums of money'.[11] Henry remained fearful of the possible foreign backing for the representative of 'the White Rose', Edmund de la Pole, Duke of Suffolk, and paid vast sums in bribes to European rulers in order to isolate the pretender. In 1505 his bribes to Philip the Fair, Duke of Burgundy, amounted to £108,000, which equated to his ordinary annual income. To find this kind of money he had become increasingly efficient in raising the revenues from his estates, which was now fourfold what it had been in the days of Edward IV. But he also sought more dubious means, undercutting the papacy's profits from its monopoly in alum (used in dye fixing), by trading illegal product and bleeding his own subjects dry with unjustified fines.

People would be informed, out of the blue, that they had broken some obscure law, hundreds of years old, for which they had to pay a massive sum. Informers earned a good trade accusing innocent men, who in turn were forced not only to pay their fines, but also to turn informer. The image of Henry as the fair unknown, chosen by God, was giving way to something ignoble: as Vergil described it, 'the good prince by degrees lost all sense of moderation and was led into avarice'.[12]

Good fortune, nevertheless, still blessed Henry. In a storm in January 1506, a ship ran aground on the Dorset coast carrying Philip the Fair and his wife Juana, elder sister of Katherine of Aragon. Henry saw an opportunity to revive the old Anglo-Burgundian alliance (enjoyed under Edward IV), and also a means of getting his hands on the 'White Rose'. Philip was showered with hospitality, but this was, in reality, a kidnap: he could not leave until he had given Henry what he wanted (and got): a promise to hand over the Duke of Suffolk.[13] As a sop to Philip's honour Henry agreed not to execute the duke, who went to the Tower instead. A few months later Philip died; but there was a further legacy of the visit: the betrothal of Henry's youngest daughter, Mary, to Philip's young son, the future Holy Roman Emperor, Charles V (grandson of Maximilian).

Almost three years after Philip's shipwreck, the Christmas celebrations at court in 1508 saw the betrothal confirmed in a binding ceremony at Richmond. The lovely twelve-year-old Mary Tudor spoke her vows 'perfectly and distinctly in the French tongue . . . without any bashing of countenance, stop or interruption'. But it was Mary's strapping seventeen-year-old brother, Prince Henry, who drew the most attention. 'There is no finer prince in all the world', a Spaniard thought: he was 'gigantic'.[14] The young prince was surrounded with admiring young courtiers looking to the future, as Henry VII was increasingly consumed by poor health.

The long, wavy brown hair Henry VII had as a young man had grown thin and white, his pale complexion had yellowed, and his expensive black clothes hung on his withered frame as bleak as a winter's night. Margaret Beaufort spent as much time as she could in the palaces of the south-east to remain close to her son. Her small, wimpled figure was seen often at his side, and when she was away her letters lavished affection on a man whose youthful loneliness returned as a widower. She called him 'my dear heart', 'my very joy', 'my own sweet and most dear king', and despite her age continued to give him practical, political help. In the East Midlands, based at Collyweston, Margaret Beaufort presided over a regional court, something no woman in living memory had ever done or would do again for a further hundred years.[15] Its scope was wide and included investigations of treasonable intent, suits delegated from the king's council, and even matters that would normally have been handled in the ecclesiastic courts, such as the case of a priest accused of baptising a cat. Such work helped spread the load of the growing burden borne by those few councillors Henry trusted.

A few weeks after the lavish wedding banquets for Mary and Charles were over, King Henry fell seriously ill. The symptoms were those he had suffered every spring for the past three years. He had a debilitating cough and an agonising infection in his throat; only this year, by the time Lent began, Henry knew he was dying and faced his last opportunity to demonstrate true repentance for his sins.

There was a story, often told in sermons, of a ghostly knight on a black horse who had appeared to a city official. The knight, breathing smoke, was dressed in burning sheepskins, and round his neck he carried a heavy weight of earth. He explained 'this horse . . . bears me to the pain of hell; for I died and made no restitution of my wrongs. I was shriven and was sorry for my sin, but I would not restore the harm I did, and therefore I am damned.' The burning sheepskins were shorn off sheep he had taken from a poor widow and the earth was the land he had stolen.[16] King Henry did not want to face such a fate. He promised that henceforth he would give promotions in the church only to those who were 'virtuous and well learned', and agreed to a general pardon of the people: the fines would end.

In March 1509 new lodgings were hurriedly created at Richmond Palace to house Margaret Beaufort's servants so she could better look after her dying son. Her hands, now cramped with arthritis, were so painful that she would sometimes cry out 'Oh blessed Jesus help me!' But to watch her son suffer was much worse. The dying king sobbed as he reflected on the lives he had ruined. His last agonies began at about 10 p.m. on Friday 20 April and lasted twenty-seven hours, but finally he was anointed with the oil of extreme unction: the seventh and last sacrament. This had the power to revive his spiritual health even as his body died. It brought him a sense of peace before he breathed his last at eleven o'clock on Saturday 21 April.

Immediately the grief-wracked Margaret had to prepare to usher in her grandson's reign. With the king's death kept secret she organised a meeting with key councillors and her co-executors of his will, to take place at the Garter ceremonies three days later. Margaret had first seen the ceremonies of the Garter as a girl aged nine. She was now a member of the Order – the last woman to be so before Queen Alexandra four centuries later. Come St George's Day – the feast day of the Order – the meeting of executors took place and her grandson, who was just two months shy of his eighteenth birthday, was informed of their next moves. Like his father, Henry VIII trusted Margaret's loyalty completely.

Late that night Henry VII's death was announced to the court and public. It emerged that a general pardon was to be issued decreeing that all debts to the Crown were cleared immediately. Convenient scapegoats were also being found for the late king's unpopular actions. Amongst them were Henry VII's tax collector, Edmund Dudley, and an equally efficient individual called Richard Empson. They had run what amounted to a gigantic protection racket in London, and their arrests – and later executions – were greeted with celebration. 'The people', the Spanish ambassador reported, 'are very happy, and few tears are being shed for Henry VII. Instead people are as joyful as if they had been released from prison.'[17]

For two weeks, Henry VII's body remained at Richmond Palace. The coffin was then placed on a chariot beneath his effigy 'crowned and richly appareled in his parliament robe, bearing in his right hand a sceptre and in his left a ball of gold'.[18] Seven great horses, trapped in black velvet bearing the royal arms, drew the chariot through the streets towards St Paul's. It was a vast procession with torchbearers and prelates singing the office for the dead; the household officers, servants and other mourners took the numbers to 2,000 people. These crowds swelled as the procession reached St George's Fields near Southwark where an enormous group of civic dignitaries and religious fraternities joined them, as did representatives from Portugal, Spain, France, Venice and Florence.

St Paul's was the great church where Henry VII had placed his banners after Bosworth, and Margaret Beaufort's confessor, John Fisher, had been chosen to deliver the obituary sermon here. If the king were still alive and suffering, 'many a one that is here present now would pretend a great pity and tenderness', the bishop noted, and urged them to be faithful servants still, and aid the king's soul on its journey from purgatory to heaven by praying for his soul.[19] Fisher claimed Henry had asked for 10,000 Masses to aid his journey. In fact, in accordance with French and Breton tradition, Henry VII's will had instituted far more than that, with money lavished on daily Masses in perpetuity, as well as gifts for churches and charitable works.[20]

At last, the procession moved on to Westminster Abbey where the coffin was taken to the Lady Chapel. There, massive wax tapers weighing 1,200 pounds were burning as Henry was lowered into his tomb to rest alongside his beloved wife, so 'pretty, chaste and fruitful'. As the coffin disappeared the choir sang 'Libera me':[21]

> Deliver me, O Lord, from death eternal on that fearful
> day, . . . when thou shalt come to judge the world by fire.

Whatever the judgement of a merciful God on Henry VII, that of historians has not always been complimentary. What are most often recalled are his last years and the accusations of avarice. Was he a better king than Richard III might have been had he survived Bosworth? Richard's abolition of forced loans to the Crown, his emphasis on the prerogative of Parliament to vote for taxes to the king, his protection of the church, and his promotion of justice for rich and poor alike, are in stark contrast to Henry VII's latter years. But Henry's had been a remarkable success story. Here was a fatherless boy and penniless exile with the name of a humble Welsh farmer who had nonetheless become a king.

Henry had been shaped profoundly by his years on the run. With his life dependent on the whims of a frivolous Breton duke he had found consolation in his religious faith, and when his fortunes changed he had looked to God for an explanation. As king, Henry had aspired to be the redeemer-hero of chivalric romance; he had been a faithful husband, a devoted father, and had continued to win his battles both on the field and off it. He founded a dynasty, and a bloodline that continues in the royal family today.

Yet the incident that had made Henry's reign possible – and without which there would have been no Tudor dynasty – was the disappearance and suspected murder of two children. Those who find it hard to believe that a man of Richard III's qualities would have killed his nephews have accused Henry and his mother of somehow being guilty of their deaths, either in the summer of 1483 or later, with it suggested that Richard hid the princes away and that they were killed after Henry became king. In reality what Henry was guilty of was failing to investigate what had happened, and it proved an error. It is very specifically the disappearance of the princes that lies at the heart of modern conspiracy theories about the origins of the Tudor seizure of power. Solving this mystery is not likely to be achieved by piecing together who was where and when, 530 years after the event; it can, however, be understood in the context of the times. This was an era of visual symbols and display. Kings projected their power and significance in palaces decorated with their badges, in rich clothes and elaborate ceremonies. The vanished princes were denied any such images; like Hamlet's father they were given no 'noble rite nor formal ostentation' in burial, no great funeral procession with effigies and banners, no hatchments over their bones, no annual Masses. The intention was to avoid creating a religious cult that would have outshone even the powerful cult of Henry VI and been immensely damaging for Henry VII, who was fearful of being regarded as a mere king consort to his wife, the sister and heir to the princes. But as Shakespeare knew, under such circumstances the royal dead would haunt the living. The absence of bodies allowed the suspicion to flourish that at least one of the princes might be alive. Perkin Warbeck's masquerade as the younger of the princes had posed a considerable threat to Henry, and even if it was a threat he eventually removed, Perkin's execution in 1499 did nothing to lay the ghosts of the princes to rest.

In 1502, three years after Perkin was hanged, a man called Sir James Tyrrell was arrested and executed. An ally of 'the White Rose' Edmund de la Pole, Duke of Suffolk, it was revealed that he had confessed to the murder of Edward IV's sons.[22] This was picked up and repeated in different forms by Polydore Vergil and Henry VIII's future Lord Chancellor, Thomas More.[23] The latter claimed he had learned that the murdered boys were first buried at the foot of some stairs in the Tower. If such a thing had become public knowledge there would have been huge pressure on Henry to have the princes reburied in sacred ground. But More was told Richard III had asked for the bodies to be moved somewhere more suitable for a king's sons, and that those involved had subsequently died, so the princes' final resting place would be forever unknown – a most convenient outcome for Henry.

In 1674, long after the passing of the Tudor dynasty, two skeletons were recovered in the Tower, in a place that resembled More's description of their first burial place. Charles II had them interred at

Westminster Abbey. In 1933 they were removed and examined by two doctors. Broken and incomplete, the skeletons were judged to be two children aged between seven and eleven and between eleven and thirteen. These bones were returned to their urn in the abbey where they remain. If these are the bodies of the princes, and if Henry VII knew where the bodies were, it is shameful that he left them in that miserable hole. It did him no good during his reign; nor would it thereafter.

14

EXIT MARGARET BEAUFORT

STANDING ALONGSIDE HENRY VIII, WITH THE PRIEST SPEAKING THE words of the marriage ceremony, Katherine of Aragon was happier than she had ever been. She had remained in England since Arthur's death, living in a kind of limbo. For nearly seven years she had waited for her father and father-in-law to make up their minds over whether or not she should marry Arthur's younger brother. In 1504, two years after Arthur died, she had been betrothed to Henry. The following year, as the tides of foreign affairs shifted, the betrothal was repudiated. By the time Henry VII lay dying at Richmond in March 1509 Katherine had despaired that the on-off marriage would ever take place. This situation was transformed, however, on the king's death. Even before his father was buried Henry VIII had told his council he wished to marry Katherine, and now the ceremony was being performed, on a glorious June day at Greenwich.

Henry VIII was a young king who needed to prove himself and was anxious to do so. As a discussion on government observed, 'the office of a king is to fight the battles of his people', and second, 'to judge them rightfully'. Henry VII had won the crown of England from the 'usurper' Richard III; Henry VIII intended to win the crown of France – rightfully England's since the reign of Edward III – from the usurper Louis XII. He had read all he could on Henry V's victories and the chivalric tales they inspired. But he needed allies. His marriage to Katherine was intended to gain him the friendship of her father, King Ferdinand, and the Holy Roman Emperor, Maximilian whose son had married her sister. Yet marrying Katherine was not about securing military alliances alone. It also held romantic appeal. A beautiful princess, for years in distress, lonely, yet unobtainable while her marriage prospects were being negotiated, Katherine was the heroine to match the hero Henry so badly wanted to be. He felt he was now rescuing her, and so it also seemed to Katherine, who was passionately in love with him.

Henry was extremely handsome. Tall and well built with clear skin, he was the image of his Yorkist grandfather, Edward IV, who had once been described as 'amongst the handsomest people in the world'. He also shared Edward's energy, conviviality and athleticism. This resemblance made Henry 'the more acclaimed and approved of', Vergil noted, for if royal status was transferable through the female line then Henry VIII, the son of Edward IV's daughter, had a better right to be king than had his father, Henry VII, whose mother was only of illegitimate royal descent. No one – least of all Katherine – seems to have considered that if Henry resembled the golden young King Edward for the better, he might come to resemble the older, bloated and brutal King Edward for the worse. She was as star-struck as the rest of the court.

The ceremony at Greenwich, in front of a handful of witnesses, was far less spectacular than Katherine's first wedding, but this one promised to be a true marriage, which she claimed her first had never been. Katherine had always maintained that she and Arthur had never had sexual intercourse. The long days of entertainments following the St Paul's wedding and Arthur's subsequent sickness meant the couple had spent no more than seven nights in the same bed, and during those nights the marriage was never consummated. It may be that, since men valued virginity, Katherine was now pretending that she had kept hers. It is also quite possible, however, that Katherine was telling the truth. Any number of diseases can cause impotence or lower the libido, including testicular cancer and tuberculosis, which are often cited as illnesses to which Arthur may have succumbed.[1] And there are other possible explanations that have yet to be considered: the sickly fifteen-year-old may have been a little uncertain how to consummate a marriage, or was overcome by anxiety that he should not carry out his duty in a sinful manner.

Henry VII had always maintained the highest standards of sexual behaviour at court, to distance his reign from the immorality with which Richard III had tarred Edward IV's later years, and which Richard had used as a tool in his usurpation of Edward V. Equally he had been keen to promote national admiration for the less than virile Henry VI. It had taken Henry VI eight years to conceive a child, during which time he had carefully policed the chastity of Edmund and Jasper Tudor, keeping 'careful watch' for flirtatious women 'through hidden windows of his chamber'. A biography of the 'saint' published in 1500 claimed that when in bed with his queen, Henry VI had never 'used her unseemly' 'but with all conjugal honesty and gravity', and that he was distressed at the sight of nudity.[2] It would not be surprising if all this had cultivated a prim atmosphere around Arthur, the future king of a new Camelot. In Thomas Malory's *Le Morte d'Arthur*, it is sexual immorality that leads to the destruction of Camelot as well as Arthur's death. Anxiety to behave chastely around the prince could well have left his sexual education somewhat limited.

Unsurprisingly, Henry VII was angered by Katherine's claims, which not only cast aspersions on his son's manhood, but also may have been taken as a criticism of the way Arthur was raised. The papal dispensation permitting Katherine's marriage to Henry VIII (who as her brother-in-law was within the forbidden degrees of kinship) tactfully observed that the marriage to Arthur at least 'may' have been consummated. For Henry VIII the consummation of his marriage that night proved to him Katherine was indeed a virgin – or so he believed at the time. Tellingly, perhaps, he would later claim that his own sexual inexperience and ignorance had not made him a competent judge. In all other respects the young couple were also proving a good match. Katherine could discuss foreign affairs with her husband while being conventional enough to treat Henry with the respect he desired as her king. She shared his energy, his love of hunting, and her good-natured seriousness proved a foil for Henry's boisterous romanticism. 'The king my lord adores her, and her highness him', Katherine's confessor reported happily to her parents.[3]

A fortnight after the wedding Henry and Katherine were crowned together as king and queen. The ceremony lasted four days and began on 21 June with Henry VIII taking formal possession of the Tower. There, the following night, he created his Knights of the Bath. This ceremony, which only took place on the eve of a coronation, involved the new knights bathing in a symbol of purification, before a vigil spent in prayer until dawn. The next day the knights led the newly-weds on the eve of coronation procession to Westminster through streets hung with tapestries. Henry was mounted on a princely horse in a jewelled costume, while Katherine, dressed in white, was carried in a litter pulled by white horses.[4] Her long auburn hair 'beautiful and goodly to behold' hung loose under a golden circlet of six crosses and six fleurs-de-lys, studded with precious stones and 'new made' for her. When a summer rainstorm broke Katherine was forced to take refuge under the awning of a draper's stall. But it passed as quickly as it had arrived and the happy procession continued in front of the cheering crowds. The next day Henry and Katherine were crowned at Westminster Abbey and Margaret Beaufort wept as many tears as she had at her son's coronation. She remained fearful, John Fisher recalled, 'that some adversity would follow'.[5]

A few days later, while staying at the abbot's house at Westminster, Margaret became ill. The cygnet she had eaten had upset her stomach. It was only two months since her son had died and Margaret did not have either the emotional or physical strength to recover. Fisher was present at her death, a mere five days after her grandson and his wife were anointed king and queen.[6] Margaret Beaufort was buried in the Lady Chapel at Westminster Abbey where her son had so recently been interred. She had decreed in her will that her Book of Hours, in which she had marked such key events as her son's victory at Bosworth and Henry VIII's birth, should be kept on display there.[7] Her black marble tomb was to be surmounted with a bronze effigy created by the Florentine sculptor Pietro Torrigiano. The face he cast expresses her forceful personality.

Margaret had survived the dangers of her son's birth. She had helped protect him during the years that followed, and risked her own life to conspire on his behalf against Richard III. In promoting her son as king, she had sacrificed her own superior claim to the throne. But although she accepted male authority she had wielded considerable influence. Margaret had used her experience of English court ceremony to place the Tudors firmly within royal tradition, drawing up the orders for future royal christenings and funerals. Her best servants became the king's, and he had continued to trust her judgement to the end. No wonder she came to sign herself in the regal style, Margaret R.

The obituary sermon Fisher gave her noted that Margaret would be greatly missed. Her female friends and relations, 'whom she had loved so tenderly', her priests and servants, 'to whom she was full dear', indeed, 'all England for her death had cause for weeping'. Margaret had been an important patroness to the universities, especially Cambridge; she had also been generous to the poor, while her passion for chivalric virtues had, Fisher said, made her an 'example of honour' to the nobility. It was her spirituality that he admired most, later commenting that although 'she chose me as her director . . . I gladly confess that I learnt more from her great virtue than I ever taught her.' If Henry VII had had a good death, reconciled to God, Fisher believed Margaret had led a good life. In later generations, however, Margaret's reputation would fall victim to religious and sexual prejudice.

In the post-Reformation England of the seventeenth century Margaret's spirituality came to be judged mere superstition and her intelligence and toughness of character were regarded with equal suspicion. The antiquarian Sir George Buck condemned Margaret Beaufort as a 'politic and subtle lady' who had killed the princes in the Tower with sorcery and poison to clear the way for her son. That Margaret was responsible for the princes' deaths is a theory becoming fashionable again and remains linked to cultural prejudices. Margaret's support for her son had been construed as those of an obsessively ambitious mother, yet for her generation she was fulfilling a duty. She was honour bound to help him regain his rightful inheritance, and later to help him restore the House of Lancaster, into which she had been born. Her strict religious devotions are, to modern sensibilities, strange, even fanatical, but amongst royal and noble women of her time they were commonplace: an effort to look beyond the vicious and ruthless political culture into which they were born, to understand humility, and the nobility of Christ's example.

The absence of portraits of Margaret Beaufort as an attractive young woman to counterbalance the images of her in old age have helped give credit to the sinister reputation she has gained. But the face that stands out from her story is not that of the widow with the hooded eyes, praying amidst the riches of a royal chapel and seen in her portraits, but a young girl, riding in the biting wet of a Welsh winter, to Pembroke Castle where she must deliver her child. Now it was for her grandchildren and great-grandchildren to continue the Tudor story.

Out of chaos God created a hierarchical, harmonious and interconnected universe in which everything had its place, and which was infused with moral purpose. The devil rebelled against this order and fifteenth- and sixteenth-century Englishmen had a visceral fear of the return to chaos the devil sought by exploiting man's weaknesses.

Catherine of Valois's marriage to Henry V, the victor of Agincourt, sealed a treaty under which their future son, Henry VI, would become heir to the French crown.

Henry VI – King of France and England – was popularly acclaimed a saint after his murder in 1471, and devotional images appeared in churches from Devon to Northumberland, as well as several in East Anglian churches such as this one at Barton in Norfolk.

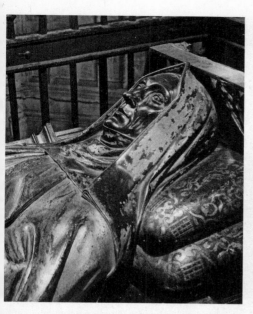

Henry Tudor's mother, Margaret Beaufort, a highly intelligent woman, has for centuries been a victim of religious and sexual prejudice. She has been condemned for doing her best to protect her only child and for conforming to the beliefs of her time.

Images of St Anne teaching her daughter the Virgin to read were commonplace in the Middle Ages. This variation, of St Anne and the Virgin teaching Christ to read, is in the Book of Hours Margaret Beaufort inherited from her mother.

In exile in Brittany and France the young Henry Tudor took on the mantle of the 'fair unknown', a stock character from romantic chivalric myth who returns from obscurity to reclaim his rightful crown, as the legendary King Arthur had done.

In this famous portrait of Richard III he shows no sign of the idiopathic adolescent onset scoliosis which meant that although five foot eight, he stood as short as four foot eight.

The white boar badge found at Fen Hole, the likely spot where Richard III fell at Bosworth, 'fighting manfully in the middle of his enemies'.

This Victorian image gives a real sense of the violence with which Edward V and his little brother – the princes in the Tower – were rumoured to have died in 1483. All we know is that they vanished: it is this that lies at the heart of the many conspiracy theories concerning their fate.

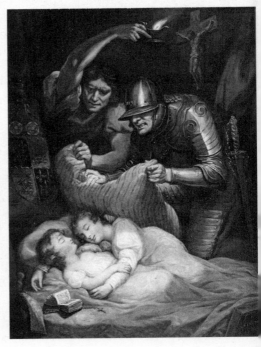

This twentieth-century stained glass at Southwark Cathedral depicts the seventeenth-century legend that Richard III's crown was caught in a hawthorn bush at Bosworth.

Allegorical miniature of a bush of the Tudor rose incorporating a Latin poem celebrating the House of Tudor, with daisies for Henry VIII's sister Margaret of Scotland, and marigolds for his other sister, Mary, and a pomegranate bush for his wife, Katherine of Aragon.

The round table that still hangs in the Great Hall of Winchester Castle was believed to be the actual round table used by King Arthur's knights at Camelot. It was painted as early as 1516 with the union rose of white for the House of York and red for the House of Lancaster.

ELIZABETHA · VXOR
HENRICI · VII ·

Elizabeth of York – the eldest
daughter of Edward IV and
wife of Henry VII. Their
marriage embodied the
union of the houses of
York and Lancaster.

Painted funeral effigy of Henry VII:
a king of many seasons, Henry VII
won the crown of England and left
his heir rich, with a kingdom at peace
at home and respected abroad.

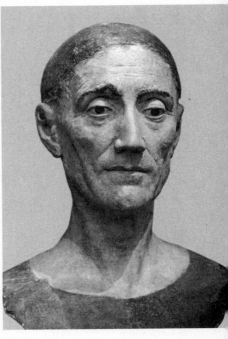

Miniature prayer books such as this one were often listed as 'tablets' in inventories of the period, and it is possible this is the tablet picture of Henry VIII that his niece Margaret Douglas described in her will.

Mary Tudor, the French Queen, younger sister of Henry VIII. The drawing is marked with the graffiti 'Plus sale que royane', that is, 'more dirty than queenly', an allusion to her, as the widow of Louis XII, marrying the lowly born Charles Brandon, Duke of Suffolk.

Margaret Tudor, Queen of Scots, elder sister of Henry VIII, with her first husband, James IV of Scots, pictured in the Seton Armorial.

The dominating presence of Henry VIII in this Holbein family portrait of the king with
his long-dead parents, and the more recently deceased Jane Seymour, mother of his son Edward,
is reflected in the words written on the central altar which boast that Henry VIII
is greater than his father for 'The presumption of Popes has yielded to unerring virtue
and with Henry VIII bearing the sceptre in his hand, religion has been restored'.

Part Two

INHERITANCE:
THE LEGACY OF ARTHUR

Avarice is expelled from the country. Liberality scatters wealth
with bounteous hand. Our king does not desire gold of gems or
precious metals, but virtue, glory, immortality.

WILLIAM BLOUNT, LORD MOUNTJOY, TO ERASMUS
ON THE ACCESSION OF HENRY VIII

15

THE ELDER SISTER: MARGARET, QUEEN OF SCOTS

QUEEN MARGARET BID HER HUSBAND, JAMES IV, FAREWELL AT Linlithgow, the palace in West Lothian he had given her as a wedding present.[1] It was here, in this towering palace by the loch, that their son James had been born on Easter Saturday the previous year. He was 'a right fair child and large for his age', and by that summer of 1513 she was pregnant again.[2] Legend has it that she had begged her husband not to leave her, for he intended to go to war with her brother and she wished to prevent it. In reality, her chief concern was for James' life. It was only four years since Henry VII's death, but the twenty-three-year-old Tudor princess was now a 'Scotswoman', as she often asserted. Under the blue painted ceiling of the Linlithgow Palace chapel, she would pray for James' victory, as well as for his safe return.

The relationship between the royal brothers-in-law had broken down in January 1512, when the English Parliament had reasserted the Crown's ancient claim to overlordship of Scotland. A furious King James had retaliated by signing a treaty with Henry's French enemy, Louis XII, in which each agreed to come to the aid of the other, were they ever to be attacked. Henry VIII was certain, however, that James would not honour it. He had joined a Holy League against Louis, inspired by the Pope's desire to see the French out of Italy, and James was threatened with excommunication if he came to Louis' defence.

Confident that James would heed the papal warning, Henry had led his army in person into France, landing at Calais on 30 June 1513.

Henry's only real concern in leaving England had been the potential threat posed by his white-rose cousins. Edward IV's nephew, Edmund de la Pole, Duke of Suffolk, had been in the Tower since Henry VII's reign, but if Henry were to lose a major battle in France – where Suffolk's younger brother, Richard de la Pole, was allied with Louis XII – it was possible he would be sprung from the Tower and crowned in Henry's place. Henry had therefore had the duke executed before his departure and his queen, Katherine of Aragon, had been left as regent of England and captain general of his armies during his absence, to deal with any unforeseen difficulties.

Henry intended the campaign in France to mark the beginning of an English reconquest of its former territories. His almoner, the priest Thomas Wolsey, who held the post concerned with the king's charitable alms-giving, had the task of ensuring the king was provided with a well fed, disciplined and equipped army. A handsome and efficient tradesman's son, Wolsey had achieved this in spades, and Henry was eager for the task ahead. 'Our king does not desire gold or gems or precious metals, but virtue, glory, immortality', a courtier told Erasmus proudly. Shakespeare's Henry V would later voice the same sentiment: 'By Jove I am not covetous for gold . . . But if it be a sin to covet honour, I am the most offending soul alive.'[3]

On 1 August, Henry began the siege of the small town of Thérouanne in Artois, hoping to make history. In pouring rain at three in the morning, Henry had walked around the camp comforting his watch by assuring them 'Well, comrades, now we have suffered in the beginning, fortune promises us better things.'[4] Henry's first victory was granted on the morning of 16 August when a small French cavalry force misjudged the position of the English army. Under artillery fire they turned and fled, pursued by cavalry. Six standards were captured, as well as a duke, a marquis and an admiral. It was called 'the Battle of the Spurs', and was quickly capped by the fall of Thérouanne.

But on 24 August, as Henry set off looking for further glory and more valuable towns, James IV crossed the border into Northumberland with the largest army ever assembled in Scotland. Within a week James had captured Norham Castle. Other lesser fortresses followed before the Scottish invader took up a high position on the Northumberland hill of Flodden Edge to await the English army. Katherine of Aragon wrote to reassure her husband that she had prepared for the coming battle and 'My heart is very good to it.'[5] For the previous fortnight she had been busy organising artillery and gunners, while also calmly sewing standards, banners and badges for the English army. Henry had no doubt this daughter of the warrior queen Isabella of Castile, who had thrown the Moors out of Spain, would prove a match for the Scot, but James was a formidable foe. He had attacked England in the past and this time the French had trained part of his huge army in the effective use of the Swiss pike. These weapons, eighteen to twenty-two feet long, had broken Richard III's cavalry charge at Bosworth, as Katherine's battlefield commander well remembered (the seventy-year-old Earl of Surrey had fought at Bosworth alongside his father 'Jack' of Norfolk, who had died in Richard's cause).

While Katherine set off northwards to prepare a defensive line, Margaret, at Linlithgow, could only await news from Flodden. The tranquillity and crystal air at Linlithgow had made this the pleasure palace of the Stuarts, and Margaret led a pampered life there. Outside King James' private chambers, the waiting room had a board game cut into the floor for people to pass the time, and a spear used to take fish from the loch is still kept at the palace. A room in the north-west tower, which has sweeping views across the open countryside, is that from which, in romantic tradition, Margaret scanned the horizon for the expected messengers. On 10 September rumours reached Edinburgh of mass casualties and a crushing defeat for the Scots, and it was not long after that Margaret learned the full, and terrible, story.

After days of appalling weather and an exchange of challenges, the battle had begun on 9 September and five phalanxes of Scottish pikemen advanced down Branxton Hill. The wind and rain battered them and the soft ground broke up their formation as men stumbled. Yet, as they continued forward in eerie silence, they had remained in good order. The English described them as 'Germanic'.

A cavalry charge against the pike was impossible and so the English had counter-attacked on foot. They used the polearm, curve-bladed weapons called bills to strike at the Scots at close quarters, but the Scots fought back ferociously. One Englishman complained they were 'such large and strong men, they would not fall when four or five bills struck them'.

A desperate struggle had been fought 'with many muckle slaughter, sweating and travail' on both sides before the battle ended in the defeat of the Scots and the death of the flower of their nobility. They included nine earls, fourteen lords, the Archbishop of St Andrews and the Bishop of the Isles.[6] This was 'The prime o' our land . . . cauld in the clay' who are still remembered in the haunting lament 'The Flowers of the Forest'.[7] But the most significant casualty was James IV.

Queen Margaret's husband was found lying near the royal banner of the red lion rampant, only a spear's length from where the English commander, Surrey, had fought.[8] James' left hand was almost severed, his throat gashed, and an arrow was shot through his lower jaw.[9] Surrey would be rewarded for the victory at Flodden with the restoration of the family title of Duke of Norfolk and an augmentation to the ducal arms, still used today, and which recalls the spectacle of James' corpse: a red lion rampant, with an arrow though its head.

With their king fallen, the survivors of James' army were chased for three miles. If the 'English had been horsed', it was boasted, '10,000 more would have been slain.'[10] That night the English toasted their victory with Scottish beer, which they commented was surprisingly good.[11] Henry claimed the horses of the Scottish dead and for weeks afterwards their loose animals were still being rounded up: 'a bay trotting horse', 'a grey mare with one eye', 'a nag with a cloudy face', all living reminders of their former riders.[12]

Katherine wrote to her sister-in-law assuring her that 'The Queen of England for the love she bears the Queen of Scots would gladly send a servant to comfort her' in her widowhood. But if she pitied Margaret, Katherine admitted in a letter to Wolsey that she regarded it as the greatest honour to have killed a king. She told Henry that she would have sent him James' head, 'but our Englishmen's hearts would not suffer it'.[13] Instead, Katherine sent him the chequered surcoat taken from James' body, which she suggested he have as his banner. Henry, then in the midst of besieging the town of Tournai, showed it 'rent' and 'stained with blood' to his ally, the emperor Maximilian.[14] His brother king had 'paid a heavier penalty for his perfidy than we would have wished', Henry commented. He would remember what Katherine was capable of in years to come, even expressing fear of her ability to 'carry on a war . . . as fiercely as Queen Isabella, her mother, had done in Spain'.[15]

Under the terms of James' will, his 'most dearest spouse' was now regent of Scotland, making Queen Margaret the first Tudor woman to rule a kingdom. She had no experience of government, but she was determined to protect her son. A general council was called at the great Parliament Hall of Stirling Castle, and the coronation of the seventeen-month-old James V took place there in the royal chapel on 21 September. Robert Carver's moving Mass for ten voices, *Dum Sacrum Mysterium*, was sung at what became known as the 'mourning coronation' because of the outpouring of grief for those who had died.

Henry returned home from France in late October, after taking Tournai, and rode hard to Richmond to see Katherine. The victorious husband and wife were reunited, and 'there was such a loving meeting as everyone rejoiced'. Margaret had hoped to build on Katherine's letter of sympathy, and asked her sister-in-law to put her in her brother's remembrance, 'that his kindness may be known to our lieges and realm'.[16] But as Henry took charge of the follow-up to Flodden, Scotland's agony continued. His captains were ordered to strike again and again north of the border, burning corn and destroying villages.

As the desperate, starving Scots began to turn on each other, Henry was sent the chilling assessment that 'there is neither law, nor reason, nor justice at this day, either used or kept in Scotland, but get what you can'.[17] It was February 1514 before he decided they had been punished enough. A treaty was signed shortly before Margaret retreated into her chamber for the period of her confinement and the delivery of her husband's posthumous child. In April Alexander, Duke of Ross was born, but Margaret had little time to recover. The Scottish council wanted a military leader, not a female regent, and there were calls for the return from exile of James IV's cousin, John Stuart, Duke of Albany. The duke's father had left Scotland following an attempt to seize the throne from James III, and the duke had been raised in France, unable even to speak Scots. The council nevertheless viewed Albany as an appropriate choice, because he was the heir to James IV's sons. Margaret, however, feared that meant he might dispose of her sons, just as Richard III had disposed of the princes in the Tower.

Margaret needed powerful backing to oppose Albany's return and planned to marry to get it. Choosing a foreign prince would mean her leaving Scotland and her children, so she looked for a suitable Scot, but the choice was limited. There was the Earl of Arran, who was middle-aged and had a dubious divorce behind him, and there was the man she did marry: the titular head of the powerful and pro-English House of Douglas: Archibald, Earl of Angus. Aged twenty-four, he had been made a member of Margaret's council in March and had a strong following of 'dependers'.[18] He was very handsome as well, and since it was believed women had difficulties controlling their sex drive it was also assumed she was marrying Angus 'for her plesour'.[19] When the news emerged of Margaret's marriage on 6 August she lost her popularity as the king's widow, and under the terms of her late husband's will her remarriage meant she also lost the regency.

It seemed Margaret had made a disastrous error, but when, just three weeks after her wedding, she agreed to Albany's return 'as governor of Scotland', she knew her brother would block the move. Following his victories in France, Henry had made peace with Louis XII, who would not wish to anger Henry by giving Albany a passport to Scotland – and it would anger Henry, as he also feared for his nephews' lives if Albany was to return.

The treaty with France was the brainchild of Thomas Wolsey, who was becoming an indispensable servant to Henry. Wolsey understood that the king's dream of becoming a new Henry V had no realistic chance of success, for he was not fighting the same kingdom his predecessors had. At the outbreak of the Hundred Years War, France had been a geographical expression rather than a political entity. The King of France had been, at best, the greatest of the feudal lords. But the fifteenth century had seen the steady erosion of feudal independence. The greatest success was when French-speaking regions of Burgundy had been brought under the French crown on the death in battle of Charles the Bold in 1477. Louis XII's kingdom now had a population six times greater than that of England, and an income sevenfold that of Henry VIII. If Louis had not been distracted by his ambitions in Italy in 1513, Henry would never have achieved his modest victories. On the other hand, Wolsey persuaded Henry that a peace, sealed by a marriage between Louis and Henry's younger sister, Mary, could gain him great rewards. The sickly fifty-two-year-old French monarch had no sons and if he were now to father one with the beautiful young Mary, and then die, there would be a long royal minority. This could give Henry huge influence in France through his sister.

The betrothal between Mary and the emperor's son, Charles, was duly cancelled, and just a week after her elder sister Margaret had married the dashing Earl of Angus, the eighteen-year-old Mary prepared miserably for her nuptials to the decrepit Louis. Margaret sent Mary a valuable Book of Hours as her wedding gift and inscribed it affectionately, 'Madam, I pray your grace, remember on me, when you look upon this book, your loving sister, Margaret.'[20] The teenage Mary hadn't seen her sister since she was eight, but she envied Margaret's marriage to a handsome young nobleman. It hardly seemed fair.

16

THE YOUNGER SISTER: MARY, THE FRENCH QUEEN

THE WEATHER WAS STORMY WHEN THE ROYAL PARTY REACHED Dover on 2 October 1514. Henry had planned to sail into the Channel to bid farewell to his sister Mary as she left for France. Now they would have to say their goodbyes on the shore where a vast crowd was gathering to see the spectacle, the townsfolk from the 400-odd houses that huddled beneath Dover Castle mixing with courtiers and foreign visitors.[1]

An Italian merchant observed that the noblemen had spent a fortune on their costumes and horses, but none outshone the princess Mary – now known as the French queen. 'Tall, fair, and of a light complexion', she was 'a nymph from heaven'. Indeed as brother and sister stood together on the shoreline, they made a startlingly good-looking pair. Henry, with his cropped auburn hair, a 'complexion very fair and bright', and 'a round, beautiful face', was the handsomest prince in Christendom; Mary glittering in a 'gown in the French fashion, of wove gold, very costly', and 'on her neck a jewelled diamond with a pear-shaped pearl beneath it, the size of a pigeon's egg' – a present from her husband, the King of France.[2]

In sight, but out of earshot of the crowds, Mary was already talking to Henry about her plans for her future widowhood, her husband's generous gifts notwithstanding. She reminded her brother she had 'consented to his request, and for the peace of Christendom, to marry

Louis of France though he was very aged and sickly'.[3] In exchange Mary wanted Henry now to reiterate his private promise to her that if she outlived Louis she could marry whom she liked for her second husband, and, 'as ye well know', she already had a groom in mind: the twenty-nine-year-old Charles Brandon, Duke of Suffolk.[4]

The handsome Brandon came from a family of impeccable Tudor loyalists. His father had died holding Henry VII's standard at Bosworth and he was raised at court, where he had proved himself an exceptional athlete at the joust. It was there on the sandy lists that he had forged a friendship with Henry and when, in February that year, Henry had granted Brandon the title Duke of Suffolk, he was recognised as the king's principal favourite. Nevertheless Brandon was not a suitable groom for a royal princess. His background was mere gentry and he had a long and messy marital history littered with illegitimate children and young brides abandoned for rich old widows. When Henry kissed his sister goodbye at the waterside and gave his word she could have her choice, he had no intention of honouring his promise.[5]

Louis XII met his young bride on a rainy day near Abbeville on the river Somme. Accompanying him were over 200 courtiers, including the Duke of Albany, Queen Margaret's rival for the governorship of Scotland. Albany was a tall, striking man of thirty-three, fair-skinned with a strong, bony face framed by a carefully trimmed beard. But Mary's attention was riveted on Louis. He had dressed as for the hunt, in the Renaissance tradition that James IV had followed with Queen Margaret, and his horse was obediently performing half-turns in order that she could see him clearly. A witness described him as looking 'very antique', in a short red jacket of cloth of gold on crimson designed to match Mary's costume. To please the gathered crowds she blew him a kiss. He promptly rode over, leaned from his saddle and kissed the teenager as passionately, it was said, as if he had been a young man of twenty-five. There was then the consummation of the marriage for Mary, Queen of France, to look forward to.

Following a magnificent ball on 9 October Louis' daughter, the fifteen-year-old Madame Claude, escorted Mary to the bed where she was to sleep with the old king. Claude was already pregnant by her twenty-year-old husband and cousin, Francis. A charismatic man with black eyes, a dark curling beard and strong nose, Francis was King Louis' nearest male relative and his heir – unless Mary produced a son for Louis. What happened in the bedchamber was therefore of particular interest to Francis. The next morning Louis boasted to the Venetian ambassador that he had 'crossed the river three times' and to a French courtier that he had 'performed miracles' with his beautiful bride. 'I certainly believe this was true', the ambassador noted dryly, 'for he was most uncomfortable.' As the days passed Louis seemed so infatuated the Venetian ambassador began to worry that 'To amuse himself with a wife of eighteen is very dangerous to his state of health.'[6] He was not alone in these concerns. In Paris they sang a ballad warning 'The King of England, has given the King of France a new young filly who will carry him off . . . either to hell or to paradise.'[7]

The French queen was miserable in those early days. Louis had dispensed with her senior English ladies-in-waiting, saying French ones were more encouraging 'when he would be merry with his wife' in the bedroom.[8] She now had no one to confide in, or to turn to for advice, except the young English maids she had been left with, and some, like the dark-eyed fourteen-year-old Anne Boleyn, were scarcely out of childhood. To add to her confusion, her brother had sent Charles Brandon, along with other leading courtiers, to attend her coronation, which took place on 5 November in the Abbey of Saint-Denis. The whole of Paris – then the biggest city in Europe – was decorated with French lilies and English roses, and the following day the French queen was driven in a carriage through the streets wearing a diadem of pearls, and a necklace of brilliant jewels. In truth she was beginning to enjoy herself. 'How lovingly the king my husband dealeth me, the Lord Chamberlain, with other of your ambassadors, can inform your Grace', Mary wrote to Henry.

Louis had once been a ladies' man, and although he was old and ill, he could be charming and gracious – as well as very generous. There were compensations, his young wife was discovering, in being an old man's darling. It may also be that, in common with Arthur Tudor, the boasts made after his wedding night were wide of the truth. 'I am certain,' his son-in-law remarked, 'unless I have been greatly deceived, that it is impossible for the king and queen to have children.'[9]

The tournament to celebrate the coronation began on 13 November and continued for three days. During the Renaissance period these games of war commonly began and ended with a procession of challengers, defenders and their retainers. Several forms of combat would follow. First, there was the joust in which mounted knights armed with lances charged at their opponents across a barrier. Then there was the melee in which mounted knights ran at each other without a tilt barrier. Finally combatants armed with blunted spears and swords fought on foot over a barrier. The French appeared to be less expert than their English counterparts, and after Francis was wounded in the hand he decided the time had come to restore French honour by fair play or foul. A huge German mercenary was hired to impersonate a Frenchman and take on Brandon, who had taken the honours on the first day. Brandon, however, proved his match. In a fight on foot with blunted swords, he seized the German by the neck and pummelled him in the face with a mailed fist. The stunned German had to be carried away, blood pouring from his nose.

On 28 December after the English had returned home, Louis wrote to Henry assuring him that 'The queen hath hitherto conducted herself, and still does, in a manner that I cannot but be delighted with her more and more each day.' He had been amused by Brandon's victory over the German, and told Henry 'I beg you to believe that, independent of the place he holds with you, and the love you bear him, his virtues, manners, politeness and good condition deserve that he should be received [by you] with even greater honour.'[10] Louis' health was in steep decline, however, and only four days later he died.

His young widow withdrew from court, veiled in the traditional white of a queen in mourning and, although it was not yet certain whether or not she was pregnant, Francis, anxious for his crown, rushed through Louis' funeral eleven days later.

In England Henry was curious to hear how this new King of France, three years his junior, measured up. 'The King of France, is he as tall as I am?' he asked the Venetian ambassador. Frustratingly he was told 'there was but little difference'. 'Is he as stout?' The diplomat said he was not. Henry then enquired, 'What sort of legs has he?' To Henry's delight, he was told they were rather thin. He promptly opened the front of his doublet, and placing his hand on his thigh, said 'Look here! I have also a good calf to my leg.'[11]

Henry was certain that Brandon's charm would succeed in engaging Francis as a friend, and decided to send him to France to bring Mary home. First, however, he made Brandon swear he would not marry her while he was in France. The sisters of kings were valuable assets on the diplomatic marriage market, and not to be wasted on a jousting partner. As Henry was to discover, however, his beautiful, spoilt, rich sister was not to be underestimated in her determination to get her way.

Mary knew Francis would have liked to see her marry a Frenchman as her second husband, and so keep her dowry in France. She suspected, though, that still more than that he wished to avoid her returning home only to be married in Burgundy or Spain, as the basis for an anti-French alliance. So when Francis came to visit her in her shuttered rooms at the Hotel de Cluny, she confided in him her wish to marry Brandon and, as she had gambled, Francis promised he would help.

When Brandon arrived in Paris, King Francis called him for a private meeting and outlined his potential support for Brandon's marriage to the French queen. The following evening the bewildered duke was summoned to see his would-be bride. No sooner had Brandon set eyes on her than Mary announced 'she must be short with him' and 'show how good a lady she was' to him. If he played his cards right, she promised she would 'would never have none but' him. 'The best in France' had warned her that Henry intended to send her off to be married in Flanders, and 'she had rather be torn in pieces than ever she should come there'. Then, fetchingly, she burst into tears. 'I never saw woman so weep', Brandon later confessed. He attempted to reassure her and promised that if she got Henry's permission he would marry her, 'otherwise' he warned 'I durst not'. The oath of a knight could not easily be broken – least of all when made to a king. She promptly threatened that if he would not marry her immediately, he should look 'never to have this proffer again', and she would refuse to return to England. Brandon married her. The question was how to break the news to Henry.

Mary laid the groundwork on 15 February in a letter insisting that she was under terrible pressure from the French to marry a groom of their choice. The fear that she would become a tool of the French would, she hoped, help a Brandon marriage look more attractive to Henry. Hoping to bring out her brother's chivalrous instincts, she added that King Francis was pestering her with sexual advances. Brandon's task was to beg Thomas Wolsey – a long-standing ally – for his help. 'The queen would never let me be in rest till I had granted her to be married,' he pleaded, 'and so, to be plain with you, I have married her heartily and lain with her.' He thought she might be pregnant. It was essential for the legitimacy of their children and her honour that they have a second, public marriage ceremony; this was usually forbidden during Lent, which began on 21 February, but Brandon told Wolsey he could get special permission from a bishop.[12]

Wolsey warned Brandon that the king had taken the news 'grievously'. Henry had believed that Brandon would be 'torn with wild horses' before he would break his oath. Wolsey suggested they get Francis to write in support of the marriage and the couple pay through the nose for what they had done: 40 per cent of Mary's dower income, and all the plate and jewels she had been given by Louis.

They were also to extract a binding promise from King Francis to send 200,000 crowns of the dowry money back to England. Wolsey ended by reminding Brandon that he was 'in the greatest danger that ever man was in'.[13]

As rumours swept Paris that their recently widowed queen had already remarried, Mary wrote a further letter to Henry. Reminding him of his promise that if Louis died she could marry whom she liked, she confirmed she had married Brandon privately, 'without any request or labour on his part', and not 'carnally, or of any sensual appetite' but only because she had feared a foreign marriage and despaired of ever seeing Henry again.[14] Francis also wrote to Henry in support of this public marriage to Brandon. The campaign worked. Francis' mother, Louise of Savoy, noted in her journal that on 'Saturday the last day of March, the Duke of Suffolk, a person of low estate whom Henry VIII had sent as ambassador to the king married Mary' in a public ceremony.[15]

Having sent Henry a stream of cash and jewels, the French queen now also sent the finest stone she had been given. A receipt dated 6 April 1515 records the arrival in England of 'the great diamond called "le Mirouer de Napples" [the Mirror of Naples], with a large pearl attached'.[16] The Italian merchant who saw her wearing it when she departed for France the previous year, claimed it had been 'valued at 60,000 crowns'.[17]

Henry was delighted with the jewel and, in a detail not yet noted by historians, he wore it just over a fortnight later. A visiting diplomat recorded being escorted on St George's Day into the royal presence at Richmond Palace, 'through sundry chambers all hung with most beautiful tapestry, figured in gold, silver and in silk'. On either side were 300 of the guard, 'in silver breastplates and pikes in their hands, and by God they were as big as giants'. At last he was introduced to Henry, who stood leaning against his golden throne. He was wearing a cap of crimson velvet tied with loops and gold enamel tags, a doublet striped in red and white satin and a flowing mantle of purple velvet.

But what dazzled the diplomat most was the jewel he wore, hanging from a gold collar, worn close around the neck, 'a round cut diamond, the size of the largest walnut I ever saw' from which 'was suspended a most beautiful and very large round pearl'.[18]

Henry duly welcomed the couple on their return to England: he was too fond of his younger sister and of Brandon to deprive himself of their company for long. Other favourites might be cleverer, or wittier, but as another Italian diplomat observed, Brandon's combination of charm and physicality reflected the king's glory.

On 15 May a third wedding was performed before the full court at Greenwich. Officially the nation rejoiced. Unofficially the Venetians observed that there were none of the public demonstrations of joy expected after a royal marriage 'because the kingdom did not approve'. In a strictly hierarchical society, people were expected to know their place – even if they were the king's best friend. Meanwhile, King Francis was reported to be 'sore displeased at the loss of the diamond called the Mirror of Naples'.[19] He scribbled angrily across a sketch of the French queen: 'plus sale que royne' (more dirty than queenly).[20]

But it was her sister who was to pay the price of the jewel's loss. Unencumbered by an English wife, as Louis had been, Francis had given Albany permission to take up the reins of government in Scotland and instructed him to send Queen Margaret's younger son, the infant Alexander, Duke of Ross, to be educated in France.[21] Scotland and France had a mutual interest in maintaining their old alliance against their English neighbour, and to Henry's dismay, on 26 July 1515, with Albany welcomed in Scotland, the Scottish Parliament approved a plan to remove the princes from Queen Margaret's care. Eight lords were chosen as their guardians, four of whom were dispatched promptly to Margaret at Stirling, to seize the princes.

17

A FAMILY REUNION AND A ROYAL RIVAL

STANDING BEHIND THE GATES AT STIRLING CASTLE, MARGARET held the hand of her three-year-old son, James V, and ordered them opened.[1] The approaching horsemen were just yards from the gate when she called on them to halt. They reined in their horses sharply. Margaret was heavily pregnant, and standing with her was not only her eldest son, but also a nurse carrying the king's infant brother, the Duke of Ross. Margaret asked the four lords to deliver their message. They replied that they were commissioned to demand the delivery of the king and his brother to them. At that she ordered the portcullis dropped. Through the lattice ironwork Margaret reminded them that the castle had been bequeathed to her 'by the king her husband, who had made her protectrix of her children'. They agreed to give her six days to consider their demands; then they would return for her sons.

Once the lords had left, Margaret returned to the castle's rooms and her husband, the Earl of Angus. They had little choice, he said, 'that the children should be given up'. Margaret insisted that they should only do so if the lords agreed she could see her children, otherwise they should seek some other solution. She had lost children before to illness; she would fight to the bitter end for those God had spared. Margaret persuaded Angus to leave to ask the advice of Henry's agents. He had not yet returned when the lords came, once again, for the children. Margaret told them she would hand them over if they would only be placed with her choice of guardians and she could 'see them when she pleased'.[2] This request was turned down flat and the Duke of Albany began immediately to cut off her supplies. Margaret soon found herself marooned in her fortress on its sheer rock face above the town.

Angus found Henry VIII's agents convinced that if the duke got his hands on the children they would 'be destroyed' and a plan had been laid for Angus to return to Stirling and rescue them. He hoped a small force of sixty men would stand a good chance of eluding detection by the duke's forces. Unfortunately, as they reached Stirling they were spotted. Sixteen of the party were killed as they fled, while one messenger got through, bringing desperate advice from Henry's principal agent in the north, Lord Dacre. He suggested she should 'set the young King of Scots upon the walls in the sight of all persons, crowned and with the sceptre in his hand'. Dacre hoped this would prevent Albany firing on the castle, and even raise the town in her support.

On 4 August 1515 Albany arrived at Stirling with an army seven thousand strong. His cannon included the infamous Mons Meg, a six-tonne muzzle-loading weapon capable of firing gunstones weighing 150 kilograms over a range of two miles.[3] 'Desolate' at the sight, Queen Margaret had no intention of putting her tiny son in the firing line.[4] Instead she agreed to surrender the castle and her children. In what time she had left with them she coached James V to ask for favour for himself, his brother and his stepfather. When the men came for him the little boy dutifully handed over the castle's huge keys, and repeated the words his mother had taught him.[5] Margaret was placed under guard as James and his infant brother were then taken from her. James was two years younger than his grandfather Henry VII had been when he was taken from his mother, Margaret Beaufort.

Queen Margaret now intended to flee Scotland for England. By the beginning of September she had gained Albany's trust sufficiently for her to be allowed to travel to Linlithgow Palace, to prepare for the birth of Angus' baby. A few days after her arrival at the palace she fled to Tantallon Castle, three miles east of North Berwick. She had only four or five servants, as well as her husband with her, but Albany soon discovered her departure. The duke needed to validate his claim that he ruled Scotland in the name of all. He could not do that with the queen in exile, and nor did he wish to risk her returning to Scotland with an English army at her back. He sent a message assuring her if she came back he would restore 'everything' to her within seven days; if she was now too near the birth to travel, she could send her husband as hostage, but as soon as the messenger arrived Margaret and Angus fled on, even leaving behind her baggage and jewels in their hurry.[6]

By the time the party had reached England Margaret was exhausted. Unable to ride as far as Lord Dacre's house at Morpeth, they stopped at the remote military outpost of Harbottle Castle. Dacre reported to Henry that there, on 7 October, 'the Queen of Scots your sister . . . was delivered and brought in bed of a fair young lady'. Henry's niece was christened the following day, 'with such convenient provisions as either could or might be had in this barren and wild country'.[7] Like her namesakes and predecessors this child, Lady Margaret Douglas, was to be a key figure in the future of the Tudor and the Stuart royal lines. But her birth had almost killed her mother. The queen proved too weak to be moved even after the religious service that marked a mother's re-entry into society three weeks later, known as churching. She could barely eat and suffered sciatica down her right leg.

It was only late in November that Queen Margaret was able to travel to Morpeth, carried in a litter borne by Dacre's menservants. The house was hung with new tapestries, Dacre's gilt plate was all put out in her honour, and she was still more pleased to discover how active her family had been on her behalf. Margaret's sister, Mary, still called the French queen, knew the Duke of Albany from France, and had extracted public assurances from him on the safety of the princes.

Henry had also sent clothes and other necessities as a public mark of his support.

Dacre was amazed by what appeared to be Margaret's obsessive 'love of apparel'. She had twenty-two gowns of cloth of gold and silks in his house, and sent to Edinburgh for more. She remained in such pain from her daughter's birth that even sitting up in bed made her scream in agony, so she could not wear them. Instead she had them held in front of her to admire. For five days, Dacre reported, Queen Margaret spoke frequently about her dresses: how she was going to have one made up in purple velvet lined with cloth of gold and another in red velvet lined in ermine. It expressed, perhaps, a wish to return to the security she had known as Henry VII's young daughter, and, later, as James IV's wife. Tellingly the traumatised queen also spoke often of her infant son, the Duke of Ross, and what a good child he was. She spoke of him even more often than of her elder son, the king. Dacre feared that the news, brought by a Scottish delegation, that the baby had died from a fever, would kill her.[8]

It was March 1516 before Dacre told Margaret. She was so distressed that her husband Angus waited a further two weeks before telling her he had decided to come to an accommodation with Albany. He returned to Scotland in April. Dacre felt that Margaret was deeply saddened by what she saw as her husband's desertion, but she was also anxious to be at court with her Tudor family, for a time at least.[9] She had not seen them since she was thirteen, that long-ago girl who had enjoyed cards, dancing, and had listened to the fine new choir singing in her grandmother Margaret Beaufort's chapel at Collyweston. Her excitement mounted as she travelled south, and from Stony Stratford she wrote to tell Henry 'I am in right good heal, and as joyous of my said journey toward you as any woman may be in coming to her brother.'[10]

On 3 May Queen Margaret entered London 'with a great company' and rested at Baynard's Castle. When the invitation to see Henry arrived, Queen Margaret found a vigorous young king very different to their old, careful, father. Where Henry VII had micromanaged state affairs, personally annotating Treasury accounts, Henry VIII delegated the daily grind, only intervening when and where he wanted.[11] He would spend days 'shooting, singing, dancing, wrestling, casting of the bar [a form of shot putting], playing at the recorders, flute and virginals'.[12] He also loved the joust, which his father had never taken part in. One ambassador described him as 'like St George on horseback' when he performed; another claimed he had never seen 'such a beautiful sight'.

The hours Henry VIII spent on such pleasures were never wasted. They lay at the heart of what it was to be a king, binding him to those who would help him win glory on the battlefield. His father had not been well loved, while the affability and largesse of Edward IV had won popular applause, and Henry VIII remained every inch his grandson. The scholar Erasmus thought Henry 'a man of gentle friendliness' who 'acts more like a companion than a king'. He had transformed the personnel of the Privy Chamber, filling it with highborn favourites and boon companions in place of the humble servants his father had used. He also expanded the size of Privy Lodgings with his many building projects, so that he would walk freely with his friends in the Privy Gallery or talk in the Privy Gardens. Henry even wrote a song celebrating his pleasure in friendships:

> Pastime with good company
> I love and shall until I die
> grudge who will but none deny
> so God be pleased thus live will I
> for my pastance
> hunt, sing and dance.

Henry's happiness and confidence had been recently boosted by fatherhood. The thirty-year-old Katherine of Aragon was the proud mother of a healthy baby: the three-month-old princess, Mary.[13] Henry had been sure that 'if it was a daughter this time, by the grace of God the sons will follow' and the couple remained very happy in each other's company.[14] Erasmus noted Katherine was 'astonishing well read, far beyond what would be surprising in a woman'. An important part of Henry's kingship was reflected in Katherine's resourcefulness and erudition, as well as her piety. Queen Margaret could see, however, that Katherine's earlier losses to miscarriage and infant death had aged her (as similar losses had also aged Margaret). Even when Katherine was 'richly attired', and surrounded by a supporting cast of twenty-five ladies on white horses, wearing dresses slashed with gold, she was judged 'rather ugly than otherwise'.[15]

Queen Margaret had chosen Henry's most trusted councillor, Wolsey, to act as godfather to her daughter and, meeting him, she could not fail to be struck by his charisma. He was now Lord Chancellor and although already forty-five he looked younger, 'very handsome, learned, extremely eloquent, of vast ability, and indefatigable'.[16] Margaret must have been particularly pleased, however, to see her sister, the French queen, and have the opportunity to watch Brandon performing in the tournaments given in celebration of her arrival. The feasting went on for a month before Margaret settled in the closed area of large houses near Charing Cross where visiting Scottish dignitaries were usually billeted, and known as Little Scotland.[17] She wanted to keep in touch with developments in her son's kingdom, and plan her return. The peace between France and England meant that, in due course, King Francis would recall the Duke of Albany from Scotland. Queen Margaret hoped again to be regent for her son, James V, or at least to see more of him.

By April the following year, 1517, Margaret had gained assurances that she could return to Scotland without fear of arrest, injury or impediment. In May she was ready to leave. Henry furnished her with more clothes, jewels, money and horses, and she bid farewell to her pregnant sister. A daughter, Lady Frances Brandon (named after King Francis) would be born in July.[18] Queen Margaret and her own little daughter, Lady Margaret Douglas, were escorted across the border in June. She was destined never to see her Tudor family again, although her daughter would one day make a life in England, returning to a very different court.

A year after Margaret had said her goodbyes, Katherine of Aragon was pregnant again. Since sexual intercourse was considered dangerous for mothers-to-be, Henry had taken a mistress, the pretty nineteen-year-old Elizabeth Blount. She was at the celebrations following the betrothal that October of the two-year-old princess Mary to King Francis' heir: the culmination of the pursuit of peace with France. The ceremonies took place at Wolsey's bishopric palace, York Place near Westminster. Wolsey had a taste for the good things in life and the Venetian ambassador described the palace as 'very fine'. You had to cross 'eight rooms before reaching his audience chamber', and each was 'hung with tapestry, which was changed once a week', while the sideboards were piled with silver worth an estimated 25,000 ducats. As for the cardinal (as Wolsey now was), his power had grown so much it seemed to the diplomat that he ruled 'both the king and the entire kingdom'.[19]

Elizabeth Blount was one of a party of thirty-six masquers that night, each dressed in 'fine green satin, all covered with cloth of gold'. She 'excelled at singing, dancing, and in all goodly pastimes', and demonstrated her skills, with the masquers dancing one at a time. When she had finished she cast off her mask to reveal her fresh young face.[20] The glow came not just from her youth and natural beauty, however: the king's mistress was in the early stage of pregnancy. A month later Katherine of Aragon delivered a stillborn daughter, 'to the vexation of everyone'. To add insult to misery Elizabeth Blount's child, born the following June, proved, 'a goodly man child of beauty like to the father and mother'.[21] He was named Henry Fitzroy, and Wolsey was once again called upon to be godfather. Elizabeth Blount was married off later that summer to a young man called Gilbert Tailboys, who was a ward of the Crown.[22]

Henry still talked of Katherine having a son, but she was now thirty-three and people began to speculate on who might become king if Henry were to die. Henry VII had hoped that in the absence of Tudor male heirs the English would look to his daughter, Queen Margaret, to provide them with a king. Having been raised in Wales and Brittany Henry VII did not share English prejudice against the Scots, or fears that having a Scottish king would result in a loss of sovereignty. Scotland, he is said to have observed, would become subsumed into England 'since the less becomes subservient to the greater'. But Queen Margaret's son, James V, was a mere seven years old and, as in 1501, when Henry VII was ill and his sons minors, many did not consider the young heirs of Tudor blood to be the best choice. In September 1519 the Venetian ambassador reported that one person who had been mentioned in 1501 as 'a noble man [who] would be a royal ruler' was again being mentioned as a future King of England: Edward Stafford, Duke of Buckingham.

A descendant of Edward III's youngest son Thomas Woodstock, and of John of Gaunt, Buckingham lived like the royal ducal magnate he was. At the siege of Thérouanne in France he had caught attention dressed in a suit of purple satin embroidered with 'antelopes and swans of fine gold bullion, and full of spangles and little bells of gold very costly and marvellous to behold'. He was currently in the process of building a vast pleasure palace at Thornbury in Gloucestershire. The ambassador noted that he was respected by the people, and 'might easily obtain the crown' if the king died without male heirs.[23]

Anxiously, Henry asked Wolsey to keep a watch on Buckingham, which the cardinal was more than happy to do.[24] Buckingham hated the low-born cardinal as a 'base fellow' and despised his peace with France.[25] In June 1520 Buckingham let it be known that he resented the expense of attending the feast of Anglo-French reconciliation Wolsey had organised near Calais. Such was the array of rich tents and pavilions that it became known as the 'Field of Cloth of Gold', but Buckingham declared the fabulous display, the tournaments and meetings, to be no more than a 'spectacle of foolish speeches' or a 'conference of trivialities'.

In November Buckingham infuriated Henry by retaining a royal servant, who was seen wearing his livery. This suggested the servant had a dual loyalty, and Henry was reported to have bellowed angrily that 'he would none of his servants should hang on another man's sleeve'. Buckingham, fearing he might be sent to the Tower, blustered to his servants that he would rather kneel before the king in submission and then thrust him through with a dagger.[26] Unfortunately a surveyor Buckingham had sacked then revealed these threats to Wolsey.

As the cardinal investigated further he discovered Buckingham believed that Henry VII's execution of the last male Plantagenet in 1499 had cursed the Tudor line. He had told his servants 'that God would punish it, by not suffering the king's issue to prosper'.[27] He also gloated to them that the prior of a Carthusian house at Hinton[28] in north Somerset had prophesied that since Henry would have 'no issue males of his body', he would one day be king adding, 'that all the king's father did was wrong, and that he had always been dissatisfied with everything the king had done'. Henry VIII 'gave fees and offices to boys rather than noblemen', while Wolsey was 'the king's bawd, showing him [which w]omen were most wholesome, and best of complexion'.[29] These complaints were reminiscent of Richard III's attacks on the immorality of Edward IV. Such, at least, was the case for the prosecution.

On 13 May 1521 Buckingham was tried on a charge of high treason and found guilty by his fellow peers of compassing and imagining the death of the king. They did so with heavy hearts. It was all too reminiscent of earlier bloodletting within the royal house, and when the jury members came to read their verdicts, they were too moved to speak. Bravely Buckingham urged them on, saying he was content to accept the punishment, 'not for the crime laid to his account, which is utterly false, but for his very great sins'.[30] Four days later, on 17 May, two sheriffs and 500 infantrymen led Buckingham to the axe-man on Tower Hill. He died, the Venetian ambassador observed, 'miserably, but with great courage'.[31] It is a mark of how shocking Buckingham's death was considered to be that a lawyer, drawing up the usually dry-as-dust yearbook of legal cases, noted beside the entry for Buckingham's trial, 'God in his love grant mercy, for he was a very noble, prudent prince, and the image of all that is courtly.'[32] The great Stafford family was never again to attain the wealth and pre-eminence they had hitherto enjoyed. And Henry still did not have a son.

18

ENTER ANNE BOLEYN

HENRY WAS IN BED ON 9 MARCH 1525 WHEN A MESSENGER ARRIVED with urgent news. Wolsey's efforts to keep Europe at peace had failed in the face of Franco-Imperial rivalry in Italy. Hoping to take advantage of this, Henry had allied with the twenty-five-year-old emperor, Charles V. His decision now seemed vindicated – King Francis had been defeated at the hands of the Imperial army at Pavia.[1] His army was massacred, and the French nobility suffered their greatest slaughter since Agincourt. But Henry was also interested to learn from the messenger the fate of an Englishman amongst Francis' commanders: Richard de la Pole, third son of Edward IV's sister Elizabeth, Duchess of Suffolk, and the last 'White Rose'.[2] He had been killed in the battle. Less than four years after the execution of Buckingham, the last serious rival to Henry VII's heirs was dead. 'All the enemies of England are gone', Henry cried out, and called for the messenger to be given more wine.[3]

Secure in England, Henry VIII believed his dream of a coronation in Paris was now within his grasp. He hoped to persuade Charles V to divide France between them, and reminded Charles that if he married his daughter, Mary Tudor, then on his death Charles could add England to his empire. But Charles was now out of money, and his need for peace was more urgent than any future prospects concerning the inheritance of England. Henry could not hope to conquer France without him, and as Charles' peace treaty with France was being signed, Henry realised bitterly that his achievements lacked the greatness he had sought. He was no Henry V. His situation more closely resembled that of Henry VI. England's power in Europe was diminishing, and like Henry VI in 1453, with no legitimate sons, he needed to bolster his position by promoting what close male relatives he did have. Henry VI had created his non-royal half-brothers, Edmund and Jasper Tudor, England's premier earls. Similarly, Henry VIII was to promote his illegitimate son Henry Fitzroy into the highest ranks of the nobility.

On 18 June the six-year-old Fitzroy left his mother, Elizabeth Blount, for good, and was brought by barge to the king's newly rebuilt palace at Bridewell on the banks of the Fleet river. Henry's former mistress would henceforth only have occasional contact with their son. After landing at the water-gate Fitzroy was conducted through a chamber hung with gold and silver hangings to a gallery where he was clothed in the robes of an earl. Fitzroy was a lively child, but this was an awe-inspiring ceremony and a crowd was gathering in the chamber below where King Henry awaited his son, standing under a cloth of estate. At last the ushers cleared a path through the court, and at a signal from the king, the trumpets blew. Fitzroy took his cue, entered and approached his proud father, who then hung a sword over his slight neck and one boyish shoulder. No sooner had the patent of the earldom been read than the next ceremony took place and Henry Fitzroy was granted the unprecedented honour of the double duke-doms of Somerset and Richmond.[4] Only afterwards could the boy relax, and there were 'great feasts and disguisings' to celebrate his new rank.

The titles Fitzroy had been granted, together with wealth and offices, prompted speculation then, as well as later, that Henry was considering making the boy his heir.[5] But these were not the titles of a Prince of Wales. Richmond was the title Henry VI had given Edmund Tudor in 1453, while Somerset was a Beaufort title. It signalled that his place was as a member of the extended royal family and made Fitzroy a potentially valuable asset on the diplomatic marriage market, while acknowledging that this situation might change under extraordinary circumstances – as it had for Edmund Tudor's heir, Henry VII. Katherine of Aragon was said to resent Fitzroy's elevation, and understandably so, for it was a public acknowledgement that she could no longer bear children. But for the time being the princess Mary was treated very much as Henry's heir, and it was as such that she was poised to play her part in Wolsey's new anti-Imperial stance.

Henry's bitterness towards the emperor Charles for ending his ambitions in France meant Wolsey was able to persuade him to re-establish his friendship with the French king. Negotiations began on yet another marriage for the princess Mary, this time to the widowed King Francis. As one foreign observer noted, 'in time of war the English make use of the princess' as if she was a 'lure' to hunt birds.[6] Mary received the French delegation sent to conclude the terms of the alliance at Greenwich on 23 April 1527. The eleven-year-old was, like her father, an exceptional musician, and her accomplishments in this regard were much praised. She was proving clever too. Her translation of a prayer by St Thomas Aquinas was being circulated so that learned courtiers might 'not only marvel at the doing of it, but further, for the well doing'.[7] But Mary was still only a child, and the delegation judged her 'so thin, spare and small as it to be impossible to be married for the next three years'.

When the 'perpetual peace' was finally signed with France on 30 April, it was agreed Mary might be married instead to Francis' second son, the Duke of Orléans. The festivities celebrating the treaty culminated on 5 May when Henry took the French ambassadors to see Mary with her mother at Greenwich Palace. The slightly built princess looked very pretty as she danced with the French ambassador that night. Her dress shone in the ubiquitous cloth of gold favoured by royalty, flattering her auburn hair, and Henry danced with one of her mother's ladies. The young woman was rather sallow-skinned, with a long narrow face and high-bridged nose, but she was graceful and striking with her dark hair and flashing black eyes.[8] King Francis' ambassadors were impressed by her knowledge of their country and fluency in their language – but then Anne Boleyn had spent many years at the French court.[9]

It was quite usual for the children of the higher gentry to leave home between the ages of eight and twelve, to be raised and educated in a great household. But Anne, the younger daughter of the ambitious courtier Sir Thomas Boleyn, had been sent further away than most – to the court of Maximilian's daughter Margaret of Austria, in Mechelen. Sir Thomas wanted her to learn French and Anne did well there until, aged fourteen, she was called upon to attend Henry's sister Mary, the French queen, at her coronation. After the French queen returned to England Anne had remained in France – perhaps so she would not expose the scandal of Mary's secret second marriage to Brandon. Anne was recalled eventually late in 1521. By then she was hardly likely to talk about a scandal concerning the king's sister, given that her own sister, Mary Boleyn, had been sleeping with him.

Henry's relationship with Mary Boleyn has generated a lot of smoke, but we know little about the fire. Anne's leading biographer, Eric Ives, believed the affair would have followed a similar pattern to that of Henry's earlier affair with Elizabeth Blount. Henry had slept with Blount when Katherine of Aragon was carrying her last baby. When Blount became pregnant with Henry's son his attentions turned to Mary Boleyn. She, in turn, may have become pregnant – or thought she was. In any event she was married off, just as Blount had been, in February 1520 to a gentleman of the Privy Chamber called William Carey. The king was the principal guest.[10] The affair may or may not have come to an end: the malicious gossip was that Henry fathered some of Mary Boleyn's children.[11]

Following Anne's return to England she had narrowly missed two possible marriages. At first her father had intended that she be married to the heir to the Irish earldom of Ormond (a title that had been held by his own maternal grandfather).[12] Irish politics, or her father's greed, had put paid to that. She had then attracted the attention of a still more eligible groom: Henry Percy, heir to the earldom of Northumberland. He served in Wolsey's household and when the cardinal was at court Percy would often visit the queen's chamber. There, according to Wolsey's servant and later biographer, George Cavendish, he would 'fall in dalliance among the queen's maidens'.[13] Amongst them, Anne Boleyn had stood out, combining French sophistication with Irish spirit, and Percy was not alone in his interest in her.

With wives left at home, male courtiers, both unmarried and married, swarmed round the few women that attended the queen. Relations between the sexes were supposed to be controlled by the code of courtly love, but a woman needed a quick wit to avoid the flirting becoming potentially ruinous: as one book on court etiquette advised, they had to learn how to 'come just to certain limits, but not to pass them'.[14] For Anne the French court had been an effective school in this art and as she became familiar with the English court she discovered how best to deploy her charms. Percy was fascinated, and in time 'there grew such a secret love between them that at length they were ensured together, intending to marry', Cavendish recalls. Unfortunately Percy was already promised to Mary Talbot, daughter of the Earl of Shrewsbury. Breaking such a commitment would anger Shrewsbury, with potentially dangerous consequences. So, when Wolsey learned of Percy's intentions, he informed the king. According to Cavendish, Henry told Wolsey to send Percy packing, admitting he was interested in Anne himself. She was the most desired woman at court and it was natural for Henry to want the star prize.

The first public hint of Henry's affections came at a joust on Shrove Tuesday, the eve of Lent, 1526. His costume was embroidered with a heart in a press surrounded by flames and the words 'Declare I dare not'.[15] Anne's other suitors soon began to notice they had royal competition. The courtier poet Thomas Wyatt compared Anne and her following of male courtiers to a hunted deer with a pack in chase, running in vain for 'graven with diamonds in letters plain, There is written her fair neck round about: Noli me tangere [do not touch], for Caesar's I am, And wild for to hold, though I seem tame.'[16] Henry Percy married Mary Talbot (unhappily) in September 1526, and as Anne's other admirers dropped away she found she was left with one suitor: Henry. But she would not sleep with him.

Anne had no desire to be a discarded royal mistress, married off to a gentleman, when she might have been Countess of Northumberland. But if Anne hoped Henry would become bored and move on, she proved mistaken. Henry was willing – even delighted – to hold back. It appealed to his love of chivalric romance and the ideal of the unobtainable mistress. Henry did not wish to break the spell Anne cast by sleeping with her. Sex was available elsewhere if he wanted it. Consciously or otherwise he was also playing out the story of his grandparents, Edward IV and Elizabeth Woodville. That had begun with Woodville refusing the king, and had ended in their marriage and the birth of two sons, as well as several daughters. Henry needed a wife with whom to have a legitimate son to continue his line, and wives must be chaste. Anne seemed to be the answer to his prayers.

Seventeen undated love letters from Henry, thirteen of which survive in the Vatican archives, record the unfolding romance from courtship to betrothal. At first Henry is 'in great agony, not knowing how to interpret' Anne's letters. Then he asks her to accept a role as his official and sole mistress. Finally she is his 'darling', and he longs to be 'in my sweetheart's arms, whose pretty dukkys [breasts] I trust shortly to kiss'. The problem for Henry and Anne (now obliged to play for the highest marriage stake of all) was that he remained married to Katherine of Aragon. There was a possible solution, however, in the new revisionist theology of a depressive German former monk called Martin Luther.

In his monastery Luther had struggled to be good, fearful that whatever he did, be it going to Mass, or confession, or helping the poor, he remained a miserable sinner. In 1515, however, it had come to him that man 'can neither will nor do anything but evil', but that acceptance by God (known as 'justification') came as His unmerited gift, through the sacrifice of Christ, for a chosen few – the elect. The church had little role in this and he came to see the clergy as just another venal interest group. Truth and certainty had to be found direct in Scripture. In 1520 Luther had published *The Babylonish Captivity of the Church*, which declared that of the seven sacraments of the church, he found no reference to support four of them in any biblical text and so considered them worthless: confirmation, holy orders, extreme unction (given to the dying) and marriage.[17] Luther argued that it was therefore permissible to dissolve a marriage and divorce.

Henry loved theological arguments, but Luther's views appealed to very few in England and certainly not to the king. With some scholarly help he had even composed a reply to *The Babylonish Captivity* defending the seven sacraments, not least marriage. Pope Leo X had been delighted by Henry's loyalty and rewarded the king with the title 'Defender of the Faith' (having toyed with the idea of naming him 'Protector of the Holy See'). Henry would never divorce and would burn Lutherans as heretics until the end of his reign. Nevertheless, he struggled to understand why God had not listened to his prayers for a male heir by Katherine. A son, Henry believed, was a blessing 'naturally desired of all men', and he feared his loss was also his kingdom's loss. Women came second to men in the divine hierarchy and if the princess Mary became queen, it was obvious to him that she could not 'long continue without a husband, which by God's law, must then be her head and direct this realm'. Either she would marry a foreign prince or an English subject, and if the latter, Henry observed it would be hard to find someone suitable for 'so high an enterprise', and still harder 'to find one with whom the whole realm could and would be contented'.[18]

An insight into his state of mind is revealed in his commission at around this time for a set of large and very valuable tapestries telling the story of the biblical King David. The themes were obedience to God, the inevitability of divine retribution on those who fail to do so, and childlessness as a curse, with the tapestries illustrating King David's adultery with Bathsheba and the death of their child, followed by David's repentance, his forgiveness by God and, finally, God granting David a military victory over his enemy.[19] It was clear to Henry that like David he had been cursed – but in what way had he failed to obey the Almighty? Henry later claimed it was the French delegation, negotiating the betrothal between his daughter Mary and the Duke of Orléans, who unwittingly suggested the answer to that question.

According to Henry the French had queried Mary's legitimacy, pointing out that he and Katherine had broken a well-known injunction from the Old Testament book of Leviticus. It warned, 'If a man shall take his brother's wife it is an impurity; he hath uncovered his brother's nakedness; they shall be childless.' This seems unlikely given the French clearly regarded Mary as legitimate, but someone else may well have helped remind Henry of it, perhaps even Anne Boleyn (in which case, no wonder he pointed the finger elsewhere). In any event, he was now genuinely convinced his marriage was cursed, that Pope Julius II had been wrong to grant a dispensation to allow him to marry his sister-in-law against divine law, and that the current Pope, Clement VII, must annul this false marriage as soon as possible. Katherine, Henry was sure, would understand the situation, and retire gracefully. She had always been obedient to his wishes. However, it was important to Henry that everyone should recognise what he himself perceived, which was that in seeking an annulment he was motivated purely by issues of conscience, and not, as he said, by 'any carnal concupiscence, nor for any displeasure or dislike of the queen's person, or age'. To ensure there was no question about his virtue he kept his intention to marry Anne secret, even from Wolsey. Henry had told the cardinal only that he required Clement VII to overturn Julius II's dispensation.

Popes were usually understanding about marital difficulties within royal families, and on 11 March 1527 the Pope had annulled Henry's sister Queen Margaret's marriage to the Earl of Angus. There had been signs that all was not well with Queen Margaret's marriage even before she had returned to Scotland in 1517. The Duke of Albany had given Angus permission to travel to England to see his wife, and when he had declined to do so, it had given 'her much to muse'.[20] After she had returned she found Angus spent his time with his mistress, Lady Jane Stuart of Traquair, to whom he had been briefly betrothed, while also depriving Margaret of her revenues. In November 1518 she had informed Henry that she and Angus had not 'met this half year' and that she planned to divorce him 'if she may by God's law and with honour to herself, for he loves her not'.[21] Margaret's annulment was granted on the basis of Angus' earlier betrothal to Lady Jane Stuart. Henry was certain that he would be similarly successful and it was with the high hope that Anne Boleyn was his future wife that he danced with her in front of Katherine, Mary, and the French ambassadors on the night of 5 May 1527. But at dawn the following morning, as Henry rested at Greenwich, in far-off Rome the world was about to change.

19

A MARRIAGE ON TRIAL

THE EARLY MORNING LIGHT ON 6 MAY 1527 REVEALED NONE OF Rome's customary beauty. The great Renaissance city was under attack: the culmination of Franco-Imperial rivalry and the role of the Renaissance popes as territorial princes. Clement VII was allied with France, Venice, Florence and Milan against the emperor, and now the war had come to Rome's very gates. By 7 a.m the enemy forces were smashing through the city walls. Despite the emperor's traditional Catholic faith, amongst his army there were thousands of Lutheran troops from Germany, mutinous, unpaid, and filled with religious hatred for Rome. As tidal waves of armed men poured down the streets, Romans fled home to protect their families and goods. Those who stood and fought alongside the Pope's Swiss Guard against the terrifying odds were annihilated.

In the Vatican, Pope Clement was interrupted while hearing Mass and told to flee immediately. A Spaniard in Rome, Francisco de Salazar, heard 'So narrow was the Pope's escape that had he tarried for three creeds he would have been taken prisoner in his own palace.'[1] Meanwhile, the emperor's army was killing everyone they came across. The little orphans of the Pieta were no more spared their lives than the sick at the Hospital of San Spirito. The Lutherans took particular pleasure in raping nuns and tormenting clerics before they were killed: one old priest was slaughtered after refusing to offer Communion to an ass. Palaces and churches were sacked and desecrated, libraries were burned, and unique manuscripts from the ancient world lost for ever.

For days the killing in Rome continued, men 'committing such atrocities that the pen actually refuses to write them down, and that there is no memory capable of recording them', Salazar wrote. When it was over Renaissance Rome was no more. At St Peter's, 'Many dead bodies lay about, so much disfigured that it was impossible to recognise them; and in the chapel itself, close to the altar of St Peter, were great pools of blood, dead horses, &c'; 'It seems all like a dream', Salazar observed, 'no one can now visit a church or go about Rome, such is the stench of corpses'.[2]

The news of what had happened was still spreading across a horrified Europe, when in England, Wolsey opened a secret court the king had instructed him to set up at York Place. Henry stood accused of having lived in an incestuous relationship with his sister-in-law, Katherine. He expected to be found guilty, and be obliged to separate from her. Then the Pope would confirm an anulment. The secrecy was intended to allow the lawyers to build up the case against Henry's marriage to Katherine before she learned about it, but she discovered what was going on within twenty-four hours of the court opening. Angry and humiliated, she kept up a pretence of ignorance as she began to work out a strategy to defend her honour and her daughter's inheritance. Henry's plans were further stymied when on 1 June England learned of the sack of Rome.

It emerged that the Pope was under siege by the emperor at the fortress of Castel Sant 'Angelo. There was no point in continuing with the court at York Place until the situation in Rome was clarified, and so the court sessions were abandoned. Henry, frustrated and impatient to get his way, decided to reveal to Katherine his 'discovery' that they were living in mortal sin, in the hope she would agree to an annulment immediately. To Henry's complete shock Katherine's reaction was instead to burst into tears. Katherine had always made Henry comfortable. This display of heartbreak was most uncomfortable. Stunned, Henry tried and failed to reassure Katherine that an annulment was for the best. He also ordered her to keep the matter secret. This too was naive, for as one observer noted, his desire to annul his marriage was by now 'as notorious as if it had been proclaimed by the public crier'.[3]

Henry's discomfort worsened as he learned of the public reaction to the news of his intentions. After eighteen years Katherine was a much-loved queen and in the streets and taverns people expressed their disgust that she was being shamed. Women in particular resented the idea that a good queen should be abandoned simply because she had grown old and had been unlucky enough not to give her husband a surviving son, for many knew the pain of losing children. On one occasion when a crowd of Londoners spotted the queen walking across the bridge from the royal residence at Bridewell, they started to shout out that her case must succeed or God would punish England and that they prayed for her victory. Katherine also needed international support, however, and in seeking it she first turned to her nephew, the emperor Charles at Valladolid in Spain. If the Pope would not take orders from the emperor whose troops had sacked Rome, he could not afford a final break with him either – and the emperor duly promised his aunt his backing.

Henry also had another major difficulty – he had chosen the wrong argument at the worst time. With papal authority being questioned by Luther and others, any threat to undermine it – such as by questioning the Pope's power to dispense with the biblical injunction against marrying a dead brother's wife – was bound to be opposed vehemently. Nevertheless, Wolsey turned to England's one internationally respected theologian, Margaret Beaufort's old friend and confessor, the Bishop of Rochester, John Fisher, for his opinion on the matter.

Fisher was a member of that fashionable group of scholars known as humanists. This referred to the study of the humanities: literature, ideas, and politics studied through the Greek and Roman classics, and is unrelated to modern humanism, which concerns the dignity of man without reference to God.[4] Amongst them Erasmus had published a New Testament in Greek and this was to become the basis of several new translations. Since a different accent on the meaning of a word could question centuries of belief, so a new importance was being placed on historical accuracy and authenticity. Some humanists would become what we would call Protestant. They are often amongst those termed 'evangelicals', because they wished to return to the '*evangelium*' or 'good news' of the Gospel, stripping away church traditions they believed had no biblical basis. Many other humanists would, however, remain orthodox Catholics.

Following the king's lead, Fisher had written powerful arguments against Luther and in favour of papal authority, fearing that without the discipline of the central authority of Rome Western Christendom was in danger of splintering. It cannot have much surprised Wolsey, therefore, when Fisher replied to his queries with the unwelcome answer that, in his opinion, the Pope did indeed have the power to dispense with the Levitical objection to marrying a brother's widow. Quoting from the Gospel of St Matthew, Fisher observed that were it not the case, 'it is in vain that Christ has said [to St Peter, the first Pope], "Whatever you loose on earth shall be loosed in heaven."'[5]

Wolsey realised there was, nevertheless, a possible way out of Henry's difficulties. Katherine insisted she had never had sexual intercourse with Arthur and that Henry's 'scruple' was therefore groundless. In doing so she had unwittingly opened up a different avenue to an annulment. Wolsey suggested to Henry that they accept that Katherine was a virgin when Henry married her. The law of 'public honesty' forbad a marriage between a woman who had been legally married, but had never consummated her marriage, to the brother of her husband. This had not been covered in Pope Julius' original dispensation. But for Henry it was vital that the basis for his annulment should vindicate his belief that his marriage was cursed and rationalise his experience in having no sons by Katherine. Henry did not want an annulment on some legal technicality, and for Wolsey even to hint that his argument was weak was seen as a betrayal.

Worse news followed in September 1527 when Wolsey learned that Henry intended to marry Anne Boleyn instead of a princess who might have gained the king foreign support for his annulment. The cardinal had just returned from a visit to France and had requested a private appointment with Henry, as was usual. The messenger reported back that he had found the king ensconced with 'a certain lady called Anna de Bolaine'. She had issued her own order to Wolsey: 'tell him to come here, where the king is'.[6] Wolsey would later call Anne the 'night crow'. In legend these were birds of ill omen, and so it was for Wolsey that 'the night crow cried, aboding luckless time'.[7] Nevertheless, for the time being at least, the glittering Anne and the great cardinal were allies with the same objective – the annulment of Henry's marriage – and to their relief the Pope agreed that Henry's case should be heard in England. The judges were to be Wolsey and a man called Lorenzo Campeggio, England's long-standing Cardinal Protector, whose job it was to act as the special advocate of England's interests in the papal Curia. Campeggio arrived in London on 9 October 1528, three days after the Pope had returned to Rome to make peace with the emperor.

Henry was anxious for matters to proceed rapidly and Anne was still more so. Her biographer, Eric Ives, estimated that she was by now already twenty-seven. This was old for a bride in an era when a woman of thirty was considered 'winter fodder'. Anne also feared that as time passed Henry might lose interest in her and in remarriage. She could not compete easily with the long familiarity of Henry's marriage to Katherine of Aragon. Court ritual meant the king and queen were often together, and the French ambassador reported that to see them you would never know there was anything wrong. Anne was grateful when Wolsey found her lodgings close to Henry and she asked him to keep her up to date on 'news of the legate; for I do hope as they come from you they shall be very good'. It wasn't until June 1529, however, that Wolsey was able to confirm that the court had opened.

The trial of the royal marriage took place in the Parliament Chamber of the Dominican friary in London known as Blackfriars, in reference to the monks' black habits. Wolsey's servant, George Cavendish, described the judges, bishops and doctors of law all sat at their tables on benches. Henry had a chair placed on a raised platform under a cloth of estate made of 'tissue', the most expensive form of cloth of gold, with raised loops of fine metal thread above a velvet or silk ground.[8] The queen was sitting 'some distance beneath the king'; 'It was', Cavendish thought, 'the strangest and newest sight' that the royal couple should 'appear . . . in court . . . to abide the judgement of their own subjects'. Henry spoke first to ask for a quick judgement. Then Katherine was called. As Anne Boleyn later observed, when Katherine was face to face with Henry, she invariably won the argument, and in court the queen put on a bravura performance.

Henry had spoken of his scruples, Katherine observed, yet 'it was not the time to say this after so long' and after twenty years of marriage. Henry blustered that his silence had been out of love for her and that nothing would please him more than if their marriage was found to be valid.[9] At this, Katherine rose up from her dais and crossed the courtroom, skirting judges, bishops and clerks, and knelt before him. 'Sir,' she said, in her accented English, 'I beseech you for all the love that has been between us, and for the love of God, let me have justice and right. Take of me some pity and compassion for I am a poor woman and a stranger born out of your dominion . . . I flee to you as the head of justice within this realm. Alas sir, where have I offended you? . . . I have been to you a true, humble and obedient wife, ever comfortable to your will and pleasure . . . and by me ye have had divers children, although it has pleased God to call them out of this world, which was no default in me.'

Twice Henry tried to raise her up. But Katherine persisted. Their fathers were both excellent kings, she reminded him, and the wise men they had consulted had agreed their marriage was allowable, 'Therefore it is a wonder to me what new inventions are now invented against me.' She asked for the right to appeal to Rome, observing that in England even her defenders would be his subjects. Finally, having committed herself to his pleasure and her case to God, Katherine rose to her feet and curtseyed. The court, watching in stunned silence, expected her to return to her dais. But instead she caught the eye of one of her servants and walked out of the court on his arm. The people who crowded the lower part of the chamber, the anteroom and the stairs, looked on as she continued walking with the king's crier summoning her to return, 'Katherine, Queen of England, come into the court.' 'On, on,' she ordered her servant, 'it makes no matter for it is no impartial court for me . . . Go on.' She never came back.[10]

The protection of women lay at the heart of the concept of chivalry and Katherine had played the 'princess in distress' to perfection. Yet Henry felt she was behaving utterly selfishly. The future of his kingdom was at stake, and to his frustration he was not granted the quick judgement he wanted. Weeks passed, with the feverish Campeggio, in agonies with gout, carried from his bed and his barge up and down the stairs to the court, day in and day out. On 12 July depositions were made concerning the witnesses to Arthur and Katherine's marriage. Amongst them was that of Henry's great-uncle, David Owen, the bastard son of Owen Tudor. Comments were made about sightings of Arthur's 'enflamed member', which suggested consummation of the marriage must have followed. Sir David would only say politely that he believed there had been 'carnal union' as they were 'reputed as lawful man and wife . . . everywhere in the realm of England in his hearing'.[11] But the deciding point in law for the legate was the full manuscript of Julius' dispensation for Henry and Katherine's marriage, which had been discovered in Spain in 1528, and which Katherine had shown Campeggio in October. He was simply reluctant to make this public while Pope Clement wished to maintain his friendship with

Henry, and recent developments in Italy were now leading to a rapprochement between Clement and the emperor Charles.

Clement was a member of the great Medici family who ruled Florence and after the sack of Rome the republicans of Florence had revolted against them.[12] Happily for Clement these republicans were close to the emperor Charles' French enemies and Charles was now moving towards making terms with the Pope in which the Medici would be restored. Campeggio remained desperate to delay any decision on Henry's annulment, knowing it would go against him, but the king was beginning to understand what was happening. On the morning of 23 July Campeggio announced blandly that since the 'reaping and harvest' season had begun the court would be prorogued, not reconvening until October. At this, Henry's brother-in-law, Charles Brandon, Duke of Suffolk, strode over to the judges and smashed his fist on the table in front of them. 'By the Mass,' he swore, 'now I see that the old saw is true, that there was never legate nor cardinal that did good in England.'[13] It was the king's anger he expressed.

The case of the King of England's marriage was soon revoked to Rome, and as Thomas Howard, 3rd Duke of Norfolk (the son of the victor of Flodden), later told the Spanish ambassador, Henry believed the Pope would now do the emperor's bidding, 'even if he were asked to dance in the public street in a jester's jacket'.[14]

Wolsey's failure to get Henry what he wanted – which had hitherto been the key to Wolsey's success – marked the beginning of the end of his career. Henry was reluctant to utterly destroy his once invaluable servant, but Wolsey had made powerful enemies, in particular Anne who had lost all faith in him. Over the following year, 1530, Wolsey was wrong-footed in divisions over foreign policy, and when, that October, news reached the king of a papal brief ordering him to separate from Anne, the cardinal was blamed. He tried to gain support for his rehabilitation from King Francis and the emperor Charles, as well as Rome, but this left him open to accusations of treason. On

4 November 1530 the broken and sickly cardinal was arrested at dinner in York. He died at Leicester, as he was being brought to London for his trial and what would surely also have been his execution. 'I see the matter against me, how it is framed', Wolsey commented on his deathbed. 'But if I had served God as diligently as I have done the king he would not have given me over in my grey hairs.'[15] When the news reached court, Anne's father celebrated Wolsey's death by putting on a farce showing his descent into hell. 'O, how wretched/ Is that poor man that hangs on princes' favours!' Shakespeare's Wolsey observes, 'when he falls, he falls like Lucifer/Never to hope again'.

20

THE RETURN OF MARGARET DOUGLAS

LADY MARGARET DOUGLAS' APPEARANCE AT NORHAM CASTLE IN Northumberland was as dramatic as her birth at nearby Harbottle Castle thirteen years earlier. Then, her mother, Queen Margaret, had been in flight from Scotland with her father, Angus. Now, in October 1528, she was a victim of kidnap. Her father wanted to flee Scotland once more. He needed a promise of free passage in England and had snatched her from her mother to send her into Northumberland as a goodwill gesture to her uncle, Henry VIII.[1]

A beautiful young girl with a long, slim nose and heavily lidded eyes, Margaret Douglas left a miserable childhood behind her. After her parents' marriage had broken down her father had seized power in Scotland. For three years he had kept her half-brother, James V, a virtual prisoner, discouraging his learning of statecraft in favour of encouraging the teenager to gamble and womanise. It was only at the end of May 1528 that Queen Margaret had been able to help James escape Angus' clutches. The young king had learned to hate his step-father and, as James had gathered an army, Angus had begun looking for refuge. Under the terms of the annulment of his marriage to Queen Margaret their daughter remained legitimate, making Margaret Douglas third in line to the English throne. She was a valuable commodity on the international marriage market, and one Henry was delighted to have in his gift.

Henry ignored the pleas of his sister, who wrote complaining bitterly of the pain of being separated from her daughter.[2] But nor was he yet ready to welcome Margaret Douglas at court. It was exactly at this time that Campeggio had arrived in London, and Henry and her godfather Wolsey were focused on the setting up of the Legatine court. Margaret Douglas was left in Northumberland under guard until March 1529, when Angus had lost the last of his castles in Scotland and left for exile in England. Her father escorted Margaret on to the house of Wolsey's then comptroller, a man called Thomas Strangways, who was a sheriff in York. There he left her with a gentlewoman-in-waiting and a manservant, but little money. She stayed for a year, with Strangways obliged to cover her costs out of his own pocket while the Legatine court farce played out and Wolsey tried, and failed, to save his career. By 6 April 1530, however, Henry was at last ready to celebrate her arrival at court, ordering a dress from the Great Wardrobe for 'our niece' as his welcome gift.[3]

Margaret found the court very changed from when her mother had last visited it and she was a baby. There was no Wolsey: he had left court for the last time. Her uncle Henry, who had always been so gay, singing of his 'pastime with good company', was now living miserably in a virtual *ménage à trois* with Katherine, who had grown 'somewhat stout', and his chic mistress, Anne Boleyn. Katherine 'always has a smile on her countenance', which must have been hard enough for Henry to live with, while Anne's temper flared like fire as she watched her youth burning away. She would remind Henry bitterly, 'I have been waiting long and might in the meantime have contracted some advantageous marriage out of which I might have had issue, which is the greatest consolation in the world.' In June, when Anne discovered Katherine was still making Henry's shirts, there were furious words. But the regular rows and tearful making up between Henry and Anne only seemed to strengthen their relationship.

To many at court the king's passion seemed a weakness, yet it was helping fuel his relentless determination to press on with his plans to marry Anne. Pressure was maintained in Rome to push the annulment forward and, with Anne's encouragement, Henry was even preparing to bypass the Pope altogether. Henry now wanted to be declared 'absolute emperor and Pope in his kingdom' and be proclaimed supreme head of the Church of England.[4] This was quite a volte-face. Less than ten years earlier Henry had written in his attack on Luther, 'I have no intention of insulting the Pope by discussing his prerogative as if it were a matter of doubt.' In England the supremacy of the Pope over the church had been an article of faith for a thousand years.[5] The overwhelming majority in England saw the papacy, with all its faults, as the 'well of grace', and the Pope as the heir to St Peter.[6] Henry, however, now believed God had appointed him, not only as a secular ruler of his subjects, but as their spiritual ruler as well. This change of heart had a great deal to do with his absolute intolerance to any opposition to his royal will. But breaking with the Pope had a positive attraction too. Henry VIII had always taken a strong interest in theological debate, even intervening in quarrels between clergy and laity.[7] As the English 'Pope' he could take this further, and be free to adjudicate the beliefs of the church within his kingdom. The greatest appeal lay, however, in the glorious title of emperor it would earn him, and which he claimed was his by ancient right.

Over a decade earlier Henry had had the round table at Winchester, said to have belonged to King Arthur, painted in the Tudor colours, with a union rose at its centre, from which rises an image of Arthur wearing an Imperial crown and depicting Henry's features. Now, more was to be made of this.[8] In January 1531 the Duke of Norfolk showed the French ambassador a seal, supposedly dating from the reign of King Arthur and inscribed 'Arthur Emperor of Britain'. The ambassador was told this 'proved' Henry had inherited a special Imperial status from his distant forebears that gave him powers over church and state.[9] There had been little effort to make any political capital out of Arthurianism since his brother Prince Arthur's death. That was changing. The difficulty for Henry was that humanist scholars were increasingly sceptical about such old legends, and the Bishop of Rochester, John Fisher, was making mincemeat of Henry's arguments.

In February 1531 a murder attempt was made against Fisher, and many believed Anne Boleyn's family were behind it. Fisher's cook confessed someone had given him powder to put in the broth he had made, as a joke, he had thought.[10] Fisher, who ate little, refused it, which may have saved his life as everyone who touched it fell seriously ill. Two servants died, as did several of the poor who were fed at Fisher's gates. Henry promptly had poisoning raised to the level of high treason. But no evidence concerning what had happened was ever presented to a jury. Instead the cook was the first criminal, guilty of a mere felony and in custody, to be condemned and sentenced to death by an Act of Parliament known as an attainder, which simply declared his guilt.[11] His execution at Smithfield was a gruesome affair, with the wretched man suspended above a cauldron of boiling water, locked in chains, and 'pulled up and down with a gibbet at divers times 'til he was dead'.[12] It is often claimed that this was a new punishment invented by Henry, who was frightened he might be assassinated by poisoning. Not so: what was new was the condemnation of a criminal without any prior judicial process.[13] It offered a grim forewarning of Henry's disrespect for the principles of common law, as well as expressing his anxiety that a man can't trust his cook.

Fisher's brush with death was still a subject of considerable interest when the princess Mary visited court the following month. Aged fifteen, Mary was just a few months younger than Margaret Douglas, petite and pretty, well proportioned with a beautiful complexion. She was devoted to her mother, with whom she stayed four or five days, but Mary loved her father too. Henry, in turn, was proud of his daughter and when he visited her household at Richmond in June they 'made great cheer'. To foreign observers it seemed that her place as his heir remained secure and the Imperial and the Venetian ambassadors were convinced the marriage annulment would not take place while 'the peers of the realm, both spiritual and temporal, and the people, are opposed to it'.[14]

At court Henry's once warm relationship with his younger sister, the French queen, had cooled over his love for his mistress. They had been the sole Tudor siblings after Arthur had died and Queen Margaret had left for Scotland; she had married, in Charles Brandon, his closest friend. But the French queen loathed having Anne, her former maid of honour, awarded a higher status than herself at court. 'Difference . . . about precedency', it was noted at the time, 'breedeth many quarrels among women, who can better endure almost any kind of injury than to have such as are of meaner degree than themselves to take place before them.'[15] Brandon tried to rake up stories from Anne's past in an effort to break her hold on Henry. Anne responded with the accusation that Brandon was having 'criminal intercourse with his own daughter'– he had two daughters by an earlier marriage, as well as two with the French queen (the eldest, Frances, was fourteen).[16] Anne remained equally defiant of public opinion. The common sort called Anne Boleyn a 'burnt arse whore', but she had her servants' livery coats embroidered with a new motto: '*Ainsi sera: groigne qui groigne*' (So it will be: complain who will).[17] And what would be was, of course, her marriage to Henry. He had made his decision.

On 16 July, Henry rode off with Anne and left Katherine at Windsor without so much as a goodbye, never to see her again. While he and Anne hunted at Chertsey Abbey in Surrey, the princess Mary hurried to see her mother. Her presence that August helped Katherine 'forget the pain of the king's absence', the Imperial ambassador believed. Mother and daughter remained together through the long summer, until Henry decided he wished to go hunting at Windsor and return to the castle. His bed and another for Anne Boleyn, each eleven feet square and with covers of gold and silver, remained in the castle even into the reign of Queen Elizabeth, when they became tourist attractions. Katherine was ordered to retire to a house called the More in

Hertfordshire, whilst Mary was instructed to return to her household in Richmond. Her cousin Margaret accompanied the princess as her senior lady-in-waiting.[18]

The warrants for the Master of the Wardrobe to supply cloth and liveries to Mary's household that October include a long list for Margaret Douglas. There was a very expensive 'gown of tinsel of 11 yards, a black velvet gown of 11yds, furred with powdered ermine [i.e. the white fur split and the black ermine tails sown in a regular pattern]; a gown of black damask, of 11yds; kirtles [outer petticoats] and sleeves of crimson satin, black velvet and black satin, of 7 yds'. There were also velvet shoes, and gloves, and more clothing for her servants, of tawny velvet and black satin.[19] This was an indication of the high status of the princess she served, as well as her own.

Margaret, who had first-hand experience of quarrelling parents, was a good companion for Mary. The princess also had the support, however, of a remarkable governess: Margaret Pole, Countess of Salisbury, the only sister of the last male Plantagenet, Edward, Earl of Warwick, executed by Henry VII. Married as a girl to one of Margaret Beaufort's half-nephews, the countess was one of the five wealthiest peers in England. As such she was a woman in a man's role and she had a high opinion of what her sex was capable of: a view she imparted to the princess. Mary's mother, as the daughter of a reigning queen, was similarly confident of a woman's capacity for rule. But the shadows were lengthening over this Indian summer of Mary's childhood. In Henry's private rooms he had chosen a new collection of tapestries telling the classical story of Aeneas, obliged by divine intervention to leave his wife Dido and fulfill his destiny.[20] Henry longed to seek his own great destiny, and a fresh mind was giving shape and direction to his ambitions: a former servant of Wolsey called Thomas Cromwell.

The surviving portrait of Cromwell, dressed in black and with piggy eyes, gives no hint of the tremendous charm he could deploy. Like Wolsey, Cromwell came from humble origins (his alcoholic father was a tradesman from Putney), he had a phenomenal appetite for hard work, a sharp intellect and, in common with Anne Boleyn, he held strongly evangelical views on church reform, as well as supporting the supremacy of the king. On 15 May 1532 Cromwell successfully engineered a formal submission of the clergy to Henry as their overlord. This ended the independence of the church guaranteed in Magna Carta, and caused Henry's Lord Chancellor, Thomas More, to resign the following day. Henry had picked More for the post precisely because he was a highly principled as well as a clever man. Henry was sure that in time More would be bound to see the virtue of his cause. But More had not: what he saw was that the supremacy, far from being a liberation from papal tyranny, left no appeal from the diktat of the king, even in matters of innermost conscience.

The way was cleared for the break with Rome on the death of the old Archbishop of Canterbury in August. One of Anne's evangelical allies amongst the clergy, Thomas Cranmer, was appointed in his place that winter. Cranmer could and would marry her to the king, she felt assured, and it was in the confident belief that she was to be queen at last that Anne began sleeping with Henry.[21] They married privately, sometime before the end of February 1533, when she was already pregnant.[22] It did not matter to Henry that he had not yet been granted his annulment. Henry believed his marriage to Anne was his first and only marriage, with the annulment of his non-marriage to Katherine a mere formality, and that would follow soon enough. On 7 April an Act in Restraint of Appeals was passed forbidding Katherine of Aragon, or anyone else, appealing to foreign tribunals. This was justified with a reference to Geoffrey of Monmouth's *History of the Kings of Britain*, arguing that 'by divers sundry old authentic histories and chronicles it is manifestly declared and expressed that this realm of England is an empire' governed by 'one supreme head and king'. The Pope's role as supreme judge on earth in matters spiritual concerning England was at an end, and the break with Rome made.

Shortly afterwards Katherine was informed formally of the king's marriage to Anne. She was further told that she was no longer to be called queen and that she was to be stripped of her servants. Katherine retorted that she would live as a beggar if needs be, but she would always be queen. At Richmond, Margaret Douglas remained in attendance on the princess Mary, who 'was at first thoughtful', and controlling her feelings as best she could, 'seemed even to rejoice' at the news. Although she was miserable to be forbidden any contact with her mother, Mary hoped that Anne's triumph would be short-lived and she needed to be well placed in her father's affections when that day came. Anne could yet lose her child, or even die in labour. After dinner Mary wrote to her father, who was delighted by her letter, 'praising above all things the wisdom and prudence of his daughter'.[23] Anne was less restrained with her feelings, boasting that she would soon have the princess for her maid, or married to 'some varlet', that is, someone base.[24] The years of waiting, fearful that Henry would abandon her, had left Anne bitter. There was a new order in England and Anne was determined all should bow to it.

On 23 May, when Cranmer at last pronounced Henry's first marriage void, the preparations for the four-day ceremonies of Anne's coronation had already begun. Her relations were to attend in force. It was a different story with the Tudor family. Henry's elder sister, Queen Margaret, offered what support she could from Scotland (which was not much); her son James V, now ruling Scotland, disapproved of the breach with Rome, as he made clear in his letters. His half-sister Margaret Douglas remained with the princess Mary, who would not attend the coronation. Henry's younger sister, the French queen, had endured poor health for some time, and also could not attend. Her daughters, Frances and Eleanor, remained with her, and although she sent him a final message of love, when she died in June the rumour was she had been killed by 'the sorrow caused by the sight of her brother leaving his wife'.[25] The final member of the Tudor family, Henry's illegitimate son Henry Fitzroy, Duke of Richmond, was in France as part of Henry's rapprochement with Francis I. Anne perceived Fitzroy as a possible threat to any children she might have and there was little love lost between them, so he was surely not too disappointed to miss the occasion.[26] It meant, however, that not a single one of Henry's Tudor blood relatives attended the ceremonies that began on 29 May.

The first day was a river pageant, last seen at Elizabeth of York's coronation over forty-five years earlier. Henry VII had used the occasion to re-engage Yorkist loyalties in the aftermath of the Battle of Stoke Field in 1487. Henry VIII also now needed to re-engage public loyalty – to his new marriage, his new queen, and their coming child. No expense had been spared, with 220 craft following the royal barges from Greenwich to the Tower; mechanical dragons belched smoke, musicians played, fireworks exploded, bells tinkled and flags fluttered as thousands lined the banks to watch the spectacle. At the Tower Henry was waiting to greet Anne.[27] Even at forty-one he remained a handsome man. A Venetian described 'a face like an angel's, so fair it is; his head shorn like Cæsar's'.[28] As Anne disembarked he kissed her to the thunder of a thousand guns. She turned round to thank the mayor and citizens, before entering the Tower where Henry was to create eighteen Knights of the Bath the following day.

Anne emerged from the Tower on the Saturday evening for the procession to Westminster, led by the new knights in their blue hoods. The roads had been gravelled to prevent the horses slipping and the weather was perfect. Anne was carried in a litter of white cloth of gold, drawn by white horses trapped in white damask, just as Katherine of Aragon had once been. Her surcoat was a glittering 'tissue', also of gold and white, as was her mantle, a cloak furred with ermine, while on her head she wore the coronet of gold crosses and fleurs-de-lys that had been 'new made' for Katherine in 1509.[29] Her dark hair flowed loose as a symbol of her chastity.[30] To make a procession so magnificent, with the streets hung with tapestry and rich cloths, all strata of society had been involved, and Henry hoped this, as well as the communal pleasure taken in witnessing it, was working its magic in binding his subjects to Anne. Yet hostile reports claimed that people did not take their hats off for her, and that the HA monogram of the new king and queen was everywhere mocked, with people pointing at it and laughing 'Ha, ha!'[31]

A story spread afterwards that Anne had worn a dress embroidered with tongues struck through with nails as a warning to those who would speak against her.[32] Ordinary people had been arrested and whipped in public for this already, so the story reflected a justified sense of fear, and a warning. Later in the summer, two women, one heavily pregnant, were 'beaten about Cheapside naked from the waist up with rods and their ears nailed to the Standard for because they said Queen Katherine was the true queen'.[33] But Anne did have her supporters. England wanted a prince to avoid the dangers of violence and possible foreign invasion if there was a disputed succession. The memories of the terrible battles of the last century and the invasions from Burgundy by Edward IV, and from France by Henry VII, were not forgotten. It was a blessing to see Anne's pregnancy so evident when she emerged from Westminster Abbey on Sunday following her coronation, wearing a crown and carrying two sceptres.[34] For Anne the seven years of being the king's mistress were over and the story of Anne the queen had begun.

21

THE TERROR BEGINS

LESS THAN FOUR MONTHS FOLLOWING ANNE'S CORONATION THE christening of her daughter was held at Greenwich and was a splendid affair. It followed to the letter the rules Margaret Beaufort had laid down for such occasions. The church of Henry VII's favourite order, the Observant Franciscans, was hung with the gold weaved tapestries called arras, and the silver font had a red silk canopy hung over it: a mark of the status of this 'High and Mighty Princess of England', the baby Elizabeth.

The ceremonies began with a procession into the hall, led by the king's cousin, Henry Courtenay, Marquess of Exeter, a grandson of Edward IV and a favourite jousting companion.[1] He carried a candle as a symbol of life and faith, which was lit at the moment of Elizabeth's baptism, along with 500 torches held by the Yeomen of the Guard, filling the room with brilliant light. The princess had been named after the late queen, Elizabeth of York, but despite the grandeur of the ceremonies and the popularity of the name, the Imperial ambassador reported Elizabeth's christening had been 'like her mother's coronation, very cold and disagreeable to the court and to the city, and there has been no thought of having the bonfires and rejoicings usual in such cases.'[2]

Henry had believed that the birth of a son would offer evidence of divine approval for his actions. This had been denied him, while his royal cousin, Exeter, was amongst those who regretted the schism with Rome. A popular mystic called Elizabeth Barton, known as the 'Holy Maid of Kent', had told Henry to his face that if he married Anne 'His Majesty should not be king of this Realm by the space of one month after, And in the reputation of God should not be king one day nor one hour'.[3] Many had hoped, and prayed, that Henry would listen to Barton. Instead, a month after Elizabeth's christening, Barton was arrested and those who had listened to her were at risk of accusations of treason. Letters from her former followers poured in to the king, begging forgiveness for having met her. They included one from Exeter's wife, who was fortunate to be spared punishment.

Henry was convinced that anyone who could not see that his first marriage was false must be evil in heart, and to demonstrate his determination to crush all opposition to his marriage he was now to turn on his seventeen-year-old daughter, Mary. Henry had decided that she was henceforth to be treated as a bastard. If he had had a son he might not have felt it necessary to make an issue of Mary's status – she would have come second to a brother even if both were regarded as legitimate – but with two daughters he felt he could not have Mary, as the elder, treated as superior to Elizabeth, the child of his only 'valid' marriage. Mary was, therefore, degraded. Her servants were told to take her badges from their livery and replace them with the king's, and she was informed she was no longer to be called princess.

Mary, with all the courage and stubbornness of adolescence, continued nevertheless to use her title. She ignored threats of the king's 'high displeasure and punishment in law' and even had the cheek to write to him expressing faux astonishment at the orders. Mary assured her father she trusted absolutely 'that your grace was not privy to the same letter, as concerning the leaving out of the name of princess, for I doubt not in your goodness, that your grace does take me for his lawful daughter'.[4] Henry realised he would have to break Mary, and to achieve that he first had to isolate her.

In December Henry shut down Mary's household, dismissing 160 servants, and her ten ladies- and gentlewomen-in-waiting. Her governess, the Countess of Salisbury, offered to pay for Mary's household out of her own pocket, but was also sent packing. To add further insult to injury Mary learned that her senior lady-in-waiting, her cousin the eighteen-year-old Lady Margaret Douglas, was ordered to join Anne Boleyn's household, while she was transferred to that of the princess Elizabeth at Hatfield.[5] There, this grandchild of the heads of four royal houses found she had been placed under the care of Anne's aunt, Lady Shelton, who was permitted to beat her if she continued to resist the king's commands to accept her reduction in title. She was also to be treated at all times as inferior to her baby sister.

As Mary wept in humiliation and anger in her rooms at Hatfield, her father was telling the French ambassador that if they wanted a marriage treaty they should favour Margaret Douglas, his 'niece, the daughter of the Queen of Scotland, whom he keeps with the queen his wife, and treats like a queen's daughter'. The French ambassador duly noted that Margaret Douglas was 'beautiful, and highly esteemed', while saying of Mary, to judge by what Henry said of her, 'he hates her thoroughly'.[6]

There were those at court, however, who were now so angered by Henry's marriage to Anne and the schism with Rome, that they wanted the Tudor dynasty brought to an end. 'They refer to the case of Warwick [the Kingmaker], who chased away King Edward', the Imperial ambassador informed Charles V, 'and they say you have a better title than the present king, who only claims by his mother, who was declared by sentence of the Bishop of Bath a bastard, because Edward had espoused another wife before the mother of Elizabeth of York'.[7] In short the king had no right to the throne through his Tudor father, but only through his mother, and that fell down if you believed Edward IV's children were the bastards Richard III had claimed them to be.[8]

Henry found it hard to accept his loss of public acclaim and he also understood its dangers. Faced with a threat, he responded as his father had always done, with massive force. A reign of terror was about to begin. In March, the Holy Maid, Elizabeth Barton, was indicted by Act of Attainder and convicted of treason without any form of judicial process.[9] It was feared a jury would find her innocent of any capital crime, so she never faced one. She was executed in April, along with a number of clergy with whom she was associated. John Fisher, the most powerful defender of the Aragon marriage, was in the Tower, simply for having met Barton. Henry's former Lord Chancellor, Thomas More, joined Fisher that month for refusing to swear an oath in support of the recent Act of Succession. This statute made Mary illegitimate in English law, but the oath's preamble also denied papal jurisdiction, which More believed was key to Christian unity and instituted by Christ. For More this was a matter of his private religious conscience; for Henry it was necessary that everyone accept the rightness of his actions, even in their private thoughts.

Yet there were still no signs of God's blessing for Henry and that summer Anne miscarried her second child. The old pattern of Katherine's pregnancies was being repeated and gossip emerged the king had an eye for other women, and even that Anne was jealous.[10] But theirs had always been a volatile love affair of sunshine and storms, and the marriage was about to be given a boost from an unexpected quarter – Rome. On 25 September 1534, Pope Clement VII died and the opportunity arose for a rapprochement between Rome and the king. The newly elected Pope Paul III was anxious for a clean slate. He saw the sack of Rome as God's punishment for the worldliness of recent popes and corruption within the church. The time for reform was long overdue and the battle to prevent the break-up of Western Christendom had begun. In May 1535 Pope Paul created a number of cardinals: men known for their sanctity, learning and integrity. Amongst them was Fisher. The Pope hoped this would both rescue Fisher from the Tower and encourage Henry on the path to reconciliation with Rome. The appointment was made, the Pope noted, not only for Fisher's virtues, but 'in honour of that king and his kingdom'.[11] The new Cardinal Fisher was to be the English representative at a council that would launch the reform of the church.

What Paul III had failed to appreciate was how important Henry's supremacy over the church was to him. What may have begun as a piece of legal and constitutional chicanery, designed to get around Pope Clement's refusal to annul his first marriage, had become, for Henry, an end entirely in itself, independent of any issues concerning the succession. It was here, Henry believed, that he would find the 'virtue, glory and immortality' he had always pursued. He had not yet achieved his boyhood dream of reconquering France, but in becoming Pope in England, with an empire over church and state, Henry had found his claim to greatness.

As always, Henry VIII genuinely believed his actions to be godly. He saw his regal prototypes as the Old Testament kings, David and Solomon, and the Christian Roman emperors, Constantine and Justinian. Henry was certain that early English kings had similarly held the title of emperor and the popes had, for centuries, usurped it. Those close to the king said he would not give up his supremacy even if St Peter were to spring to life again.[12] When Henry learned of Fisher's elevation he retorted that he would send Fisher's head to Rome for his cardinal's hat, and he had recently created the capital crime for which the bishop would die.

A new Treason Act had made any denial of the royal supremacy punishable by death. The first to suffer were members of the contemplative order of the Carthusians (regarded widely as amongst the holiest men in England – Londoners often went to them for advice and counselling, even staying for days or weeks of peace and prayer). Their jury had refused to convict them until Thomas Cromwell threw any pretence of justice to the wind and threatened the jurors with terrible consequences if they did not return the verdict the king had wanted. People could hardly believe their eyes to see men once so respected being dragged through the streets on hurdles that May, to be hung, drawn and quartered in their distinctive white robes. But

Henry was making the point that no one could expect mercy on this issue, and one he wished his courtiers also to witness.

Amongst those who attended the execution was the king's fifteen-year-old son, Henry Fitzroy. He was obliged to stand close to the scaffold and watch each monk hanged in turn for a short time, cut open while conscious and disembowelled.[13] Being killed one at a time ensured the monks saw the slow and horrible deaths of the companions who preceded them to the scaffold, and suffered the additional terror of knowing they too were about to die thus. After this group were all dead, further Carthusians were executed before a restive gathering of Londoners in the middle of June. Fisher would be next.

The colour scarlet, worn by cardinals, was supposed to represent their willingness to die for their faith. But in the 1,000-year history of the cardinalate only one member of the Sacred College has ever been called upon to do so, and that was Fisher. Margaret Beaufort's old friend, strikingly handsome as a young man, but now well into his seventies, was emaciated and almost blind, and had to be carried on a mule to the scaffold on Tower Hill.[14] He was well aware of the corruption of recent popes and had been a leading advocate of reform of the church. But he believed in the institution of the papacy, just as he believed in the institution of the English monarchy. On the scaffold Fisher prayed for his king, as well as his country, and then he died before a stunned and silent crowd.

It is the death of Thomas More, the family man and politician, beheaded in July, that is now better remembered. But at the time it was Fisher's death that was considered the more notable. An outraged Pope declared Fisher a greater martyr than Thomas Becket – whose tomb was one of the three top pilgrimage sites in Europe – because Fisher had died for the universal church. It followed that Henry VIII was worse than Henry II who had caused Becket to be killed. On 1 September the Pope decreed that until such time as Henry should repent, he was to be cast out of the Christian family as a heretic, schismatic and rebel.[15] This made it certain that the annulment of

Henry's marriage to Katherine would never be recognised in Europe. Yet Henry's honour, as he saw it, rested on the rightness of his second marriage. The reports of Henry's extramarital flirtations faded as he launched on a long summer progress with Anne. It was now all the more essential for Henry that they have a son, not only for the sake of the dynasty, but so he might feel exonerated in his actions.

Courtiers travelling with Henry and Anne from palace to palace that summer of 1535 hunted and enjoyed themselves as best they could. The king's niece, Margaret Douglas, enjoyed the new sensation of being surrounded by admiring young men and she made several friends. A book, now known as the Devonshire Manuscript, preserves the verses they copied and wrote for each other, and which reflected the lives they were leading and their feelings about it. These compositions include those of Norfolk's twenty-three-year-old younger brother, Lord Thomas Howard, Henry Fitzroy's wife, the fifteen-year-old Mary Fitzroy, Duchess of Richmond, who was also a daughter of the Duke of Norfolk, and another of Anne Boleyn's cousins, her maid of honour, Mary Shelton.[16]

Like Margaret, Mary Shelton was exceptionally attractive. She had briefly even caught the attention of the king, but others had now taken up the pursuit. The Devonshire Manuscript features a poem written for her, which spells out her name in the first letters of each of the seven stanzas. The theme is that of an admirer bemoaning a mistress who does not notice his attentions, and it ends: 'till she knows the cause of all my pain/content to serve and suffer still I must'.[17] Mary Shelton and Margaret Douglas scribbled a few tart comments under it, poking fun at the poet's insincerity. All the while Margaret was falling in love, however, with Thomas Howard.

Anne was expected to help keep her young women's romantic fancies under control, and reprimanded Mary Shelton when she spotted her scribbling poetry in her prayer book in the chapel. But Anne was the most successful woman in England at the game of love

– it had won her a king – and in the febrile atmosphere of the summer progress, she found she enjoyed it too much to give it up. She flirted with the twenty-five-year-old Sir Francis Weston, accusing him of preferring Mary Shelton to his wife, a comment that prompted his reply that there was one he preferred to both, and then confirming: 'it is yourself'. It remained the king's attention that mattered most to Anne, however, and by early November she was pregnant again. She hoped for a son, but she did not neglect her daughter in the meantime. Anne lavished Elizabeth with attention, personally selecting the silks and velvets that would clothe her. Elizabeth's position, honour and dignity were a guarantee of Anne's own. Equally, Anne regarded any honour given to her stepdaughter, Mary, with fear. Henry had assured her that Mary would not marry while he lived. But Anne observed how courtiers who accompanied her to see Elizabeth would often slip off to pay their respects to Mary. Few regarded it just that Mary was declared illegitimate. Under canon law, if parents had good reason to believe their marriage was valid when their children were conceived, those children remained legitimate when the marriage was annulled. Even those who were prepared to accept that Henry's Aragon marriage was invalid regarded Mary as a true princess and the king's rightful heir. If Henry were to die, Anne's position, and even her life, would be in grave danger.

Many courtiers were also concerned that Henry's marriage to Anne would lead to war with Katherine of Aragon's powerful nephew, Charles V. For the moment the emperor was hoping to draw Henry away from France. He had even persuaded the Pope not to publish Henry's excommunication, so releasing his subjects from their duty of obedience. But Charles was certain Henry's marriage would prove a passing aberration. If it proved otherwise then he might ally with his aunt, and Henry too was fearful that, though Katherine's health was poor, she might one day, in her daughter's interests, 'carry on a war against him as openly and fiercely as Queen Isabella, her mother, had done in Spain'.[18] It came as a huge relief, therefore, when news reached the court that Katherine had died in Huntingdonshire on 7 January 1536. 'God be praised that we are free from all suspicions of war!' he announced.

Katherine had spent her last days worried that the deaths of 'good men' were her fault, and asking bystanders to pray for the husband she had loved and lost. There was no grief in Henry, however, for the woman with whom he had once been so happy. That Sunday Henry dressed in yellow and after dinner, carrying Elizabeth in his arms, he showed her off first to one courtier and then another, 'like one transported with joy'. [19] He felt rejuvenated, and on 24 January he continued to celebrate at the joust. He was now forty-four, however, older than Edward IV had been when he died, and like his grandfather he was growing stout. No longer as fit as he once was, his pride came before a crashing fall when he was tipped from his saddle. He was left unconscious for two hours.

It is sometimes suggested that this caused a head injury that had a deleterious effect on the king's character. But his executions of the Carthusian monks the previous year were amongst the most shocking of his entire reign. What the accident did do was remind Anne how precarious her situation was. It left the mood at court sombre, and Anne was without any trace of her former gaiety. The Imperial ambassador reported that it had occurred to her that one day, 'they might deal with her as they had with the good queen [Katherine of Aragon]'. On 29 January, the day that Katherine was buried in Peterborough Abbey, Anne miscarried her third pregnancy. [20] It was said that her baby had been a boy.

Henry came to see Anne, as she lay bleeding in her bedchamber, but rather than offer sympathy he announced self-pityingly, 'I see that God will not give me male children.' [21] This was troubling for Anne. Although Henry was not pointing the finger of blame at her, it was evident he believed God had passed judgement on him again. His affair with Anne's sister, years earlier, also meant he had good reason to wonder if his second marriage was as cursed as his first.

Desperately, Anne assured him that it was only the shock of hearing of his fall at the joust that had triggered the miscarriage. By nature hot-tempered, she could not prevent herself adding, however, that his 'loving another woman' had also left her 'broken-hearted'. As in the past when his wives were pregnant, Henry had been looking to other women for sex. Anne's suggestion that his own actions had caused the miscarriage infuriated Henry, and he left her rooms with the brusque comment, 'When you are up I will come and speak with you.'[22]

The Marchioness of Exeter claimed Henry was soon complaining he had been seduced and trapped into marrying Anne.[23] Within a fortnight the Imperial ambassador, Eustace Chapuys, had also learned the name of a woman in whom the king was showing romantic interest: Anne's maid of honour, Jane Seymour. A gentleman's daughter, of average height and average looks, Jane Seymour was somewhat older than Margaret Douglas's group of high-spirited, literary friends. And she was different in every respect from Anne. With her light-red hair, she was as fair as the queen was dark, and utterly lacked her mistress' brio. Her cool, arrogant poise attracted Henry nevertheless – the old appeal of the unobtainable maiden.

Anne assured Margaret Douglas and her other ladies that all would be well, given time. She would have another child and, with Katherine of Aragon now dead, her next baby would carry no taint of illegitimacy. Her difficulty was how could she conceive a child, for it seemed Henry's anxiety about the validity of his second marriage had rendered him impotent.[24] Opponents of the Boleyns were also moving quickly to exploit the opportunity Anne's weakness offered them. When Jane's brother, Edward Seymour, joined Henry's Privy Chamber in March he found those who regretted the break with Rome most anxious to promote his sister with the king. Amongst them was Edward IV's grandson, Exeter. The royal marquess and his allies were certain that if Anne were out of the way Henry would recognise the legitimacy of the princess Mary. They suggested to Jane that she should play on

Henry's fears that his marriage was invalid while refusing his bed. She did exactly that.

At the end of the month Henry sent Jane a letter along with a bag of coins. Instead of opening the letter, with its possible suggestion of a liaison, Jane fell to her knees. She begged the messenger to tell Henry 'to consider that she was a well-born damsel, the daughter of good and honourable parents, without blame or reproach of any kind; there was no treasure in this world that she valued as much as her honour and on no account would she lose it, even if she were to die a thousand deaths'.[25] The Marchioness of Exeter was soon reporting that Henry's interest in Jane had increased 'marvellously'. They hoped to see Anne trounced at her own game, and Mary restored as Henry's rightful heir – but they had badly misjudged the king they thought they knew so well.

22

THE FALL OF ANNE BOLEYN

As soon as Anne's aunt, Lady Boleyn, was out of sight, Margaret Douglas would sneak into the chamber of her friend, Mary Fitzroy.[1] With the coast clear, Margaret's lover, Lord Thomas Howard, then followed. He and Margaret met regularly to talk privately, kiss and exchange gifts. One day Margaret gave Thomas her picture, and on another, a diamond. He in turn gave her a ring blessed by Henry in the royal chapel. This, it was believed, had given it healing qualities through a special power granted to the Lord's anointed.[2] Their surreptitious meetings remained well hidden from the rest of the court, but there was a warning to secret lovers recorded on the opening page of the book of verses they shared with their friends:

> Take heed betime lest ye be spied
> Your loving eyes you cannot hide
> At last the truth will sure be tried
> Therefore take heed![3]

It may have been written about the king and his once hidden love for Anne Boleyn. But now it was for Margaret and Lord Thomas to take heed. Tensions were high at court with rumours raging over the worsening relationship between the king and queen.

On 30 March 1536 the Imperial ambassador Eustace Chapuys even asked the king's chief minister, Thomas Cromwell, if there was a possibility of divorce. Cromwell confided that Anne regarded him as an enemy and so it gave him no pleasure that 'notwithstanding that the king was still inclined to pay attention to ladies [such as Jane Seymour] he believed the marriage to Anne would continue'.[4] The ambassador wondered if Cromwell's body language – he kept his hand over his mouth – indicated he was lying. But dissolving the marriage to Anne was a more complex issue for Henry than Chapuys realised. As was later explained to the ambassador, Henry believed 'he could not separate from the Concubine [Anne] without tacitly confirming not only the first marriage, but also, what he most fears, the authority of the Pope'.[5] If Henry were to get rid of Anne some means other than simple divorce had to be found. Happily for the Boleyns it was by no means clear how this might be achieved and Henry was, by nature, dilatory.

On 2 April Anne felt sufficiently confident in the security of her position to confront Cromwell on a major issue that divided them: what to do with the money made from the dissolution and reform of small and failing monasteries. Anne hoped to see many of the reformed monasteries become teaching establishments, a role that monasteries had always played, with all the money raised ploughed back into charitable enterprises. Cromwell, by contrast, intended to pour the monasteries' wealth into the king's pocket and those of men whose support the king needed. He also disliked monasteries on theological grounds, seeing them as promoters of the 'superstitious' veneration of saints and their relics.

That morning Anne's almoner, John Skip, delivered a sermon in the king's chapel that broadcast her opposition to Cromwell's activities. Skip complained about indiscriminate abuse being heaped on the clergy, claiming it was done out of greed for the church's possessions; he reiterated Anne's view that the money from the dissolved monasteries should be going on education, laying the blame for the money going elsewhere on evil counsel. Without naming names, he went on to compare Cromwell to Haman, the corrupt minister of the biblical King Ahasuerus, and Anne to that king's wife, Queen Esther, who had saved the Jews from persecution. Finally the chaplain reminded his audience that Haman had gone to the scaffold.

What Anne had not grasped was that Henry badly wanted the church's wealth. By threatening Cromwell's life Anne had united Henry's vague hope that one day he might be free to choose a new wife with Cromwell's ability to get a nasty job done, and given the king another reason to wish to see the back of her.[6]

For a short while there was nothing to suggest any change in the king's attitude. Indeed, on 18 April, Chapuys was invited to kiss Anne's ring before meeting Henry at Greenwich Palace. Since this would have been a public recognition of Anne's status as queen, the ambassador made excuses not to do so. But standing in the king's chapel for Mass he was tricked into being positioned in such a place that he was obliged to acknowledge Anne as she entered. Later the same day, the rattled ambassador informed Henry that the emperor wished for an alliance – but only as soon as the princess Mary was restored to the succession and he was reconciled with Rome. A furious Henry shouted back that his relationship with the Pope was none of the emperor's business, and as for his daughter Mary, 'he would treat her according as she obeyed him or not'.[7]

Henry was soon sending letters to his diplomats across Europe insisting that his marriage to Anne be recognised wherever they had been posted. Yet this was not about any personal attachment to Anne, only his desire to protect the royal supremacy with which their marriage was, for the time being, associated. His interest in Jane Seymour continued unabated and Cromwell now sought allies amongst her promoters. The first sign of his success was his giving up his rooms at Greenwich to Jane's brother, Edward Seymour, which allowed Henry to meet her more discreetly and conveniently. Meanwhile, that other court romance, between Margaret Douglas and Thomas Howard, had culminated at Easter in a secret betrothal.[8]

Henry had seemed to smile on his niece's relationship in its early days, but the couple only confided their decision in a few friends. The situation at court remained volatile. From the close quarters of the queen's Privy Chamber, Margaret could see that Anne was extremely angry with her husband. Anne's brother, George Boleyn, would spend time with his sister laughing with her about the clothes the king wore and the ballads he wrote. George let slip once that Anne had even complained about Henry's abilities as a lover, telling him that her husband had neither talent nor vigour in bed.[9] Some wondered if he was suggesting that the princess Elizabeth was not her father's child. If she was complaining that Henry was such a poor sexual performer, it followed that she might have a lover. Many noticed the pleasure the queen was taking in the dangerous game of courtly love. Even lowly servants were speaking to her in a familiar manner.

On Saturday 29 April Anne stopped by the round window in the Presence Chamber and addressed a young musician called Mark Smeaton. She asked him why he was looking sad. It was 'no matter', he replied sulkily. It was an attempt to draw her into romantic banter and Anne reminded him that she couldn't speak to him as if he were a nobleman. 'No, no madam,' he replied, evidently stung; 'A look sufficed, and so fare you well.'[10] On the same day the king's close body servant, Sir Henry Norris, came to see one of Anne's maids. Anne asked him teasingly why he had not yet married his betrothed. Norris answered that he preferred to 'tarry a time', to which Anne joked, 'You look for dead men's shoes, for if ought came to the king but good, you would look to have me.' No sooner were the words out of her mouth than Anne realised that she had overstepped the line. Imagining the death of the king was a treasonous offence. Norris, aghast, replied that 'if he should have any such thought, he would [wish] his head were off'.[11]

The next day Anne and Henry had a row. A Scottish visitor at court later recalled seeing Anne in a courtyard, with the princess Elizabeth in her arms, pleading with the king who was looking down at her from a window. It was clear he was very angry, 'although he could conceal his anger wonderfully well'.[12] That Henry had accused Anne of being unfaithful, and that she believed he suspected Norris, is suggested by the fact that on the same day Anne asked Norris to go and see her chaplain and assure him she was a 'good woman'. But had Anne got it wrong? Was Henry referring to Norris or someone else? Smeaton was being questioned that very same day on whether or not he had committed adultery with her.

Smeaton's interrogation took place at Cromwell's house in Stepney. We do not know if Cromwell had taken the initiative in arresting him, or if it was on the king's orders. But accusing the queen of adultery would have been very dangerous for Cromwell. He could not be certain how Henry would react. On the other hand, if Henry had learned of a rumour concerning Norris or Smeaton it makes sense that he demanded Cromwell get to the bottom of it. The French learned that 'the discovery was owing to words spoken by [Smeaton] from jealousy', and according to Cromwell, 'some of his grace's council . . . with great fear' declared 'what they heard unto the king's highness'.[13] Anne's conversation with Norris gave Cromwell a means of accusing her of treason. But Norris was unlikely to confess to adultery and so make a charge of plotting the king's murder plausible. A weaker man was required if Anne's chastity was to be besmirched – and Smeaton would fill that role.

Before that evening Smeaton had confessed to having committed adultery with the queen on three occasions. According to later gossip Smeaton was kept in a sweetmeat cupboard with Anne calling for marmalade when she desired him. Had this really happened? Anne would go to her death denying any such activity, and to have lied on the eve of eternity was to risk hellfire. Despite later tales of a knotted rope being tightened around Smeaton's head, and of his being racked, there is no evidence that torture was used in his questioning, but it is not uncommon for people to make false confessions under psychological pressure. Strangely, perhaps, suggestible people will sometimes even come to believe that they have committed a crime of which they are completely innocent, and this too may be true of Smeaton, for he never withdrew his confession.[14]

On the Sunday evening Henry postponed, but did not cancel, a trip he had planned to take with Anne to Calais in June. He could not yet be certain how matters would continue to unfold. Cromwell had more interviews to conduct. The next morning, May Day 1536, was warm and sunny: the perfect day for the jousts taking place at Greenwich Palace. The king, sitting to the front of the royal stand between the twin towers of the tilt-yard, was enjoying himself. Henry's brother-in-law, George Boleyn, was the leading challenger, while his old friend Sir Henry Norris led the defenders. Also watching them was Anne Boleyn and her ladies. The pennants flew, and horses galloped down the sandy list where only a few months earlier Henry had fallen, and come close to being killed. As the tournament ended a message was passed to the king. Abruptly he rose from his seat and left for Westminster, taking with him only a handful of attendants. Norris was called to join him, while an astonished Anne was left to oversee the closing of the competition.

As the king's party rode off Henry asked Norris an extraordinary and terrifying question – had he committed adultery with the queen? It was usual for courtiers accused of a serious offence to be kept away from Henry since this spared him the embarrassment of their pleading for mercy to his face. But Henry, having read Cromwell's message, had chosen to have Norris ride with him and was acting as his chief interrogator. He made it clear to Norris he wished to play the roles of judge and jury too. He offered the horrified man a pardon if he admitted to sleeping with Anne. Norris was a fellow member of the Order of the Garter, Henry's equivalent to the Knights of the Round Table, and now found he was being cast in the role of Lancelot.[15] Norris angrily – desperately – asserted his innocence. It did him no good. He joined Smeaton in the Tower that night. Anne was taken there the following day.

'Shall I go into a dungeon?' the terrified Anne asked the Lieutenant of the Tower on her arrival. 'No madam,' he replied, 'you shall go into the lodgings you lay in at your coronation.' This reduced the queen to hysterical laughter and bouts of weeping. Anne had heard, she said, that she would 'be accused [of adultery] with three men'. She knew the names of those already in the Tower. 'O Norris,' she wondered, 'hast thou accused me? Thou art in the Tower with me, [and we shall] die together; and, Mark, thou art here too.'[16] Since adultery was not a capital offence, Anne expected to be accused of imagining the death of the king. In fact further capital offences were being sought.

As Anne prepared to spend her first night as a prisoner, Henry kissed his son Henry Fitzroy goodnight and, with tears trickling down his face, Henry claimed that Anne had intended to dispose of both his children, poisoning Fitzroy and his half-sister Mary. It also emerged that Anne's brother, George Boleyn, who had followed her to the Tower, was accused of adultery with his sister. This was intended to demonstrate Anne was capable of any horror or perversion and it rapidly became evident she would be accused of adultery with more than merely three men. Interviews with Norris and Anne's own comments led to the arrest of the young Sir Francis Weston, who had flirted with Anne in the summer of 1535, and another courtier called William Brereton was also arrested. A couple of knights and the courtier poet Thomas Wyatt followed, but they had sufficiently powerful friends to escape trial.[17]

The evidence against Anne and her remaining co-accused was extremely weak, as even Chapuys was moved to comment. According to one of the judges the adulteries had been revealed by a former lady-in-waiting 'who shared the same tendencies' as the queen and had described Anne's crimes on her deathbed in 1534.[18] But how did this confession reach Cromwell two years after the woman had died? The answer may lie in the fact that her family were clients of Anne's old enemy, Charles Brandon, Duke of Suffolk, widower of Henry's sister, the French queen. Here was a man always ready to oblige the king, and who disliked Anne. Wyatt blamed Brandon for his arrest and the accusation that Anne had committed incest with her brother suggests revenge for her accusation in 1531 that Brandon had slept with 'his own daughter'.

Two of Anne's current ladies were also named as giving evidence for the trial.[19] The first was the Countess of Worcester, whose sister-in-law was married to one of Anne's supposed lovers, William Brereton.[20] He had few links with Anne, but he was a troublesome figure in the Welsh Marches, and one Cromwell was happy to see out of the way. The second woman named was Anne, Lady Cobham, whose husband was to be one of the trial judges.[21] In later generations a case was built to suggest that George Boleyn's wife, Jane, Lady Rochford, was a third, and that she informed against her own husband. This is inspired, however, by later gossip rather than contemporary fact.[22] Indeed there is little to suggest that any of Anne's women deliberately betrayed her. The frightened women were pressed hard on what they had seen and heard of Anne's behaviour. Anxious not to be accused of withholding anything, they repeated the jokes between Anne and her brother about Henry's impotence, his gaudy clothes and dull poetry. The pregnant Lady Worcester had been so distressed by the pre-trial interrogations that Anne Boleyn had feared her friend would miscarry her baby (a little girl destined to be named Anne).

At the trial Anne's complaints about the king's abilities as a lover made it easy to assert that she had found her sexual satisfaction elsewhere. George Boleyn was described leading Anne in dances in her Privy Chamber, passing her on to other men, and kissing her. This brotherly affection became, in the hands of the lawyers, sexual perversion: with George's tongue in Anne's mouth, and him passing on his sister not merely to dance with other partners, but for sex. As one judge noted, 'all the evidence was bawdy and lechery'.[23] On Friday 12 May 1536 the four commoners were found guilty of plotting to see the king dead and replaced by one of them. George Boleyn and his sister were condemned on the Monday. All were doomed.

23

LOVE AND DEATH

ANNE WAS SENTENCED TO DEATH IN THE KING'S HALL AT THE Tower, right next to the rooms where she was imprisoned. As the gruesome details were read out one of the judges, her former beau, the Earl of Northumberland, collapsed. With 2,000 witnesses looking on from the newly built stands, he was helped from the room. The king, meanwhile, was at court, and in a merry mood. The Imperial ambassador thought no man had ever been so content to advertise he was a cuckold, or to show so little sign he minded. When Henry claimed he had heard Anne had slept with over a hundred men it sounded like a boast.

On 17 May the men accused of being Anne's lovers were processed to their executions on Tower Hill. An anonymous verse later circulated at court remembered each of them: Norris the flirt, George Boleyn with his wit and pride, Weston, 'that pleasant was and young', Brereton, loved by his friends, and Mark Smeaton who had enjoyed the high life, and whose confession destroyed them all, 'thy death thou hast deserved best', it concluded damningly.[1] The same day they died Archbishop Cranmer annulled Anne's marriage to Henry on the grounds of his previous relationship with her sister. Since Henry was soon to be a widower, the decree's principal purpose was to bastardise their daughter, Elizabeth.

The two-and-a-half-year-old princess, described by her governess 'as toward a child and gentle of conditions as any I have known in my life', had not lost her father's affection, despite what her reduction in status suggests.[2] It is true that by late summer she was beginning to grow out of her clothes and her governess had to remind Cromwell that she needed new ones. But this reflected only the absence of her mother's attention. Elizabeth was still dining in state every day, something her governess begged to be stopped as it meant she could not prevent the toddler from helping herself to wine, or whatever food she wished.[3] Elizabeth was not capable of doing anything personally to anger Henry; he had decided simply to re-acknowledge that his daughter Mary – whose mother had been royal and loyal – was the elder sister. As Chapuys observed it would have been far simpler for Henry to have it decreed that Elizabeth was Norris' child than to have his marriage to Anne anulled.[4] The fact he did not do this implies a strong conviction that Elizabeth was his. It also suggests he did not really believe Anne was the nymphomaniac he claimed – what Anne was guilty of was seducing him into a cursed union.[5]

When his sexual inadequacies were paraded during the trials Henry could console himself that it was only proper that he was unable to copulate in a damned marriage. Cranmer reassured him that Anne's adulteries were indeed 'only to her dishonour not yours'. Nevertheless Henry felt it necessary to advertise his masculine vigour by staying out all hours, banqueting with beautiful girls, seemingly full of 'extravagant joy'.[6] In private he comforted himself in a different way, taking a close interest in the details of his wife's coming death. In Thomas Malory's *Le Morte d'Arthur*, King Arthur had sentenced his adulterous Queen Guinevere to death by burning, although it was never carried out. Henry decided Anne would be beheaded with a sword. It was the preferred method of execution for the nobility in France where Anne had spent so many happy years in her girlhood, and this has given rise to the myth that Anne requested it. But there is no evidence for that. The choice of a sword – the symbol of Camelot, of a rightful king, and of masculinity – was Henry's alone. He also pored over the plans for the scaffold. Taking control of the minutiae of how his wife was disposed of helped Henry to convince himself that he was empowered rather than diminished by her fall.

On the morning of 19 May Anne walked to the scaffold Henry had designed for her within the walls of the Tower. Ever elegant, she was dressed in grey damask. The poet Thomas Wyatt, who had been amongst her admirers, looked down from his prison window in the Bell Tower to seek out her procession. Wyatt's literary predecessor, Geoffrey Chaucer, had described in 'The Knight's Tale' a hero spotting a beautiful maiden from a tower window, on a morning just such as this. Although it was not possible for Wyatt to see Anne, he could see men coming and going as preparations were made for what was to follow. He could imagine the rest. 'The Bell Tower showed me such sight/That in my head sticks day and night', he wrote, *circa regna tonat* [around the throne the thunder rolls].[7]

The rituals of Anne's beheading followed a strict cultural code. Prisoners were expected to give a last speech in which they would pronounce themselves judged guilty by the laws of the land and so content to die, as prescribed by the law. If they were innocent they knew that God was punishing them for something, and did not doubt they deserved death. Their speeches concluded with a request for forgiveness and the hope their sovereign would reign long and happily. Anne's followed these conventions. Of Henry she said, 'a more merciful nor more gentle prince was there never, and to me he was ever a good, a gentle and sovereign Lord'. There was no insistence that she was innocent. She hoped her killing would be quick and clean, and had joked earlier that she had 'but a little neck'. Carefully, she tucked her skirts in around her feet so that she would keep her modesty when her body fell. Then she turned her head, uncertain when the blow would come. When it did her head was struck off with one stroke, her famous black eyes and lips still moving as her head landed in the straw. She was buried that same day in the Tower church of St Peter ad Vincula.

Archbishop Cranmer had already issued a dispensation to free Henry to marry Jane Seymour, his fifth cousin.[8] Henry still needed a male heir – and to prove his virility. On 30 May 1536, eleven days after Anne died, his third wedding took place with his niece, Margaret Douglas, carrying Jane Seymour's train. Margaret had shared in the trauma of pre-trial interrogations with Anne's other ladies. Wyatt wrote of being made an 'instrument/to frame others' and they copied his words into the book of verses they collected: 'I was made a filing instrument/To frame others, while I was beguiled/But reason hath at my folly smiled/ And pardoned me.' Yet the terrors of the summer were far from over.

That Henry had no intention of legitimising Mary, as many assumed he would on Anne's death, became clear on 22 June. Only five weeks after Anne's execution, Mary was threatened with her death and that of several named friends, until she accepted the royal supremacy and her illegitimacy. The Imperial ambassador advised Mary to sign the articles without reading them and so make the intolerable, bearable. The twenty-year-old princess hated it, but she bowed to the threats. She was learning to be a survivor and she composed an abject letter designed carefully to win back her father's favour: 'Here', she wrote, 'is my poor heart which I send unto your highness to remain in your hand, to be for ever used, directed and framed ... at your only pleasure.'[9]

With Mary and Elizabeth now illegitimate, James V of Scots became Henry's heir under the usual rules of primogeniture and Margaret Douglas followed her half-brother in line of succession.[10] It was, however, possible – even probable – that if Margaret were married to an English nobleman her claim would be preferred in England over that of the Scottish James. Significantly, Henry was having it written into a new Act of Succession that if he died without legitimate children, he could appoint his heirs so James V could be excluded, if Henry wished it. Astonishingly on 4 July, when the new Act was ready, it emerged that Henry had chosen not to name an heir. The Act explained that he feared 'such person that should be so named, might happen to take great heart and courage, and by presumption fall into inobedience and rebellion'. It further stated that anyone who attempted to stake their own claim in preference to any heir he might appoint in the future, would not only be guilty of treason, their heirs would also forfeit any right to the throne. This reflected Henry's extreme anxiety that he would not be able to pull off what he was now considering, which was to appoint his illegitimate children over the legitimate royal heirs born to his sisters.

Foreign ambassadors had picked up rumours that Henry Fitzroy, Duke of Richmond would be the leading beneficiary of Henry's will. Fitzroy's name had been raised in council at the beginning of June when it was argued that of the king's three illegitimate children he was, at least, a boy.[11] But Fitzroy was terminally ill with 'a rapid consumption'. This left the way clear for Mary, whose submission – and carefully composed letters to her father – led, seemingly, to her rehabilitation.[12] On 6 July, Henry and Jane Seymour visited the princess and gave her 1,000 crowns 'for her little pleasures', as well as a diamond.[13] Henry also promised that she would soon be restored to a full household and be received at court. Nothing further would be done until he felt she had proved her loyalty; however, Henry still hoped for a son.

Two days later Henry learned of Margaret Douglas' betrothal. His daughters, illegitimate and unmarried, would make weak claimants: far weaker than the legitimate Margaret Douglas if she married into the powerful Howard family. Even if Henry had a son, the boy would be vulnerable until he reached adulthood. Henry ordered the couple arrested and taken to the Tower. The twenty-five-year-old Thomas Howard admitted to his interrogators that he had been in love with Margaret Douglas for a year; that they had been betrothed at Easter and that he considered Margaret to be his 'sweet wife'.[14] She described the gifts she had given him. In their youthful naivety they hoped that when the king's anger had abated their promise of marriage would be recognised. After all, they had not committed any crime under prevailing law. In the Tower, Thomas Howard composed romantic verses describing the pain of seeing 'her daily whom I love best in great and intolerable sorrows'. Margaret, in turn, celebrated having 'the faithfullest lover that ever was born' and kept a couple of Thomas Howard's servants to wait on her, as a mark of her good faith.[15] But they were about to discover just how angry and fearful Henry was.

On 18 July an Act of Attainder proclaimed it was 'vehemently suspected and presumed' (i.e. there was no proof) that Thomas Howard, having been 'led and seduced by the devil' had 'contemptuously and traitorously contracted himself by crafty, fair and flattering words to and with the Lady Margaret Douglas'. His object, it was decreed, was to usurp the throne, trusting people would prefer the English-born Margaret to her half-brother, the King of Scots, 'to whom this Realm has, nor ever had, any affection'.[16] The attainder sped through Parliament and created the law for which Thomas Howard was to be convicted. Marrying into royal blood, or for those of royal blood to marry without the king's consent, was now treason. On 23 July Chapuys reported that Thomas Howard had been condemned to death and that the twenty-year-old Margaret Douglas was spared only because the marriage had not been consummated.[17] There was, in fact, a further reason. The annulment of the marriage of Margaret's parents had left her legitimacy intact. The attainder nevertheless referred on several occasions to Margaret Douglas as being her mother's 'natural [i.e. bastard] daughter'. This was a clear attempt to demote her in the succession, and ensure Henry's children had the superior claim.[18] Henry's sensitivity on the issue was the more acute because Henry Fitzroy had just died. Anxious to downplay the significance of this Henry had ordered Norfolk – Fitzroy's father-in-law – to take the body out of London in a closed cart and bury his beloved son without any public ceremony.

Margaret's father, Angus, who was living in England on a pension from the king, could or would do nothing to help her. But in August her mother, the dowager Queen of Scots, wrote to Henry crossly observing that she believed her daughter's betrothal had taken place 'by your grace's advice'.[19] Queen Margaret could not understand why, therefore, Henry should mind if she 'should desire or promise such'. If he was angry with her daughter he should, she suggested, return the girl to Scotland forthwith. Instead, Henry sent Cromwell to Margaret Douglas to offer her advice. Margaret believed Cromwell was responsible for the king's decision not to have her condemned and so she paid close attention to what he had to say. After their meeting she agreed to send away Thomas Howard's servants and promised she would ensure that no one thought 'that any fancy remains in me touching him'.[20] In November, when Margaret fell ill in the Tower, Henry was sufficiently mollified to permit her to be released into the care of the nuns at nearby Syon Abbey.[21] The following month he also allowed parcels to be sent of 'deep crimson silk', 'fringe of silver' and 'crimson velvet' to upholster a suitable chair for her. Henry promised Queen Margaret that her daughter would continue to be well treated provided she remain 'convenient'.[22] But she remained under arrest as Henry now faced a major political crisis provoked by the succession issues, and his associated religious policies.

Promoting the jurisdiction of the Pope had been made an offence and informers were being encouraged to report anyone suspected of it. People were expected to accept that they would do as well to pray to Christ as to any saint. Purgatory had ceased to exist by name and praying for the dead was endorsed, less as a means of helping souls pay for their sins and go to heaven and more as a matter of 'custom'. When Owen Tudor's son, Sir David Owen, had died the previous year, he had left money to be lavished on Masses to be said for his soul, those of his parents, for his half-brothers Edmund and Jasper Tudor, and for his nephew, Henry VII. Already this was largely wasted, as were his other bequests to the church at the priory of Easebourne where he was buried: gold and silver gilt crucifixes, silver bells and candlesticks, fine chalices and Mass books in parchment, paper and vellum, rich fabrics of green damask with red roses, swallows and wolves for altar hangings and vestments. The priory was dissolved, granted in July 1536 to the Treasurer of the Royal Household, Sir William Fitzwilliam.[23]

The trigger for the revolt, which began in Lincolnshire on 1 October, was a visitation of the churches by Henry's church commissioners with instructions against 'superstitious' practices concerning the cult of saints. The local people loved their saints and the Henrician regime was now widely regarded as avaricious, sacrilegious, and led by evil men. A nearby Cistercian abbey had recently been closed and the congregation of St James's in Louth were convinced that their church was about to be stripped of the treasures their ancestors had bequeathed for generations. As they gathered that day for a religious procession behind their valuable processional crosses, a member of the choir called out bitterly, 'Masters step forth and let us follow the crosses this day. God knows whether we shall follow them again.' This despairing cry lit the touchpaper; by the end of October rebellion had convulsed northern counties from the river Don in Yorkshire to the Scottish border.

The scale of the rebellion against Henry VIII had not been seen since the shattering Peasants Revolt of 1381. The most serious uprising, the so-called Pilgrimage of Grace, called for the reversal of religious change and the overthrow of the king's 'heretical' councillors, but also for the repeal of the 'statute of illegitimacy' against Mary and the king's new power to leave the 'crown of this realm by will'. Ordinary people, as well as courtiers, were united in seeing the princess Mary as the champion of traditional religion, because, as the legitimate child of her parents' valid marriage, she embodied resistance to the break with Rome. They also saw her as the king's rightful heir. Since Henry VII and Henry VIII both drew their royal blood through female lines, people believed the princess could play a similar role, and be married to a suitable nobleman of royal blood. The rebels blamed Cromwell in particular for his role in the recent changes. It was even being said he was behind Thomas Howard's attainder and wanted to marry the beautiful Margaret Douglas himself: in short, that he aspired to the crown.

On 16 October rebel nobility, gentry, clergy and commoners entered York under their badge of the five wounds of Christ. On the 19th, Hull capitulated. With over 30,000 people involved the Pilgrims were too powerful to be defeated in battle. Henry bought them off instead with promises of pardons and the answering of grievances. It was a humiliation for the king, but Henry was biding his time to gain revenge. When it emerged in the New Year that Henry would not keep his promises, further unrest followed, but it was fragmented, disorganised and easily defeated. In the spring of 1537 the gentry leaders of the rebellions were brought to London for trial. Over 144 executions followed in the capital, with the beautiful young wife of one rebel burned alive. In the north there were further executions, with Henry demanding that 'the inhabitants of every town, village, and hamlet that have offended' should suffer such 'dreadful' deaths 'as they may be a fearful spectacle to all others hereafter'. The Duke of Norfolk chose to keep the numbers of the deaths down; nevertheless six abbots and thirty-eight monks were amongst those executed.

Henry now saw the monasteries as foci of resistance to the break with Rome, and instead of the programme of reform that he had previously intended, every monastery, large and small, good, bad or indifferent, was to be suppressed. The process took only four years. They had all gone by the end of January 1540, and their works of art, relics and libraries were either pillaged or destroyed. Out of 600 books in the library of Worcester Priory, only six remain. Three volumes survived the destruction of the Augustinian friars of York out of a total of 646. Amongst the greatest losses were many unique manuscript books of English church music.

Some of the empty buildings were converted into houses for new owners (including Easebourne Priory) and a few monastic churches continued as cathedrals or were bought by a parish to serve as their local church. Amongst them is Tewkesbury Abbey, bought for £453, the value of the bells and lead roof that otherwise would have been salvaged for the king. A brass plaque in the choir today commemorates Prince Edward of Lancaster, the son of Henry VI and Margaret of Anjou, who is buried there. For the most part, however, all that was left of the monasteries by the end of the Tudor period were Shakespeare's 'bare ruin'd choirs where late the sweet birds sang'.

Most monks and nuns were retired with a pension, although the remaining Carthusians from the London Charterhouse were not to be so lucky. There were to be no trials or public executions, which might stir up further unrest. They were simply taken to Newgate that May, chained to wooden posts in their cells and left in their own filth to die of starvation. Henry did not give them much thought. On 27 May 1537, two days before the monks were taken to Newgate, the great hymn of thanks, the 'Te Deum', was sung at St Paul's Cathedral 'for joy at the queen's quickening with child'. After all the years of disappointment, the king was to have a son at last.

24

THREE WIVES

THE CHRISTENING OF THE KING'S SON EDWARD AT HAMPTON COURT on 15 October 1537 was a subdued affair. There was an outbreak of plague in the London suburbs, and guests who had stayed recently in those areas had been asked to stay away. Edward's half-sisters Elizabeth and Mary were there, however. The four-year-old Elizabeth was carried in a courtier's arms, clutching the chrism cloth which was to be laid on his head during the baptism, while Mary made a happy godmother. She was relieved that the burden of being the king's 'true' heir was taken from her, and those of all religious persuasions rejoiced with her that England now had a legitimate prince.

A few days later the prince's mother, Jane Seymour, haemorrhaged in her rooms. She died on 24 October, to Henry's great sadness. It was said she had once angered Henry by begging him to save the monasteries. If the story is true it was a rare foot wrong. Her motto, 'Bound to Obey and Serve', expressed a similar understanding of Henry's psychological needs to that Katherine of Aragon had possessed as a young wife. Jane Seymour had been an intelligent and astute woman and came from what would prove a clever – if not always astute – family. For over a year Jane had shared Henry's bed, hunted with him and ridden in royal processions, she had been kind to his daughters Mary and Elizabeth, and at Christmas her pale, placid face had been ever present at the court celebrations and ceremonies.

Writing to King Francis of the birth of their son, Henry confessed that 'Divine Providence has mingled my joy with the bitterness of the death of her who brought me this happiness.' She was to be the only one of his wives to be honoured with a state funeral.

Jane's stepdaughter Mary acted as chief mourner that November, riding solemnly behind the chariot that bore Jane's coffin in procession to Windsor. Behind Mary, in the first of the chariots bearing the great ladies of the court, sat her cousin, Frances Brandon, the twenty-year-old elder daughter of the late French queen. Named after King Francis, she was married to Harry Grey, Marquess of Dorset, a 'young, lusty' nobleman 'of great possessions', who was a descendant of Katherine Woodville's first marriage to a Lancastrian knight.[1] The couple had a baby daughter, aged about six months, who they had named Lady Jane Grey after the queen. And although no one could have guessed it, little Jane Grey was destined also to be a queen.[2] Lady Margaret Douglas, who had been freed from arrest earlier that month, should have been sharing her cousin Frances' carriage, but she was absent from the funeral.[3] Her lover, Thomas Howard, had died 'of an ague' in the Tower and she had taken the news 'very heavily'.[4] Her last entry in her collection of poetry expressed the hope she would soon be with 'him that I have caused to die'.[5] Clearly she was in no fit state to appear in public just yet, let alone to consider why Henry had chosen to bury Jane at Windsor and not the Lady Chapel at Westminster Abbey. But it was to prove a highly significant decision – for it was at Windsor that Henry also intended to be buried.

Henry had stopped work on his tomb in the Lady Chapel at Westminster Abbey in the aftermath of the Pilgrimage of Grace the previous year.[6] The old divisions of the Wars of the Roses were being replaced by religious strife, but faced with the evidence of the turmoil he had created, Henry remembered the promise of the union rose – of national healing – and associated it with himself. He would be buried in St George's Chapel at Windsor because it was there that his Lancastrian great-uncle, Henry VI, and his Yorkist grandfather Edward IV were buried. The name chosen for his son should be seen in this context. The boy had been born on the eve of the Feast of Edward the Confessor after whom it is often claimed he was named. But Henry showed little attachment to this royal saint, whose shrine at Westminster he stripped of its valuables. Rather, he was doing what his father had never done: honouring his mother's family.

The evidence of a psychological break with his father is still more evident in the fresco Henry now commissioned from Hans Holbein. When completed it covered most of one wall at Whitehall (formerly Wolsey's York Place). It was a family portrait, but one that boasted how much better Henry VIII had done than his father. At the centre of the fresco was an enormous altar. Above were the slight figures of Henry VII and Elizabeth of York. Below, to the left of the altar was Jane Seymour, the mother of the prince, and to the right the much larger figure of Henry VIII standing astride, his oversized codpiece thrust forward, 'so majestic in his splendour, [and] so lifelike that the spectator felt abashed, annihilated in his presence', one viewer commented.[7] The Latin inscription on the altar asked who was the greatest, Henry VII or Henry VIII? 'The former often overcame his enemies and the fires of his country and finally gave peace to its citizens'; but 'the son, born indeed for greater tasks, drives the unworthy from the altars and brings in men of integrity. The presumption of popes has yielded to unerring virtue and with Henry VIII bearing the sceptre in his hand, religion has been restored.'[8]

Although Henry wished for further sons he was in no hurry to remarry. His priority was to build on this claim to greatness. Henry was now determined to forge a new religious unity within a reformed English Catholic church that was humanist, Christo-centric, anti-papal and biblical. Where Henry VII had commissioned a silver gilt image of himself in the shrine of Thomas Becket, and another at the famous shrine to the Virgin at Walsingham, Henry VIII had the tomb of Thomas Becket fired out of cannons and the towers of Walsingham with their 'golden, glittering tops' were levelled to the ground.[9] Yet Henry was ready to create as well as destroy, commissioning a new Bible in English by Miles Coverdale. It was to have an image of Henry at the top of the page, as the Vicar of Christ, handing the Word of God to Cranmer and Cromwell, who would in turn pass it on to his subjects. There were concerns an English Bible would encourage heresy with individuals interpreting what they had read in their own way, but Henry was prepared to police the beliefs of his subjects personally.

In May 1538 an Observant Friar was convicted of heresy for his traditional Catholic beliefs, and burned with exquisite cruelty over 'a slow fire' fuelled by an ancient image of a Welsh saint.[10] A campaign was being led against all statues and objects linked to cults, and killing the monk in this way sent out a strong message to parishes. But Henry also burned evangelicals, and in November 1538 stepped in to oversee the trial of a man who, influenced by European reformers, denied the Real Presence of God in consecrated bread.[11] This was an issue that would come to be a defining difference between Catholics and Protestants – and Henry decisively rejected what would come to be called Protestantism. The miraculous transformation of bread and wine into Christ's body and blood at the moment of consecration, which lies at the heart of Catholic belief, also lay at the centre of his Christianity. Henry, dressed symbolically in white, insisted the man die at the stake.

Henry's self-appointed role as Grand Inquisitor and his destruction of pilgrimage sites was, however, now attracting the threat of a crusade. The papal sentence of excommunication, suspended since Henry's marriage to Anne Boleyn, was issued and Pope Paul III asked the English cardinal, Reginald Pole, to persuade Charles V and Francis I to launch an invasion. The cardinal's family in England were already suffering for their connection to him. On 9 January 1539 his elder brother, Henry, Lord Montague and his cousin, Henry Courtenay, Marquess of Exeter, were executed for being in contact. Even Pole's old mother, the Countess of Salisbury, the princess Mary's former governess, was attainted and eventually executed. The axe-man, a 'blundering youth', was said to have 'literally hacked her head and shoulders to pieces'.[12]

Henry faced the threat of invasion equally robustly, by creating the greatest fortifications of the realm since the reign of Edward I. Coastal forts were built or rebuilt and a strategic alliance was made with the House of Cleves, which held the dukedom between the Low Countries and the German Empire. To seal this, Cromwell pushed the idea of a marriage with the Duke of Cleves' second daughter, Anne. With infant mortality high it was also the case that the more sons Henry had the better. He had shown Edward off in the spring of 1538, holding the prince in his arms at a window with 'much mirth and joy' and 'to the sight and comfort of all'.[13] A painting of Edward aged fourteen months, dressed in red velvet and holding a golden rattle, depicts a fat and beautiful baby. But even the healthiest baby could be snatched away suddenly by disease, and having seen Holbein's attractive portrait of Anne of Cleves, Henry agreed to marry her.

The king's first meeting with his new wife, on New Year's Day 1540, was intended to be in the romantic tradition of royal grooms meeting their brides by chance, seen already with Henry's sisters.[14] But instead of preparations and warning, Henry played it for real, bursting into her room at the Bishop's Palace in Rochester in the guise of a servant, while she was watching a bullfight from a window. 'She looks about 30 years of age, tall and thin, of medium beauty, and of very assured and resolute countenance', the French ambassador reported. 'She brought 12 or 15 ladies of honour clothed like herself [in German fashion], a thing which looks strange to many.'[15] Henry offered a New Year's gift as 'from the king'. She accepted graciously, but to her astonishment the 'servant' then seized and kissed her. Confused, and evidently appalled, she thanked him, before turning back to the window, and studiously ignoring him. It had been a disaster. Humiliated, Henry later turned to the men around him commenting that Anne appeared to be 'no maid'; that is, she was not a virgin.[16]

The artist Barthel Bruyn produced a portrait of Anne of Cleves very similar to Holbein's, but which better reflects the French description of her. Especially notable is the ugliness of her dress. In Anne Boleyn, Henry had fallen in love with the most chic and elegant woman at court. The English still favoured the French fashions she had loved, with smooth silhouettes, natural waistlines and conical skirts. The German style Anne and her ladies wore was quite different. Their necklines were high, their gowns were short-waisted and tightly laced with alternating bands of contrasting fabrics, often embroidered with lace. It was 'heavy' and 'unbecoming', and the fact Anne of Cleves spoke no English meant there was little chance of compensating for her hideous dress with a flash of courtly wit. Deeply disappointed, Henry's reaction was immediately to consider how he might extract himself from this unwelcome marriage – hence his desperate comment that Anne was 'no maid'.

Henry knew that Anne of Cleves had been betrothed aged twelve to the heir to the dukedom of Lorraine. After enquiries were made, at Henry's request, it emerged the Cleves ambassadors had failed to bring a copy of the Lorraine contract with them that would prove they were not legally man and wife. Reassurances were issued and vows sworn that Anne of Cleves was free. But when Henry married her on 6 January 1540, it was solely to cement the alliance with her father, and although he slept with Anne, he told Cromwell he could not consummate the union. Her stomach and breasts were those of a married woman, he insisted.

Cromwell decided Anne simply needed to improve her sexual performance and instructed the Earl of Rutland to ask her to behave more 'pleasantly' to Henry. The unlucky earl did so in as polite a manner as he could, and through an interpreter. Anne's English ladies later claimed she knew so little about sex that she believed a kiss was enough for consummation. Given the language barrier, such conversations seem unlikely and it is significant the women made their claims only when the king's lawyers began looking for proof of non-consummation in order to annul the marriage.

Franco-Imperial relations had quickly become strained, and as soon as Henry no longer needed the Cleves alliance his marriage was doomed. An impotent man could not legally marry, but Henry had his lawyers argue that he was only impotent with Anne. As evidence that he could have intercourse with other women he described how he had wet dreams and justified his lack of attraction to Anne with reference to her contract with the son of the Duke of Lorraine. Henry may well have chosen not to have sex with Anne hoping that the time would come when he could annul his marriage, but it is also possible that his impotence had a physical basis. Earlier wives had all conceived children. His later wives never would. Here his growing weight was surely a contributing factor.[17] The illuminations in a psalter painted that year has an image of Henry in his favourite guise of the biblical King David, but he more closely resembles a hippopotamus in scarlet hose, even if he had not yet reached the massive proportions of the following decade.[18]

Parliament confirmed the annulment of the marriage on 12 July. The chief casualty of this third annulled marriage was not Anne of Cleves, however, but its architect, Thomas Cromwell. The old nobility had spotted an opportunity to be revenged on the parvenu who had helped dispose of so many of them. On 10 June, when Henry was already courting the flirtatious twenty-two-year-old Katherine Howard, a niece of the Duke of Norfolk, Cromwell was arrested on charges of treason and heresy. His associations with Sacramentarians in Calais had left him vulnerable to the accusation that he denied the Real Presence of Christ in the Eucharist. Convicted under an Act of Attainder, he begged Henry fruitlessly for 'mercy, mercy'. Cromwell was beheaded on 28 July, the same day that Henry married Katherine Howard.[19] It was a botched job and Cromwell's skull was smashed to pieces.

* * *

In October 1541, Henry's elder sister, Margaret, the dowager Queen of Scots, died aged fifty-one, following a stroke.[20] The queen hadn't seen her daughter Margaret Douglas since she had been kidnapped and taken to England aged thirteen. She had been reassured, however, that life had improved for her daughter in the four years since Thomas Howard had died in the Tower. Margaret had served Anne of Cleves as a lady-in-waiting and was now serving the new queen, Katherine Howard. She was even falling in love again, this time with the queen's brother, Charles Howard, a nephew of Thomas'. Happily there was nothing to fear in her new romance for Henry was gloriously happy with Katherine.

Just as Henry's response to the stories of his impotence in the Boleyn trials was to banquet with beautiful women, following his admission of impotence with Anne of Cleves he liked to show off his passion for his young bride. 'The king', the French ambassador reported, 'is so amorous of her that he cannot treat her well enough and caresses her more than he did the others.'[21] Unfortunately, that October Archbishop Cranmer learned something disturbing about Katherine. Despite the king's ability, self-proclaimed during his marriage to Anne of Cleves, to tell from a woman's appearance if she was a virgin, it seemed that Henry might have been fooled in this regard where the new queen was concerned.

Cranmer's source was a former servant of Katherine Howard's grandmother, Agnes, the dowager Duchess of Norfolk. Katherine had spent her early teenage years in the dowager's household, in line with the aristocratic practice of sending daughters off to a well-connected family to improve their education. As was usual, when the dowager was away her wards were left in the care of servants and they were less concerned to keep an eye on the behaviour of these girls than the old duchess. Katherine would flirt with her music teacher, and after she became interested in another man she had agreed to let him touch her in a 'secret place' if he would stop pestering her. He masturbated her in the family chapel, later boasting how he had 'had her by the cunt' and would 'know it among a hundred'.[22] Katherine Howard had gone still further, however, with the man for whom she left the music teacher: her kinsman Francis Dereham.

According to the young women who had shared Katherine's room as teenagers, she and Dereham would kiss like 'two sparrows'. They even shared a bed, the other girls in the room giggling over the 'huffing and blowing' emerging from Dereham under the covers. Under canon law any promise Dereham and Katherine had made each other, followed by intercourse, constituted a valid marriage, placing the king in a bigamous union. The news was a political gift to Cranmer who hoped to use it to break Howard's influence: the Duke of Norfolk had once said that England was merry before the 'new learning' came up – hardly a ringing endorsement of the Reformation. For Cranmer a girl's life was a small price to pay to damage Norfolk's standing with the king.

When Cranmer informed Henry what he had learned of Katherine Howard, the king's reaction was quite different to when he had been told of Anne Boleyn's misdeeds: he refused to accept it. He ordered that Dereham and the musician be questioned in order to clear her name, but to Henry's horror they confessed to everything. 'His heart was so pierced with pensiveness', the council reported, 'that long it was before his majesty could speak, and utter the sorrow of his heart unto us.' When he did so there were 'plenty of tears which was strange in [one of] his courage'.[23] Again the contrast to his reaction on 'discovering' Anne Boleyn's adultery is striking. This time he had had no concerns that his marriage was cursed, and no wish that his wife was no more.

On 6 November Henry deserted Katherine Howard at Hampton Court never to see her again. By 11 November Dereham had confessed under torture that after Katherine became queen he was replaced in her affections by a gentleman of the Privy Chamber called Thomas Culpepper. It was also decided Katherine would be sent to Syon and stripped of all but four of her servants, with the rest sent home.[24] First, however, the queen's ladies all had to be interviewed. Margaret Douglas' lover Charles Howard had already been banished from court, and Margaret must have been terrified their flirtation would be discovered – as it was.[25] The interrogators learned of Margaret's relationship the following day. The king was informed and she was delivered a chilling warning. She had 'demeaned herself towards His Majesty, first with the Lord Thomas Howard, and second with Charles Howard', to whom she had shown 'overmuch lightness'. She was advised: 'beware the third time'.[26] It was considered sufficient on this occasion that she 'fully apply herself to please the king', and claims that she was imprisoned again are mistaken.[27] But the queen was not to be so fortunate.

It had emerged that Katherine had met Culpepper many times in private, beginning as soon as within seven or eight months of her marriage to the king. In this she had some help from an old friend called Katherine Tilney, and a great deal more help from Jane Boleyn, Lady Rochford, the widow of Anne Boleyn's brother, George. Given Jane Boleyn's position in Anne's court Katherine may have assumed that she would know how a queen might conduct a secret love affair. But if this explains why she was asked for help, it is more difficult to understand why she agreed to give it. She was short of money and it is possible she helped Katherine in exchange for payment, or perhaps she was simply silly and enjoyed the thrill of being 'important' again in the queen's bedchamber. In any event, she was the conduit for Katherine's love letters to Culpepper.

Katherine would meet Culpepper in a 'vile place', her stool house, or lavatory, where Jane Boleyn would stay with them awhile before leaving. Katherine and Culpepper never confessed to having had full intercourse. Penetration would have imperilled the succession, and as Katherine had once assured Dereham, she knew how to 'meddle with a man' without risking having a child by him. But Culpepper admitted that he had wanted to, very much, as did she. 'It makes my heart to die to think what fortune I have that I cannot always be in your company', she wrote to him, 'yours as long as life endures, Katherine.'

Dereham and Culpepper were tried for treason and found guilty. Dereham was hanged, drawn and quartered on 10 December 1541. Culpepper, who Henry knew from court, was granted the mercy of a beheading the same day. On the 22nd several of Katherine's friends and relations were found guilty of failing to reveal knowledge of acts of treason. These were to be defined subsequently by the Act of Attainder used against the queen and Jane Boleyn. The Act made it a treasonous offence for an unchaste woman to marry the king without first confessing it to him, and declared that it was treason for a queen, or the wife of a Prince of Wales, to commit adultery, or for anyone to commit adultery with them. Once again Henry was sending people to the block for actions that were only made a capital crime retrospectively.

On 10 February 1542 Katherine Howard was taken, angry and struggling, on to a covered barge and brought from Syon to the Tower. She passed under the bridge where the heads of her lovers had been rotting for two months. In the Tower, she and Jane Boleyn broke down, as Anne Boleyn had when terror reduced her to laughing, weeping hysteria. Jane was judged to be half mad, but Katherine recovered her poise and even practised laying her head on the block in the privacy of her chamber. The executioner had made a mess of Cromwell's head on the day she was married; she wanted her death to be more dignified. It was to be so.

Jane Boleyn waited in her rooms as her former mistress was beheaded, hearing the gasps of the crowd, before she took her own last walk to the scaffold and stepped to the block. Somehow she managed to keep herself steady. She said her prayers, laid her head down on the blood-soaked wood and died quickly, as Katherine had done, at the fall of the axe.

25

THE LAST YEARS OF HENRY VIII

THE ROADS WERE COVERED IN SNOW WHEN JAMES V REACHED HIS wife, Mary of Guise, at Linlithgow Castle. It was here that his mother, Margaret Tudor, had learned of the death of his father at Flodden. James now carried the knowledge of another defeat at English hands. He had ordered a raid into England in retaliation for an invasion attempt, but on 24 November 1542 his forces were defeated at Solway Moss, his banner taken, and senior members of his household seized.[1] He told the queen what had occurred, and although she was pregnant and the birth of their child was imminent, he explained he could not stay. Preparations had to be made to continue the campaign and reverse his humiliation.

The aim of Henry's invasion attempt had been to cripple Scotland before he turned his attention, once again, to France. The prestige of Henry V's victories had helped protect the throne of his infant son Henry VI well into his majority. Henry VIII hoped that territorial gains in France would, similarly, secure the throne for his son, Edward, were Henry to die before the boy reached adulthood.

For James V there was little hope of peace with Henry and the difficult task he faced in defending his country from his belligerent Tudor uncle was made still harder by illness. On 6 December, at the end of a long day of military planning, James left Edinburgh for Falkland Palace, twenty-one miles from his capital. He was exhausted by the time he arrived, and went to bed. The next day he was too sick to be moved, vomiting copiously, and suffering severe diarrhoea. Feverish and anxious he 'did rage and cry out, and spake but few wise words thereafter'.[2] On 8 December the dying king learned that his wife had delivered a daughter at Linlithgow. The Scottish crown had come to the Stuarts through a woman.[3] Unless James' daughter married another Stuart it seemed certain the dynasty would end with one as well. 'It cam wi' a lass and it will gang wi' a lass', are the last coherent words James is reported by tradition, as having said.[4]

James V had ruled Scotland since he was sixteen, when he escaped the damaging control of his stepfather, Angus, with the help of his mother, Queen Margaret. He was only thirty when he died on 14 December, his body grotesquely swollen. In England his death was ascribed to 'regret, sorrow and rage' over Solway Moss. Certainly James had been bitterly angry at times, but his symptoms are suggestive of cholera rather than depressive illness. He had fought for his life as his body ran dry, fearing what his country and his daughter, the new Mary, Queen of Scots, would face without him.

At Henry's court James' twenty-seven-year-old half-sister, Margaret Douglas, mourned him, as was her duty. She was back in favour and, with the king's daughters, was amongst eighteen attendants at his wedding at Hampton Court on 12 July 1543. Henry's sixth wife, the twice-widowed Katherine Parr, was thirty-one years old and the kind of woman who had always attracted him: strong-willed, clever, passionate and sensual. He had spotted her amongst his daughter Mary's ladies-in-waiting. At the time Katherine Parr was in a love affair with Prince Edward's younger uncle, Thomas Seymour, a vivid figure, 'fierce in courage, courtly in fashion, in voice magnificent'.[5] But when the king's interest became clear Katherine had little choice but to sacrifice her love for Seymour to marry Henry.

A few months later, in February 1544, the secretary of the Spanish nobleman Juan Esteban, Duke of Najera, was invited to Whitehall with his master to meet the queen. They travelled to the palace by barge, admiring the Thames on the way. 'It is not possible, in my opinion, that a more beautiful river should exist in the world', the Spaniard noted, 'the city stands on each side of it, and innumerable boats, vessels and other craft are seen moving on the stream', and 'never did I see a river so thickly covered with swans'. Whitehall had a well-laid-out garden with walks decorated with statues, and carvings of birds, monsters and other creatures. Inside Katherine Parr greeted them in her chambers. She was extremely animated with 'a lively and pleasing appearance', and was dressed in a magnificent gown of cloth of gold, worn with sleeves lined with scarlet satin and trimmed with red velvet. 'Suspended from her neck', he also noted, were 'two crosses, and a jewel of very rich diamonds'.

Having asked her visitors to sit down, Katherine called for music. While the queen danced with her brother, Margaret Douglas and the princess Mary danced with other gentlemen. Margaret was in silk and Mary in a violet gown set off with a petticoat of cloth of gold, her auburn hair glittering with her jewelled headdress. At the end of the evening the duke kissed the queen's hand, and asked if he could also kiss Mary's, but the princess insisted on a kiss on the lips, in the English manner. The Spanish secretary thought her very pretty and 'well shaped', and was told she was 'so much beloved throughout the kingdom that she is almost adored', but that she was careful 'to conceal her acquirements'.

Mary had learned from experience that it can be helpful to be underestimated and was now at court only because her father no longer regarded her as dangerous. Henry believed a husband could yet make her so, so he had no intention of having her married, even if it meant she died a childless spinster. He wanted no potential challengers to the claims of his son. For Mary's friend and cousin, Margaret Douglas, a wedding also seemed far off. Happily, however, that was about to change. Instead of using resources to invade Scotland, Henry intended to build up a body of Scottish support for a marriage between the infant Queen of Scots and his son Edward, thus uniting the kingdoms under the English crown. Margaret Douglas was to be a pawn in these plans, with Henry offering her as a bride to a man who regarded himself as the rightful holder of the Scottish throne: Matthew Stuart, Earl of Lennox.

A descendant of James I of Scotland, Lennox had returned from exile in France the previous year, only to be disappointed in what he could achieve in pursuit of his ambitions. He hoped he would do better leading a pro-English Scottish party from England.[6] Under the treaty Lennox made with Henry, he had to agree to recognise Henry's 'right' of overlordship in Scotland and convert to the religion of Henry's Church of England. Then he was introduced to Margaret. It had been agreed that both parties would have the opportunity to accept or reject the marriage after they had seen each other.[7] Margaret proved delighted with Lennox. Described as 'a strong man of personage well shaped . . . with a good and manly countenance . . . he was most pleasant for a lady'.[8] Lennox was equally delighted with Margaret, who he found as beautiful as others had judged her as a girl, and talented and clever as well.

With the match settled, the princess Mary showered Margaret with wedding gifts of balas rubies, table diamonds, sapphires and pendant pearls, brooches and girdle buckles. Henry gave Lennox still more substantial gifts of land, principally in Yorkshire, where they were to reside at Temple Newsam, a house only completed in 1520, and which had belonged to one of the executed leaders of the Pilgrimage of Grace. On the morning of 29 June Margaret and Lennox married in front of the king and queen.[9] It was to prove a love match as well as an effective political partnership, but the Lennoxes had been obliged to stomach some disappointment. Margaret's name was not mentioned in the Third Act of Succession, which had been given the royal assent that spring.

Henry was aware it was unlikely he would have more children and so he had Mary and Elizabeth named as Edward's heirs, following any children he might have with Katherine Parr. Neither Margaret

Douglas nor Henry's other nieces, Frances and Eleanor Brandon, was mentioned, however. The Act merely stated that Elizabeth's heirs would be named later in letters patent. As the previous Act of 1536 had observed, he feared named heirs might 'take great heart and courage, and by presumption fall into inobedience and rebellion'. Unlike his spinster daughters, his nieces were married, and into great noble families: Margaret Douglas to Lennox, Frances Brandon to Harry Grey, Marquess of Dorset, and her younger sister, Eleanor Brandon, to Henry Clifford, Earl of Cumberland.

Henry's decisions on the succession were about defending the rights of his children and on a personal level Henry was very fond of Margaret. He wrote to her from Calais that September, as the French campaign continued, sending the new bride his special 'recommendations'.[10] Six days later Henry's army enjoyed a great victory with Boulogne surrendering to English forces. As had happened in the past, however, Henry was let down by his ally. On 18 September, Charles V concluded a peace treaty with Francis I. England was left to fight on alone through 1545, defeating invasion attempts and attacks on Boulogne, while launching massive raids into Scotland in answer to the arrival of French reinforcements there. It dissipated the wealth Henry had taken from the church and smashed the economy. Henry's oldest friend and one-time brother-in-law Charles Brandon was worn to the bone, and died of pneumonia in August shortly after he had returned home from fortifying Portsmouth. In June 1546, his money exhausted, Henry was obliged to make peace with France.

Only recently recovered from the birth of her son, Henry, Lord Darnley, Margaret Douglas was by this time already back at court.[11] Appointed with her cousins, Frances and Eleanor Brandon, as a lady-in-waiting to Katherine Parr, she was now to have a front-row seat to the paranoid and bloody denouement of Henry's reign.[12]

The fifty-five-year-old king was increasingly bedridden. His waist, once measuring a trim thirty-two inches, was a gross fifty-four inches, and his legs suffered recurring ulcers. Yet Henry found it hard to forget his youthful chivalric glory. In his favourite psalter, where Psalm 37:25 read 'I have been young and now am old', he wrote in the margin 'a grievous saying'. It was all the more so when it meant he had so little time left to protect Edward. He wanted an awe-inspiring image for the little boy and had his son painted in the famous Holbein pose: skinny legs spread, his fresh, eight-year-old face looking commanding, straight at the viewer. But however Henry had him painted, Edward was still just a boy, 'the most amiable, and the gentlest thing of all the world', one of his tutors observed.[13]

Edward was fond of the queen, and fonder still of his elder sister Mary, the nearest thing he had had to a mother since babyhood, and in whose company, he said, he felt a 'special content'. 'Although I do not frequently write to you, my dearest sister,' he wrote to her that year, 'yet . . . I love you quite as well as if I wrote to you more frequently'; indeed he observed, 'I love you most.'[14] As Edward's nearest royal relative, Mary was the obvious choice for regent if Henry died while Edward was a minor.[15] But if Mary married, would Edward be safe from an ambitious prince? Henry feared not. And what of Edward's council? What dangers might they both face there?

Since 1533 and the break with Rome the quarrels of the Wars of the Roses had been replaced with religious divisions. Courtiers were now driven not only by personal ambition, but also by competing ideologies; some wished for further evangelical reform; some wanted to maintain the status quo, and others wished to reverse the break with Rome. In Italy the Council of Trent had recently opened. The church's teachings were to be discussed and defined anew, and this threatened to leave Henry's Reformation behind. Humanism was to be hugely influential in what became known as the Catholic Revival or (more negatively) the Counter-Reformation. Henry's anti-papal stance meant England could not be part of that, yet he persisted in seeing Lutheranism and the still more radical Swiss Reformed Churches as heretical.

In Parliament in December 1545, the same month that the Council of Trent had opened, Henry had berated both houses for their quarrels, complaining that the Bible was being 'disputed, rhymed, sung and jangled in every ale house and tavern'. His role as the arbiter of religious truth was a power he was now determined to remind his subjects forcibly was his alone, and would be inherited by his son. As in 1534 and 1536, when he threatened his daughter Mary to demonstrate that he would not tolerate any opposition to his royal will, so in 1546 Henry's queen was the first to be used as an example and warning that it was for the king alone to declare on religious issues.

Katherine Parr had a strong interest in religious reform. She had promoted evangelical tutors for Edward and every afternoon evangelical chaplains were invited to preach to her ladies. The historian David Starkey believes it was the princess Elizabeth who unwittingly brought to the king's attention the true radical nature of Katherine's religious inclinations.[16] Aged twelve, Anne Boleyn's daughter was proving an excellent linguist, and in imitation of her great-grandmother, Margaret Beaufort, she had begun to do her own translations of religious works. In 1546 she gave her father a New Year's gift of a translation into French, Italian and Latin of a composition of her stepmother's: a book of prayers and meditations printed in 1545. It reflected the Lutheran belief that faith alone, without the necessity of carrying out good works, was all that was necessary for salvation, and Starkey suggests that far from pleasing the king, the gift made him realise that Katherine was involving herself in theological matters and encouraging Elizabeth to do so too.

Katherine further exposed herself to danger, however, in a forceful letter that she wrote to the University of Cambridge on 26 February 1546. Responding to a request for her intercession with the king on the university's behalf, Katherine once again waded into her husband's preserve of theology, chiding the Cambridge scholars for writing to her in Latin and instructing them that the purpose of learning was only to set forth Christ's teachings, and that all else was vanity. The very next day the Imperial ambassador reported to Charles V that there were rumours circulating that Henry would discard Katherine and marry again. These spread rapidly and circulated at least into early April, after which they faded. A famous story later told by the Elizabethan martyrologist, John Foxe, may well reflect something of what had happened.

Foxe described how Katherine enjoyed debating religion with the king. But one day, after they parted, he had expressed irritation over it. Foxe then claims that conservative councillors seized the opportunity to fan Henry's anger and a warrant for her arrest was drawn up. Henry, however, decided to warn Katherine about his displeasure through one of his doctors. She took the hint, and when she went to Henry that night she reassured him humbly that she had only debated with him for her own instruction and to take his mind off the pain in his leg. 'And is it even so sweetheart?' Foxe records him as asking her, 'then perfect friends we are now again'. Katherine Parr had indeed survived danger, much as Foxe's story later relayed, but the source of the danger was Henry, not the dark forces of conservatism that Foxe preferred to blame. Henry had made a point, as well as indulging his cruel streak: religious policy came from him alone.[17]

Katherine Parr proved immune from the ferocious heresy hunts that followed. But while Henry countenanced, and even encouraged, the zeal of conservatives in this regard, he also chose this moment to break the intellectual leader of religious conservatism in England: the Bishop of Winchester, Stephan Gardiner. Hitherto the bishop had been one of his most effective servants, but Henry believed that the only man who could control a figure as brilliant as Gardiner was Henry himself, and he did not want Gardiner coming to dominate his son, or those around him. Although Gardiner had helped frame the arguments for the Royal Supremacy, Henry may also have suspected (rightly) that Gardiner would come to question its ability to protect England from heresy. In November 1546 Gardiner discovered Henry was mysteriously angry with him over the exchange of some lands. The king would never see him again.

It was, however, to be the Duke of Norfolk's eldest son, Henry Howard, Earl of Surrey, who unwittingly provoked Henry's deepest fears for his son. One of the great poets of his generation, Surrey was the brother of Margaret Douglas' friend Mary Fitzroy, Duchess of Richmond (widow of the king's bastard son), and was close to their fellow poet, Mary Shelton. He was, however, also known with good reason as 'the most foolish, proud boy that is in England'. Surrey had quartered the royal arms into his own heraldic bearings, and made it plain he believed his father, as England's premier nobleman, should be Protector when Henry died. The king had not forgotten that the last Protector was Richard III, in whose cause Surrey's grandfather had fought and his great-grandfather had died. Henry's son Edward, now aged nine, was three years younger than Edward V had been when he disappeared with his brother. On 12 December 1546, the glamorous Surrey was arrested on suspicion of treason and shortly afterwards he and Norfolk were sent to the Tower.

On 26 December, shut up away from all but his closest servants, Henry called for his will to draw up his final plans for Edward's protection. He knew he was now dying and that this was his last opportunity to ensure Edward's survival. His daughters, Mary and Elizabeth, had been nominated as Edward's heirs under the Act of Succession. This would remain the case. Being illegitimate and female, they posed no threat to Edward – unless they married – and Henry's will now added the proviso that their inheritance depended on them marrying only in accordance with the wishes of the executors of his will. Henry was to name sixteen men as his executors, whom he envisaged sharing the authority of the crown equally until Edward reached the age of eighteen. He was not going to trust any one individual with the powers of either a Protector or a regent.

To prevent factions Henry further instructed that no one would be allowed to join his privileged circle of oligarchs before Edward's majority, and none was to be expelled. It was a sealed entity. Those who were on the king's list included Edward's senior maternal uncle,

Edward Seymour, supported by his chief ally on the council, John Dudley. They had been key figures in the king's recent wars, as well as pivotal members of the evangelical and reformist grouping at court. Another was Katherine Parr's brother-in-law, the flame-haired William Herbert, who was expected to guarantee the interests of a child born to the queen, should she prove to be pregnant after Henry's death.[18] Henry also now settled the unresolved matter of the long-stop heirs – the successors to a childless Elizabeth.

Henry's great-niece Mary, Queen of Scots – daughter of James V – was the most senior heir in blood. But whom she married was outside the control of anyone in England. It was likely to be a King of France or Spain, and Henry was not going to give a foreign monarch any help in laying claim to Edward's throne. Edward was born while England was in schism with Rome, so it was possible to argue he was not legitimate. To protect Edward, Mary, Queen of Scots and her heirs were therefore ignored in his will.[19]

The claims of Margaret Douglas, who was next in line, also went unmentioned. Historians have said Henry's decision followed a quarrel Margaret had with her uncle that autumn, and have suggested it was over religion. The numerous payments Margaret and her husband made that year to chantry priests, who prayed for souls in purgatory, indicate they were conservative.[20] But Henry VIII asked in his will for Masses to be said for his soul (albeit on nothing like the scale of his father). There is no evidence that Margaret ever quarrelled with Henry over his religious policies, and the sole basis for the claim of there being any quarrel at all is a much later, self-serving story spun by a disgruntled former Lennox servant.[21] In reality the evidence is that Henry had wished to demote Margaret in the line of succession since 1536 when she was referred to as her mother's 'natural' child. Her claim to the English throne was now united with her husband's claim to the crown of Scotland, making it potentially powerful enough to draw support in England, Scotland and France (where Lennox had spent many years). Alone amongst Henry's nieces Margaret also had a son,

Henry, Lord Darnley. Margaret was not named in Henry's will to limit the potential threat she posed, not because of any quarrel.[22]

In place of the descendants of his elder sister, Margaret of Scotland, Henry looked to those of his younger sister, Mary, the French queen. The senior heir was his niece Frances, but her husband was denied a place on Henry's list of executors and her name was passed over in favour of her young daughters, Lady Jane, Katherine and Mary Grey. These three unmarried girls, all under the age of ten, and with only a distant claim under Common Law, were chosen because they were weak candidates who posed little threat to Edward.

With the matter of the succession decided on, the dying king moved to complete the destruction of the Howards. It proved difficult to persuade a jury to convict Surrey of treason and Henry intervened personally to convince them to do so. The 'proud boy' was executed on 19 January. A final Act of Attainder was used to deal with the still trickier case against Norfolk, who Surrey had argued should be Protector. The execution was due to take place on 28 January, but by the evening of Thursday 27 January it was clear to all around the king that his death was imminent. Henry was asked if he wanted to confess his sins, but he was not troubled by his conscience in the way his father had been. Henry was as sure as ever that his actions as king had had the purest motives, and that all those he had destroyed had received their just merits. 'I will first take a little sleep', he said. 'And then, as I feel myself, I will advise [you] upon the matter.' Henry VIII never woke.

26

ELIZABETH IN DANGER

IN THE THIN LIGHT OF THE NEW DAY, LEADING COURTIERS ARRIVED at Whitehall to view the royal corpse. Henry's body lay on the vast state bed expanded in 1542 to bear his weight. It was the most valuable piece of furniture in the palace. Six craftsmen had worked for ten months to carve its gilded frame and the rich hangings cost even more than the bed itself.[1] It was in Henry's waxy face, however, that the power he had wielded was best recalled. 'If all the pictures and patterns of a merciless prince were lost in the world, they might again be painted to the life out of the story of this king', the Elizabethan Sir Walter Raleigh would later write. Now that power was gone Henry's trusted servants were free to ignore his dying commands.

If Henry could have walked during the last night of his life he would have seen two figures in the gallery outside his chamber door: his private secretary, Sir William Paget, instantly recognisable by his forked frizzy beard, and the tall, fair figure of the young Edward's uncle, Edward Seymour, Earl of Hertford. Henry had wanted a council of equals to rule during Edward's minority, but Paget believed this was impossible in a kingdom so used to being ruled entirely by the will of one man, and for weeks he had helped prepare the ground for Edward Seymour to take charge of the council as Lord Protector of England. He had pressed the king to grant land and titles to potential supporters, and as the instructions were always verbal Paget could mishear or misunderstand them in such a way as helped their cause. His price, he had told Edward Seymour, was to be his principle adviser. As the king drew his last breaths the deal had been sealed and now they were ready to gain the agreement of other key figures.

All that day, as the great men came and went, the usual ceremonies continued without interruption. No news was released of the king's death, and at dinner a choice of fish and fowl was delivered to the sound of trumpets. The following morning, as the same rituals were repeated, Edward Seymour arrived at the medieval palace of Hertford to collect his royal nephew and escort him to London. Henry had been poised to make Edward the Prince of Wales, and the grey-eyed boy believed this was the purpose of their journey.[2] Only when they stopped at the Princess Elizabeth's residence at the plain brick quadrate palace of Enfield, were he and his thirteen-year-old sister told that their father was dead. The children wept bitterly in each other's arms. Neither had yet faced the dangers and physical threats that their sister Mary had known. Edward was Henry's longed-for son, and despite some physical resemblance between Elizabeth and her disgraced mother, Henry had always loved her, sending her his 'heart blessings' when he was away at war in France.[3] Without their father, they were both now extremely vulnerable.

At 8 a.m. on Monday 31 January 1547, the Lord Chancellor announced Henry's death in Parliament, and an hour later Edward was proclaimed king. That afternoon, with carefully synchronised timing the new Edward VI arrived at the Tower in front of the watching crowds, together with Edward Seymour. There were brave salutes from cannon fired from the fortress and battleships on the Thames to greet the new king, but the fact that Edward was a child was a cause for national anxiety. While some in the crowds rejoiced, at least inwardly, that Henry was dead (with pro-papal Catholics claiming visions of the king surrounded by fire), most grieved that he had died too soon. Their fears would soon prove justified. Henry's executors had already organised the first meeting of the new reign. There they renamed themselves the 'Privy Council', added Edward VI's younger uncle Thomas Seymour to their number, and made Edward Seymour Protector of England.

The term 'Privy Council' had first been used in 1540 when Henry VIII had given the old, more informal council a fixed membership, a hierarchy based on the ranking of offices, a secretariat and an official record, as well as powers to summon individuals before it by legal process. It had met more or less daily for the rest of Henry's reign and had proved an extremely effective executive body.[4] Nevertheless, recreating it had broken the closed circle of equals Henry had envisaged ruling during Edward's minority. For all the terror Henry had instilled, his will had been overturned before he was even buried.

Preparations now began for Henry's funeral. On the Wednesday night, the feast of Candlemas, Henry VIII's coffin was carried from the Privy Chamber to the royal chapel. There a huge 'hearse' had been built. The term then referred to a static structure big enough to hold the coffin and to allow the principal mourners to sit within it. Each corner was adorned with the banners of saints beaten in fine gold on damask, and it held forty candles. As the coffin was set within the hearse, the light bounced off the precious stones glittering in the cover of cloth of gold.

Following medieval royal tradition, Mass was said in the royal chapel continually for the next ten days. Behind the scenes, however, was a less spiritual mood. Details were still being thrashed out about who was going to get what in the distribution of land, office and titles being used to bolster the Protectorate. Edward Seymour was to be made Duke of Somerset, the family title of the Beauforts through whom Henry VII had claimed his right to the throne. The new Protector Somerset's close ally, John Dudley, became Earl of Warwick, a title that had been held by the last male Plantagenet.

The carve-up of royal property and appointment of honours paused only as the funeral began on Sunday 13 February. Three bishops took it in turns to officiate at three Masses: the first in white in honour of the Virgin, the second in blue to celebrate the Trinity, the last in black for the requiem. But Henry was not to be buried just yet. The next day his body began a two-day journey to Windsor, with hundreds of official mourners assembling at Charing Cross at first light.

Two gentleman porters began the march at eight o'clock, on that clear winter's morning. Each carried a black stave, 'to stay, that neither cart, horse, nor man should trouble or cumber them in this passage'. Behind walked the sergeant of the vestry with his verger carrying a huge cross: then the singing children and priests of the Chapel Royal; then 250 poor men in long hooded gowns, each carrying a burning torch. These were the traditional 'beadsmen' paid to pray for the soul of the deceased.[5] They were followed by the royal standards, and behind them other mourners were grouped in ascending order of precedence. The most senior, François van der Delft, the ambassador of the Holy Roman Emperor Charles V, walked with Archbishop Cranmer close to the chariot carrying Henry's coffin. It was covered with blue velvet and cloth of gold, the colours of the Order of the Garter, and the coffin was surmounted with its life-size representation of the king, dressed as a Garter knight and wearing 'a crown imperial of inestimable value'.

Bells rang in the villages ahead to warn of the procession's arrival so that as it passed by the churches, the local curates and clerks were ready outside, dressed 'in their best ornaments' and praying loudly. The procession stopped for the night at Syon before continuing the following morning, the chariot surrounded with the banners of the Trinity, the Virgin and St George.[6] The only innovation was a new banner of 'King Henry the saint' – that is, the last Lancastrian king, Henry VI.[7] Henry VIII's attacks on the cult of saints had ensured that Henry VI was never to be beatified, but he had remained keen, nevertheless, to be associated with his pious predecessor. In his will, he asked that the tombs at Windsor of Henry VI and his Yorkist grandfather Edward IV be made 'more princely', as well as ordering his own magnificent tomb to be 'made up'.

No expense had been spared in crafting the vast marble edifice that was to mark Henry's last resting place. It reused much of the tomb that Cardinal Wolsey had commissioned for himself, including gilded bronze torch-bearing angels by Benedetto da Rovezzano, who later collaborated with Michelangelo. In addition, however, were four life-size images of Henry and Jane Seymour, as well as a statue of the king on horseback under a triumphal arch, 'of the whole stature of a goodly man and a large horse'. A further 134 figures, including St George, the Apostles and the Evangelists, 'all of brass gilt as in the pattern appeareth', were planned.[8]

At last, Henry's coffin was borne into St George's Chapel, and another Mass was said, Katherine Parr looking down through the carved windows of the Queen's Closet dressed in robes of blue velvet. The next day came the interment with sixteen tall Yeomen of the Guard lowering Henry's body into the vault he was to share with Jane Seymour. The Bishop of Winchester, Stephen Gardiner, threw earth into the grave, and Henry's chief officers and gentlemen of the Privy Chamber then broke their wands of office on their heads, casting 'them after the corpse within the pit' with tears and sighs.[9]

When Henry VIII had become king in 1509 the young prince had represented an ideal of chivalric kingship come to life: pious, romantic, athletic, musical. It was an image that still held a powerful hold over the English imagination. Much of what Henry had done since the break with Rome had been deeply unpopular, but he had worn the trappings of a king so well that he had retained the devotion of a majority of his subjects. In 1544 the bloated and crippled Henry was being described to the secretary of the Spanish nobleman Juan Esteban, Duke of Najera, as if he were still the beautiful young man of his youth. The people are 'martial, valorous . . . full of suspicion', one visitor noted. 'But towards their king they are wonderfully well affected . . . so that the most binding oath which is taken by them is that by which "the king's life" has been pledged.'[10] Even with Henry's power gone, his reputation would help protect his children. It would not, however, protect his church.

Henry's tomb was, he noted in his will, 'almost complete'. It promised to be a powerful statement of the power and glory of his godly reign. Yet it would never be built. This was due in no small part to the actions of his last weeks. Destroying the Duke of Norfolk, and his decision to exclude Bishop Gardiner from his list of executors, were acts intended to protect Edward. But it had amounted to a rout of the religious conservatives and this was to have seismic consequences for England. Henry had decreed that the king was head of the Church of England and the king defined its theology. But the king was now a nine-year-old boy entirely in the power of the reformist Somerset and his allies. The way was open for the Reformation to be driven forward by those who shared neither the tastes nor the theology represented by Henry's tomb with its angels and saints.[11] As planks were laid over Henry's open grave, the Garter King of Arms proclaimed that the king lived, now as Edward VI; and a cultural revolution was about to begin.

The nine-year-old Edward VI made his formal entry into London on the following Saturday to a pageant sequence that had been written for the coronation of the seven-year-old Henry VI. Ambassadors were lined up at the Tower where he arrived dressed in purest white and mounted on a horse trapped in crimson satin and gold damask. The Imperial ambassador greeted the boy in French, but was stopped by the Protector who told him to address the king in Latin, which he said Edward understood better. The ambassador did as he was asked, but commented in his dispatches that 'truth to tell, he seemed to me to understand one just as little as the other, although the Archbishop of Canterbury had assured me that the king knew Latin as well as he did himself'.[12]

The procession to Westminster took four hours, but the boy king barely seemed to notice the numerous pageants that had been organised by the City authorities. The only moment when Edward showed his natural childish delight was when an acrobat whizzed down a tightrope from the battlements of St Paul's, jumped about and made him laugh. The next day, at Westminster Abbey, Edward was sat on several cushions and dutifully read the new coronation oath written by Archbishop Cranmer. The protections of the clergy guaranteed in Magna Carta were deleted, and it was now for the people to consent to the king's laws, not the other way round. These powers were to be used to impose dramatic religious change, with Cranmer explaining in his address that Edward was called upon to emulate the youthful biblical king Josiah, purging his kingdom of idolatry and images as well as papal 'tyranny'.[13] While Henry's injunctions had ordered the removal from churches of images that were judged to be the objects of worship, the view was now taken that all religious images must go.

Edward soon saw the statues and pictures of saints in his rooms taken away, while beyond the palace an orgy of iconoclasm was launched. In churches rood screens, tombs with their prayers for the dead, and stained glass windows, were smashed. The Elizabethan antiquarian John Stow complained that because some of this Christian Taliban 'judged every image to be an idol', not only religious art, but even the secular thirteenth-century carvings of kings in Ludgate were broken.[14] In place of crucifixes the royal arms were painted. This emphasis on the monarch, and his divine link with God, made it all the more important for the regime that Edward be seen as the driving force behind their actions and not a mere puppet. Hence Cranmer's claim about Edward's excellent Latin, which was of a piece with the more general claim that his abilities were so remarkable 'it should seem he were already a father' to his people, rather than a boy 'not yet ten years old'.[15]

It was still more vital that Edward grow up to applaud their actions and not to condemn them. To this end Edward was sat daily before preachers whose sermons advocated the changes he saw around him, and his reformist tutor, John Cheke, was ever at his elbow 'to inform and teach him'. The fatherless Edward, told that he was now a father to his people, did his best to be the kind of father he would have wanted – loving and attentive – and he listened and learned for his subjects' sake. A new Book of Homilies was soon printed which unambiguously promoted the Lutheran teaching on justification by faith alone. By August the rosary was banned, and the Mass, so evident during Henry's lying-in-state, began to be attacked with 'much speaking against the sacrament of the altar, that some called it Jack in the box, with divers other shameful names'.[16]

The Protector Somerset foresaw no difficulties coming from Edward's half-sisters. They had been given substantial land grants, giving them incomes far in excess of £3,000 a year due to them under their father's will. Mary was dealt with particularly generously, with an income that placed her on a par with dukes.[17] Many in Europe considered that Mary, as Edward's nearest royal relative, should have been given the role of regent. Somerset did not wish to risk any dangerous accusations that her rightful place had been usurped. With this new income Mary left Katherine Parr's household in May 1547 to set up her own establishment. She made clear her anger over the religious changes, which she argued were illegal during her brother's minority, but Somerset told her he was certain that she would soon come round to the reforms, as she had previously to her father's.

Elizabeth, who was too young to be independent, remained with Katherine Parr and her life would now take a very different path from that of her sister. Mary had always been affectionate towards her. She used to write to their father praising Elizabeth and she made gifts for her, like the box she personally embroidered in silver thread.[18] But while Mary continued to write to Elizabeth, her family became the small band of servants with whom she lived, many of whom were related to each other and who had a strong emotional bond. They were often keen religious reformers, and amongst these was the most important member of the household to the princess: her governess, the jovial and sophisticated Kat Astley, who had been with Elizabeth since 1536 and was married to a kinsman of the Boleyns called John Astley.[19]

Elizabeth's stepmother, Katherine Parr, was also a loving and maternal figure. But unfortunately for Elizabeth, the same month that Mary left Katherine Parr's household the dowager queen had married in secret. Katherine Parr's choice was the man she had been in love with before she had married Henry – the Protector Somerset's charming but power-greedy younger brother, Thomas Seymour, Baron Sudeley. He had wanted a position that recognised his close blood relationship with the king, specifically the Governorship of the King's Person. This would have given him close access to the king, with all the possibilities for influence that suggests. To his frustration, however, the Protector Somerset had taken the post for himself. Seymour was now intent on promoting his place within the royal family by other means, and judged that marrying Katherine Parr would add considerably to his status. The question for the couple was how to make their marriage public.

Katherine suggested to Seymour that he persuade Edward and Mary to write letters giving their permission for the marriage and later make the announcement that it had taken place. Both were extremely fond of Katherine, but Mary was deeply shocked by their plans. It was 'strange news', she told Seymour, her father being 'as yet very ripe in mine own remembrance'.[20] Seymour had better luck with Edward who was easily persuaded into doing what was asked of him. The letter proved no help to the couple when the marriage became public, however. Katherine's behaviour in marrying within five months of Henry VIII's death was considered still more sexually incontinent than Margaret Tudor, Queen of Scots' remarriage within a year of the death of James IV. Their manipulation of Edward also meant their future access to him was to be limited.

The marriage Katherine Parr had chosen for love was furthermore to prove a short and tragic one. By May of the following year, 1548, when she was six months pregnant, she was filled with fears that if she were to die in childbirth Seymour would replace her with Elizabeth. Kat Astley had been complaining that Seymour would visit the princess in her bedchamber dressed only in his nightshirt and would try to kiss her good morning. At first Katherine Parr had made light of it, but vulnerable in her pregnant state, she became more suspicious about his intentions. Elizabeth left her household the week after Pentecost, with Katherine Parr warning her that her good name was at risk. The princess did not need reminding that as the daughter of the infamous Anne Boleyn, she had still more reason to be careful than most women. Shocked and humiliated, Elizabeth wrote to Katherine afterwards, assuring her that she had listened to her advice, 'albeit I answered little, I weighed it more deeply when you said you would warn me of all evils you should hear of me'.[21] But she would never see the sensual and once-ebullient Katherine again. Henry VIII's last wife died shortly after giving birth that summer. The baby was a girl, destined to die before her second birthday.[22] And Thomas Seymour was, indeed, soon plotting to marry Elizabeth.

The law against unauthorised marriage into the royal family, introduced by Henry VIII in 1536, had been repealed in November 1547. But even if what Thomas Seymour planned was not treason, Elizabeth's place in the succession remained subject to her marrying in accordance with the wishes of the Privy Council. Elizabeth was also mindful of what Katherine Parr had said to her when they last met. She refused even to write to Seymour to commiserate the death of the queen, fearful that it might be taken as an encouragement. Elizabeth was not, however, fully in control of her adult servants. Kat Astley began working with Elizabeth's cofferer (or accountant), Thomas Parry, to arrange the princess' marriage, even discussing Elizabeth's property with Seymour, without her permission. This stopped only in January 1549 when Seymour was arrested.

When Elizabeth's terrified servants were questioned, Seymour's visits to her bedchamber were described. Kat Astley and Thomas Parry also confessed their role in pushing for a marriage. But each made it clear that Elizabeth had refused to be drawn into their plans. The young princess, who was emerging as brave and quick-witted, also remained consistent in her denials that she had intended to marry anyone without the council's permission. She even pleaded for Kat Astley, 'who hath taken great labour and pain in bringing of me up in learning and honesty', claiming she had heard Kat 'many times say that she would never have me marry' without the council's consent.[23] But if her position was safe, for Seymour it was a different matter. He had plotted not only to marry Elizabeth, but also to overthrow Somerset. Poor Edward, who was fond of his uncle Thomas, was obliged to give his assent to the Act of Attainder that condemned him on 10 March 1549. Seymour was executed ten days later.

In a famous but invented story, when Elizabeth heard the news of Seymour's death she commented that he had been 'a man of much wit and very little judgement'.[24] Elizabeth's actual views on Seymour were expressed in writing in a book of psalms and prayers, which still survives at Elton Hall near Peterborough. It had once belonged to Katherine Parr, and is inscribed with words of affection from Henry VIII to his last wife: 'Remember this writer/When you do pray/For he is yours/None can say nay.' He had signed it 'H' with a superimposed 'R' for Rex. On a separate page Elizabeth now wrote in Latin, 'Vanity of Vanities, and the height of Vanity. T. Seymour.' Beneath was a 'T' and superimposed 'R' in mimicry of the signature her father had used.[25] Elizabeth believed ambition had destroyed Thomas Seymour. It would also destroy his brother.

27

MARY IN DANGER

THE PRIESTS IN MARY'S CHAPEL WORE VESTMENTS OF WHITE AND gold on Whit Sunday 10 June 1549. The Protectorate – Somerset, Archbishop Cranmer and their allies – had banned ashes on Ash Wednesday and palms on Palm Sunday. Every church candle, save two on the altar, was snuffed out by political decree. Now, a new religious service had been commanded. Written in English it reflected the view that Christ was not present, body and blood, in consecrated bread and wine. This was an attack on the heart and soul of Catholic belief. Mary had been arguing that her father's religious settlement could not be overturned while Edward was a minor. Central to this was the Mass. For Mary the time had now come for an act of defiance. The full Henrician Mass was being celebrated in public at her house of Kenninghall in Norfolk according to the Sarum Rite, said in the British Isles for 500 years.

Across England other congregations listened to the words from the new Book of Common Prayer with growing anger. They had been taught to obey royal decrees as a religious duty, for God had appointed the king to rule over them. Yet their king was only a boy, and what was being asked of them was sacrilegious. The following day, at Sampford Courtenay in Devon, villagers forced their parish priest to say Mass once more. Their rebellion spread rapidly and by 2 July there was violence across the Midlands, the Home Counties, Essex, Norfolk and Yorkshire, while in the west Exeter was under siege. Only ten days later Norwich was also threatened, with an army of 16,000 rebels at its gates, but there it was largely those receptive to the new religious ideas who had joined the rising. The great men who had benefited from the lands confiscated from the church under Henry VIII had continued to expand their estates, and were enclosing the common land that saved the landless from starvation when paid work dried up. 'The pride of great men is now intolerable, but our condition miserable', ran the Rebel's Complaint; 'We will rather take arms, and mix heaven and earth together than endure so great a cruelty.'

In the end foreign mercenaries were paid to crush the rebel armies. Some 2,500 farm boys were killed in the west and 3,000 in the east, where John Dudley, Earl of Warwick used Germans used to particularly dirty and difficult work. As a percentage of the population the deaths that summer are equivalent to the entire English military casualties of World War II. It left much of the country cowed, but come October Somerset realised he was also under threat from erstwhile allies on the council. They blamed the scale of the risings on the duke delaying the use of force and ignoring advice, even from Henry VIII's former private secretary, William Paget, who had helped plot his rise to power as the old king lay dying.

The unfolding coup was a frightening experience for Edward, who had just turned twelve. Somerset told the boy that the plotters would kill them both if they succeeded in their plans. Edward was seen riding from Hampton Court to Windsor with his uncle, waving a little sword from his horse, begging those on the roadside, 'My vassals will you help me against those who want to kill me?' When the guards came to Windsor to arrest Somerset and entered Edward's chamber he reacted with terror. He was soon reassured, however, and there were no plans, as yet, to execute Somerset, who was lodged in the Tower. He was merely replaced by a Privy Council now chaired by John Dudley, who would be named Lord President a few months later.[1]

The son of Edmund Dudley, one of the most notorious of Henry

VII's henchmen, John Dudley was a devoted family man adored by his wife and children. He could, however, also be extremely intimidating. He had clawed his way up the greasy pole in the shadow of his father's execution at the outset of Henry VIII's reign and it was later said that he 'had such a head that he seldom went about anything, but he conceived first three or four purposes beforehand'.[2] The Imperial ambassador judged him a pragmatist and hoped the overthrow of the Protector would be good for Mary. She told him doubtfully on 7 November that 'the councillors have not as yet pressed her or exacted from her anything against her will . . . and so . . . she is awaiting the upshot of the matter, not without apprehension'.[3] Meanwhile, at Mary's turreted house of Beaulieu in Essex on 26 November, she prepared to receive her cousin, Frances Brandon, who was accompanied by her daughters.[4]

A slim, elegant woman, Frances was the elder daughter of Mary's late aunt, the French queen, and only a few months younger than Mary.[5] She had served in the princess' household when her eldest child, Lady Jane Grey, was a baby. Mary recalled with gratitude the support Frances' mother had given Katherine of Aragon against Anne Boleyn. But Frances found the arguments of Swiss and German religious reformers inspiring and she was amongst those who most welcomed the religious changes that Mary opposed. Having carefully erased all mentions of the Pope and Thomas Becket from a Book of Hours she had inherited from her mother, she now found all the images of saints and devotions of the Virgin so distasteful that she would give it away the following year.[6] Her daughters Jane, aged twelve, Katherine nine, and Mary Grey, four, were all being raised as what we could now term Protestants and she was particularly close to Jane, who she helped with her studies.[7] An exceptionally clever child, Jane was also proving passionate about her faith. According to the Protestant martyrologist John Foxe, Jane even deliberately insulted Mary's belief in the Real Presence of Christ in the Eucharist while she was staying at Beaulieu.

On the altar in an antechapel, at right angles to the main chapel at Beaulieu, there was the exposition of the Blessed Sacrament: that is, the consecrated host was displayed after the Mass in a golden sunburst stand known as a monstrance.[8] For Mary the host was the transformed body of Christ. Jane saw it as nothing more than the idolatrous worship of a piece of unleavened bread. When one of Mary's servants dropped to one knee in genuflection as they passed the chapel, Jane asked her sarcastically 'whether the Lady Mary were there or not?' The servant retorted that she had made her curtsey 'to Him that made us all'. 'Why', Jane commented acidly, 'how can He be there that made us all, [when] the baker made him?'[9]

On 29 November, three days after Frances' arrival at Beaulieu with her daughters, their father, Harry Grey, Marquess of Dorset, was appointed to the Privy Council. Described as 'an illustrious and widely loved nobleman', Harry Grey was much admired for his learning and his patronage of the learned. But he had all the arrogance of the ideologue and the Imperial ambassador described him as being without good sense.[10] He had never previously been trusted with a council place, and that John Dudley had now given him one was taken, correctly, as a signal that Dudley had decided to base his regime on the most enthusiastic reformers.[11] Edward VI, like his mother Jane Seymour, was by nature keen to please, and Dudley had discovered that Edward's tutors had been successful in raising a reformist prince. An enthusiasm for further reform would help him to gain Edward's trust. Within a month orders had gone out to destroy all Latin service books. By mid-January the Imperial ambassador was expressing fears that the new regime would 'never permit the Lady Mary to live in peace . . . in order to exterminate [the Catholic] religion'.[12]

Over the next few months reform was driven fast and hard, with Harry Grey and John Dudley spearheading action on the council, along with Katherine Parr's brother, William, Marquess of Northampton. Statutory approval was given for clergy to marry, stone altars destroyed and replaced with simple wooden Communion tables, organs were ripped out of churches and elaborate music expunged, while in Oxford the Edwardian bonfires appear to have consumed nearly every book in the university library.[13] Mary also found that she was under attack for continuing to have Mass said publicly in her chapels, but she was determined to hold fast. Who could better defend the Catholic beliefs of her brother's subjects than the most senior adult royal in England? She could not be as easily disposed of as the peasants of Norfolk and Devon. She had to show courage and hope that one day, soon, her brother would overthrow his erstwhile guardians.

Harry Grey and William Parr were at Edward's side that Christmas of 1550, when Mary came to court to see the king. At thirteen Edward was growing up and like his father dressed magnificently, favouring reds, whites and violets embroidered with pearls.[14] This helped disguise the fact he was small for his age, slightly built and, like Richard III, he had one shoulder distinctly higher than the other. He may have inherited scoliosis with his Yorkist blood. Edward had once told Mary that she was the person he 'loved best'. But instead of fraternal kisses, Mary was subjected to a tirade, with Edward demanding to know why she still held the Mass in her chapels. Shocked, she burst into tears. This, in turn, prompted Edward to cry. He would have preferred that she understood her duty to him better and that they need not quarrel. He found it painful: that much was obvious to Mary, who was convinced that Edward had been put up to making his comments.

The following year Mary continued to use her influence to defend her father's religious settlement – and her influence was considerable. To her servants and affinity Mary was a quasi-sacred figure, who cared for them body and soul as their sovereign princess, sitting before them daily under a cloth of estate, in rooms hung with tapestries that boasted her royal lineage. Of Mary's four grandparents, three had been reigning monarchs and all were the senior representative of their royal house.

She was, above all, heir to the throne. In March 1551, when Edward called Mary to Westminster for a further dressing-down, she arrived in London in force 'with fifty knights and gentlemen in velvet coats and chains of gold afore her, and after her four score gentlemen and ladies'. Each of them carried their banned rosary beads, prominently displayed.[15]

Mary soon discovered, however, that she had failed to intimidate the regime. Edward would turn fourteen that year, the age at which a boy could marry under common law. John Dudley and the council had decided this would mark his majority. The implication would be that she was no longer defying them, but that she was defying the king. At Easter 1551 several of Mary's friends were arrested after attending Mass in her house. By July she feared she was on the point of being imprisoned, or even murdered. Matters came to a head in August 1551, just as Edward began attending his first council meetings. Three of Mary's servants were ordered to go to Beaulieu and prevent other members of the household from hearing Mass. They refused and were duly imprisoned. Mary was obliged, nevertheless, to give way. As she noted, if they arrested her chaplains too she could not hear Mass, however defiant she remained. Mary made it clear, however, that she would lay her head on the block before she heard the Prayer Book service.

Come the autumn the aggressive attacks on Mary began, mysteriously, to recede. The reasons were not immediately obvious, but behind the scenes John Dudley was facing a threat on which he was obliged to focus his attention. Edward had been ill over the summer and, although he had soon recovered, it was a reminder that Mary remained only a heartbeat away from the crown. There was anger amongst the political elite over the way the heir to the throne was being treated. The Protector Somerset, who had been released from the Tower in February 1550, was hoping to take advantage of this to bring Dudley's regime down. Dudley intended to deny Somerset that support and strike first.

During the second week of October the young king was given the shocking news that his uncle Somerset was planning to murder Dudley and Katherine Parr's brother, William Parr. Edward promptly empowered Dudley further, by creating him Duke of Northumberland, his ally Harry Grey, Duke of Suffolk, and William Parr's brother-in-law, William Herbert, Earl of Pembroke. William Parr already had the great title of Marquess of Northampton. Five days later Edward saw his uncle arrive at court at Whitehall, noting in his diary that he was 'later than he was wont and by himself'. Edward then added the chilling comment, 'After dinner he was apprehended.' The former Protector was returned to the Tower, and this time he would not be released. Somerset was to be executed early in the following year.[16]

Mary soon found she was again being invited to court. The pretext was a reception given in November for Mary of Guise, the widow of her cousin James V, who had died in 1542. Mary declined the invitation, perhaps because she feared being asked to attend a religious service with the king. Instead, Edward's diary records that he sat on Mary of Guise's right, under a shared cloth of state, while on the other side were his cousins Frances Brandon and Margaret Douglas. Frances was often at court, because her husband, Harry Grey, was regularly at the king's side, but Margaret and her husband Lennox had also maintained cordial relations with Edward and his councillors. They were discreet about their conservative religious inclinations and Lennox was useful to Edward, running an effective network of spies in Scotland.[17] The women dressed to flatter Mary of Guise, in the Scottish style with their hair loose, 'flounced and curled and double curled'.

Strikingly, the princess Elizabeth was no more present at the reception than her elder sister, Mary. But she made her presence felt when she did appear at court, by dressing so plainly that it was 'to the shame of them all'.[18] Edward had recently received a work promoting modesty of dress in women, and Elizabeth was keen to remind him that, in contrast to Mary, she was the good Protestant princess her reformist governess had raised her to be, as well as (less convincingly) modest and chaste. It did her little good. While Edward noted Lady Jane Grey's attendance at the reception, he made no mention of his half-sister's presence on any of the days when Mary of Guise was being welcomed and entertained. It seems he was not encouraged to be any closer to her than he was to Mary.

That Christmas, after Mary of Guise had left, there were further entertainments to be enjoyed at court with plays, masques, tournaments and a tilt on the last day, 6 January, which Edward enjoyed enormously. John Dudley had ensured Edward had been taught to ride and handle weapons, and Edward had begun 'arming and tilting, managing horses and delighting in every sort of exercise', although he did not yet take part in the competitions.[19] Dudley was extremely astute in his handling of Edward. According to the French ambassador, Edward revered Dudley almost as if he was his father. Yet Dudley was careful to emphasise that, as Lord President of the king's council, he was only a senior member of a team working for Edward, whom he involved ever more deeply in matters of state.

In March a core of the king's senior servants began to meet with him each Tuesday to brief him on policy matters. High on the agenda was the work that was about to begin on a new and more radical prayer book, which would rename the Eucharist the Lord's Supper, have Communion tables brought into the church chancel or nave so people could stand around them as for a communal supper, and where they were given bread in their hands rather than unleavened wafers in their mouths. It would also rewrite the baptism and confirmation service, and remove all mention of prayers for the dead at burial services. Edward's cousin Margaret Douglas remained at court, but in early April there was a measles and smallpox outbreak and on 7 April she asked permission to return to Yorkshire.[20] Even Edward had fallen ill, but happily by the 12th, when Margaret was heading north, Edward was reporting that 'we have shaken that quite away', and in the summer Edward was hunting again.

That October, when Edward turned fifteen, a famous Italian astrologer was invited to cast the king's horoscope.[21] He predicted Edward would reign a further forty years and would achieve much. The revised Book of Common Prayer, published in November 1552, was to be followed by the publication of forty-two articles of faith that would become the basis for the Elizabethan thirty-nine articles that today remain the founding beliefs of the Church of England.[22] The future would not be untroubled: the country was suffering dire financial problems, stemming in part from the wars of the 1540s against France and then Scotland. Cranmer and Dudley had fallen out over the execution of Somerset and the push for a further confiscation of church assets. But the longer-term prospects were bright: it was, the astrologer assured Edward, all in the stars.

28

THE LAST TUDOR KING

EDWARD HAD A PERSISTENT COUGH IN JANUARY 1553 THAT HE WAS having trouble shaking off.[1] The fifteen-year-old king recalled, however, that he had had a 'grave sickness' in the summer of 1550, and both measles and smallpox in April 1552. He would surely soon recover again.[2] The cough had worsened when, on Saturday 7 February, Elizabeth wrote a letter to her brother, telling him that while on her way to see him on the Thursday, she had been stopped on the road and told he was too ill to give her an audience. She alluded to gossip that she had lost his favour. She was sure, she said, this was not true, and whatever others thought, Elizabeth noted, 'your grace's goodwill . . . I trust will stick by me'.[3] There is no record of a reply.

Mary, who had arrived in London the previous day attended by a retinue 200 strong, had been better treated than Elizabeth. John Dudley had met her on the outskirts of the city along with a number of knights and gentlemen who had escorted her to Whitehall. There she was entertained with great magnificence, and a few days later her ailing brother had agreed to see her. Edward had maintained the ban on the Mass in Mary's private chapels, despite the Imperial ambassador pleading with him 'several times to let my sister Mary have her Mass'.[4] Whatever passed between brother and sister that February he was determined not to change his mind on this, and may have tried, unsuccessfully, to change hers. On 21 February

John Dudley called in one of her leading servants, for another dressing-down on the subject.

Edward began to feel better, at last, in April 1553 when the weather got warmer. Nevertheless, the time had come, he felt, to practise writing a will before drawing up a more formal document in the event that he should fall seriously ill again. Headed 'My Device for the Succession', his efforts covered barely more than one piece of paper, but its contents were explosive.

The first decision Edward made was to pass over the claims of his sisters, Mary and Elizabeth.[5] Dynastic issues took second place for Edward to religious ideology and, as he later admitted, he feared Mary would undo the religious reforms of his reign, not least his replacement of the Mass with the Lord's Supper and the destruction of images. Since there was no precedent for ignoring Mary's claim on grounds of her Catholic faith, he chose to use her illegitimacy under the Act of Succession of 1536 as the legal basis for his actions. With Elizabeth described as illegitimate in the same Act, it was necessary that she also be passed over. But in any case, as Edward later reminded his lawyers, Elizabeth's mother had died a traitor to his father.[6]

Edward then looked to other heirs of their Tudor grandfather, Henry VII. It was said that the first Tudor king had hoped that in the event of the failure of his son's line England would look to the heirs of his daughter, Margaret of Scots. But Margaret Tudor's senior heir, Mary, Queen of Scots, was a Catholic and betrothed to the French dauphin. The next in line, Margaret Douglas, was, if not a papal Catholic, then certainly no Protestant, and her husband had been a Scot and a Frenchman before he became an Englishman. Both had been ignored in Henry VIII's will and so a precedent had also been set for ignoring them now, as Edward did. This left the heirs of his junior aunt, Henry VIII's younger sister, the French queen, and her husband, Charles Brandon.

The French queen's eldest daughter, Frances, was a staunch Protestant. But Henry's will had bypassed her in favour of her daughters: Lady Jane, Katherine and Mary Grey. In any case, Edward wanted a male heir in line with the precedents for royal women transmitting their rights to their sons. Edward therefore left his throne to the sons Frances might yet have (she was thirty-five), followed by the sons of her daughters in line of succession. Failing the Grey line, the crown was to pass through Frances' fifteen-year-old niece, Margaret Clifford, the sole heir of Frances' younger sister, Eleanor, who had died in 1547.[7] Having written the document, it must have seemed unlikely to Edward that it would ever see the light of day, but he was not yet well.

On 11 April Edward travelled by barge from Westminster to the airy rooms of Greenwich Palace, where he hoped he would continue his recovery. Those around him had to consider, however, what would happen if he did not. Under the terms of his will the throne would be vacant until a male heir was born, with Frances acting as governor.[8] An empty throne was likely to attract the predatory attentions of the King of France, acting in favour of his future daughter-in-law, Mary, Queen of Scots, and of the emperor Charles V acting for his cousin, the princess Mary. As the Tudor claimant, and accepted as Edward's heir for a decade, the princess was by far the stronger candidate, and if she became queen there was every reason to suppose she would revenge herself on those who had bullied her for years and overthrown the Mass. To prevent her accession a male heir was needed as soon as possible, and to this end all the women of royal blood would have to be married. Even if a son wasn't born in time, the marriages could be used to bind the leading families of the regime to a common purpose: preventing Mary's accession.

According to Edward's Secretary of State, Sir William Cecil, it was William Parr's wife who suggested Frances' eldest daughter, Lady Jane Grey, be married to Dudley's fourth son, Lord Guildford Dudley.[9] William Parr had no legitimate children and Guildford was the elder of two unmarried sons available to Dudley.[10] The Lord President proved enthusiastic. Unlike the other leading figures in Edward's regime – William Parr (brother of the late queen, Katherine Parr), William Herbert (the widower of Anne Parr, the late queen's sister) and Harry Grey (whose wife Frances was Henry VIII's niece) – John Dudley was not a member of the extended royal family. The previous year he had tried, and failed, to pressure Eleanor Brandon's widower, the Earl of Cumberland, into marrying his daughter Margaret Clifford to Guildford. He was delighted his son was to make this still greater match, and it was one to which Harry Grey soon agreed.

Lady Jane Grey, who was about to be sixteen, had matured into a remarkable young woman, only averagely attractive, but with far better than average brains. She spoke Latin, Greek, French, Italian and some Hebrew.[11] She was a patron of the first pastor of London's 'Strangers Church' for European Protestant exiles, and was admired amongst a circle of clever Protestant women that included William Cecil's intellectual wife, Mildred. There is no evidence to support the later romanticised gossip amongst Italians that Jane married at the 'insistence of her mother and the threats of her father'.[12] It was usual for the daughters of the nobility to have an arranged marriage made around their sixteenth birthday, and even if Edward lived, Jane's marriage had great promise. When her father died his title, Duke of Suffolk, was likely to pass to Guildford, who was close to her age and remembered by contemporaries as a 'comely, virtuous and goodly gentleman'.[13]

Poor Edward, meanwhile, found his health was deteriorating once more. On 28 April 1553, as the Imperial ambassador recorded the news of Jane's betrothal, he also reported that every day Edward's agonising cough was growing worse. 'The matter he ejects from his mouth is sometimes coloured a greenish yellow and black, sometimes pink, like the colour of blood', the ambassador noted. 'His doctors and physicians are perplexed and do not know what to make of it. They feel sure the king has no chance of recovery unless his health improves in the next month.'[14] The symptoms and Edward's medical history suggest he had contracted tuberculosis in 1550. It was then suppressed by his immune system and reactivated by the measles he suffered in the spring of 1552.[15] Mary's allies at court were keeping her informed of the developing situation – and so was John Dudley, who in a remarkable turnaround was also now emphasising Mary's right to her full arms as Princess of England.[16] In September 1551 Dudley's ally William Parr had told the Imperial ambassador not to refer to Mary as 'princess' but merely as 'the king's sister'. This had been followed by Somerset's attempt to ally with Mary's sympathisers against the Dudley regime. The ambassador suggested Dudley was now attempting to conciliate Mary in order to forestall further trouble – and indeed it appears this exactly explains Dudley's actions, for something else was also being done in that regard. Mary had been obliged to surrender lands to the Crown in December 1552, before the serious nature of Edward's illness was understood. In May, ostensibly in compensation for these, she received prime lands, castles and manors worth far in excess of what she had lost. They included the royal castle of Hertford and the manor castle of Framlingham, which had been the principal seat of Thomas Howard, 3rd Duke of Norfolk, before he was sent to the Tower in 1546.[17]

John Dudley and his allies were confident Mary would accept the overthrow of her father's will by her brother, just as she had accepted those parts overthrown by the Protectorate in 1547, with land grants once again being used to sweeten the pill. As for Elizabeth, the Imperial ambassador heard that John Dudley's eldest son would be divorced so he would be free to marry her. But from Elizabeth herself there was silence. Like Mary she was playing her cards close to her chest, watching and waiting on events. Edward's Secretary of State, who also happened to be the surveyor of her estates, William Cecil, may have been her eyes and ears at court.

At Greenwich on 10 May there was a brief and brilliant distraction from the gloom cast over the court by Edward's illness. The Company of Merchant Adventurers had sent three ships down the river to Greenwich to salute the king before they headed to seek a north-west passage to China. When news reached the palace of the ships' approach, 'the courtiers came running out and the common people flocked together standing very thick upon the shore, the Privy Council they looked out of the windows of the court and the rest ran by to the tops of the towers.'[18] The ships were being towed by rowboats filled with sailors dressed in blue, while other sailors stood on the ships' decks waving to their friends. There was no sign of the king, however, and as the guns fired their salutes before the ships sailed away on their voyage of discovery, he continued to lie in agony in his rooms.

Two days later the Imperial ambassador reported that it was considered certain Edward would die, and to contain the rumours that this was the case, three people who were overheard talking of it had 'their ears torn off'. The marriages or betrothals of all the royal women who were still single, and not passed over in Edward's will, were now to go ahead. The first were those of Lady Jane Grey and her pretty blonde sister, the twelve-year-old Katherine Grey. They took place during the last week in May, with Katherine's groom, the fifteen-year-old son of William Herbert, brought from his sickbed to the ceremony.[19] Edward sent gifts 'of rich ornaments and jewels', but it was becoming rapidly evident that he would not live long enough to see Jane or Katherine bear a son.

About a week later Edward made a small but important change to his will. He drew a line through the provision that Frances would rule as governor if he died before any male heirs were born, and inserted two short phrases above the line. The throne was to pass to Frances' male heirs, but in the absence of such issue 'before my death' the throne was to pass to Lady Jane Grey 'and her' heirs male. Since Frances was not pregnant and had no sons, she was, effectively, ruled out as governor with the throne passing directly to Jane as queen regnant. The doctors suggested that Edward might live until September when Parliament was due to assemble, and his will could then be confirmed by statute. But since his survival for that length of time was uncertain, Edward summoned his senior judges to ratify his will immediately.

Edward could no longer hold down food and was weakened by a violent bout of fever. Nevertheless, when his judges arrived he gathered what strength remained to give them his instructions and secure his legacy of a Protestant England. The judges would later claim they only drew up the document after threats issued by John Dudley. But one way or another, they gave the will legal force, and Edward then summoned Frances to see him.[20] She had little choice but to accept his decisions, as others would now be asked to do. On 21 June the nobility and leading officials were all asked to sign the document the judges had drawn up. It drew attention to the illegitimacy of Edward's sisters, who were, Edward noted, only of 'the half blood', and gave stark warnings of the dangers of their marrying foreigners.[21] By contrast there was praise for the Grey sisters, described as 'natural born here within the realm, and . . . very honourably brought up and exercised in good and godly learning, and other noble virtues'.[22] The Privy Council, Archbishop Cranmer, the officers of the household, civic dignitaries, and twenty-two peers all signed it and swore a solemn oath to uphold its provisions.

Elizabeth's acceptance of the will was to be bought, as Mary's had been, or so Dudley believed. On 26 June he acquired a reversionary interest in several of Elizabeth's estates, including her largest land-holding at Missenden, Buckinghamshire; this gave him first refusal if the property became available either through the death of the owner or a proposed change of ownership, such as reversion to the Crown.[23] Elizabeth would only have agreed to this if she had been promised something better in exchange. We don't know what this was, but her first biographer, William Camden, recalled she was offered 'a certain sum of money and great possession of land' to accept Jane Grey as queen. Elizabeth had chosen to make the best of a bad situation.[24]

With the September parliament less than three months away, doctors and faith healers were ordered to do anything they could to keep Edward alive. This included, reputedly, dosing him with arsenic, and Edward's subjects began saying that John Dudley was poisoning the king and intended to hand the country over to the French.[25] It was clearly in France's interest that Charles V's cousin, Mary Tudor, not inherit, and the rumours grew after Dudley was seen entering the residence of the French ambassador.[26] What he actually sought was the promise of French backing in the event that the emperor attacked England on Mary's behalf when Edward died. The French were happy to give it.

On Sunday 2 July the contents of the king's will were signalled to the public for the first time, with church services excluding the usual prayers for Mary and Elizabeth.

The following day, as Mary travelled to London to see her brother, she was warned Edward's death was imminent. On 5 July news reached John Dudley that Mary was heading away from court for her house, Kenninghall, at the heart of her estates in Norfolk. From there she could flee to Flanders and the emperor. Dudley was persuaded to play it safe and ordered his third son, Guildford's elder brother, Lord Robert Dudley, to pursue Mary with a small number of horsemen and bring her to London.

Edward was fading fast. Between eight and nine in the evening of 6 July he sighed 'I feel faint.' Gathered into the arms of a gentleman servant, he began to pray: 'Lord have mercy on me and take my spirit.' Edward's reputation is that of a cold boy, remembered for signing the death warrants of his uncles, and whose religious beliefs associate him with the dour Puritanism of the Commonwealth a century later. But what little we glimpse of Edward the boy, rather than Edward the king, is of an affectionate youth prone to hero worship, keen to do the right thing, and with a boyish enthusiasm for funny acrobats, exciting sports and adventure. As Edward drew his last breaths, far away in the North Sea two of the three ships that had fired their salutes in farewell in May had scattered in the winds; but one captain heading into the unknown held his course, until he 'sailed so far that he came at last to the place where he found no night at all, but a continual light and brightness of the sun shining on the mighty sea'.[27] Edward's suffering was over and the last Tudor king was dead. But the Tudor women were not finished yet.

Henry VIII is depicted looking straight at the viewer with the late Jane Seymour, and their son and heir, Edward. To the left and right are the princesses Mary and Elizabeth. It has been suggested that the view behind them hints at a possible life outside the royal palaces, with marriages and households of their own.

(*Left*) Katherine of Aragon.

(*Right*) Anne Boleyn's daughter Elizabeth wore this ring after she became queen.

(*Left*) Dress was important at the Tudor court with Anne Boleyn one of its most fashionably dressed women. By contrast the ugly German costume worn here by Anne of Cleves made her repulsive to Henry VIII.

(*Right*) Jane Seymour by Hans Holbein.

(*Left*) The jewellery in this portrait has prompted historians to claim it is Katherine Howard, but it has also been suggested that it is a portrait of Margaret Douglas, and certainly it resembles portraits of her as an older woman. (*Right*) Katherine Parr, attributed to Master John.

Mary Tudor by Master John.
The physical similarities suggest the
Tudor sisters have more in common
than history has credited.

A portrait of Elizabeth in a crimson
dress is listed in an inventory of
Henry VIII's possessions at his
death so this picture may date
from as early as 1546.

The infant Edward Tudor, dressed
to mimic his father and offering
an apparent blessing on the viewer
like the Christ child. The Latin
inscription urges him to imitate
or even surpass the achievements
of his father.

PARVVLE PATRISSA, PATRIS, VIRTVTIS ET HÆRES
ESTO, NIHIL MAIVS MAXIMVS ORBIS HABET.
GNATVM VIX POSSVNT COELVM ET NATVRA DEDISSE.
HVIVS QVEM PATRIS, VICTVS HONORET HONOS,
ÆQVATO TANTVM, TANTI TV FACTA PARENTIS,
VOTA HOMINVM, VIX QVO PROGREDIANTVR, HABENT
VINCITO, VICISTI, QVOT REGES PRISCVS ADORAT
ORBIS, NEC TE QVI VINCERE POSSIT, ERIT.

Edward VI, attributed to William Scrots. Behind the public image of the godly prince was a boy keen to please, prone to hero worship, anxious to do the right thing and fond of boyish pursuits.

This famous nineteenth-century painting of Jane Grey's execution encapsulates the myth of Jane as an innocent virgin, sacrificed on the altar of adult political ambition. In reality Jane was a religious leader and no mere victim.

Mary I, already drawn and ill, is here wearing La Pelegrina, the largest pearl in the world at that time, and a gift from her husband Philip of Spain. It would later be bought by the actor Richard Burton for Elizabeth Taylor. Mary holds the red rose of the House of Lancaster from whom she and her husband both claimed descent.

The earliest known portrait of an English mother and her child, this depicts Lady Katherine Grey – the heir to Queen Elizabeth I under Henry VIII's will – and her son, Lord Beauchamp, as Madonna and child.

Elizabeth I's face is a mask of beauty and eternal youth, although when the Rainbow portrait was painted she was already an old woman, missing several teeth.

This portrait was sold in the nineteenth century as Lady Jane Grey/Dudley. The style of the costume, however, dates the portrait much earlier. If it is an English court lady, as is the current view (despite the style being French), then it may well be Margaret Douglas, which would fit with the sitter's buttons marked with the initial D. Like her ancestress and namesake, Margaret Beaufort, whom she in many ways resembled, Margaret Douglas has suffered from the absence of authenticated portraits of her in her youth.

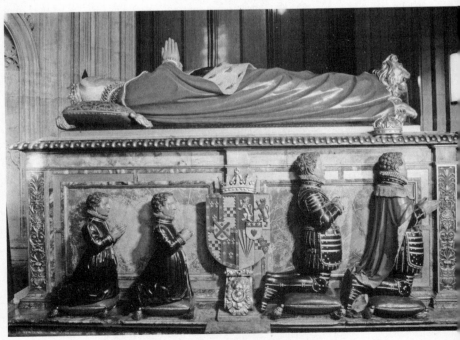

Funeral effigy of Margaret Douglas and four of her eight children.

When this limning of Mary, Queen of Scots was painted by Hilliard she had already been Elizabeth's prisoner for over a decade.

The spoilt, vicious, doomed, Henry Lord Darnley – later King of Scots – and his brother Charles.

James VI of Scotland, aged twenty.

Arbella Stuart, child of Margaret Douglas' son Charles Stuart, and Bess of Hardwick's daughter, Elizabeth Cavendish.

This seventeenth-century family tree depicts the Tudor descent of James VI
of Scotland and I of England.

Part Three

SETTING SUN:
THE TUDOR QUEENS

Let men that receive of women authority, honour, or office, be
most assuredly persuaded, that in so maintaining that usurped
power, they declare themselves enemies to God.

JOHN KNOX, *THE FIRST BLAST OF THE TRUMPET AGAINST THE
MONSTROUS REGIMENT OF WOMEN* (1558)

29

NINE DAYS

AT TWO O'CLOCK ON THE HIGH-SUMMER AFTERNOON OF MONDAY 10 July 1553, Jane Grey's barge arrived at the Watergate near the Tower. A sparse crowd was gathering to watch her formal procession to the fortress, which she would claim as all monarchs did on the eve of their coronation. Her young husband Guildford Dudley was with her, along with her mother and ladies, while other members of the nobility followed behind in their barges. As Jane reached the top of the steps John Dudley and his fellow councillors greeted her. A famous account given by the Italian merchant and knight Baptista Spinola adds an intimate description of the sixteen-year-old as the procession gathered and began to make its way slowly and with due pomp down the streets:

This Jane is very short and thin, but prettily shaped and graceful. She has small features and a well-made nose the mouth flexible and the lips red. The eyebrows are arched and darker than her hair, which is nearly red. Her eyes are sparkling and light hazel. I stood so long near Her Grace, that I noticed her colour was good, but freckled. When she smiled she showed her teeth, which are white and sharp. In all, a *graziosa persona* and *animata* [animated]. She wore a dress of green velvet stamped with gold, with large sleeves. Her headdress was a white coif with many jewels. She walked under a canopy, her mother carrying her long train, and her husband Guilfo [Guildford] walking by her, dressed all in white and gold, a very tall strong boy with light hair, who paid her much attention. The new queen was mounted on very high chopines [clogs] to make her look much taller, which were concealed by her robes, as she is very small and short. Many ladies followed, with noblemen, but this lady is very *heretica* and has never heard Mass, and some great people did not come into the procession for that reason.

It paints a vivid picture of Jane before the great gates of the Tower closed behind her. Unfortunately, like so much about Jane's life and reign, Spinola's report is a clever mixture of fact and fiction. The description of a smiling girl was composed in 1909 by a historical novelist turned biographer called Richard Davey and has been slavishly quoted by historians ever since.[1] In describing a teenager so small she has to wear stacked shoes to give her height, he paints a picture of innocence and vulnerability that chimes with myths concerning Jane Grey developed over centuries. They depict her in the appealing guise of a child victim who is never a player in her own fate. The real Jane was a far more interesting, as well as more ambivalent figure, than the idealised girl of this tradition.

On the eve of her coronation Jane Grey was less than two years younger than Henry VIII had been when he became king. She had not sought the crown that Edward had bequeathed her, but she believed that the Mass, for which Mary risked so much, was evil. Since only God could make a king, it can have been of little surprise to Jane that she had been chosen over Mary.[2] The gathering crowd watching her procession were puzzled, however, not only that Mary (who had been accepted as Edward's heir for a decade) had been passed over, but so had Jane's mother, who was carrying her train. If Frances Brandon had transmitted her place in line of succession to a son this would have been understood and accepted – Margaret

Beaufort had transmitted her right to her son, Henry VII – but for Henry VIII's niece to serve her own daughter was a worrying reversal of the natural order.

At around four o'clock Jane and her glittering following disappeared behind the Tower's huge walls. The gates closed, trumpets blew and the heralds began to read the royal proclamation of 'Jane, by the Grace of God, Queen of England, France and Ireland'. It explained that Edward had appointed Jane his heir in letters patent, signed by himself along with his nobles, councillors, judges and 'divers other grave and sage personages'; that Mary and Elizabeth had been excluded as illegitimate and because they might choose a husband who would impose a foreign government, and bring a 'free realm into the tyranny and servitude of the Bishop of Rome'. When the heralds had finished reading they again proclaimed 'Jane, Queen of England' and cheered. In the crowd, however, people were shocked and some were also angry.

This was not yet a Protestant country. The break with Rome was recent in historical terms and had been deeply traumatic, while to the majority of Englishmen Protestantism remained an alien creed, begun in Germany.[3] The proclamation also begged the question, what qualifications did Lord Guildford Dudley have to be a King of England? He had no royal blood. His grandfather was Henry VII's servant Edmund Dudley, remembered for running a virtual protection racket in London and executed for treason in 1510. His father, John Dudley, Duke of Northumberland, had been Lord President of a hated regime. When in the previous year he had tried to marry Guildford to Jane's cousin, Lady Margaret Clifford, there had been malicious rumours that he was aspiring to the crown. This was easier to believe now: after all, wives were expected to obey their husbands, and Jane's husband was his son.

When the proclamation was read again at Cheapside a boy cried out that Mary was the rightful queen. Not that this mattered much. Even the Imperial ambassadors judged that Queen Jane had achieved a fait accompli. They advised Mary's cousin and most powerful ally, Charles V, to accept that she had been passed over, arguing that 'All the forces of the country are in [John Dudley's] hands, and my Lady [Mary] has no hope of raising enough men to face him.' As for the common sort, 'there are troops posted everywhere to prevent the people from rising in arms or causing any disorder'.[4] Mary was, however, about to demonstrate that she was made of sterner stuff than the Imperial ambassadors.

Mary's reputation has, like Jane's, been shaped for centuries by a combination of sexual and religious prejudice. In Mary's case this is further complicated by the fact it is the heirs of her ideological opponents who have written her story. Even in the twenty-first century some popular historians continue to describe her as a hysterical, weak little woman, easily dominated by men. We are told 'her upbringing ... had not given her the skill of leadership' and that she had 'none of the guile and shrewdness necessary to succeed in the fickle world of Tudor politics'.[5] She is ever the dark, damp little cloud to her sister Elizabeth's glorious sun. Yet the truth is that Elizabeth had enjoyed far less useful training in the 'skill of leadership' than Mary had.[6]

Mary had been raised as her father's heir until well into her teens and since 1543, aged twenty-seven, she had been her brother's heir. For the previous five years Mary had also been a great landed magnate, a role held almost exclusively by men, but one in which she had had the example of her childhood governess, Margaret Pole, Countess of Salisbury. The influence of Mary's mother, Katherine of Aragon, also remained important. The late queen had played up to gender expectations, but the same woman who had sewn the banners for the army at Flodden had been prepared to send James IV's head to her husband as a personal gift. Even Henry VIII had spoken with awe of Katherine of Aragon's fierceness in war. Mary, far from having 'none of the guile and shrewdness necessary' for Tudor politics, knew very well the necessity of compromise and duplicity when playing for high stakes, especially from a position of weakness. She was also capable of acting with extraordinary courage and ruthlessness.

That morning a messenger from Mary had arrived at the Tower. When the message was read at Jane's council table, those who heard it were 'greatly astonished and troubled'. It demanded their allegiance to her as their rightful queen, 'by act of parliament and the last testament and will' of Henry VIII, and promised if they now returned to their duty, she would take their support for Jane thus far 'in gracious part'. Mary needed the backing of the elite and this was her first bid to win back their loyalty. The shock for Jane's council was that this meant the peaceful transition of power they had expected was to be denied them. Jane would have to fight for her crown. Fear of a brutal and protracted struggle, such as the wars of the previous century that had ended in the extirpation of the houses of York and Lancaster, was even more profound than the personal fear that if they picked the losing side they would pay for it with their lives. When Jane's mother and mother-in-law were told of Mary's letter they burst into tears.[7] Bloodshed was inevitable.

The next day Jane's proclamation was posted across London. It warned of severe punishment for those who opposed her and an example was set immediately with the boy who had cried out for Mary at Cheapside: he had his ears cut off. Jane now had to raise an army, and on Wednesday 12 July, Londoners were offered ten pence a day to fight in defence of her crown. It was not expected to be a long war. Jane announced that her coronation would be delayed for only two or three weeks and, in anticipation of her victory, she was brought the crown jewels to peruse.[8]

Yet worrying news was coming in by the hour. Mary had issued her own proclamation, declaring herself queen in Norfolk and parts of Suffolk, and it was evident she was using her tenants and wider affinity as the platform from which to launch her claim. Mary's household officers had been preparing for weeks, possibly months, for her exclusion from the succession, using her networks as the leading

Catholic in England, as well as those of a great landowner. Knights and gentlemen were reported to be rallying to her cause, along with 'innumerable companies of the common people'.[9]

Something had changed in England: in 1501 when Henry VII was ill, his children were overlooked as his possible heirs, with people showing a preference for the de la Poles, children of Edward IV's sister, Elizabeth, Duchess of Suffolk, or Edward Stafford, Duke of Buckingham, senior descendant of Thomas of Woodstock. In 1519 – ten years after Henry VIII came to the throne – the Venetian ambassador reported a continuing preference for Buckingham, while the last de la Pole was still in Europe hoping for his chance. By 1525 these two men were dead, and at the end of Henry's reign the Tudors were being associated in the public mind not with their obscure Welsh antecedents, but as the family of the union rose, just as he had wished. In striking contrast to the fate of Edward V, the elder of the princes in the Tower, Edward VI had reigned for his natural lifespan, and now ordinary English people were rallying to a Tudor queen.

John Dudley, who had defeated the 1549 rebellion in Norfolk, was given the task of commanding Jane's army against Mary. He left London on 14 July at the head of 'the fairest band of gentlemen and others that hath been lightly seen upon a sudden' and a 'fearsome' artillery train. But as he headed north-east, to the west a gentry-led rebellion exploded in the Thames Valley. Jane's claim was a complex one, easily derided as no more than a clever fraud. Mary was soon being proclaimed in Buckinghamshire, while other counties were also turning against Jane as a 'queen of a new and pretty invention'.[10] It was in East Anglia, however, where the towns had been quick to proclaim Jane queen a few days earlier, that the rebel numbers were growing fastest. Mary had raised her standard at Framlingham Castle in Suffolk and even the Protestant elite of the region was being recruited to her cause.

On 15 July, as John Dudley and William Parr made for Bury St Edmunds to cut off Mary's support in the Midlands, Jane received news that the five royal ships at sea off the Norfolk coast had mutinied, the sailors forcing the officers to go over to Mary's side. Reports were also coming in that the tenants of noblemen loyal to Jane were refusing to serve against Mary – an extremely troubling development. It promised social unrest on a scale even more threatening than that of the rebellions of 1549, which had only been crushed with the help of foreign mercenaries.[11]

Mary pushed home her advantage with promises of reconciliation. On 18 July she issued a proclamation that avoided any mention of Edward's Device for the Succession; Mary did not want to advertise the fact her brother had excluded her from the throne. Indeed the proclamation did not even name Jane. Instead Mary placed the focus on John Dudley, her 'most false traitor'. The crisis was explained as the consequence solely of his ambition to make Guildford king, 'by marriage of a newfound lady's title'.[12] Mary was signalling to the elite that she intended John Dudley be made the scapegoat for the crisis. They had not been able to bring the English people with them in following King Edward's wishes to exclude Mary from the throne – and she was offering them a way out of their dilemma.

As the support of Jane's councillors fell away, John Dudley and William Parr received 'letters of discomfort' from their friends in the Tower. Jane continued, however, to play her role as queen. While Mary was issuing her proclamation, Jane was raising troops against the Buckinghamshire rebels, naming William Herbert, Earl of Pembroke (the father-in-law of her sister Katherine Grey) as one of two commanders who would deliver 'such punishment or execution as they deserve'.[13]

On the morning of the 19th a christening ceremony went ahead in the church on Tower Hill. Jane had been asked to stand as godmother to the infant son of a minor court figure called Edward Underhill, and one of her mother's cousins stood in her place.[14] By tradition, the godmother chose the child's baptismal name, and Jane had chosen that of her husband, Guildford. Other proxies stood in for Jane's father, who remained by her side in the Tower, and for William Herbert, who was at his London home, the former royal palace of Baynard's Castle.

Herbert had claimed he was to meet the French ambassador to discuss bringing foreign auxiliaries from the Netherlands to aid Jane. In reality he was concerned that Mary's promise to take the councillors' actions 'in gracious part' would not apply to him if he led Jane's troops into Buckinghamshire, and he was planning with others to desert Jane's cause. That afternoon, the lord mayor arrived at Baynard's Castle along with a number of councillors that Herbert had summoned. All were desperate for a peaceful resolution to the crisis. When the City aldermen were also gathered, William Herbert announced they were to ride together to Cheapside to proclaim Mary as queen. Several officials wept with relief. As the men rode towards Cheapside word of their intention spread and a huge, excited crowd gathered. Herbert read the document proclaiming Mary queen, and when he concluded by throwing a hat full of coins in the air, the crowd erupted. 'From a distance the earth must have looked like Mount Etna', the Imperial ambassador reported of the cheers and shouts; 'the people are mad with joy'. To the ambassador's amazement, Mary's gamble had paid off. 'Not a soul could have imagined the possibility of such a thing', he recalled.

As the council's soldiers arrived at the Tower, Jane's father, Harry Grey, ordered his men to put down their weapons. He was informed the council's soldiers had orders to arrest him if he did not leave willingly and sign the new proclamation. Reluctantly he did as he was asked. Jane's cloth of state was taken down in the throne room and all the symbols of her reign defaced – 'a sudden change!', one of her shocked ladies commented.[15] Jane now found herself a prisoner in the Tower from where she had reigned, as was Guildford and his mother.[16] 'Thus Jane was queen for only nine days and those most turbulent ones', a friend of the Greys wrote to a Swiss divine.[17] This referred to the number of days since Jane had been proclaimed at the Tower. In fact her reign, from the death of Edward VI, had lasted thirteen days.

The sobriquet 'the Nine Days' Queen' would stick nevertheless. Turning her reign into a mere 'nine days wonder' helped diminish its significance, and that was something from which both Mary and her Protestant opponents would benefit. Mary did not want it remembered that Jane had once had serious backing, while Protestants were later embarrassed by their treasonous support for Jane against the Tudor sisters – not just Mary but also Elizabeth; far better for everyone to treat Jane's reign as a small aberration, engineered by Dudley alone.

The details of Mary's victory reached John Dudley in Cambridge that night. The tears streamed down his face as he expressed the pitiful hope that 'Queen Mary was a merciful woman, and that he doubted not thereof.'[18] Edward's entire Privy Council had signed the king's will, and John Dudley's confession later confirmed that William Herbert, William Parr and Harry Grey had all been involved in the decision to marry Jane to Guildford. But the Imperial ambassadors told the emperor, 'it was thought best not to inquire too closely into what had happened.'[19] On the eve of his execution in August John Dudley reconverted to Catholicism. He may have hoped it would save his life, but since he believed he was about to face the judgement of God it is more likely he felt misled and betrayed by those former Protestant allies who had now abandoned him. It was a propaganda coup for Mary, but would do nothing for his posthumous reputation. He died damned as a traitor by Catholics, and by his former allies as an apostate as well. For centuries afterwards the crisis of July 1553 would be ascribed to John Dudley's ambition alone.

On 30 September Mary's coronation procession through London began, with the Tudor queen carried on a litter in triumph. She was dressed in a 'mantle and kirtle of cloth of gold', and with 'circlet of gold set with rich stones and pearls' on her head.[20] The next day, for the ceremonies in the abbey, she changed into the red velvet robes that would later become her state robes for the opening of Parliament. Carried out for a female monarch for the first time ever, the ceremonies followed closely the crowning of earlier kings, and it was as a king she intended to rule; a right soon confirmed by Parliament. Mary later announced in a speech to Londoners that if she had 'been established and consecrated as your queen, by the Grace of God only', so they would owe her 'respect and due obedience solely on account of the holy unction' of the coronation. Yet, she noted, 'How much more entitled as I am now to expect all these things from you' who had won the crown on the battlefield, and was also queen 'by the Grace of God, by rightful law of succession, confirmed by your unanimous acclamations and votes' in Parliament.

Mary was a warrior queen, established by God, by blood, and by law, and she had now 'taken charge of the supreme authority and administration of the Realm of my forefathers' as England's first ruling queen.[21]

30

REVOLT

QUEEN MARY SAT UNDER HER CANOPY OF ESTATE AT WHITEHALL, A slight figure, with light-coloured eyes.[1] Her cousin Margaret Douglas, and her half-sister Elizabeth, watched her from a gallery and enjoyed the music Mary had ordered for the feast. There were harps and choirboys to entertain the new Imperial ambassadors, who had just arrived that October 1553. People wondered if they had come to arrange a marriage for the queen. Aged thirty-seven, Mary had grown accustomed to spinsterhood and claimed she preferred the single life, but she would need to choose a husband, and soon, if she was to have children.

The popular choice of husband for Mary was a great-grandson of Edward IV called Edward Courtenay. Royal and English, he might have been the perfect candidate had he not been imprisoned in the Tower since 1538, the year his father, the Marquess of Exeter, had been executed by Henry VIII for his pro-papal loyalties. Courtenay had been only twelve then, and when he had emerged from the Tower in August, aged twenty-seven, he was a damaged man. Like Edward Plantagenet, Earl of Warwick, who had grown up in the Tower in the reign of Henry VII, Courtenay was childish and petulant. Mary did not appear at all interested in him as a husband, and so Courtenay began annoying Elizabeth instead, claiming there were 'amourettes' between them.[2]

What was not yet public knowledge was that Mary was already considering a marriage proposal she had received a few days earlier from Charles V's son, her cousin Philip of Spain.[3] Mary was concerned that her country was threatened by French ambitions, and while Courtenay was of 'small power and authority', she believed Philip would 'be able from his own resources to prevent an enemy attack'.[4] Before Mary would accept the proposal, however, she wanted Philip to agree that he would have no role in the government of her kingdom. This was an issue that the new ambassadors would have to grapple with, and indeed accept, before negotiations progressed. Meanwhile Mary was also considering who should succeed her if she proved unable to have children.

Mary confided to one of the Imperial ambassadors that she would not allow her current heir, Elizabeth, 'to succeed [to the throne] because of her heretical opinions, illegitimacy and characteristics in which she resembled her mother'. Sitting in the gallery alongside Mary's contemporary, Margaret Douglas, the twenty-year-old was a vision of shining youth, her hair the same corn gold as her late brother Edward's, her long face, sallow skin and black eyes those of the mercurial, shamed, Anne Boleyn. Since Jane Grey's imprisonment Elizabeth had become the new focus for the Protestant opposition and it was a role she seemed to flaunt. She continued to affect the plain dress she had worn during her brother's reign, her servants were all Protestant, and Mary complained she 'talked every day with heretics and lent an ear to all their evil designs'.[5]

Mary wanted to name Margaret Douglas as her heir in Elizabeth's place, but she had been warned that overturning the Act of Succession would be extremely problematic. Although Elizabeth remained a bastard under parliamentary statute and canon law (as Mary did not), she was still King Henry's daughter. The importance of that had been underscored by Mary's own victory over Jane Grey.

Mary's former rival remained in the Tower but, in contrast to her attitude to Elizabeth, Mary was putting the best possible complexion on all Jane's former actions and a future pardon was expected. It was assumed Mary was acting from feminine instincts for mercy. In fact Mary's motives were hard-headed. It remained important to Mary that people ascribe the attempt to exclude her from the throne to John Dudley's ambitions, not Edward's wishes, and that peace was re-established within the royal family. To this end the Grey family were cast almost as Mary's co-victims. Harry Grey had been pardoned in July and although the Imperial ambassadors had dissuaded Mary from pardoning Jane too, she persisted in describing Jane as an innocent dupe.[6] Mary had always claimed Edward was a puppet of the adults around him. If it were accepted that Jane had been a Dudley puppet, it would support her contention that Edward's religious settlement and its abolition of the Henrician Mass had been illegal, since it was implemented when he was a minor and too young to know his own mind; and that his Device for the Succession, also written when he was a minor, was in reality John Dudley's Device.

Venetian reports, later written up by three Italians, include what may be a garbled account of a deposition Jane made in the Tower, aimed at securing her pardon. These repeat the official line that Jane's reign was all the fault of the Dudleys, with Jane forced to accept the throne with many tears. The French went so far as to claim that Jane had said all along that Mary was the rightful queen. Further stories circulated suggesting that when the crown jewels had been brought to Jane she had expressed shock that a crown was also to be made for Guildford, and when she had bravely insisted she would only make him Duke of Clarence, Guildford and his mother had continued to pressure Jane into having him declared king. This was all nonsense. It had been fully expected that Guildford would be granted the title of king, most likely in the September parliament (the two subsequent consorts of reigning English queens were both given the title).[7] He had already been referred to as such. But there are no sources written before Jane's overthrow that suggest she was under any pressure to pre-empt Parliament's decision on this matter.

The Imperial ambassadors warned Mary that pardoning Jane would risk 'scandal and danger', but to Mary the new focus on Elizabeth suggested that Protestants saw Jane as a busted flush, and she had no wish to taint her reputation with the execution of a young girl. Jane was due to be tried for treason in November, and Mary intended that the trial play a role in the sixteen-year-old's rehabilitation. In Tudor England treason trials were more about advertising guilt than establishing it, and since Jane clearly had committed treason she would certainly be found guilty. Mary intended to then pardon Jane in recognition that she had been manipulated and as a demonstration of royal mercy and power. These plans began to go awry, however, as the true nature of the Greys' opposition to Mary resurfaced.

In early November, Harry Grey led the parliamentary opposition in the Lords to the repeal of the Edwardian religious legislation, which he had done so much to promote. On 13 November Jane too chose to advertise her religious sympathies. That morning she left the Tower to walk in procession to the Guildhall where the trial was to take place. A man carrying an axe led the way, as a reminder that the prisoners were being tried for a capital crime. Guildford was dressed dashingly in a black velvet suit slashed with white satin. Jane, behind him, had chosen plain black, and, strikingly, she was carrying an open prayer book in her hands with another, covered in black velvet, hanging from her waist.[8] It was a public statement of Protestant piety. Transcripts of Jane's trial do not survive, but it was said she remained composed even as judgement was read and she was condemned to be burned at the stake – the default punishment for all women convicted of treason.[9]

Mary focused her anger on Harry Grey and, anxious to protect his daughter, he duly apologised for the trouble he had caused in Parliament. He also withdrew his vociferous opposition to the Spanish marriage, which, it had emerged, was to go ahead. The queen responded graciously and in December the conditions of Jane's imprisonment were relaxed. But although Jane enjoyed walking in the Queen's Garden in the Tower, the teenager was also horrified when, on

15 December, the Mass was re-established by royal proclamation. From the Tower Jane composed an open letter to a former tutor who had recently reconverted to Catholicism. The letter described him (and by implication all Catholics) as 'the deformed imp of the devil', and called on good people to make a stand against the Mass, which she described as no better than a form of satanic cannibalism. 'Christ', Jane reminded her readers, 'came to set one against another', and she exhorted them to 'Return, return again unto Christ's war.'[10]

Whether or not Jane intended a literal call to arms, her father was now plotting with a group of like-minded Protestant gentry to rebel against Mary, prevent the Spanish marriage and the legalisation of Catholic ceremonies. They did not plan to restore Jane as queen, however. They recognised the English people wanted a Tudor and intended that Mary should be replaced with Elizabeth, who was to be married to Courtenay. Mary I was right: her sister Elizabeth now posed a dangerous threat. Harry Grey may have feared for his daughter in the Tower, but he knew she could not be judged guilty of the revolt and believed that Mary's pardon of his earlier crimes proved she was no ruthless Henry VIII. She would surely spare Jane. His allies also assured him that as soon as their revolt succeeded they would free his daughter and imprison Mary in her place.

Mary's seventy-four-year-old Lord Chamberlain, and a few poorly armed members of the guard, were beyond the outer gates of St James's Palace when they came under rebel attack.[11] As they ran back to the palace the old man fell in the icy mud. His armour of steel plates sewn on to cloth weighed him down, but his men hauled him to his feet as they fled on.[12] Mary, in the gallery by the gatehouse, could see them running back into the courtyard, and heard her ladies screaming 'We shall all be destroyed this night!' Her Guard battered at the doorway of the hall before running on through the kitchen and back ways, slamming doors, and seeking their escape at the Watergate. Shouts of 'Treason! Treason!' punctuated the clatter as word spread that the royal commander, William Herbert, Earl of Pembroke, had gone over to the rebels.[13] Yet the porters, who were in charge of palace security, proved both loyal and brave, closing the gates under a shower of rebel arrows.

The planned revolt of Harry Grey and his allies, intended for March, had been exposed by 21 January. The risings had gone off early and Harry Grey's attempt to raise the Midlands with the rallying cry 'Resistance to the Spaniard' had failed. But in Kent it had been a different story. The London militia had deserted en masse to Thomas Wyatt (son of the poet). The Privy Council had urged Mary to leave London. Instead, a week earlier, on 1 February 1554, she had given the speech of her life to City officials at London's Guildhall. 'I was wedded to the realm', she had said in her deep, loud voice, 'the spousal ring whereof I wear on my finger, and it ever has, and never shall be left off.' Her subjects, she told the City worthies, were her children, and 'if the subjects may be loved as a mother doth her child, then assure yourselves that I, your sovereign lady and your queen, do earnestly love and favour you.'[14] If Parliament did not think her marriage to Philip of Spain beneficial she would not go through with it, she promised. The speech was greeted with loud cheers – but had it been enough?

'What a sight is this to see the queen's chamber full of armed men; the like was never seen nor heard of', the women complained.[15] Mary had only about seventy experienced soldiers with her at St James's Palace and they included Protestants such as Edward Underhill, father of Jane Grey's godson, Guildford, baptised on the last day of Jane's reign. Having done her best to rally London's citizenry at the Guildhall seven days earlier, Mary now had to rally these men in an impromptu speech made from the gallery window. They were, she told the soldiers, 'gentlemen in whom only she trusted', and asked them to stay close to the palace for her security.[16] Her words appealed to the old chivalric values at the core of which was the protection of defenceless women. As her handful of personal defenders began to march up and down beneath her window, Mary knew that, nevertheless, her humiliation and death could be imminent.

The scene in London remained confused, but there were no further attacks on the palace and in the late afternoon it became clear that the rebels were defeated. As the rooms in the Tower filled up with new prisoners the time came to make some hard decisions about those already there, amongst them Jane and her husband. Already condemned at their trials, Mary had signed their death warrant that morning. It was possible that Mary would, once again, show mercy and allow the warrants to lapse. Yet her long-advertised claims that the Greys were merely victims of Dudley ambition now looked foolish, as well as way off mark. Stories would emerge claiming Mary was persuaded only with difficulty to confirm the executions of the young couple. But then queens were expected to be merciful, and although Mary sent Jane her personal chaplain in the hopes of gaining her conversion, becoming a Catholic had not saved John Dudley.

Jane was, in any case, set on martyrdom. The brave and passionate teenager wrote down her conversation with Mary's chaplain so it might be used to stiffen Protestant resolve after her death. She also composed a farewell letter to her thirteen-year-old sister, Lady Katherine Grey, which she wrote on the blank pages of her Greek New Testament. Such books were treasured objects so it guaranteed the letter would be preserved and read as her last testament. The letter warned Katherine that if she accepted the Catholic faith, 'God will deny you and shorten your days.' The damnation of the apostate would await her. 'As touching my death, rejoice as I do', Jane continued, 'for I am assured that I shall for losing a mortal life find an immortal felicity'; 'Farewell dear sister', her letter concluded, 'your loving sister, Jane Dudley.'

It fell on the Bishop of Winchester, Stephen Gardiner, to explain why the harshest punishment was necessary. That Sunday he preached a public sermon before the queen. After the death of Henry VIII, heresy had been preached in England, he reminded his congregation, and, against the Protestant doctrine of an elect predestined to heaven, he argued that God had given man free will and good works were a means to heaven. It was heretics, Gardiner reminded his listeners, who had threatened the queen in 1553. Mary had been merciful then, but from this 'open rebellion was grown'. He asked 'that she would now be merciful to the body of the commonwealth' and that 'the rotten and hurtful members thereof' be 'cut off and consumed'.[17] As his congregation were invited to pray for Edward VI and the souls of the faithful departed – as only Catholics did – they were in no doubt that 'sharp and cruel execution' would follow.

Jane composed a final note for her father in a prayer book she shared with Guildford. Her husband would be much maligned in later myth, but she describes him in her own hand to her father as one who would be in heaven with her, as a co-martyr: 'though it has pleased God to take away two of your children, yet think not, I most humbly beseech your grace, that you have lost them, but trust that we, by losing this mortal life, have won an immortal life . . . Your grace's humble daughter, Jane Dudley.' There is no finger pointing at Guildford for anything in the past and Jane uses her married name.[18] Just before ten in the morning of Monday 12 February 1554, Jane saw the 'comely, virtuous and goodly gentleman' she had married being led to the scaffold on Tower Hill.[19] There was no priest to attend on Guildford, which suggests he had refused one. He simply said his prayers and laid himself flat on the block. It took one blow to take off his head.

Jane had the misfortune to see Guildford's body brought back in a cart, his head wrapped in a bloody cloth. Bravely Jane kept her composure as she walked behind the Lieutenant of the Tower, in the last procession of her life to the scaffold within the privacy of the Tower walls. Jane had donned the black dress she had worn to her trial and again she read from a prayer book. There was a final message for the lieutenant inscribed in it: 'there is a time to be born, and a time to die; and the day of death is better than the day of our birth. Yours, as the Lord knows, as a friend, Jane Dudley.'[20] Executions are always grim affairs, and the brutal killing of this brilliant young girl was particularly horrible. There was a terrible moment at the end when Jane, blindfolded and feeling desperately for the block, was heard crying out 'What shall I do? Where is it?' Eventually someone – possibly the executioner – stepped forward to guide her. As Jane died in a fountain of blood other scaffolds were already being built all over London. Further executions began the next day and Elizabeth was summoned to London.

31

MARRIAGE AND SONS

ELIZABETH ARRIVED AT WHITEHALL FROM HER HOUSE AT ASHRIDGE in Hertfordshire on the same day that Harry Grey was beheaded, 23 February 1554. He had confessed before he died that the rebels had intended to make Elizabeth queen. It had further emerged that his brother, Thomas Grey, had carried messages to her household outlining their plans, and a copy of one of Elizabeth's letters was discovered in the diplomatic bag of the French ambassador.[1] This was evidence that the rebels had friends at the heart of Elizabeth's household, at the very least. Mary was not prepared to use an Act of Attainder against her sister; she had greater respect for the law than their father Henry VIII had shown. But Wyatt and other captive rebels were being interrogated for further incriminating evidence to be used against Elizabeth at her trial.

Three weeks later Harry Grey's widow, Frances Brandon, married her Master of the Horse: a zealous Protestant called Adrian Stokes.[2] Marrying a commoner would ensure that Frances could not be accused of aspiring to the crown herself – and she had good reason to be fearful. The Spanish were talking of the necessity of wiping out the Greys in the male line to protect the Catholic faith. Frances' brother-in-law, Thomas Grey, was sentenced to death on 9 March, the same day she married Stokes. It was one of almost a hundred executions that would follow the Wyatt revolt. She needed to distance herself from the rebels, not least in case it emerged that Jane's letters and writings were being prepared secretly for publication – amongst them the letter to Frances' second daughter, Katherine, who was in her care. As the Elizabethan William Camden later commented, the marriage was 'to [Frances'] dishonour, but yet for her security'.[3]

The tense nature of those weeks in March was underscored on the 17th when Elizabeth learned that she was to be placed in the Tower. The twenty-year-old princess wrote a frantic letter to Mary swearing she had no knowledge of any treasonous contacts and begged to see her. She told her sister that she had heard that the Protector Somerset had once observed that if he had seen his brother Thomas Seymour at the time of his arrest, he would have spared his life, but that others had convinced him that his life was at risk while his brother lived. 'I humbly crave but one word of answer from yourself', she pleaded with Mary, 'Your highness' most faithful subject that hath been from the beginning and will be to my end, Elizabeth.' Mary did not reply, and was extremely angry that Elizabeth had been allowed to write to her.

Mary's anger was justified. The Seymour analogy Elizabeth had made in her letter carried an implicit threat. Thomas Seymour had been arrested after plotting with Elizabeth's servants to marry her. Elizabeth was claiming that once again her life had been put at risk by actions taken by members of her household without her knowledge. But Elizabeth's recollection of Thomas Seymour's fate also offered a warning. Many believed that Somerset's execution in 1552 was God's punishment for the fratricide of Thomas Seymour in 1549, when he was condemned by Act of Attainder and beheaded. Did Mary really wish to travel down the same route and risk God's wrath by executing her own sister? That was the subtext, and Mary would not have missed it.

The next day Elizabeth was lodged in the same royal apartments in the Tower from which her mother had gone to her death. Her life, however, proved to be safe. Wyatt used his speech from the scaffold to exonerate her, and the Privy Council was divided on whether

Elizabeth should be prosecuted for treason. The shocking execution of Jane Grey, aged only sixteen, would make it that much more difficult to get a conviction from a jury. Mary decided to hope that the worst of the danger Elizabeth had posed was past. On 19 May, Elizabeth was removed from the Tower to house arrest at the Oxfordshire palace of Woodstock. In any case, she believed, Elizabeth would soon be rendered irrelevant: Mary was poised to marry Philip and with God's blessing they would quickly have children.

Mary met her twenty-seven-year-old prince at Winchester, four days after his ship had landed on 20 July. He was brought by torchlight to the house of the dean of the cathedral, 'the lords going before him, and the queen's guard in their rich coats standing all the way'. A servant of Margaret Douglas' husband Lennox noted his appearance: 'Of visage he is well favoured, with a broad forehead and grey eyes, straight-nosed, and manly countenance' and 'so well proportioned of body, arm, leg, and every other limb to the same, as nature cannot work a more perfect pattern'. After dinner, at ten o'clock, Philip was brought by 'a private way' to the queen, who 'very lovingly, yea, and most joyfully received' him. It was with a sense of duty rather than delight, however, that Philip met a bride who was eleven years his senior. Philip had accepted the marriage as his father Charles V's wish, and it was clear Mary was a woman he could respect. 'Not only is she brave and valiant', a diplomat observed, she possessed 'a wonderful grandeur and dignity, knowing what became a sovereign as well as any of the most consummate statesmen in her service'. Unfortunately the strain of the past twenty years was written in her face, which was 'lined more by anxieties than age'.[4] Philip showed no sign of disappointment, however, and went out of his way to charm everyone present, even speaking a few words of English. This was enough for him to be pronounced a prince of 'a stout stomach, pregnant witted, and of most gentle nature'.[5] Mary's kingdom wanted a king, and although the notoriously xenophobic English would have preferred an Englishman of royal blood, Philip – a descendant of

John of Gaunt – was far more acceptable than Guildford Dudley had been. Indeed he would remain well regarded in England, even if his compatriots were not.

The marriage was celebrated at Winchester Cathedral on 25 July 1554, with the royal couple dressed in white and gold and glittering with diamonds. Music was a shared passion and the sung Mass was judged outstanding. But the most important details reported by observers were those concerning precedence. The marriage treaty with Spain had given no powers or land to Philip, and he could not inherit England if Mary died childless. Parliament had confirmed that Mary had the full rights of a king and at their marriage Mary stood on Philip's right as a mark of her superior status. When the Bishop of Winchester, Stephen Gardiner, displayed the marriage treaty, he reminded the wedding congregation that it had been approved by Parliament. Mary was to be married in accordance with the wishes of the realm, as she had promised in her speech at the Guildhall during the Wyatt revolt. Now all she had to do was give her country, and her husband, the heirs they so wanted.

Over the following weeks, a Spaniard recorded that Philip and Mary appeared 'the happiest couple in the world, and more in love than words can say. His Majesty never leaves her, and when they are on the road he is ever by her side, helping her to mount and dismount.'[6] In short, Philip continued to play the role expected of him to perfection. By November Mary was convinced she was pregnant. On the 27th, dressed in robes of velvet and ermine for the opening of Parliament she was processed to the Presence Chamber at Whitehall and sat 'richly apparelled, and her belly laid out, that all might see she was with child'.[7]

The future of Mary's child and her kingdom was to lie within the Catholic Church. Edward's reign had seen the Royal Supremacy fail to protect England from heresy. Now Cardinal Pole, a younger son of Mary's former governess the Countess of Salisbury, had returned after twenty years in exile to help Mary achieve reunion with Rome, and this parliament was set to play a key role. On the 29th, both Houses of Parliament again presented themselves at Whitehall. With vigorous opponents of Mary's Catholicism now silenced, a petition was presented to the king and queen asking that they intercede with Pole so that England might serve 'God and your Majesties' in 'perfect obedience' to the Apostolic See.[8] When Pole accepted the petition the schism with Rome was over, 'since the day of which', one contemporary wrote, 'all such things as were amiss or out of order here begin now to come to rule and square'.[9]

The restoration was generally welcomed. In the provinces one parish quickly sold 'the table which served in the church for the Communion in the wicked time of the schism' and replaced it with an altar, while in others parishioners returned images and vestments they had hidden from state officials, or bought replacements.[10] Choirs were set up again and processions taken up with enthusiasm. But the clock was not going back simply to the days of Mary's youth. Mary was now to launch an English Counter-Reformation. With Mary's support, Pole, as papal legate and later Archbishop of Canterbury, brought to life a humanist vision of a reformed Catholic Church in England. A new translation of the New Testament was commissioned, support was given for the printing of other religious texts in English as well as Latin, clerical education was encouraged and great attention was paid to beauty in worship, especially liturgical music.

Church attendance and vocations to the priesthood had dropped dramatically under Henry VIII and still more under Edward VI. The Marian reforms brought a new sense of energy. Far from being backward-looking, Mary's English Catholic renewal anticipated measures not formally adopted in the wider church until the Council of Trent's final sessions in 1562–3 after Mary's death.[11]

At court too there was vigour and life. With King Philip at Mary's side there were masques and sporting combats to enjoy. Mary had never lived surrounded solely by pious Catholics, as is sometimes claimed.[12] She soon welcomed even the return of the Greys to court, placing Jane's sister, Lady Katherine Grey, in her Privy Chamber. Amongst other former enemies were Guildford Dudley's brothers, who competed in some of the combats. All, however, were expected to conform to the religion of the state. Those who were incorrigible were encouraged to go into exile. Those who did not leave, or could not do so, were dealt with under the heresy laws revived in January 1555. The queen expected a few exemplary punishments of heretics to follow, but this proved wide of the mark. Although Protestants remained a minority there was a strong Protestant commitment, in the south-east of England in particular, where people had embraced the Edwardian reforms and iconoclasm with enthusiasm.[13] 284 people, most of them ordinary men and women, stood bravely by their beliefs and were burned at the stake during Mary's reign. It would earn her the late seventeenth-century sobriquet, 'Bloody Mary', that has come to define her.[14]

To those of us for whom capital punishment is barbarous, it remains difficult to appreciate the mindset of this earlier age. In the sixteenth century it was commonplace to be hanged for theft. The promotion of heresy was considered a worse crime, for it was, potentially, to steal souls. Several of those Mary burned had themselves overseen burnings under Henry VIII. Amongst the most remembered deaths under Mary is that of Hugh Latimer, the Bishop of Worcester. Burned alongside the Bishop of London, Nicholas Ridley, he spoke the famous, if apocryphal, last words, 'Play the man, Master Ridley; we shall this day light such a candle, by God's grace, in England, as I trust shall never be put out.' Yet it was Latimer who had overseen the execution of the Observant Franciscan suspended in chains over a 'slow fire' fuelled by a famous effigy of a Welsh saint during the reign of Henry VIII. It had taken two hours for the monk to die, during which time he was mocked by his executioners as Latimer stood by.[15] Anabaptists (who believed in adult baptism and would not bear arms or take oaths) had been burned even under Edward VI, and would be burned under Elizabeth I too.[16]

Nevertheless, the numbers Mary burned are striking: they were unprecedented in England and unmatched in Europe.[17]

The queen's actions were in the past ascribed to those of a bigoted woman in thrall to priests, an act of revenge, or born of sheer desperation. In truth she was behaving as the ruthless Tudor monarch she was. The burnings began in February 1555 when she was at the height of her power, and her reasons concerned the future, not the past. She wished to eliminate a destabilising minority that had grown exponentially during her brother's reign. Reaction varied. In some areas people would hide wood to thwart the authorities as they built the stake and bonfire, in other areas people sold strawberries amongst a cheerful crowd. The image, however, of those burning pyres still haunts the imagination, along with the stories of the lowly who died: an old man hobbling to the stake 'willingly, angrily and pertinaciously', and behind him a young blind boy, also put to death.

It was Mary's baby that was most crucial, however, in securing the future she envisaged, and in April there were whispers that it was not proceeding normally, even that she was bewitched. It was decided that a close eye should be kept on Elizabeth, and Mary called her sister to Hampton Court, where a superficial reconciliation followed, with Elizabeth falling on her knees swearing she was a true subject.

The twenty-two-year-old princess had matured into a young woman described as 'attractive rather than handsome', 'well formed with a good skin, although olive'.[18] This was in stark contrast to her sister Mary, who looked unwell and old. In May it emerged that Elizabeth's household had employed the magician John Dee to cast the queen's horoscope. He was arrested. Rumours sprang up in the same month that Mary had delivered a son, and there was an explosion of joy with street parties set up across London. Then it emerged that the expected birth date had passed without any sign of a child and new whispers began that Mary was not pregnant at all, merely ill. Mary clung on to her hopes of impending motherhood until August, when at last she accepted there was no baby.[19]

It is impossible to be certain what had caused Mary's phantom pregnancy. She had for years suffered menstrual abnormalities and was by this time very thin. Her symptoms are suggestive, however, of autoimmune hyperthyroid disease, which affects a sufferer's mental state, and this includes documented cases of delusional pregnancy.[20]

The public were relieved to see Mary at the end of August when she and Philip rode from Hampton Court through London to Greenwich. They thronged the streets and as she came into view there were great shouts in acclamation. But everything Mary had fought so hard to achieve was now unravelling. Will-power, courage, intelligence, ruthlessness; these could do nothing to change her fertility, or improve her health. No one except Mary now believed it was still possible she would have a child, and it was evident Elizabeth, established in law as Mary's successor, would one day succeed her.

Two days later Mary bid farewell to her husband, who was obliged to return to the Continent. His father now wished to end ruling his vast empire and retire into private life. In October 1555 Charles V renounced his sovereignty of the Netherlands in favour of Philip, and in January 1556 the crown of Spain.[21] Philip suggested his distressed wife immerse herself in matters of business, but Mary dreaded facing what she knew was coming. Her enemies scented weakness, for without a child Mary's plans had no future, and soon she would be facing repeated attempts on her throne and her life.

32

A FLICKERING LIGHT

QUEEN MARY WAS RARELY SEEN IN PUBLIC IN THE SUMMER OF 1556. In private, however, she appeared drawn and was sleeping badly. A plot to overthrow her had emerged that spring and left her badly shocked. When a conspirator from inside the exchequer informed on his friends several senior Protestant gentry were exposed. Ten were executed, but it had since emerged that members of Elizabeth's household had known of the plot. They included Elizabeth's governess Kat Astley, whom the princess was said to love with a strength 'to be wondered at'.[1] Kat was sent to the Tower for several months, and to Elizabeth's distress, was then dismissed from service. However, Mary also had to reconsider what to do with Elizabeth.

Philip wrote begging Mary to do nothing to imperil Elizabeth's future accession for, in default of her claim, the English throne would pass to Mary, Queen of Scots and into French hands. Mary decided, reluctantly, to try and make amends with her sister. Two servants delivered a diamond ring to Elizabeth as a mark of Mary's faith in her. But then in July yet another plot was uncovered. A schoolmaster in Yorkshire claimed to be Courtenay and announced his intention to marry Elizabeth. It was a further reminder that Elizabeth was the intended beneficiary of all the plots against Mary. The pretender was executed in short order and the real Courtenay died in Padua in September. But when, in November, a plan by leading Protestants to surrender Calais to the French was uncovered, Mary's depression worsened. She spent her time, it was said, 'in tears, regrets and writing letters to bring back her husband'. Philip replied to her in as kindly a manner as he could, but he had his own kingdoms to run and his demands that Elizabeth be married to an Imperial ally were painful reminders of Mary's childlessness. After reading one such letter she threw her mirror across the room in self-disgust.

Yet Mary also did her best to do her duty to her husband and her country, calling Elizabeth to court that Christmas. The princess arrived in London with 200 liveried men on horseback and was cheered through the City in scenes reminiscent of Mary's visit to her gravely ill brother in February 1553. Elizabeth had written telling Mary she wished that there were such 'good surgeons for making anatomies of hearts that they might show my thoughts to your Majesty'. These thoughts were all loyal, Elizabeth promised, and she assured her sister her deeds would supply what 'my thoughts cannot declare'.[2] Mary was now to take her up on that. Having received her with great honour and displays of kindness, she asked Elizabeth to accept a marriage with Philip's cousin, the Duke of Savoy.[3] Elizabeth would later smile at the memory of her conversation with her sister.[4] Mary would not force an unwanted marriage on her and she therefore had the upper hand. Three days later Elizabeth headed back to Hatfield in Hertfordshire, still happily un-betrothed. When Philip wrote insisting Mary try harder to bring Elizabeth round, Mary shot back that perhaps he should come to England to help her achieve this feat. When Philip did at last return, in March 1557, he brought his illegitimate sister, Margaret of Palma, as well as Christina of Denmark, to also set them on the task of Elizabeth's marriage.

To Mary, Philip was again the attentive spouse. 'His manner and character are such as to capitivate anyone', a Venetian recorded, and in truth 'no one could have been a better husband to her and so good a one'. Mary saw increasingly, however, 'that no one believes in the possibility of her having progeny, so that day by day she sees her authority, and the respect induced by it, diminish'.[5] While Mary always received Elizabeth 'with every sort of graciousness and honour' and never conversed 'with her on any but agreeable subjects', it was clear that in seeing her sister Mary was transported back to the humiliations of her youth and was tormented by the knowledge this 'illegitimate child of a criminal' held the eyes of the nation as her successor.[6] Elizabeth never forgot Mary's humiliation, or the dangers Mary faced, and she was determined she would never be placed in a similar situation. Meanwhile, to Philip's continued frustration, Elizabeth easily batted away the enticements of his sister and Christina of Denmark to marry his cousin. She had no intention of limiting her future freedom of action.

Philip had better luck in his desire to engage his reluctant wife in his war against France. Shortly after his arrival in England there was yet another plot against Mary. A group of between thirty and a hundred Protestant exiles landed at Scarborough from a French ship. The traitors were rounded up and executed with twenty-four others. But Mary had grown tired of French provocation and, encouraged by her husband, she declared war on France that summer. She certainly had a better cause for war with France than her father had ever had.

There was early success for Mary's armies with the English capturing Saint-Quentin along with their Spanish allies. 'Both sides fought most choicely', a Spanish officer wrote, 'and the English best of all.'[7] But the war had triggered a falling out between Mary and France's papal ally, Paul IV. This did not amount to a religious division between the papacy and England, but it was a grave political row nonetheless. Born before the battle of Bosworth, Paul IV was an ultraconservative Neapolitan, violently anti-Spanish and so bad-tempered it was said that sparks flew from his heels as he walked. To punish Mary for her war he recalled Cardinal Pole to Rome, intending to try him as a heretic for his past efforts to find an accommodation with the Lutherans on the theology of justification by faith alone. Mary, astonished at the Pope's ingratitude for all Pole's work in healing the schism, refused to send him.

Relations with the Vatican embittered, things also now went badly in France. On New Year's Day 1558, 27,000 French troops attacked Calais, which was quickly lost. Although Calais had long cost as much to defend as it made in trade, this was a national humiliation; a reminder of all England had lost in France since the death of Henry V, and it marked the beginning of a terrible year. An influenza epidemic struck down a population weakened by successive harvest failures. Up to 18 per cent of the English population succumbed to sickness or hunger in 1557–8: the highest death rate recorded in England for another 200 years and equivalent to about ten million deaths today.[8] With Philip absent again in Europe, Mary's health also worsened with bouts of insomnia, depression, loss of vision, headaches and weakness.[9] She had another false pregnancy and in March, when she wrote her will, she bequeathed her throne to the child she insisted she was carrying eight months after last seeing her husband. By then, the more hard-headed Elizabeth was already planning with the surveyor of her estates, the thirty-seven-year-old Sir William Cecil, for Mary's death and her own accession.

Aged twenty-four, 'her forehead large and fair', her nose 'somewhat rising in the midst' and the whole 'compass of her countenance some-what long', foreign observers found Elizabeth 'proud and haughty'. She defended her mother's honour by arguing that Anne Boleyn had refused to live with the king unless they were married. She also defended her own, claiming that since her parents had believed them-selves to be married when she was born, she was legitimate. Above all she 'gloried' in her father, 'with everybody saying she resembled him more than the queen does and he therefore always liked her'.[10] She was certainly proving as capable as her father in spotting a good servant.

Cecil had served as Secretary of State to Edward VI and Jane Grey, and even his enemies thought him 'able and virtuous'.[11] He was a man who inspired confidence, he had a proven record as a talented political operator, and was adept at keeping his hand hidden. Although an ideological Protestant he was often at Mary's court, playing the

Catholic, dining with Cardinal Pole, while keeping Elizabeth abreast of political developments and dangers. He may have been her principal informant during the crisis of Edward VI's last months and Jane's accession. He certainly played such a role over that summer of 1558 as Mary's health declined. By October, when it was accepted the ailing queen was dying, Elizabeth's and Cecil's plans were in place.

Mary did not place any difficulties in her sister's way. On the contrary she added a codicil to her will on the 28th confirming that her successor was her heir in statute. On 7 November she went further, and named Elizabeth before a parliamentary delegation. Whatever Mary thought of Elizabeth, she had no desire to leave England at risk of civil strife. Elizabeth had sworn she was a Catholic and, although Mary surely did not believe her, she chose to leave the rest to God.

Philip was unable to come to England to attend on his dying wife. He was caught up in the funeral arrangements for his father Charles V, and dispatched his Anglophile Captain of the Guard, the Count of Feria, in his place. Feria arrived in London on 9 November to find Mary's councillors very fearful of how Elizabeth would treat them once she became queen. The next day Feria went to see Elizabeth at the house of a neighbour near Hatfield. She was much less serious than Mary: not as personally kind, but funnier, and not as terrifyingly implacable, but shrewd, as the ambassador discovered. They had dinner and 'we laughed and enjoyed ourselves a good deal', he recalled. Nevertheless the private meeting he had with her after dinner was a glum experience for the Spaniard. Feria tried to persuade Elizabeth that she owed her crown to Philip, who had protected her life and her place in the line of succession, despite her links to plots against Mary. Elizabeth made it clear, however, that she felt her sister had treated her most unjustly and that she had the ordinary people of England to thank for her present position; neither Philip 'nor the nobility of this realm had any part in it'.

Elizabeth had not forgotten the events of 1553 when the ordinary people had backed the Tudor sisters, while the political elite had supported Jane Grey. 'She is a very vain and clever woman', Feria concluded, adding perceptively, 'She is determined to be governed by no one'.[12]

Mary died aged forty-two during a private Mass in St James's Palace on 17 November. Pole, who died the same day, had described her life as 'like a flickering light buffeted by raging winds for its utter extinction, but always kept burning by her innocence and lively faith'.[13] Even Philip, who had not loved her, felt 'regret' at her passing. Mary was unlucky that her health had broken down within not much more than a year of her accession and in the very public manner of a phantom pregnancy. She had failed in the essential task of having a child and, as she suspected, Elizabeth would undo much of her religious legacy – but not all. Although England was not to be a Catholic country by the end of Elizabeth's reign, Mary's Counter-Reformation had restored a Catholic identity that would survive centuries of propaganda and persecution.

Inevitably Mary's reputation would suffer from being recorded by the eventual Protestant victors of the English Reformation struggle. The result is that she is remembered better for her failures than her successes. But Elizabeth respected her sister's abilities as a queen and recognised the difficulties she had faced. Mary's rule had also set a template for Elizabeth in the role of an English queen regnant.

Although it is often claimed that Mary lacked Elizabeth's charisma, her qualities in this regard had been demonstrated before her illness took hold: in 1553, when Mary confronted Jane, and 1554, when her speech at the Guildhall roused London in her defence. Mary had spoken then of her marriage to her kingdom, describing her coronation ring as a wedding band, and her love of her subjects as that of a mother for her children. These were phrases and motifs that Elizabeth would use repeatedly and which became absolutely central to her queenship.

It was thanks to Mary that Elizabeth could expect to claim the powers of a king, and Elizabeth further intended to shape a religious settlement of her choice, as Mary had. Finally Mary's reign forewarned Elizabeth of dangers ahead. England was at war with France and while

Elizabeth hoped to make peace, Mary, Queen of Scots was now married to the dauphin (and even had dinnerware quartered with the arms of England, claiming it by right over the illegitimate Elizabeth). Mary I had faced the French threat with a Spanish husband, but Elizabeth was highly sensitive to the fact that announcement of the marriage had triggered a revolt. And who else was there as a possible husband? One councillor expressed the view to Feria that for Elizabeth 'there was no one she can marry either outside the kingdom or within it' with safety.[14] It was a conclusion with which Elizabeth concurred, yet there were still other dangers in ruling alone.

That summer the Protestant polemicist Christopher Goodman had argued in print that the obedience of a subject was dependent on a monarch obeying divine law, and that this excluded women from rule. The same view would be restated more forcibly a few weeks later in John Knox's *The First Blast of the Trumpet Against the Monstrous Regiment of Women*. According to Knox, a reigning queen was 'repugnant to nature; an insult to God, a thing most contrary to his revealed will and approved ordinance; and finally, it is the subversion of good order, of all equity and justice'.

Although many assumed Elizabeth's anger over her treatment at Mary's hands meant she would act vengefully when it came to Mary's burial, no one was more aware than Elizabeth what they had in common as sisters, as Tudors, and now as queens. Elizabeth ordered that King Henry's funeral book be followed to the letter.

The final ceremonies of Mary's funeral began on 13 December when her body was processed from St James's Palace to Westminster Abbey. The coffin was placed in a chariot surmounted by the traditional carved image of the deceased monarch, dressed in crimson velvet with a crown on its plaster head. Mary's cousin and friend, Margaret Douglas, acted as chief mourner, dressed in black trailing to the ground. Margaret had served as Mary's senior lady-in-waiting when Mary was Henry VIII's heir and had watched Mary's humiliation as her household was broken up after Elizabeth was born. She had seen Mary's restoration to her father's favour, and been close to her, once more, when she became queen. In all those years, a Venetian commented of Mary, she had shown, 'neither in adversity nor peril . . . any act of cowardice or pusillanimity, maintaining always, on the contrary, a wonderful grandeur and dignity'.[15]

At the church door the abbot met Queen Mary's body. Along with him were four bishops who incensed the coffin. A hundred gentlemen in black coats kept watch that night along with the queen's guard holding burning torches, as the prayers for the dead were repeated. The next day Mary's requiem was held, and her obituary sermon was given by John White, Bishop of Winchester, who had been present at her death. 'She was a queen and by the same title a king also', he said of her, and it was in 'this church that she married herself to the realm, and in token of faith and fidelity did put on a ring with a diamond on her finger, which I understand she never took off after in her life'. She had remained until her death careful 'of her promise to her realm' and her subjects. He was less hopeful of the future, however. The bishop could only bring himself to say that Elizabeth held the kingdom 'by the like title and right' to Mary, and wished her 'a prosperous reign in peace and tranquillity'.

Mary was buried in the Lady Chapel along with her brother Edward VI, her grandparents, Henry VII and Elizabeth of York, and great-grandmother, Margaret Beaufort. Her wooden effigy was set up on display, the new modern jointed arms and legs allowing it to be enthroned. In life it was said Mary's eyes were so piercing they inspired not only respect but fear in those on whom she gazed, and her voice was loud enough that she could be heard far off. But in painted wood she was silent, the wide eyes staring blankly in the coming years as the statues, the altars, and stained glass in the abbey were destroyed once more, and a new Protestant order established.

33

A MARRIED MAN

DISTURBINGLY, THE FAMOUS MAGICIAN NOSTRADAMUS, WORKING for the French court, was predicting disaster for Elizabeth's reign: 'There shall be difference of sects, alteration, murmuring against ceremonies, contentions, debate, process, feuds, noise, discord . . .' With a Protestant queen ruling a Catholic country, this seemed all too likely, and in an effort to calm national nerves the council commissioned the magician John Dee to cast a more positive horoscope.

It was Dee whom Elizabeth had employed to cast Mary's horoscope when Mary was supposed to be pregnant in 1555, and it is often said that Dee also picked the day of Elizabeth's coronation. This is not so, but Elizabeth's state entry into London was intended as a kind of manifesto for her reign, a political prophecy.[1] The day began at the Tower on Saturday 14 January 1559. The court gathered outside at midday while the queen dined in her apartments. There were flurries of snow and as the light bounced off the tumbling petals of ice a Venetian onlooker thought 'the whole court so sparkled with jewels and gold collars that they clear the air'. When Elizabeth emerged early in the afternoon the procession began.

Both sides of the street, from Blackfriars to St Paul's, had wooden barricades, on which the merchants and artisans of every trade leant in their long hooded gowns of red and black cloth, standing alongside their ensigns, banners and standards. The bad weather and crowds of people and horses made the streets muddy, but sand and gravel had been laid – and just as well. The Venetian counted 1,000 horses before the queen appeared 'in an open litter, trimmed down to the ground with thick gold brocade, and carried by two very handsome mules covered with the same material'.

Elizabeth's strawberry blonde hair hung loose over Mary's old coronation mantle of cloth of gold, and she carried a pair of gloves in her fine long hands. Alongside walked 'a multitude of footmen in crimson velvet jerkins, all studded with massive gilt silver, with the arms of a white and red rose on their breasts and backs, and laterally the letters ER for Elizabetta Regina wrought in relief'.[2] Directly behind the queen rode her Master of the Horse, a handsome man in red cloth of gold, 'of tall personage, a manly countenance, somewhat brown of visage, strongly featured, and thereto comely proportioned in all lineaments of body'.[3] He was a reminder to the people pressing against the barricades, and leaning from windows, that many of the unpopular Edwardian elite were back in power. His name was Lord Robert Dudley; a son of John Dudley, Duke of Northumberland, and an elder brother of Jane Grey's husband, Guildford.

At several points the procession stopped for the queen to admire a series of pageants that her Secretary of State, William Cecil, had helped organise. These colourful exhibitions each signalled a political message directed not only at the people, but also at the queen. The first on Gracechurch Street was a huge triumphal arch, divided into three floors. On the lower level was Henry VII, with a large red rose in front of him, and Elizabeth of York, with a white rose in front of her, both in royal robes. On the second floor was Henry VIII, with a white and red rose in front of him, and Anne Boleyn at his side, as if there had been no divorce or execution. Officially that was to be forgotten. On the third floor of the pageant was Elizabeth's own image, standing alone as if just waiting for her pair. It was a reminder to Elizabeth that her key duty as a sovereign was the establishment of peace and harmony. A marriage would settle the direction of religious policy and, if there were children, offered the best guarantee of future security.

The next three pageants suggested that under Queen Mary religion had been misdirected, and that the future was going to be greener, happier and more godly under Elizabeth. It was, however, the last pageant, on Fleet Street, that was of most interest to Elizabeth for this offered the official answer to John Knox's attack on female rule. Elizabeth was depicted in parliamentary robes, with figures at her feet representing the three estates: nobility, clergy and commons. This was intended to remind Elizabeth 'to consult for the worthy government of her people'.[4] The theme was expanded in a treatise already commissioned by the council. Entitled 'Against the Late Blown Blast Concerning the Government of Women' it argued that Elizabeth was far superior to most women, who are by nature 'fond, foolish, wanton, flibbergibs ... in every way doltified with the dregs of the devil's dunghill'. Nevertheless a godly queen always ruled with the advice of her male councillors, peers and Members of Parliament, and 'it is not she that ruleth but the laws'.[5] In other words, rule by a woman – even Elizabeth's rule – was allowable only when it was a cipher for male government. But of Elizabeth's response to the pageant's message, we hear nothing. She played her role and kept her counsel. '*Video et taceo*', as one of her mottos ran, 'I see and say nothing'.

The following morning Elizabeth was crowned at Westminster Abbey in a ceremony that was so discreetly handled – with Elizabeth taking Communion behind a curtain – that few could be certain how Catholic or Protestant it was. Elizabeth had no wish to institute a rapid and radical shift in religious policy against the wishes of her people, despite pressure from the returning Protestant exiles and their allies. But nor could things stay as they were under Mary. Elizabeth was the physical embodiment of the break with Rome that had followed her parents' marriage, and she had been raised by reformers. Change there would be, albeit carefully handled.

With the coronation ceremony concluded Elizabeth walked out of the abbey door carrying the sceptre and orb in one hand, and in the other the Imperial crown. She had 'a most smiling countenance for everyone, giving them all a thousand greetings'. To the Venetian onlooker it seemed Elizabeth's smiles exceeded 'the bounds of gravity and decorum'. Mary had always shown 'extraordinary dignity and grandeur' in her public performance as queen, but later even Elizabeth's enemies would admit she had 'the power of enchantment'. She was wooing the ordinary people to whom she owed her crown and, in time, she hoped, they would help her secure it. Yet Elizabeth was still a novice queen, and less than three weeks after the coronation she made a dangerous misjudgement of the popular mood.

On 2 February 1559, a Commons select committee presented Elizabeth with a formal request that she marry. To their horror, however, in her reply Elizabeth declared that she would be happy never to marry, and that 'in the end this shall be for me sufficient: that a marble stone shall declare that a queen, having reigned such a time, lived and died a virgin'.[6] Chastity was considered the principle virtue of womanhood and Mary I had often said she preferred the single life – but that was before she became queen. As a monarch Mary had made the point that she married because it was necessary for the stability of her kingdom. Elizabeth had seen the announcement of Mary's marriage bring something quite other than stability. But if she wanted to kick the issue into the long grass, she had gone the wrong way about it. Her remarks shocked all who learned of them. Elizabeth offered to choose a worthy successor, but this only prompted rumours that she could not have children.[7] Then another possible explanation emerged: that she was secretly in love – with a married man.

Elizabeth's Master of the Horse, Robert Dudley, was frequently in her company and they would often be seen touching casually and sharing private jokes. He had been married as a teenager to a gentle-woman called Amy Robsart. It had been a love match, but that love was now in the past. In April Count Feria reported 'It is even said that her Majesty visits him in his chamber day and night. People talk of this so freely that they go so far as to say that his wife has a malady in one of her breasts, and that the queen is only waiting for her to die to marry Lord Robert.'[8] They had a physical energy in common, humour and a sense of pragmatism. Both had known danger after losing their powerful, charismatic fathers. They had been in the Tower at the same time during her sister's reign and Elizabeth claimed he had later lent her money when she needed it. But the nearest Elizabeth ever came to explaining why she loved him as she did was when, in comparing him to one of his brothers, she said she thought he had a special 'sweetness'.

From Feria's perspective it remained essential for Spain to remain on good terms with England, whatever happened with Dudley. Elizabeth had signed a peace treaty with France, and if this developed into an alliance it would threaten Spain's empire in the Netherlands.[9] Feria advised King Philip to consider coming to an accommodation with Dudley, in case he ended up as King of England. He warned, however, that the unpopularity of the Dudley name was such that any future marriage to the queen could trigger unrest in England. That would open the way to an invasion by Henri II of France on behalf of his daughter-in-law, the sixteen-year-old Mary, Queen of Scots. If Elizabeth was overthrown Philip needed to have his own candidate in place. Feria suggested the best candidate for this role was Elizabeth's heir under Henry VIII's will – the blonde, eighteen-year-old younger sister of the executed Queen Jane: Lady Katherine Grey.

During Mary's reign Katherine Grey had been well treated and despite her sister Jane's exhortations that she die a martyr, Katherine had attended Mass at court, where she had waited on the queen. She was a pretty, good-natured and romantically inclined girl, whom Feria believed (wrongly) remained a Catholic. Where he was correct was in his assessment that Katherine resented her treatment by Elizabeth. The new queen had demoted her from serving in the exclusive quarters of the Privy Chamber to the Presence Chamber to which the entire upper gentry had access. This so infuriated Katherine that she had

had a fit of temper one day, using 'very arrogant and unseemly words in the hearing of the queen'. Katherine told Feria she believed that 'the queen does not wish her to succeed' to the crown, and this was quite true.[10] Elizabeth was fearful that if she did not marry an acceptable husband and produce a son, or prove to be as Protestant as some wished, then one day they would back Katherine Grey against her, just as they had once backed Jane against Mary.

Elizabeth's concerns were all the more acute as she faced the complex issues of shaping her religious settlement. The queen is sometimes depicted as an essentially secular figure. She was not. Like Henry VII, she believed that it was the 'exceeding goodness of God' that had protected her 'through difficult times' until 'coming to this, our crown'.[11] She was not doctrinaire, however, and was now trying hard to shape a religious settlement that would appeal to as broad a Protestant constituency as possible – Lutherans and Swiss reformed Protestants – with some Catholic dressing that would ease the change for her conservative subjects. Although there was to be a return to the Protestant 1552 Book of Common Prayer, she forced through some concessions against the wishes of Cecil and his former Edwardian friends. These included distinctive vestments for priests at Communion and sentences on the administration of the bread and wine that could be taken as implying Christ was present, at least in some spiritual sense, in the elements. Like her father's church, it was an idiosyncratic creation, and like her father she intended to keep a personal grip on religious policy.

There would be relentless pressure on Elizabeth – especially from the returning Protestant exiles – to go further, not least in banning vestments, and in facing them down the queen deemed it vital that Katherine not become a more attractive candidate by marrying and producing a male heir. Shunning Katherine was Elizabeth's way of making Katherine as unattractive a bride as possible. The Spanish, hoping to take advantage of Katherine's frustration, and having been told by Feria that she was Catholic, began to discuss how she might be smuggled out of the country. These plans were dropped after 30 June, when Henri II of France was involved in a fatal jousting accident.[12] The new king, Francis II, husband of Mary, Queen of Scots, was only fifteen and too young to take on an invasion of England. Innocent of the plot to take her to Spain, Katherine instead accompanied the queen on the first of the summer progresses of her reign.

Elizabeth intended to visit several palaces and private houses, be seen by the people, and enjoy herself balling, masking and hunting. That summer proved to be everything she hoped, with Robert Dudley constantly at her side. His wife Amy had expected to spend more time with him. She wrote on 7 August to their agent apologising for failing to discharge a debt, explaining 'I forgot to move my lord thereof before his departing, he being much troubled with weighty affairs, and I not being altogether in quiet for his sudden departing.'[13] Such weighty affairs had included his ensuring that the queen had the best horses for her progress, and his 'sudden departing' was so that he did not miss a moment with her.

On the day that Amy was writing her letter, Dudley was with Elizabeth enjoying some of the most expensive entertainments ever to be staged in England. Hosted by Henry Fitzalan, Earl of Arundel, at the intimate palace of Nonsuch in Surrey, they included banquets, masques and parties that went on until three in the morning. The forty-seven-year-old earl was hoping that Elizabeth would see him as an acceptable king consort. He had an ancient lineage, but he too was rather ancient, in Elizabeth's eyes at least, as well as 'loutish' and flabby. He struck diplomats as 'a flighty man of small ability' and Elizabeth had told Feria already that she did 'not get on with him'. Elizabeth's eyes remained on her 'Sweet Robin', although she had not entirely forgotten the warnings her late stepmother, Katherine Parr, had given on guarding her reputation, not least where married men were concerned.

To counter the growing rumours that she had a sexual relationship with Dudley, Elizabeth and her former governess, Kat Astley, conspired to produce a piece of public theatre. In an act of supposed spontaneity Astley threw herself at her mistress' feet, begging Elizabeth to end the malicious gossip about her relationship with Dudley; Elizabeth was then able to respond by pointing out that she could not possibly behave dishonourably when she was always surrounded by her ladies, and to explain that she needed Dudley's company as she had 'so little joy' in her life.[14]

Amongst Elizabeth's greatest pleasures was to ride with Dudley, and the 'gallopers' he ordered from Ireland were spirited, beautiful horses with names like Bay Gentle and Great Savoy. He noted nervously that 'she spareth not to try as fast as she can go. And I fear them much, but she will prove them', as indeed she did, often wearing out everyone who tried to keep up. She loved the sensation of escape.

While the progress continued visitations were taking place in the parishes to ensure the royal articles and injunctions on religion were being carried out. The enthusiastic Protestants of Rye had taken their altar down already, but more often it was found that Catholic sacred objects were being concealed. In part this was because people liked them. But it was also because no one could be sure if Elizabeth and her religious settlement would survive long. In France Elizabeth's ambassador reported Mary, Queen of Scots had been overheard saying that 'As God has so provided that ... she is Queen of France and Scotland, so she trusts to be Queen of England also.'[15] Instead of destroying altars, parishioners were placing simple boards on them to make temporary Protestant Communion tables.[16] One day the altars could be used again. To prevent this happening, and Mary, Queen of Scots ever coming to the throne, was to be William Cecil's life's work, and while Elizabeth enjoyed her summer, he was busy considering how best to take advantage of a rebellion that had broken out in Scotland.

A band of Protestant lords had moved to overthrow the Catholic regent, the Queen of Scots' mother, Mary of Guise. Cecil saw an opportunity to create a Protestant Britain that would help secure England's northern border, and he pressed Elizabeth to agree to giving military support to the rebels. Elizabeth was extremely loath to give any support to men fighting against a rightful sovereign, but after months of Cecil's pleas and threats of resignation she gave way.

The English contribution in favour of the Scottish rebels proved decisive and, in July 1560, shortly after Mary of Guise died, a peace treaty was signed. A Protestant reformation was then pushed through the Scottish Parliament repudiating the Pope, suppressing monasteries and prohibiting the Mass. But the future for a Protestant England could only be secured if Elizabeth had a son, and to Cecil's dismay Dudley was closer to the queen than ever.

Elizabeth knew she could not just have Dudley's marriage annulled and marry him in the same way her father had annulled his marriage to Katherine of Aragon and married Anne Boleyn. She had already been warned that a queen was expected to take counsel, not take control. She would never be able to impose her will in the way her father had done. But where she could not take positive action, she could stall, and this is what she was doing on the vital issue of her marriage. Her claim that she wished to remain a virgin had backfired, and she understood that she needed to put on a convincing pretence that she was looking for a suitable husband. This was proving impossible while she was so clearly smitten with her handsome Master of the Horse. A murderous resentment was now growing at court against the royal favourite. Even Cecil freely admitted he wished Dudley were dead.[17]

34

DANGEROUS COUSINS

ELIZABETH RETURNED TO HAMPTON COURT FROM THE HUNT ON the morning of 7 September 1560 with dramatic news. The latest Spanish ambassador, Bishop Alvarez de Quadra, was astonished to learn from her that Robert Dudley's wife, Amy, 'was dead or nearly so'. The man she loved would be free to marry – but they would need powerful support to be able do so. If Elizabeth now hoped that Quadra would immediately offer Spanish backing she was disappointed. He thought it a 'shameful business', and although he did not voice this, she saw enough in his reaction to ask him to keep the news secret for the time being. Her own feelings were better hidden and to Quadra it seemed impossible to tell whether she would now marry Dudley or not.[1]

Later that day Elizabeth confirmed publicly that Amy was dead, explaining in Italian that the twenty-eight-year-old 'broke her neck'.[2] It emerged that Amy's body had been found the previous evening at the bottom of a flight of stairs at a house which belonged to a friend of Dudley. She had never been 'almost' dead, as Elizabeth had told Quadra. What made the news all the more shocking to the ambassador was that only the day before William Cecil had confided his fears that Dudley's supporters were thinking of killing Amy to free him to marry Elizabeth. It was also clear that while some courtiers believed the official line, that Amy's death was an accident, many others suspected Dudley had ordered his wife's murder.

The recent discovery of Amy's post-mortem reveals she had head injuries. These could have resulted from a fall in which she hit the edge of the stone steps. There were reports she had been unwell, and she might have fainted. Equally, they could be the result of deliberate blows inflicted on her. The coroner's jury, who later viewed the body, brought in a verdict of death by misadventure, which suggests the further possibility of suicide. Amy and Dudley had married as love-struck teenagers, and there had been signs that she had grown unhappy during his absences: Cecil summed up the course of events sourly as 'a carnal marriage' which had 'begun for pleasure and ended in lamentation'. Significantly for Elizabeth and Dudley, however, it had also ended in scandal and the consequence was uproar.

It seems possible that Dudley's servants had carried out what they assumed would be his wish, but he was under no illusions that Amy's sudden demise had actually damaged his hopes. He asked a cousin to find out what had happened – his chief concern being 'how this evil should light upon me, considering what this wicked world will bruit [i.e. gossip]'. At court, in addition to the dismay that the queen might marry a murderer were significant concerns that if she did marry Dudley, he would seek revenge on those who had allowed his father to be made the scapegoat for Jane Grey's reign in 1553. Tensions ran so high that Ambassador Quadra reported there could be a revolt: 'The cry is that they do not want any more women rulers, and [the queen] and her favourite may find herself in prison any morning.' Cecil feared that she was determined to 'do as her father did', and marry whom she wished despite public feeling.[3] But if so, Elizabeth had to consider how easy she might be to replace.

During the Wars of the Roses, Henry VI had been threatened by his cousin Richard, Duke of York, and he was later overthrown by York's son. Elizabeth had not only one cousin to fear, but many – a Tudor hydra – although happily all her near heirs were female.[4] Of these, three women would dominate the family story and succession issues of Elizabeth's reign. Elizabeth now had to consider their relative strengths.

Her senior heir under Henry VIII's will, Lady Katherine Grey, was unmarried – an unattractive proposition as a future queen to courtiers angered by Elizabeth's behaviour with Dudley. Elizabeth's heir in blood, Mary, Queen of Scots was married, but to the hated King of France, so she too was not a popular choice. And then there was Henry VIII's senior niece, Margaret Douglas: Elizabeth's last surviving Tudor first cousin (following the death of the ailing Frances Brandon in 1559).

The passage of time and the birth of eight children had taken its toll on the forty-five-year-old's once famous beauty, but Margaret's husband, Lennox, still adored her. Margaret Douglas knew how to charm and the couple had done remarkably well in negotiating the lethal riptides of the changing Tudor courts. Indeed Margaret had matured into a political operator to match her great-grandmother and namesake, Margaret Beaufort. She had been involved for years in intrigues in Scotland, working for the restoration of her husband's rights as Earl of Lennox, and for her own as the heir to her father, the Earl of Angus (who had died in 1557). But what concerned Elizabeth most was that Margaret Douglas' two sons were the nearest male heirs in blood to the crowns of Scotland (through their father) and England (through Margaret).

Margaret was well aware she was being closely watched and complained bitterly to Quadra that she felt a virtual prisoner. But Elizabeth had good reason to watch her, as was evident in Margaret's request for financial aid from Spain in support of her claim.[5] Quadra decided he would rather see how things played out. Cecil had told him that in their desperation for an adult male ruler, courtiers were keenly considering a claim outside the Tudor family, a white-rose candidate, Henry Hastings, Earl of Huntingdon, who was a Protestant descendant of Edward IV's brother, the Duke of Clarence. Cecil was also working hard, however, to hammer home to Elizabeth that if she married Dudley she would be overthrown.

Elizabeth liked to imagine what it would be like to be a former queen, free of the burdens of her office, and thought she would do rather well: 'I thank God I am indeed endowed with such qualities that if I were turned out of the realm in my petticoat I were able to live in any place in Christendom', she later observed.[6] But that was fantasy. Since the deposition of Richard II in 1399, all those who had lost their crown in England had first lost their freedom, and then, later, their life.

Cecil's dire warnings were convincing, and in October Elizabeth assured him she would not marry Robert Dudley. The pain of this decision was revealed the following month when she had, on her desk, a patent that would have raised Dudley to the peerage – a necessary move if he were to become her husband. Faced with a choice between her happiness and her throne she chose her throne, stabbing and slashing at the patent with a knife. Cecil remained concerned that, nevertheless, Elizabeth had not yet made a final decision on marrying Dudley. And if the immediate danger to the queen had passed, events in France were about to put her in fresh peril.

Francis II had always been sickly, and that November his health deteriorated sharply. For three weeks his young wife tended him but on 5 December he died, leaving Mary, Queen of Scots a widow just three days short of her eighteenth birthday. Whoever now married Mary could one day be King of England, as well as Scotland, and that made her an international prize. In England, Margaret Douglas was amongst those who began calculating the new political possibilities. Margaret's younger son, Lord Charles Stuart, was still only five years old.[7] But the eldest, Henry, Lord Darnley, was already fifteen and Margaret believed he was an excellent choice as a potential groom for her half-niece, the Queen of Scots. Exceptionally tall and good-looking, Darnley was a fine dancer, horseman, musician and poet. He had even contributed to the collection of poetry Margaret and her friends had built up during King Henry's reign. More significantly, he was English-born, as well as being of royal blood. Marrying him would go some way to answering criticism of Mary's foreign birth, and so strengthen her claim to the English throne.

Margaret Douglas wrote promptly to the new widow to propose a match.[8] By February 1561 there were rumours in Scotland that Darnley was in France. He had, in fact, met Mary, Queen of Scots in 1559, when Margaret sent him to congratulate Francis II on his accession. There is no evidence that he had returned, but at Easter Margaret did send messengers, to both France and Spain, to garner support for her marriage project.[9] Six weeks or so later she also made contact with members of the Scottish peerage. That summer of 1561, Mary, Queen of Scots would return to rule the homeland where her late mother, Mary of Guise, had been regent until her death in 1560. When she did, Margaret was ready to contact her again, and her messenger soon arrived at Stirling to see the queen.[10]

Mary, Queen of Scots had inherited all the height and beauty of her Yorkist ancestors, standing at five feet eleven inches, with slanting eyes, sensuous grace and great personal charm. Walking with the messenger in her chamber, only her maids present, it became clear that she didn't recall much of her earlier meeting with Darnley in 1559 but she seemed pleased with what she heard now of his 'stature, age, qualities, ability and friends'.[11] Following this successful meeting Margaret Douglas continued her secret correspondence into Scotland, using the code name 'hawk' to denote Mary, Queen of Scots.[12]

William Cecil was, however, already recruiting spies in Margaret's household. For a zealous Protestant like Cecil, any Catholic heir was a particular danger and Margaret Douglas' religious beliefs now made her vulnerable to accusations of criminal activity. She obeyed Elizabethan law and attended a weekly Protestant service to avoid a fine, but she also continued to hear Mass in private.[13] This had been acceptable to Elizabeth until Easter when Cecil had manufactured a threat to the queen's life. Several Catholic gentlemen had been arrested and convicted, on charges of plotting with foreign powers to kill Elizabeth by witchcraft. Elizabeth, a firm believer in the occult, had been sufficiently frightened to permit Cecil to then launch the active persecution of English Catholics.[14]

Elizabeth did not share Cecil's profound concerns about the religion of her Catholic heirs, however. Indeed she disliked the efforts made by Protestants in the 1550s to associate the nature of 'true' kingship with their own beliefs. Rather than attack Margaret Douglas through her religion, Elizabeth preferred to build on Henry VIII's claim that Margaret was illegitimate. Elizabeth could do nothing about her own bastard status. To have asked Parliament to remove the stain of her illegitimacy would have been to stir up memories of her father's affair with her aunt, Mary Boleyn. But she could damage Margaret's status, and to this end information was now being sought in Scotland concerning the marriage of Margaret's parents.[15] As yet, however, Elizabeth feared the claims of her Protestant cousin Katherine Grey far more than she did that of Margaret Douglas. It was, after all, Katherine's sister, Jane, who had usurped the throne in 1553. Cecil was equally anxious to allay the queen's fears in this regard. If anything happened to Elizabeth it was likely to be Katherine he would back as queen.

Cecil was deeply concerned when, in the spring of 1561, he learned that the twenty-one-year-old Katherine was spending her time enjoying the 'company and familiarity' of the dashing Edward Seymour, Earl of Hertford.[16] Aged almost twenty-two, slim, and with an aquiline nose, Hertford was the heir of the Protector Somerset, and his mother a descendant of Edward III: in short he was a most appropriate choice as the king consort of a Protestant queen. A marriage between such a pair as Hertford and Katherine would both terrify and anger Elizabeth, so to separate the couple, Cecil arranged a long trip around Europe for the earl. He left in May, leaving Katherine behind to, once again, accompany the queen on a summer progress.

Travelling from Greenwich on 14 July the progress arrived later the same day at Wanstead and Havering, near Romford, Essex. A tour of the eastern counties lay ahead. Elizabeth had requested Hertford to commission a French goldsmith to make jewelled hat feathers, chains and bracelets for her ladies, 'to be gay in this court, towards the progress'. She was pleased to see the expected package had arrived from France, with everything she had asked for.[17] If she also noticed that Katherine was despondent not to have any letter from Hertford herself, the queen did not say so.

On 16 July the progress moved on to Pirgo on the edge of the park at Havering. There Robert Dudley awaited the queen with his servants dressed in a new green livery. She was still in love with him, and Dudley remained with her as the court's progress continued through Essex and into Suffolk. At Ipswich, a town notable for its enthusiastic Protestantism, Elizabeth was infuriated to discover that church ministers were not wearing surplices for Communion services and that many were married with children. Most Protestants had hoped, in 1559, that her religious settlement was just a first step towards England being cleansed more thoroughly of 'Popery'. Vestments worn at Communion suggested a belief in the Real Presence of Christ in the Eucharist and so were particularly disliked. But Elizabeth was determined to keep religious policy under her own control, and as far as she was concerned her kingdom's religion had been settled for the duration of her reign. Although it was permitted for clergy to marry, she didn't like it, and on 9 August she issued an order forbidding women from living in cathedrals or colleges. As for the matter of surplices, in the future she would make the wearing of vestments a test of obedience to her religious settlement. The abusive term 'puritan' would come to describe those who failed that test.

The following morning Elizabeth and her ladies attended a Communion service. There was a great deal of whispering amongst the congregation, but this had nothing to do with surplices or women living in cathedrals, as Elizabeth discovered the next day when Dudley asked to see her. Katherine Grey had visited him the previous night at his lodgings in Ipswich. Dudley's younger brother, Guildford, had been married to Jane Grey so he was family, and on her knees, Katherine had asked for his help. The pretty twenty-year-old had explained that she had married Hertford in secret before Christmas, and was now eight months pregnant. She had realised by 'the secret talk she saw amongst men and women' that morning 'that her being with child was known and spied out', and she had begged him, weeping, 'to be a means to the queen's highness for her'.[18] Her hope that Dudley would be able to mitigate the queen's anger was to be disappointed.

Elizabeth listened to what Dudley had to say with mounting fear and fury. Katherine's marriage had taken place in the immediate aftermath of the crisis of the previous autumn, when Robert Dudley's wife had been found dead. Elizabeth was convinced it was part of a plot to replace her if she had decided to marry Dudley. She was acutely aware that, as an illegitimate daughter, she owed her legal right to the throne to an Act of Parliament that another Act could easily supersede. Katherine was sent under guard to the Tower where she was imprisoned in Jane's former lodgings, while Hertford was recalled from France, also destined for the Tower.

The subsequent interrogations revealed the story of the young lovers' feelings for one another. There had been a summer romance in 1558, but they had only fallen deeply in love during the progress of 1559. They had decided to marry in the winter of 1560 with a flurry of secret assignations, a diamond betrothal ring, and a gold wedding band engraved with the promise their union was a 'knot of secret might' that no man could break.[19] The spinster queen had at her fingertips even the details of the consummation of the marriage. The documents describe them as naked, save that Katherine had kept on a small wedding veil, and for two hours they had lain together, 'sometimes on the one side of the bed, sometimes on the other'. They had got up from the bed once, but in their passion soon returned, staying until the time came when Katherine had to return to court for supper.[20] Elizabeth learned that over the following months Katherine and Hertford had met for sex in half the royal palaces of England, as well as his London house. No proof emerged that anyone of significance was linked to the marriage, but

Quadra also suspected there was more to the story than a simple love affair.

One name mentioned to Quadra was that of Henry Fitzalan, Earl of Arundel, the flabby, middle-aged nobleman who had courted Elizabeth in the summer of 1559. Having been humiliated in his hopes of marrying the queen he had begun courting Hertford's nineteen-year-old sister, Lady Jane Seymour. She had died that spring of 1561, but it emerged that she helped the lovers meet and had witnessed her brother's marriage. The earl had perhaps hoped to become if not a king consort to Elizabeth, then a king's brother-in-law, with Hertford and Katherine made king and queen on Elizabeth's fall.[21]

The most significant name Quadra mentioned was, however, that of William Cecil. He had begun his career as servant to Hertford's father, the Protector Somerset and was a kinsman of the Grey family. Quadra believed Cecil had arranged the marriage in the immediate aftermath of Amy Dudley's death, fearing Elizabeth would marry Dudley with the backing of King Philip. He had then dropped the matter when he was back in the queen's good graces.

Elizabeth, seeing treachery all around her, and knowing nothing could be proved, became deeply depressed. She had been in great danger during the Protectorate of Hertford's father – and now another Seymour was aspiring to be king! An emissary of Mary, Queen of Scots, who joined the progress at the royal palace of Hertford on 8 September, found the frightened queen 'extremely thin and the colour of a corpse'.[22]

Mary, Queen of Scots' advisers had proposed that Mary renounce her immediate claim to the English throne (a claim based on the grounds she was the senior legitimate descendant of Henry VII) in exchange for formal and binding recognition as Elizabeth's heir. Mary was working with the incumbent Protestant regime in Scotland, she accepted Protestantism as the national religion while she, in turn, had assurances that she could hear Mass. It was a possible template for a future role as Queen of England, and William Maitland of Lethington, the 'flower of the wits of Scotland', had arrived to negotiate the issue with Elizabeth. Cecil feared he might be successful, with Elizabeth moving to dispose of the Grey/Seymour claim once and for all.

Elizabeth began by stating her preference for Mary's claim. 'I have noted', she told Maitland, 'that you have said to me . . . that your queen is descended of the royal blood of England and that I am obliged to love her as being nearest to me in blood of any other, all which I must confess to be true.' She dismissed the claim of Katherine Grey, saying that while 'It is true, that some of them have made declaration to the world that they are more worthy than either [Mary] or I, by demonstrating that they are not barren, but able to have children', the pregnant Katherine and her younger sister, Lady Mary Grey, were unable 'to succeed to the crown by reason of their father's forfeiture' for treason in 1554. Elizabeth reassured Maitland that 'despite the recent war with Scotland' she never 'meant ill towards' his queen, and though she had offended her 'by bearing my arms and acclaiming the title of my crown', she had blamed others for what had happened.

Elizabeth warned Maitland the succession was not a matter she wished to discuss formally, but as the meeting closed she reiterated her personal support for Mary's claim: 'I here protest to you, in the presence of God, I for my part know no better [claim] nor that I myself would prefer to her, or yet, to be plain with you, that case that might debar her from it.' Maitland hoped that if he pressed Elizabeth, she might offer her direct backing for a parliament's recognition of Mary, Queen of Scots as her preferred choice. At his final audience, however, Elizabeth gave three reasons why she would never do so.

'First', Elizabeth reminded Maitland, the uncertainty caused by changing laws of succession and controversies over marriages 'lawful and unlawful, of legitimate and base-born children', had been responsible for a series of crises in England. Elizabeth did not wish to provoke further unrest. This was also why 'I have hitherto forborne to match with any husband', she explained. Elizabeth's reasons for not marrying have long been speculated on. Often it is assumed she had some psychological hang-up associated with her mother's death, or the execution of Katherine Howard when Elizabeth was at the impressionable age of nine. But there seems to be no reason to disbelieve her own explanation that she didn't marry because she feared making a divisive choice. Elizabeth had witnessed the damage done to both Jane Grey and Mary I by their marriages, and in the tensions at court following Amy Dudley's death she had experienced a taste of what would happen if she married Robert Dudley,

'Now', Elizabeth said to Maitland, as she came to her second point, 'where you said that by declaring your queen my successor our affection should become more firm. I rather fear it should be the seed of a most bitter hatred.' How could she trust that a powerful monarch, from a neighbouring country with a long history of enmity to England, would not take advantage of her new position? 'But', Elizabeth continued, 'the third consideration is the most weighty of all.'

Elizabeth remembered how men had looked to her during the previous reign, hoping to use her to replace her Catholic sister. One day, she feared, such men might wish to overthrow her too: 'I know the inconstancy of the people of England, how they ever mislike the present government and have their eyes fixed upon that person that is next to succeed, and naturally there are more that look, as it is said, on the rising than the setting sun.' In that light, she asked Maitland to judge for himself how dangerous it would be for her to name the Queen of Scots as her heir. 'I was married to this kingdom, whereof always I carry this ring as a pledge', she concluded, and 'howsoever things go I shall be Queen of England so long as I live, when I am dead let them succeed who have the best right.'

As with the issue of her marriage, the safest option for Elizabeth in naming a successor was to stall: 'let them succeed who have the best right'. If Elizabeth had left few in any doubt that she believed Mary, Queen of Scots had the 'best right' she had done so largely to weaken the claim of Katherine Grey who posed the immediate threat. What Elizabeth could not do was prevent the young mother-to-be from carrying out the primary purpose of a royal princess – the delivery of a son. On 24 September Katherine Grey gave birth to a boy: Edward Seymour, Viscount Beauchamp.

Katherine's newborn baby posed a threat not only to Elizabeth, of course, but also to the Stuart claim, and within a week Margaret Douglas had sent a message to Mary, Queen of Scots. It asked cryptically 'whether she would keep her promise made in France, or not'.[23] Elizabeth's agents intercepted it. The family competition for the Tudor crown was becoming acute, and Elizabeth would have to decide carefully what to do next.

35

ROYAL PRISONERS

ELIZABETH'S INVITATION TO SPEND CHRISTMAS AT COURT PUT Margaret Douglas 'in great alarm'. Acutely attuned to any indications of political trouble Margaret realised her letters to Scotland must have been intercepted. She feared she could be thrown in the Tower; even that her son Darnley's life was at risk. Yet she was also defiant. What was wrong, she asked the Spanish ambassador, in giving marital advice to her niece, when a marriage between Mary, Queen of Scots and Darnley would protect England from a civil war on Elizabeth's death? Quadra knew the answer to that. A childless spinster who was already twenty-eight, Elizabeth based 'her security on there being no certain successor should the people tire of her rule'.[1]

The Christmas season came and went with the Lennox family all at court. It must have been grim for everyone, not least Elizabeth, who seemed to spend her life dealing with people planning for what would happen on her death. Beside the Lennox family, there was the danger posed by Katherine Grey's son to face. On 10 February 1562 Elizabeth set up a Church Commission 'to examine, inquire, and judge of the infamous conversation and pretended marriage betwixt the Lady Katherine Grey and the Earl of Hertford'.[2] According to canon law all that was required for a valid marriage was consent by the bride and groom to marry in the presence of witnesses, followed by intercourse. The death of Hertford's sister, Jane Seymour, the sole witness to the wedding, along with the disappearance of the priest, simplified the commissioners' task in deciding the marriage was invalid and Katherine's son a bastard. This left Elizabeth free to concentrate once more on the threat from the Lennox family.

Cecil had gathered a great deal of incriminating information from Lennox's former secretary, a professional spy called Thomas Bishop. This information included their contacts with the Spanish ambassador. Margaret, however, suspected Bishop's disloyalty after spotting one of his men at court, and she launched an attack on Bishop's character. He was a coward, a sexual reprobate, a thief and a troublemaker, who had even tried to come between her and Lennox in their early marriage, to the fury of Henry VIII, she warned Cecil. Bishop defended himself vociferously, claiming that Margaret had always been determined to damage his reputation in order to 'rule' Lennox and that Henry VIII had been so angry over her slanders against him that he had passed her over in his will.[3] No one took that claim seriously, but Bishop was throwing a lot of mud at the family – he even claimed that Margaret was behind Mary I's decision to place Elizabeth in the Tower in 1554 – and some of it began to stick.[4]

Lennox was placed under guard with the Master of the Rolls, and then sent to the Tower on 11 March. Margaret and her sons were also imprisoned, by 2 April, at the former Carthusian abbey of Sheen. With Lennox and Hertford in the Tower, and their wives and children also locked up, the Spanish ambassador was moved to comment 'The prisons will soon be full of the nearest relations of the crown.'[5] Lennox's imprisonment was particularly onerous with him kept 'close' prisoner while, to Lennox's irritation, Hertford was granted certain privileges, including having messages carried to Katherine[6]. Margaret Douglas ascribed this to Lennox's robust defence of their actions and reputation.[7] But it was she who was considered the tougher nut to crack. As Margaret's interrogators complained, she was 'very obstinate in her answers to the council' concerning the new charges that were laid against her that month.[8]

The fresh accusations could hardly have been more serious. Margaret was said to have committed treason in the recent war in Scotland, of being in secret communication with a foreign monarch (her niece Mary, Queen of Scots), and also with the French and Spanish ambassadors. It was further alleged that there were 'proofs' that she did 'not love the queen'. Servants claimed that she referred to Elizabeth as a bastard and that her fool at Temple Newsam in Yorkshire often roundly mocked Elizabeth and Robert Dudley, who she despised.[9] She had described Dudley and his siblings as 'traitor's birds', and Robert Dudley also as a pox-ridden wife-murderer.

The greatest danger to Margaret was, however, that she would be accused of attempting to kill the queen with witchcraft, like the Catholics Cecil had arrested at Easter the previous year. Cecil was already planning to frighten the queen with a more dangerous version of the 1561 plot. His aim was to turn Elizabeth against Mary, Queen of Scots by convincing her that her cousin was at the heart of these satanic conspiracies to end her life. Cardinal Pole's nephew Arthur Pole (who had been arrested, but released in 1561) was already being lined up to implicate the Scottish queen.[10] Margaret was at risk of being used similarly. Not only had it emerged that Margaret was a Catholic who heard Mass said 'by one little Sir William', it was also alleged that she was in contact with 'witches and soothsayers', even that she had conjured the lightning that had burned down the steeple of St Paul's in 1561, on the feast of Corpus Christi.[11]

An atmosphere of fear and paranoia was being stoked in Parliament where witchcraft was, at this very moment, being made an offence in common law. Parliament was similarly reviving a law against 'fond and fantastical prophecies', and here too Margaret was in trouble.[12] Her servants had revealed that when her first son had died as a baby, she had been comforted by a prophecy that Darnley would one day unite the crowns of England and Scotland.[13] Margaret asked to see Elizabeth to defend herself, quoting an old proverb that the greater the distance a person was from the court, the greater the slanders about them could grow. Lennox weighed in, describing their accusers as mere 'exploiters, hired men and other fantastical persons'.[14] But the accusation that most angered Margaret was not that concerning treason or witchcraft, which she rightly thought Elizabeth did not intend to pursue (Elizabeth suspected she was being manipulated), it was the attack on her legitimacy that had been planned for over a year. After Lennox's disloyal former servant, Thomas Bishop, had described Margaret as 'a mere bastard', she fired off a furious missive to Cecil reminding him 'Even as God hath made me, I am lawful daughter to the Queen of Scots [Margaret Tudor] and the Earl of Angus which none alive is able to make me other without doing me wrong.'[15]

No further charges were made against Margaret, but as summer turned to autumn she became increasingly concerned about Lennox's health. She bombarded Cecil with requests he be placed with her, or that they both be released. This worry was understandable. Her first love, Anne Boleyn's uncle Lord Thomas Howard, had died in the Tower in October 1537 and he had been a much younger man than Lennox. On 25 October Margaret wrote again, begging Cecil 'to be a means that the queen shall consider the long time of her husband's imprisonment . . . especially he being in the Tower and the winter coming on, and that house both unwholesome and cold'.[16] Unfortunately Elizabeth was in no state to do anything to help.

On 10 October 1562, when Elizabeth was at Hampton Court, she had begun to feel unwell, with aches and pains in her head and back. She had decided to have a bath and take a short walk to shake it off. When she returned to her chambers, however, she became feverish. A physician was called. To Elizabeth's irritation he diagnosed the potentially deadly smallpox. Since there were as yet no blisters she refused to accept the diagnosis, but sickness and diarrhoea followed and she became delirious. By 16 October the queen could no longer speak. On the 17th she was unconscious.

Elizabeth had been on the throne almost four years: only a year short of her sister's reign. If she died, as many feared she would, how would her reign have been remembered? Elizabeth's religious settlement was not viewed as settled by anyone save the queen. One of her own bishops called it 'a leaden mediocrity'. In military matters, while Mary I's loss of Calais is still remembered, Elizabeth's failed efforts to recover Calais by taking Le Havre and using it as a bargaining tool are completely forgotten. The campaign had ended that August 1562, with the huge loss of 2,000 men. Most troubling at the time, though, was what was likely to happen next. Mary I had named Elizabeth as her heir, despite her personal feelings towards her sister, and so allowed the crown to be inherited peacefully. Elizabeth continued to refuse to name anyone. Instead, when she woke up briefly, believing she was dying, she asked for Robert Dudley to be made Lord Protector with an income of £20,000. Her councillors promised her wishes would be fulfilled, but behind the scenes they had begun to argue furiously how the succession should actually go.

Since Elizabeth's immediate heirs were all female, some remained willing to look outside the Tudor family in order to pass the throne directly to a man. Cecil was sufficiently concerned about this to have sprung his 'witchcraft' trap early. Arthur Pole, and his brother Edmund, who were descended from Edward IV's brother, the Duke of Clarence, had been arrested and put in the Tower as an argument against their claims. Others were prepared to consider another of Clarence's heirs: the Protestant Henry Hastings, Earl of Huntingdon.[17] But a far larger proportion of the council looked to the Tudor family rather than to any faded remnants of the white rose.

As the frantic arguments continued, the pox blisters on Elizabeth's body began to appear. They broke first in her throat and mouth, before spreading outwards to her face and body. But she began to feel better and after a few days she could speak again. On 24 November Lennox was freed from the Tower on the queen's orders and permitted to join Margaret at Sheen. Having him die in the Tower was an embarrassment Elizabeth wished to avoid now that she faced renewed pressure to settle the issue of the succession once and for all. The council was determined to address the controversy during the coming parliament and Elizabeth remained most concerned about the threat posed by Katherine Grey.

The queen looked magnificent at the procession for the state opening on 12 January, all golden hair and red velvet. It was a wise queen who appeared 'most royally furnished . . . knowing right well that in pompous ceremonies a secret of government does much consist, for that people are both naturally taken and held with exterior shows. The rich attire, the ornaments, the beauty . . . held the eyes and hearts of men dazzled between contentment and admiration.' But Elizabeth also bore the scars of smallpox, a reminder that while her life had hung by a thread, so had the fate of her kingdom.

A debate on the succession began immediately with a petition soon drawn up, humbly requesting Elizabeth to marry, while also insisting that even if she did so, she must name an heir. Elizabeth's reply to the Lords reminded them fiercely that the marks she now had on her face left by smallpox weren't wrinkles and that, like the aging St Elizabeth, mother of John the Baptist, she could still have children. If she declared a successor, she warned, 'it would cost much blood in England'.[18] Yet the debates continued, and as they did so the shocking news broke that the twenty-two-year-old Katherine Grey was about to have a second child.

It emerged that in May Hertford had managed to bribe two guards to unlock his door and those to Katherine's nearby chambers. On the 24th they had spent an hour making love on her bed, with its covers of silk shot damask. Four days later he had returned, and once again they had lain together.[19] The guards had then got cold feet, or someone senior had got wind of what had occurred. When Hertford visited his wife on a third night he had found the door to Katherine's rooms locked.[20] He had not been able to return, but evidently those two nights had been enough for Katherine to conceive. It would now be difficult to deny they were married. They had been interrogated by the Archbishop of Canterbury and senior councillors and told them all they considered themselves man and wife. Under canon law such a statement, followed by intercourse, was a legal marriage.

At 10.15 in the morning on 10 February 1563 Katherine delivered another son, Lord Thomas Seymour. Elizabeth ordered the Lieutenant of the Tower be imprisoned in one of his own cells for his failures in keeping Hertford locked up, but ordinary people were demanding 'Why should man and wife be [prevented] from coming together?'[21] Elizabeth persisted, however, in refusing to recognise the marriage, and come the summer, when a virulent plague hit London, Elizabeth took the opportunity to move the couple out of the Tower to separate and far-flung country houses.

Katherine desperately missed Hertford. 'I long to be merry with you, as I know you do with me, as we were when our sweet little boy [Thomas] was begotten in the Tower', she wrote of their lovemaking; 'I wish you to be as happy as I was sad when you came to my door for the third time, and it was locked. Do you think I can forget what passed between us? No, I cannot. I remember it more often than you know . . . such is my boundless love for my sweet bedfellow, that I once lay beside with joyful heart and shall again.'[22] Katherine pleaded with the queen for her forgiveness, but she was kept apart not only from Hertford, but also from her elder son.

A miniature of Katherine with the infant Lord Beauchamp, painted at around this time by the female court artist Levina Teerlinc, remains the earliest known portrait of an English mother with her baby: a sad reminder for Katherine of all she had lost. But for others it represented the future: an icon of a Madonna carrying the Lord's anointed, the next King of England. Copies were made and even after 450 years several still survive. Katherine and Hertford had many friends who hoped that the queen could yet be pressured into naming Katherine, or one of her sons, as her heir.

Amongst Katherine's supporters was an MP called John Hales who spent the following months composing a book clarifying her succession rights and attacking those of Mary, Queen of Scots. Here, his greatest success was in unearthing a law, dating back to the reign of Edward III, which excluded those born outside the realm from inheriting land in England. Elizabeth's reaction was compared to a tempest when she learned of Hales' book in the spring of 1564; he was to spend a year in the Tower and a further four under house arrest for it. She complained particularly about Hales 'writing the book so precisely against the Queen of Scotland's title'.[23] It interfered with her latest plan of defence, which involved stalling Mary's remarriage.

Elizabeth could bastardise Katherine's sons, but she would have no such ability when Mary, Queen of Scots married – so she had to delay her from doing so for as long as possible, preferably until she was no longer able to bear sons. Elizabeth planned to convince Mary that to gain the English throne she had only to marry the one man she trusted: Robert Dudley. Bringing Mary round to marrying a mere subject of England would take time, and once that was achieved Elizabeth intended to come up with some last-minute impediment to the very marriage she was promoting. Although Elizabeth had accepted she could not marry Dudley herself, she was no less possessive of him than she had ever been.

As a sign of her commitment to the Stuart claim, Elizabeth had begun showering the freed Lennox family with marks of favour. Lennox had been permitted to return to Scotland to pursue the rights lost when he had come to England to serve Henry VIII, while Margaret Douglas and her children had been invited to court. There the thirty-year-old Elizabeth had long given up the modest attire she had worn during the reigns of Edward VI and Mary I. In a portrait from this period Elizabeth is wearing a beautiful scarlet dress with the cone-shaped skirts that were then fashionable, glittering with gold thread. A queen was expected to dress like a queen, and Elizabeth now followed her elder sister who had delighted 'above all in arraying herself elegantly and magnificently'.[24]

Darnley was greatly flattered by the attention of the glamorous Elizabeth that summer. She made a great show of enjoying his lute playing, and on 29 September he was given a prominent role in the ceremonies in which Elizabeth raised Robert Dudley to the royal title, Earl of Leicester: a necessary move if Dudley was to be considered seriously as an attractive groom for Mary, Queen of Scots.[25] Darnley preceded Elizabeth in the procession at St James's Palace, carrying the sword of state before her into the room where the ceremonies were to take place. There was something spoilt and effeminate about Darnley; 'a polished trifler' was the verdict of the French court.[26] The Scottish emissary agreed. His view, shared with Elizabeth, was that this tall boy 'was more a woman than a man, being very lusty, beardless and lady faced'. Mary would surely prefer Robert Dudley as a husband, Elizabeth believed, and when Dudley knelt before her and bowed his dark head, she could not resist 'putting her hand in his neck to kittle him smilingly'.[27]

Elizabeth was confident that Margaret Douglas had been tamed by her imprisonment. Cecil agreed and Margaret had used her considerable charm and intelligence to build up a relationship of mutual respect with him, even playing co-godparent to his daughter, Elizabeth Cecil, in July 1564.[28] Margaret also appeared to have befriended Robert Dudley, whom she had earlier accused of being a pox-ridden wife-killer. Events suggest that it was, in part, at Robert Dudley's persuasion that Elizabeth permitted the trifling Darnley to join his father in Scotland. Elizabeth soon realised, however, that she had made a disastrous miscalculation. Margaret and Robert Dudley had become, if not true friends, then political allies. Dudley was making it evident he had no intention of leaving England, and his supposed match with Mary, Queen of Scots was dead in the water by early 1565. England needed a successor, and Robert Dudley had come down on the side of the Queen of Scots, while leaving open the possibility that he might one day marry Elizabeth.

As it dawned on Elizabeth that she had been persuaded to grant Margaret's son a passport so that she could be pressured into allowing him to marry Mary, Queen of Scots and name them as her co-heirs, she panicked. To make it quite clear that she would not be bullied into naming any heir, Elizabeth delivered the devastating news to Mary that she had decided not to name a successor until 'she shall be married or shall notify her determination never to marry'. In doing so, however, she had lost her leverage over Mary, who noted icily, 'I . . . fear it shall turn to her discredit more than my loss.' The English ambassador begged Mary's advisers to dissuade her from acting hastily, but they cut him short. Mary would marry soon and to her own choice, they told him: 'The die is cast.'[29]

36

MURDER IN THE FAMILY

QUEEN ELIZABETH HAD ENJOYED HER EVENING AS SHE SAT DOWN to supper at court, on 5 March 1565. Her cousin, Margaret Douglas, had joined her to watch a joust and a tourney on horses. The combat, with twenty-four challengers and opponents, had been organised by Robert Dudley, who had also taken part in what had proved an excellent competition. He had planned more entertainments to come, and following supper all the guests congregated for a comedy he had set up in the queen's apartments. It featured two goddesses debating the virtues of marriage over those of chastity. 'All this is against me', Elizabeth commented wearily. It was only when the dancing began that Elizabeth's good spirits returned. There was a masquerade of men dressed as wild gods and satyrs who danced with the ladies, as did the men who had taken part in the combats, still wearing weapons. The evening ended with everyone flushed with excitement, hungry again, and eating from a huge table laden with snacks of herring and other small fish, cakes and sweets.[1]

When the latest Spanish ambassador, Don Diego Guzman de Silva, saw Elizabeth nearly three weeks later, she spoke again about the pressure to marry: 'I promise you, if I could today appoint such a successor to the crown as would please me and the country, I would not marry. It is something for which I have never had any inclination. My subjects, however, press me to do so. I must therefore marry or take the other course, which is a very difficult one. There is a strong idea in the world that a woman cannot live unless she is married, or at all events that if she refrains from marriage she does so for some bad reason. They said of me that I did not marry because I was fond of [Robert Dudley] the Earl of Leicester, and that I would not marry him because he had a wife already. Although he has no wife alive now I still do not marry him . . . But what can we do? We cannot cover everybody's mouth, but must content ourselves with doing our duty.'[2]

When the conversation moved to the saga of Margaret's son Darnley seeking to marry the Queen of Scots, Elizabeth assured Silva that the boy would be returning to England in May, along with his father. Margaret, however, had already told the ambassador Darnley had 'no such intention'.[3] Mary, Queen of Scots had realised that she could not trust Elizabeth and that she needed a party of supporters in England if she wished to inherit the English crown. Margaret Douglas had spelled out to her the advantages of marrying her son in this respect. The tract on the succession written by the MP John Hales, with its claims that a foreigner could not inherit the English throne, had also made Darnley's English birth more attractive to Mary. Margaret told Silva that negotiations were far advanced, and she was sending rich jewels into Scotland to secure the support of key figures.

It was sometime over the next few days that Elizabeth and Cecil discovered that a marriage between Darnley and Mary, Queen of Scots might actually take place. They were appalled. Cecil believed the majority of English people saw Mary as Elizabeth's rightful heir. A marriage to Darnley would strengthen Mary's candidature still further, and Elizabeth feared this would interfere with her policy of ensuring there was 'no certain successor' to her crown.[4] She sent increasingly frantic messages to Mary warning her not to marry Darnley. Come late April, with Mary still ignoring her messages, Elizabeth decided the time had come to remind Darnley that his mother was at her mercy.

When Margaret Douglas next visited Elizabeth at Whitehall

Elizabeth snubbed her. This was followed up with an order confining her cousin to her quarters. Margaret's crime, she learned, was 'having received letters from a foreign prince [Mary, Queen of Scots] without the queen's permission and without conveying the contents to her'. Margaret insisted she had just been on her way to show these letters to Elizabeth when she was arrested. This time Elizabeth was not to be fooled. On 22 June Margaret was sent back to the Tower to which she had last been consigned nineteen years earlier in 1536, by Henry VIII.[5]

Elizabeth's action did nothing, however, to alter Mary, Queen of Scots from her path. Darnley was proclaimed King of Scots and on 29 July 1565 he and Mary were married. The new royal couple gambled that Elizabeth would never dare harm Margaret, and together, as king and queen, they reiterated Mary's promises to maintain the Protestant religion as established in Scotland. All they needed now was to have a son, and in due course the crown of England would fall into their laps. The prophecy that Margaret's heir would one day unite the crowns of England and Scotland had never looked closer to being fulfilled, and Margaret rejoiced.

When Silva saw Elizabeth the following month she was under pressure from the French to release Margaret. Robert Dudley had asked if Silva 'would go and see the park' at Richmond. They duly wore out 'three horses and saw a large quantity of game'. Returning, they 'came round by the footpath leading to the riverside through the wood to where the queen lodges, and when we came to her apartments Leicester's fool made so much noise calling her that she came undressed to the window'. Elizabeth once admitted 'I am no morning woman.' When business was urgent she might see officials before 10 a.m, but still wearing something akin to a dressing gown. Usually she liked to read for a while, or sit by her window to watch the world go by. Having seen them she came downstairs – though it took an hour and a half for her to get dressed – and together Elizabeth and Silva had 'walked for a long while talking'.[6] Elizabeth confirmed that she had no intention of bowing to French pressure on Margaret just yet.

In the Tower, as the months passed, the servants who waited on Margaret Douglas whiled away the hours, engraving their names on the principal fireplace in the Queen's House where their mistress was confined. Margaret also kept busy, corresponding with her contacts across Europe, England and Scotland in an effort to keep informed. Nevertheless, she could not see the disastrous turn her son's marriage was soon taking. The nineteen-year-old Darnley found having to play second fiddle to his reigning wife intolerable, while she had concluded he possessed neither aptitude for hard work nor the wisdom required to rule a country as volatile as Scotland. As their marriage broke down, he began spending his nights in the brothels of Edinburgh, and she refused him the 'crown matrimonial' that would have given him an equal share of royal power. Darnley had done his duty as a king consort in one respect only: by the time he passed his twentieth birthday in December, Mary was pregnant.

Margaret, blinded by her love for her son and cut off from events, blamed Mary, Queen of Scots for the couple's quarrels and wrote her furious letters, at which Mary was 'greatly offended'.[7] In Scotland Mary was facing a dangerous enough enemy in the form of her Protestant half-brother, James V's illegitimate son the Earl of Moray and his allies. They had begun to play on her effete husband's sense of impotence, using Mary's trust in her Italian secretary, David Riccio, to make him jealous. The overthrow of 'bad' councillors was the traditional pretext for a noble seizure of power, and Riccio was being set up in that role to justify a coup. The first thing Margaret knew about this was when, in the spring of 1566, she learnt that Riccio had been murdered – and that her son Darnley was involved.

The details of the killing that reached England were horrific. Mary had been having supper with Riccio in her private rooms when Darnley had appeared with a group of men. She had tried to prevent them taking Riccio away, but she was held at gunpoint while Darnley prised

Riccio's fingers from her skirt. He had then held her back while Riccio was thrust out of the room. Fifty-five stab wounds were found in Riccio's body, as was Darnley's dagger, which his allies left embedded in the corpse to prove his involvement. Elizabeth was astounded: 'Do you think the Queen of Scotland has been well treated to have armed men entering her chamber, as if it were that of a public woman, for the purpose of killing a man without reason?' she asked Silva. He agreed 'it was a bad business', but he also believed that 'if [only Margaret] had been in Scotland . . . her son would not have been led astray, nor would these disputes have taken place, as she is prudent and brave, and the son respects her more than he does his father'.[8]

Lennox was furious with Darnley, but also afraid what would happen next. He was hugely relieved when Mary, Queen of Scots chose to reconcile with his son and so forestall Moray's intended coup. Margaret did her best to make up for her mistakes by encouraging the family reconciliation, and as the birth of her first grandchild approached she sent Mary gifts. On 19 June 1566 Mary, Queen of Scots bore a son. He was christened Charles James: Charles after his godfather Charles IX of France, and James after his grandfather, James V of Scots. It was as James that he would always be known. Margaret promptly contacted the Pole brothers, who had been in the Tower since 1562, and persuaded them to pass on to Mary all the royal claims of their Plantagenet descent.[9] This well-meant gesture was hardly necessary. James' birth had greatly enhanced the virtues of Mary's already strong claim to the English throne. 'From what can be heard the people of this country are delighted at the good news of the birth of the Queen of Scotland's child' Silva reported. The same was certainly not true of the queen, although she put on a show of delight to the ambassador and suggested mischievously that she might send Cecil to the christening.[10]

If Margaret hoped that the birth of her grandson would also revive Mary and Darnley's marriage she was to be disappointed. At the beginning of February 1567 Margaret was writing to the Spanish ambassador, telling him how it grieved her to see her son was quarrelling again with his wife.[11] She was also, she said, desperate to leave the Tower, even if only to house arrest. The person most likely to persuade Elizabeth to allow this was Cecil, so Margaret was delighted when Lady Cecil arrived to see her on the 19th, along with a very old friend. Lady Howard was a sister-in-law of Lord Thomas Howard, the man to whom Margaret had been betrothed in 1536, and had been her confidante all those years ago. But it soon emerged the women had not come just to pay Margaret their respects. Elizabeth had chosen them as the kindest bearers of terrible news: Margaret's twenty-one-year-old son Darnley had been assassinated, the fate of so many earlier Kings of Scots.

The murder had been discovered nine days earlier after the people of Edinburgh had been awoken at two in the morning by a violent explosion. Some ran towards the apparent origin of the blast at Kirk o' Field. There they found the Old Provost Lodging, where Darnley had been sleeping, a heap of rubble. Nearby in the orchard, his strangely unmarked body had been laid out, dressed only in a night-gown, alongside a dead servant. Margaret Douglas immediately assumed that Darnley had been killed on the orders of his wife, as did almost everybody else. Revulsion and grief overwhelmed her, and she 'could not by any means be kept from such passion of mind as the horribleness of the fact did require'. After a doctor was called, Elizabeth agreed to release her grief-stricken cousin from the Tower. Margaret was now reunited with her younger son Charles and placed in the secure care of a family who backed Katherine Grey's cause.[12]

Darnley's murder had also deeply shocked Elizabeth, but her concern was chiefly for her sister queen. She had always been fascinated to hear about Mary. In 1564 she had demanded to know from the Scottish emissary how Mary compared to her in height, looks and musical talent, just as her father, Henry VIII, had once asked how Francis I measured up to him. Yet although there was a sense of rivalry, and concerns about the danger that Mary posed as her heir, nevertheless while Mary was secure on her throne in Scotland, Elizabeth, as a fellow reigning queen, had felt that little bit more so herself. 'Madame', Elizabeth now wrote to Mary, 'My ears have been so astounded and my heart so frightened to hear of the horrible and abominable murder of your husband and my cousin that I have scarcely spirit to write: yet I cannot conceal that I grieve more for you than him. I should not do the office of a faithful cousin and friend, if I did not urge you to preserve your honour, rather than look through your fingers at revenge on those who have done you "tel plaisir [this pleasure]," as most people say. I counsel you so to take this matter to heart that you may show the world what a noble princess and loyal woman you are.'[13] These urgings to find and condemn her husband's murderers, and so end the rumours of her involvement, went unheeded.

In Scotland Mary was 'deeply afflicted, and in great fear' that Darnley's assassins would now kill her, and make her infant son a puppet king.[14] Then the extraordinary news emerged that in May 1567 Mary had married the Protestant Earl of Bothwell, one of the principal suspects in Darnley's death. She said – and many historians now accept – that she did so only after she had been captured and raped.[15] Others believe that she was looking for protection. Whatever her true motives, her marriage provided the pretext for a rebellion led by Bothwell's erstwhile allies amongst the Protestant lords. Bothwell became a fugitive, and Mary was soon imprisoned in a castle on an island on Loch Leven. Her infant son, James, was crowned King of Scots in her place on 24 July 1567, with the misogynist John Knox giving the sermon.

Elizabeth raged against the rebels; Cecil only managed to dissuade her from sending an army to free Mary by warning such action could trigger Mary's assassination. The queen had always been more fearful of Katherine Grey's claim (so much closer to home, and in light of Jane Grey's earlier usurpation), and now it seemed Katherine's cause would be unstoppable. Elizabeth had all the keys to her chambers, save one, hidden away, and the imprisonment of Katherine's husband,

Hertford, was made stricter.[16] By the time Katherine was moved to the distant Cockfield Hall in Suffolk that winter, the twenty-seven-year-old Protestant heir to the throne rightly despaired of ever being freed.

The house that was to serve as Katherine's fifth prison in seven years belonged to a future Lieutenant of the Tower, a man called Sir Owen Hopton. Cecil had always been careful to find jailors he hoped would be kind to Katherine, and Sir Owen was a relative of hers. Remarkably, he was a grandson of Owen Tudor's illegitimate son, David, knighted by Henry Tudor when he landed in Wales in 1485.[17] Sir Owen was distressed to discover that Katherine was in a state of suicidal depression. He wrote to Cecil warning that Katherine was ill, and worse, that she welcomed her death.[18]

The doctor sent from the court could do nothing for Katherine. On the night of 26 January 1568, Katherine told those at her bedside that she was dying. They tried their best to raise her spirits, telling her that 'With God's help you shall live and do well many years.' But Katherine replied firmly, 'No, no. No life in this world.'[19] At about six or seven the next morning Katherine gave Sir Owen Hopton her last messages. Elizabeth she begged to 'be good to my children and . . . to my Lord [Hertford], for I know this my death will be heavy news to him.'[20] To her husband she sent the pointed diamond he had given her on their betrothal, her gold wedding band, and a memento mori ring, engraved with the words 'While I lived, yours.'[21] Katherine's death at nine o'clock that morning, Tuesday 27 January 1568, brought to a close another tragic love story in the Tudor family. Elizabeth put on a show of grief, as expected at the death of a relative, but it was judged an unconvincing performance. 'She was afraid of her', the Spanish ambassador noted.[22]

Of the three Grey sisters only the youngest, Lady Mary Grey, remained alive – and she was also in disgrace. In 1565, aged nineteen, undersized, and judged by the Spanish ambassador to be 'crook backed and very ugly' Mary Grey had married a giant of a man called Thomas Keyes who was the sergeant porter, in charge of palace security. It is possible she had a severe form of the scoliosis that afflicted Richard III and Edward VI. Clearly this hadn't bothered the strapping Mr Keyes, but Cecil described their physical disparity as 'monstrous'.

Lady Mary Grey hoped that Elizabeth would forgive her actions, because in marrying a commoner she had ruled herself out of the succession. But she too had been kept in country-house prisons, while Keyes was crammed in a tiny cell in the Fleet prison. It had been the porters in charge of palace security who had saved Mary I when St James's Palace came under attack from the Wyatt rebels in 1554, slamming shut the palace gates, while the guard had fled. Elizabeth felt betrayed by Keyes and he was cruelly treated in prison. As for Lady Mary Grey, although she posed no threat, Elizabeth intended to use her fate to act as a warning to any of the next generation of Tudor blood to obey her in the matter of their marriages, or expect severe punishment.

As one head was cut from the hydra of royal cousins another, inevitably, grew stronger. Elizabeth, aged thirty-four, was increasingly unlikely to have children, and now the future of England lay once again with the twenty-five-year-old Queen of Scots. But four months after Katherine's death, in May 1568, Mary made another miscalculation. Having escaped her island prison in Scotland she sailed for England, from where she sent Elizabeth a letter. Mary had little doubt her fellow queen would help restore her to her throne and expressed 'the confidence I have in you, not only for the safety of my life, but also to aid and assist me in my just quarrel'. She also looked forward to their first ever meeting: 'I entreat you', 'Mary continued' 'to send to fetch me as soon as you possibly can, for I am in a pitiable condition, not only for a queen but for a gentlewoman, for I have nothing in the world but what I had when I made my escape'. Her adventures, riding across country and travelling at night, 'I hope to declare before you, if it please you to have pity', Mary concluded.

Elizabeth did not want Mary, Queen of Scots at court since she would have been obliged to treat her as a visiting sovereign, and so raise Mary's profile as her heir. But it was useful to have Mary in her power, and that is how Elizabeth intended things should stay. She ordered that Mary be kept under guard in the north, while her council debated what they thought she should do next with her reluctant royal guest. Mary hoped the moderate Protestant establishment who had supported her in the past would do so again, and so they did – at first. Robert Dudley was amongst those who continued to take the pragmatic view that England's long-term security demanded a named successor. They believed they could still resolve the difficulty of Mary's Catholicism by marrying her to England's premier nobleman, Thomas Howard, 4th Duke of Norfolk. The great-grandson of the victor of Flodden, he was Protestant, as well as young, handsome and popular. Mary responded positively to the suggested marriage and even began using the Protestant Book of Common Prayer for spiritual contemplation. It was certain that Cecil's political ruin would follow if Mary was named as Elizabeth's heir, but many believed it was time he was cut down to size. Unfortunately, Elizabeth was not among them.

When it emerged that Elizabeth would never allow Mary to marry Norfolk, the court campaign behind the proposal collapsed. As Cecil emerged victorious his opponents assumed he would wreak revenge. Most fearful were Norfolk's allies in the north, the Catholic Earls of Westmorland and Northumberland. Rather than risk dying in prison, and encouraged by their wives, the earls raised a rebellion in the north 'against a new-found religion and heresy' and 'for the preservation of the person of the Queen of Scots'. Elizabeth had long feared a revolt in favour of her successor. Now it was happening. Yet this northern rebellion was no Pilgrimage of Grace. In November 1569, when the rebel earls took Durham, their force of around 4,000 foot soldiers and 2,000 horse was already dwindling. Within six weeks it was over. But it had touched a raw nerve with the queen, and her vengeance was to be on a scale unmatched by any of her Tudor predecessors.

Elizabeth ordered hangings in every village involved in the revolt. On 23 January 1570 one of her officers in the North Riding of Yorkshire reported 'six hundred and odd' executed, and that the people were 'in marvellous fear so that I trust there shall never such thing happen in these parts again'; twelve days later another official confirmed they had 'already executed above five hundred of the poorer sort'.[23] The estimated total is around 800–900. This was four times more than Elizabeth's father had hanged, beheaded and burned in the aftermath of the Pilgrimage of Grace, which had seen 30,000 rebels in the field. It was also nine times the number her sister Mary I had executed after the Wyatt revolt, which had come so close to overrunning the court. In 1570 Elizabeth, too, had earned the sobriquet 'Bloody'.

The Elizabethan bishops pressed the queen to go further. They informed Elizabeth it was her duty to execute the Queen of Scots, along with all those who threatened the security of the Protestant religion. Elizabeth refused. Mary's situation was a little too reminiscent of her own position under Mary I, when her name was repeatedly linked to plots against her sister. 'I have', she recalled, 'tasted of the practices against my sister', and she remembered well, 'There were occasions in me at that time, I stood in danger of my life, my sister was so incensed against me.'[24] Imprisoning her female cousins had served Elizabeth well enough in the past, and she believed she had no need to set a dangerous precedent in the execution of a monarch. Mary, Queen of Scots realised, however, that she was now as trapped as a deer at bay, the hounds barking at her throat awaiting only the huntsman's signal to end her life.

37

EXIT MARGARET DOUGLAS

A HEART-SHAPED LOCKET KNOWN AS THE LENNOX JEWEL IS TODAY one of the most important pieces in the royal collection. Commissioned by Margaret Douglas and her husband, it tells the story of their happy marriage, of their grief for Darnley and of their determination to protect the interests of their grandson, King James. The case is gold, studded with precious stones, and has a white enamel border which reads in Scots: 'Who hopes still constantly with patience shall obtain victory in their claim': that is, their claims to the thrones of Scotland and England, united in James.

Opening the locket reveals two hearts pierced by arrows and the initials MSL for Margaret and Matthew Stuart Lennox. Only 'Death will dissolve' their marriage, it says, and a further motto in Scots forewarns 'What we Resolve'. On the back is the image of the fallen Darnley with a crown at his side. This is the crown of Scotland, which he had worn as king consort. From it springs a sunflower – James – turning towards the sun, which represents the English crown. A further image known as the Pelican in its Piety depicts a bird drawing blood from its own breast to feed its young, just as Margaret and Lennox will do everything possible to nourish James until he is King of England.[1]

Margaret and Lennox had good reason to be anxious for James' future. There was a sharp reminder of Scottish violence on 23 January

1570, when Elizabeth's ally, the regent Moray, was shot and killed in Scotland. Margaret and Lennox had come to see Moray as James' protector. Now Moray was dead Margaret was determined they should take control of James' care. 'I doubt not you know partly how many sorrowful grieves I have passed', Margaret wrote to Cecil, and shared her fears that she faced more losses. She had been married to Lennox for twenty-six years, she reminded Cecil, yet she could not calm her husband in his distress because 'he sees plainly the destruction of that innocent little king near at hand'. She urged that any anxieties concerning their religious affiliations be put out of the queen's mind, and Lennox be given permission to return to Scotland for James' protection.[2]

It was a mark of how remarkably persuasive Margaret could be that Cecil and Elizabeth allowed Lennox to return to Scotland to replace Moray as James' regent, while Margaret remained in England as his ambassador at court. The couple kept in close touch, with Lennox relying on his 'Good Meg' for her advice and intelligence. But the following year, 1571, Lennox was shot in the back during a raid on Stirling made by supporters of Elizabeth's prisoner, Mary, Queen of Scots. The five-year-old King James would never forget seeing his grandfather brought back into the castle with his 'bowls cut'. As Lennox lay bleeding he begged the Scots lords to protect James. 'If the bairn's well, all's well', he said, and with his last breath he sent his love to Margaret: 'Thus treason bereft me of my son and my mate', a memorial verse about Margaret Douglas later recalled.

Elizabeth too was soon to be threatened with assassination. Only a few months later William Cecil – by now granted the title of Lord Burghley – uncovered a plot that shocked Elizabeth to the core. It involved a Florentine banker and double agent called Roberto di Ridolfi, and a plan to capture Elizabeth during her summer progress, then replace her on the throne with Mary, Queen of Scots, and Norfolk, backed by an invading army of 6,000 Spaniards. The Duke of Norfolk was tried and convicted of treason in January 1572 and executed early in the summer morning of 2 June. Elizabeth continued in her refusal to execute Mary but she had undergone a sea change in her attitude to her fellow queen. Mary had been the focus of the rebellion of the northern earls, and now of the Ridolfi plot. Elizabeth had no doubt there would be others, and in verse she described Mary angrily as 'The daughter of debate, That discord aye doth sow.'

In a nod to please the backers of the Grey claim, Elizabeth had permitted the widowed Hertford to return to court in the aftermath of the Northern rebellion. A few days after Norfolk's execution she also now released Hertford's sister-in-law, Lady Mary Grey, from her long imprisonment. Thomas Keyes, her husband, had died the previous September and Mary Grey's bitterness at being freed only when she was a widow is recalled in her portrait, which hangs today at the prime minister's country residence, Chequers. In her hair Mary Grey wears carnations and gillyflowers for love, fidelity and remembrance, while her hand is raised to show her wedding ring to the viewer. She would live quietly for a handful more years before dying, childless, in 1578 during an outbreak of plague.

Only one of the grandchildren of Henry VIII's sisters still remained unmarried – Margaret Douglas' youngest son, Charles Stuart. Margaret was desperate to find him a bride, but after the harsh treatment of the Grey sisters and their spouses, not to mention the execution of Norfolk, no nobleman was willing to cross Elizabeth by agreeing to a match. Margaret hoped Cecil might help her and hinted to him that her teenage son needed a father figure.[3] She hoped he would agree to become the boy's guardian, so taking on some of the responsibility of arranging a marriage. Cecil declined to take the bait, but in 1574 one of the most upwardly mobile women in Elizabethan England, Bess of Hardwick, did approach Margaret.

The clever red-haired Bess had once served as a lady-in-waiting to Frances Brandon, the mother of the Grey sisters. She had married her second husband, Sir William Cavendish, at the Grey family seat in

Leicestershire, and at least four members of the Grey family had played godparent to their children. She treasured a portrait of Lady Jane Grey, as well as her letters, almost as if they were holy relics. Bess was currently on her fourth and richest husband: George Talbot, 6th Earl of Shrewsbury, the jailor to Mary, Queen of Scots. She had married her eldest son and daughter to two of Shrewsbury's children. But she couldn't find anyone she considered suitable for her third daughter, Elizabeth Cavendish, and so Bess had decided to use the immense wealth she had acquired through her marriages as bait to catch Charles Stuart, the unmarried heir of Tudor blood. Margaret responded positively to Bess's approach. Bess was no fool, she knew, and Elizabeth had always liked Bess, which would help when news of the marriage emerged.

The two mothers laid their plans around the midsummer of 1574 and in October they were ready to carry them out.[4] Margaret set off with her nineteen-year-old son from London, ostensibly travelling north to her home in Yorkshire. The bells were rung in villages as Margaret's train approached, and people came out from their homes to see Henry VIII's last niece and her son pass by. When the horses, carriages and carts reached Nottinghamshire, a messenger was sent to Bess, who was staying 'by chance' at her husband's seat at Rufford Abbey. She rode out to meet Margaret and Charles, and invited them to stay. A little while later Shrewsbury received a letter from his wife. Bess told him that Margaret had fallen ill shortly after arriving at Rufford and had spent five days in bed, during which time Charles Stuart had fallen in love with her daughter. The love was so intense, Bess warned her husband, that Charles was sickening and she believed it was necessary for his health that he should marry the girl as soon as possible.[5] Shortly afterwards – certainly before anyone could intervene – they were, indeed, married.

Charles Stuart's marriage to a commoner was far less threatening to Queen Elizabeth than his elder brother Darnley's marriage to Mary, Queen of Scots had been. But Elizabeth did want to know if

Mary had played some hand in the marriage. Margaret had been in touch with some of Mary's close allies since at least the midsummer of 1574 and when she had expressed an interest to Elizabeth in visiting Bess, Elizabeth had warned her not to go to Sheffield Lodge where Mary was imprisoned.[6] If she did people might think she 'did agree with the Queen of Scots', Elizabeth had explained pointedly. To this Margaret had retorted that she was 'made of flesh and blood and could never forget the murder of my child [Darnley] . . . for if I would, I were a devil'.[7] Margaret now explained to Cecil that as Rufford was only a mile out of their way on the road north, and Bess had invited her and Charles to stay in person, she could hardly have refused her friend. She assumed Rufford was not considered off limits by Elizabeth, it 'being near thirty miles from Sheffield' where the Queen of Scots was held.

Elizabeth eventually concluded that the arrangement of the marriage between Margaret's son and Bess's daughter had only 'money at the ground of it', and, with nothing else 'that may cause twitch', Margaret was released after a few months of house arrest at her home in Hackney.[8] As for Bess, she managed to buy back the queen's good favour with little more than the gift of an expensive cloak she embroidered for Elizabeth as a New Year's gift.

Margaret was, however, soon establishing a rapprochement with Mary, Queen of Scots, just as Elizabeth had feared she might. Margaret had not forgotten the murder of Darnley, but she had become convinced that Mary was innocent of any involvement in his death. Mary's guilt had supposedly been proven in 1568 when a tribunal in York and Westminster had established the authenticity of a series of papers known as the Casket letters, sent by the Scottish government as 'evidence' of Mary's role. We now know the letters had included a number of forgeries, but since there was no chance whatever of any independent forensic analysis at the time, the easiest way to debunk them was to retaliate in kind. This Mary's friends had now done with a forged deathbed confession by Bothwell which exculpated Mary of any involvement in Darnley's death, and pointed the finger instead at the nine-year-old King James' latest regent, James Douglas, Earl of Morton.[9] He had admitted knowing of the plot, and that was enough to convince Margaret, whose hatred was now directed at 'the wicked governor', rather than Mary, Queen of Scots.

James' safety was a shared source of concern for his mother and grandmother, and in a letter to Mary dated November 1575, Margaret Douglas confided her fears that 'our sweet and peerless jewel in Scotland' was not safe in Morton's care. But Margaret also now had another grandchild to think about: Charles and his wife had a baby daughter: Arbella Stuart. Mary had sent the little girl gifts and Margaret expressed the hope that Arbella 'someday may serve your highness'.[10] The two women continued thereafter to exchange tokens as well as letters. They included a piece of extremely fine and expensive needlework Margaret had worked with her own hair as a mark of her devotion. This remarkable turnaround in Margaret's attitude to Mary had an important pay-off: Mary revised her will, naming Charles as the heir to his nephew, King James.

When Charles died of an unknown cause in 1576, Margaret had yet another 'sorrowful grief' to endure. But her pain at the loss of the last of her eight children was ameliorated when the little Arbella and her mother came to live with her. A picture she had painted of Arbella, aged twenty-three months, depicts a hazel-eyed infant clutching a fashionably dressed doll, and around Arbella's neck, hanging from a triple chain of gold, hangs a shield with the countess' coronet along with the Lennox motto in French, 'To achieve, I endure'. Arbella's place in the line of succession was very similar to Margaret's in the 1530s. Where, by the tradition of primogeniture, Margaret had been second in line to James V, but had the advantage of her English birth, so Arbella was second to James VI, but also had the advantage of being English-born. Nevertheless, as far as Margaret was concerned the English throne remained destined for James, and was rightfully his.

From her houses in Yorkshire and Hackney Margaret kept in contact with her growing grandson, sending James works of history, and on one occasion a pair of beautiful pearl-embroidered hawking gloves. But her servant, John Philips, recalled that by 1578, when she was aged sixty-two, Margaret seemed worn down by the loss of her beloved husband and children. Money was tight, too. Margaret had to pay £500 a year to Bess alone in interest on loans. Yet, despite everything, Margaret remained engaged in politics and continued to entertain the powerful and influential. At a dinner in February 1578 she had Robert Dudley as her guest. This was a woman who could remember Henry VIII intimately, and had witnessed the falls of Anne Boleyn and Katherine Howard from the close quarters of the queen's Privy Chambers. But she and Robert Dudley also had memories to share, as well as a future to argue over.[11]

Robert Dudley was no longer a supporter of Mary, Queen of Scots. After the rebellion of 1569 and the Ridolfi plot, he had become, instead, a protector of the Puritans: those Protestants who wanted further reform in the Church of England. In this he had little in common with Margaret and it was later claimed that he poisoned her at this last dinner. Perhaps the food disagreed with her and she fell ill, just as her ancestress Margaret Beaufort had after eating swan almost sixty years before.

Margaret wrote her last testament on 26 February 1578, still in 'perfect mind' and 'good health of body'. It asked that when she died the body of her son Charles be moved from his tomb at her house in Hackney, to be buried with her in Westminster Abbey. She had already chosen the spot for her tomb in the Lady Chapel where her grandfather Henry VII was buried. £1,200 was put aside for her funeral and burial expenses. She matched this with a gift of £1,200 for the poor. William Cecil was bequeathed a black enamel ring set with four diamonds, and Robert Dudley a chain of pomander beads netted with gold. She also left him her tablet picture of Henry VIII. Even in death it was important to grease the right palms – especially if you wanted a grand funeral in Westminster Abbey.

Margaret Douglas died on 10 March and on 3 April she had a funeral appropriate for a royal princess, and with a service of which Elizabeth would approve.[12] Nothing had been written in her will that distinguished her as Catholic or Protestant and there were no marks of Catholic belief at her funeral.[13] Margaret obeyed the letter of the law, as she was obliged to do and had always done in public. The tomb she had wanted was later set up by her secretary Thomas Fowler. In an echo of the Lennox motto, 'To achieve I endure', it celebrated 'a lady of most pious character, invincible spirit, and matchless steadfastness' who was 'mighty in virtue' and 'mightier yet in lineage'. Few tombs in the abbey matched the royal ancestors she had listed on her tomb, but she was prouder still to be 'a progenitor of princes' in her son Darnley, known as Henry, King of Scots, and in her grandson King James. One day, she had hoped, he too would lie in this abbey, as a King of England.

38

THE VIRGIN QUEEN

WAS IT BETTER FOR A QUEEN WHO COULD NOT MARRY NEVER TO have felt love? In verse Elizabeth begged 'let me live with some more sweet content/Or die and so forget what love e'er meant'.[1] Her father, Henry VIII, had feared it would be hard to find a king consort for a Tudor queen 'with whom the whole realm could and would be contented', and so it had proved.[2] The anxieties she had expressed to the emissary of Mary, Queen of Scots in 1561, that she could not marry without triggering unrest, had deepened following Mary's disastrous marriages to Darnley and Bothwell. Elizabeth continued to look publicly for a husband to fulfil national expectations, and surely hoped it was not impossible that she might find someone suitable, but in their absence she had settled for something akin to a celibate marriage with Robert Dudley. It was a kind of 'sweet content'.

People always rushed to see Elizabeth and Dudley together. The antiquarian John Stow recalled witnessing them meeting in 1566. Dudley had entered London with a train of 700 lords, knights and gentlemen accompanied by the queen's footmen, as well as his own. They marched from Temple Bar, through the City, across London Bridge into Southwark while the queen came 'secretly [across the water] taking a wherry with one pair of oars for her and two other ladies'. When she landed Elizabeth got into a blue coach and as Dudley and his army reached her on the highway, she came out and greeted him with kisses, before she mounted a horse and they rode on together to Greenwich Palace. That night Stow had watched Dudley return to London in advance of the queen, his way lit by the strange glow of the Northern Lights.[3]

Nine years later, in 1575, Robert Dudley had prepared a magnificent eighteen days of entertainment for Elizabeth's visit to his seat at Kenilworth Castle in Warwickshire. When the great day came Elizabeth had enjoyed a feast in a specially built pavilion before Dudley rode with her to his castle, the flickering flames of the candles from the windows reflected in the lake and glittering like a vision from a fairy tale. Over the following two and a half weeks there were masques, pageants and dramas, with the subject of marriage a constant theme. But Elizabeth would turn forty-five in 1578, suitors had come and gone for two decades, and the pretence that she would ever marry was coming to an end.

One last serious discussion of a match was under way with Elizabeth courted by the twenty-four-year-old brother of the French king Henri III, the Duke of Anjou. The old friendship with Spain had soured over their religious differences and the English piracy of Spanish gold brought back from their colonies in the New World. Elizabeth needed France as a friend, but to England's beleaguered Catholics the marriage proposal also represented the desperate hope of an end to the increasingly vicious persecution to which they were being subjected.

On Elizabeth's accession new legislation had required all clerics, lay office holders and the heirs to large estates to swear an oath denying papal authority. In notable contrast to the Henrician bishops, all but one of the carefully picked Marian bishops had refused to take it and had consequently been deprived of office. In Oxford the head of all but one of the colleges had also resigned or were sacked. This had left Catholics in the parishes largely leaderless, as priests either became Protestant ministers or left their posts.

Over the following years bewildered congregations had seen remaining rood screens, with their images of Christ, Mary and St John, replaced with the royal arms of the supreme governor of the Church of England. Newly whitewashed walls were decorated only with biblical quotations, there was no holy water with which to cross themselves, no candles, everything was plain and without colour, while elaborate music too was frowned on as a distraction from prayer.

This cultural revolution was not entirely to Elizabeth's taste. She employed the Catholic composers Thomas Tallis and William Byrd in the royal chapels. She issued proclamations in an effort to protect ancient monuments, fonts and altars from wholesale destruction. Elizabeth believed that rood screens were 'rather for the advantage of the church' and she retained candles and a crucifix on the Communion table in her chapel.[4] In 1565, when the dean of St Paul's gave a sermon attacking Catholic writing in praise of the Cross, she interrupted him saying loudly, 'Do not talk about that.'[5] But even the queen's plain silver crucifix, described as a 'foul idol' placed 'on the altar of abomination', was twice broken and attacked in sermons by members of her clergy. Her subjects were far less able to protect their churches from zealous iconoclasts.

In 1562 the Bishop of Durham, James Pilkington, had sneered at his parishioners, imitating them wailing, 'What shall I do at the church? I may not have my [rosary] beads, [and] the church is like a waste barn; there are no images or saints to worship and make curtsey too . . . there is nothing but a little reading or preaching that I cannot tell what it means. I had as leaf keep me at home.'[6] But avoiding church was not permitted, with ever-heavier fines for those who did, with the result that a generation had grown up used both to white walls and to the new pattern in which Morning Prayer replaced the Mass. Some old habits, such as placing crosses on graves, were hard to break, and many remained ignorant of basic Protestant doctrine. Ordinary people continued to believe that good deeds played some part in their salvation and couldn't, or wouldn't, understand the Protestant doctrine of predestination for an elect few. As one contemporary noted, 'heaps' of people had 'cast away the old religion without discovering the new'.[7]

But by and large acceptance for the new ways of worship was successfully being reinforced by the desire to be loyal to the Crown, by propaganda such as the copies distributed to parishes of Foxe's *Book of Martyrs*, with its descriptions of the deaths of the Protestants burned by Mary I, and also by fear of the consequences of opposition.

As the Catholic communities had shrunk so they had also become subjected to intense attacks at the hands of the Elizabethan regime. These had worsened dramatically following the 1569 northern rebellion, especially after Pope Pius V had answered a request by the rebel earls to excommunicate the queen, pronouncing her 'deprived of her pretended title to the . . . crown'. The vast majority of Catholics had remained loyal – and there had been no signs of revolt in counties like Hampshire where Catholicism remained strong.[8] Nevertheless it had meant Catholics could be painted as traitors by reason of their faith alone, and in 1577 the first of many Catholic priests to be executed by Elizabeth had been hanged, disembowelled while alive, and quartered.

English Catholics reasoned that Elizabeth's fears would be greatly reduced if she were married to a Catholic, but their hopes for the Anjou marriage were matched by Protestant opposition. Steeped in dread of the biblical apocalypse and deeply aware of the religious divisions within their own ranks, at home and abroad, pious Protestants greatly overestimated Catholic unity. A massacre of Protestants in Paris by Mary's Guise relatives in 1572 tapped into fears that they faced possible extinction at Catholic hands, and English priests who had trained in Europe, and who began returning to tend to their abandoned flocks, were seen as a dangerous fifth column. These divisions over the Anjou match were to be played out during the royal progress into East Anglia that summer.

As usual a book was drawn up of the proposed route of the progress, which the queen would then agree, and she picked the clothes she was to wear. Elizabeth's face now had the squarer jawline of middle age and her aquiline nose drooped a little at the tip, giving it a hooked appearance. But what she had lost in youth she made up for in the increasing magnificence of her dress. The Spanish-style cone-shaped skirts of the 1560s had given way in the 1570s to much fuller skirts, thickly embroidered fabrics, and still more elaborate ruffs. Elizabeth did not always remember all the clothes, ruffs and jewels she needed for each stop of her progress and she once overheard a carter, who was being sent back on a third trip to the royal warbrobe, slap his thigh, complaining, 'Now I see that the queen is a woman . . . as well as my wife.' More than her Tudor predecessors, Elizabeth had a sense of humour, and having asked loudly from her window, 'What a villain is this?', she sent him three coins 'to stop his mouth.'[9]

The progress of that summer arrived in Norwich on Saturday 16 August 1578, where amongst the composers of the coming entertainments was a poet called Thomas Churchyard. One of his patrons was Katherine Grey's widower, Hertford, and a principal theme of his shows was to be the virtues of chastity. He had been rehearsing in Norwich for weeks but he was uncertain when and where his performances could go ahead and the weather was unsettled. When the Monday proved dry, Churchyard was determined to seize the opportunity to put on his opening pageant.

Sometime before supper the queen was spotted standing at a window with her ladies. As Churchyard's players swung into action Elizabeth saw an extraordinary coach appear in the gardens beneath her. It was covered with painted birds and naked sprites and had a tower decked with glass jewels, topped with a plume of white feathers. As the coach rattled by, a boy dressed as Mercury jumped off, made a leap or two and delivered a speech. The subject was God's desire to 'Find out false hearts, and make of subjects true/Plant perfect peace, and root up all debate.' Elizabeth looked pleased – but his show was not over yet.[10]

The next day a friend gave Churchyard advance notice of the path the queen was taking to dinner. They set up quickly in a field where a crowd was gathering. Churchyard had a whole morality play organised, in which the forces of Cupid, Wantonness and Riot were ranged up against Chastity and her lieutenants, Modesty, Temperance and Shamefastness. When Elizabeth arrived it unfolded before her, in praise of the celibate life. She acknowledged Churchyard's efforts politely with 'gracious words', unaware as yet of the true significance of what she had just witnessed.[11]

The famous phrase the 'Virgin Queen' was coined in the parting pageant on Saturday, but Churchyard's show in the open field was the first to celebrate Elizabeth as such. The sobriquet associated Elizabeth with the cult of the Virgin Mary, and when the Anjou match eventually came to nothing like the others before it, a new iconography was born, with classical as well as Christian associations. A favourite theme in the pictures of Elizabeth that courtiers commissioned was the classical story of the Vestal Virgin who proved her chastity by carrying water in a sieve from the river Tiber to the temple of Vesta. At least eight pictures from the period 1579–83 survive depicting Elizabeth holding a sieve. In several of her portraits icons of empire were included, with the abandonment of the Anjou marriage linked to an aggressive foreign policy in which England would found a Protestant empire. But although these are the images of the great queen we still remember, behind the icon stood an isolated figure.

Elizabeth is supposed to have written the verses of yearning 'to live with some more sweet content' when Anjou left England. But the pain and passion they describe surely have their inspiration in the man she had truly loved: Robert Dudley.

> I grieve and dare not show my discontent,
> I love and yet am forced to seem to hate,
> I do, yet dare not say I ever meant,
> I seem stark mute but inwardly do prate.
> I am, and not, I freeze and yet am burned,
> Since from myself another self I turned.

My care is like my shadow in the sun,
Follows me flying, flies when I pursue it,
Stands, and lies by me, doth what I have done.
His too familiar care doth make me rue it.
No means I find to rid him from my breast,
Till by the end of things it be supprest.

Some gentler passion slide into my mind,
For I am soft and made of melting snow;
Or be more cruel, Love, and so be kind.
Let me or float or sink, be high or low.
Or let me live with some more sweet content,
Or die, and so forget what love e'er meant.[12]

If Robert Dudley had been the son of a king she would have married him, Elizabeth had told the Spanish ambassador Silva in 1565. But Dudley had long since ceased to dream of being her husband. He was desperate now only for a son to carry on his title and inherit his lands. On 21 September 1578, a month after the 'Virgin Queen' sobriquet was coined, Dudley married Mary Boleyn's granddaughter, Lettice Knollys, the widowed Countess of Essex. The fact that Lettice resembled a younger Elizabeth only added to the queen's anguish when she heard the news over a year later in the winter of 1579. Reportedly it was the French ambassador who told her, in revenge for Dudley's opposition to the Anjou match. Dudley was out of favour for weeks and Elizabeth would never forgive Lettice.[13]

And there was another unpleasant reminder of the cost to Elizabeth of her spinstershood in the summer and following winter of 1579. It concerned a friend of Robert Dudley, one who was second only to Elizabeth at court in terms of royal blood. She was yet another royal Margaret, the last surviving granddaughter of Henry VIII's younger sister, the French queen. Born Margaret Clifford, only child of Eleanor Brandon, she was now the Countess of Derby. Under the terms of

Henry VIII's will she had become Elizabeth's heir following the death of her cousin Mary Grey in 1578. The countess had joined forces with Robert Dudley in opposition to the Anjou match, and in August 1579, when the Duke of Anjou had visited Elizabeth secretly, she made the news public. The countess was arrested and her servants interviewed, in the course of which it emerged that she had employed a magician to cast the queen's horoscope and discover when she would die. This was reminiscent of Elizabeth's household when it was apparent that Mary I's pregnancy was not proceeding normally and they had employed the magician John Dee. Imagining the death of a monarch was treason. But Dee's activities seemed to have scared Elizabeth more than they had Mary I. Dee had escaped with his life in 1555 and his prophecies would be used into the 1590s by William Cecil, to raise fears of Catholic threats. Margaret Clifford's magician (she claimed he was only her doctor), on the other hand, was executed. Although the countess lived until 1596, she was never restored to royal favour.[14]

There remained, however, the certain knowledge that Elizabeth could not live forever, and her likely successor was a far more dangerous figure than the ambitious and foolish Margaret Clifford. Elizabeth had once been 'a second person' to Mary I, and as such, as she often recalled, she had 'tasted of the practices against my sister'. 'I did differ from her in religion and I was sought for divers ways [to overthrow her]', Elizabeth had recalled in 1566. Such was the position now held by Mary, Queen of Scots, and if the brutal crushing of the northern rebellion of 1569 ensured there would not be further such revolts, there remained the dangers to Elizabeth of assassination and invasion. With the failure of the Anjou match, the shrinking Catholic community split and divided. While the vast majority still sought compromise with the state, hoping for some measure of religious toleration, a few were determined to fight back.

Members of the Counter-Reformation order of the Jesuits were amongst the priests recently returned from Europe, and they stiffened the resolve of Catholics to refuse to attend Protestant services, even if it meant fines, imprisonment or death. Further executions followed, both of priests and of those who sheltered them. Blood spilt demanded a blood price, and a small number of radicalised Catholics were prepared to do whatever it took to overthrow Queen Elizabeth, including murder.

39

THE DAUGHTER OF DEBATE

ELIZABETH'S COUSIN AND RIVAL, THE THIRTY-SIX-YEAR-OLD MARY, Queen of Scots, was still lovely in 1579 with fashionably curled hair. Nevertheless a miniature by Nicholas Hilliard depicts a fuller face than in her youth. Like her great-grandmother Elizabeth of York, she was growing stout in middle age and this was exacerbated by the sedentary life she was obliged to live as Elizabeth's prisoner. A woman of great physicality who associated fresh air and vigorous exercise with good health, she had been deprived of both for a decade, and suffered frequent illness. She was grateful when her life was enlivened by the arrival of the lively little Arbella Stuart, in the household of her jailors, the Earl of Shrewsbury and his wife, Bess.

After Margaret Douglas had died Elizabeth had permitted Arbella to live with her mother and both were in Bess's care. 'I am utterly unable to express the manifold causes I have to yield your majesty my most humble thanks', Bess wrote to Elizabeth of her 'gracious goodness' in this regard. Bess was aware there had been several bids for Arbella's wardship, and 'so much the more am I bound to be your faithful and thankful servant', she acknowledged.

Mary, Queen of Scots grew very fond of Darnley's niece. She tried to persuade her son King James to recognise Arbella's right to inherit the Lennox title, and in her will she even bequeathed Arbella one of her most personal possessions, her French Book of Hours. Unfortunately, however, by 1582 when Arbella's mother died, Mary's affection for her niece had become complicated by Bess's behaviour.

The Shrewsburys' marriage had collapsed and Bess blamed Mary. As a queen, who also happened to be a prisoner, Mary reigned at the centre of a macabre court, waited on by a full household of servants, paid for and watched over by Shrewsbury, with only intermittent repayment by Queen Elizabeth. He and Bess quarrelled over money and Bess grew jealous of the amount of attention he was obliged to expend on his royal prisoner. Although Mary was becoming crippled by arthritis and had developed a stoop, she remained good company, with an uncanny ability to make whoever she spoke to feel good about themselves. Shrewsbury's respect and affection for her infuriated his wife, who began to spread malicious gossip that Mary and Shrewsbury were having an affair. Mary was still more angered by Bess's growing ambitions for Arbella. 'Nothing has alienated the countess more from me', Mary wrote to the French ambassador in March 1584, 'than the vain hope she has conceived of setting the crown on her granddaughter Arbella's head, even by marrying the Earl of Leicester's son.' That particular plan died with the little boy shortly afterwards, and Mary paid Bess back for her malicious gossip with a letter to Elizabeth repeating Bess's stories from court.

As the astute Spanish ambassador, the Count of Feria, had observed in 1558, Elizabeth was extremely vain and, according to Bess, courtiers would vie with each other in offering the aging queen the most outrageous compliments, trying not to laugh as they outdid each other. Bess had also claimed to Mary that Elizabeth had had sex with Robert Dudley and others – at least as she was able to, for, it was said, Elizabeth was deformed internally. When Mary's letter ended up on William Cecil's desk he chose not to show it to Elizabeth, but Mary was transferred out of Shrewsbury's care in August 1584.

Negotiations had begun for a treaty with the now eighteen-year-old King James that would see Mary, Queen of Scots freed, under his assurances of her good conduct, and those of the King of France. Mary was desperate to believe they would succeed, but fresh anxieties over Elizabeth's security emerged as news reached England of the assassination of William of Orange, the leader of a Dutch revolt against the Spanish in the Netherlands. A month earlier a lone fanatic had shot him dead in his palace – the first ever political assassination carried out with a gun.[1] It raised to boiling point fears that Elizabeth's life was in similar danger.

William Cecil and Elizabeth's other councillors were determined that if she died, Mary, Queen of Scots should also be killed. That October they drew up what amounted to an assassins' charter, known as the Bond of Association. Its signatories were sworn to kill anyone they judged might be responsible for Elizabeth's death and that included any Catholic heir to the English throne. It was sent around the country for local county worthies also to sign. That so many proved willing to commit their names to Mary's murder is a mark of how much England had changed since the 1560s when much of the political elite remained Catholic in sympathy, and many Protestants on the Privy Council, amongst them Robert Dudley, had considered Mary the best candidate for the succession. The wider acceptance of Protestantism, and the Catholic threats posed to Elizabeth since the northern rebellion of 1569, had combined to turn Mary, Queen of Scots into a national bogeywoman.

Cecil planned to follow the Bond of Association with a law that would bring a Grand Council into effect on Elizabeth's death with the power to choose her successor.[2] Elizabeth put paid to this neo-republican scheme for the election of a monarch, but the Bond of Association remained, and left Mary terrified that if she stayed in England she would be killed, and sooner rather than later. Her only hope was that the son she had not seen since babyhood would come to her rescue. Mary had sent a man called Albert de Fontenay as her emissary to James in Scotland in August 1584 and so she had some idea of how much she could, or could not, rely on that.

Fontenay had been well received in Scotland and was even invited to stay at Holyrood Palace, which, with its great stone courtyard and towers, bore a resemblance for the Frenchman to the chateau of Chambord. Fontenay found James, Elizabeth's closest male heir, to be 'a young, old man'. Broad-shouldered and of average height, the eighteen-year-old dressed plainly and wore his reddish hair cropped short. His lower body had some weakness, possibly the result of childhood rickets, and Fontenay observed 'his gait is bad, composed of erratic steps', 'but he is in no wise delicate'. Indeed James was a mass of energy. Hunting gave this some release, and Fontenay learned he would often ride six hours in a day, 'chasing all over the place with loosened rein.'[3] Fontenay gained regular access to James, often hunting with him, and soon a detailed assessment of the king's character, appearance and abilities arrived in England addressed to Mary's secretary, Fontenay's brother-in-law, Claude Nau.

Apart from hunting, James had no time for the usual courtly pastimes. 'He hates dancing and music in general', Fontenay reported. James also disapproved of elaborate courtly dress, and men with long hair, 'not abiding above all ear-rings'. The lack of his mother's influence was obvious and James was 'very rude and uncivil in speaking, eating, manners, games, and entertainment in the company of women'. On the other hand, Fontenay also found James highly intelligent. As a child he had had the brilliant humanist scholar George Buchanan as his principal tutor, and it showed.

'For his age he is the most remarkable prince who ever lived', Fontenay remarked; 'Three qualities of mind he possesses in perfection: he understands clearly, judges wisely and has a retentive memory. His questions are keen and penetrating and his replies are sound . . . He is well instructed in languages, science, and affairs of state, better, I dare say, than anyone else in his kingdom. In short he has a remarkable intelligence, as well as lofty and virtuous ideals and a high opinion of himself.'[4]

There were other areas, however, in which Fontenay perceived weaknesses of character. The first was James' provincial arrogance, which made him 'overconfident of his strength and scornful of other princes'. Second was his self-indulgence. Fontenay complained that James loved his male favourites recklessly. He was also lazy, avoiding administrative work. A final concern was that James appeared severely traumatised by the violence of his childhood. Fontenay felt that, 'nourished in fear', James would never have the courage to stand up to the great lords.

James took the criticism Fontenay directed at him remarkably well, assuring the Frenchman that he worked very quickly when he did work, and 'That nothing was done secretly by the lords that he did not know, by means of having spies at the doors of their rooms morning and evening, who came and reported everything to him'.[5] But if James was canny, Fontenay was astute, and while James promised all sorts of help for his mother, Mary, Fontenay noted that 'he has never enquired anything of the queen or of her health, or her treatment, her servants, her living, and eating, her recreation, or anything similar'.[6]

The truth was that Mary, Queen of Scots was a stranger to her son, and one of whom he had rarely heard a good word. For years James had been told that she had murdered his father. And whatever he believed, his principal concern was his own survival. His subjects, James later commented, were 'a far more barbarous and stiff-necked people' than the English. His main objective was to inherit Elizabeth's crown and get the hell out of Scotland as soon as he could.

The following year, 1585, Mary discovered James had made an agreement with Elizabeth that made him a pensioner of the English crown and left her in prison; James' letters to Elizabeth even referred to the English queen as his 'Madame and mother'. Bitter and afraid, Mary began to look urgently for some other means of escape from England. If her son would not help her, she believed, 'In all of Christendom I shall find enough heirs with talons strong enough to grasp what I may put in their hand'.[7] At the top of the list was Philip of Spain, a descendant of John of Gaunt, and whose bitter enmity Elizabeth gained in August 1585, when she gave military aid to his Dutch Protestant rebels.

By early 1586 Philip was already planning an invasion of England. His objectives were to end English aid to Dutch rebel forces and also to halt the relentless attacks of English privateers against Spanish shipping with its cargoes of gold from his colonies in the Americas. But Philip did not wish his invasion to be seen merely as an act of Spanish conquest or punishment. As the husband of Elizabeth's sister Mary I, he had been the king of a Catholic England subsequently dismantled and then persecuted, almost to extinction. Philip wanted his invasion to be a religious crusade. For that he needed the backing of the energetic new Pope, Sixtus V, who was reluctant to give it.

Born in the papal states and now in his sixties, the Pope believed 'The King of Spain's foreign policy is about his interests, not those of the church.'[8] Philip was by now King of Portugal as well as Spain and Pope Sixtus complained he felt like a fly compared to an elephant, against the king on whose great empire the sun never set. He did not relish the prospect of Philip becoming more powerful still. Nevertheless, he had to consider the interests of England's Catholics whose priests were now being executed under a law that made it treasonous merely to be ordained abroad. The Pope decided to back Philip, on condition that after Philip's victory Mary, Queen of Scots, was given the English throne.

Mary's great fear was that even if Philip's invasion were successful, she would be killed before anyone could rescue her. She realised she needed English help if she was going to survive and, in her desperation, she began to hope that she might be saved by a group of young Catholic courtiers who had contacted her and were plotting to kill Elizabeth. It did not seem a difficult task. Queen Elizabeth was well aware there were threats to her life, but she continued to walk abroad with her ladies and a few courtiers, acknowledging the displays of public affection from the crowds that would dash to see her whenever she appeared. 'They are seeking to take my life, but it troubles me not',

Elizabeth commented, 'He who is on high has defended me until this hour, and will keep me still, for in him do I trust.'[9]

The leader of the group of courtiers planning Elizabeth's death was one Anthony Babington. 'Attractive in face and form, quick of intelligence, agreeable and facetious', the twenty-four-year-old was to prove a poor conspirator.[10] A government spy had been placed amongst the traitors' ranks and the Privy Council knew at an early stage that Babington had contacted Mary. His letter to the Queen of Scots promised 'the dispatch of the usurper' at the hands of 'six noble gentlemen, all my private friends, who, for the zeal they bear the Catholic cause and for your Majesty's service will undertake that tragical execution.'[11] Fatally, in July 1586, Mary responded and in August her secretaries, Babington, and his fellow conspirators were arrested.

Elizabeth was determined to punish her would-be assassins in a manner that would act as a deterrent to others. In 1569, after the northern rebellion, she had ordered hundreds of hangings, one in each village that had taken part in the revolt led by the Earls of Northumberland and Westmorland. Nearly twenty years on there had been no further risings. Now she took a special interest in the details of the execution of Babington and his friends, asking the council that their agonies be made as extreme as possible, 'for more terror'.[12] In answer to her orders, it was ensured the prisoners were hanged for only a short time before being disembowelled and castrated while conscious and screaming on a huge public scaffold. Mary would die next.

The principal concern for Elizabeth and her Privy Council was James' potential reaction to his mother's execution. It was possible that he would break Scotland's new treaties with England and turn to Spain, or France, to avenge his mother's death. They tried to sound James out, but he did not grasp what was being asked, and merely let it be known that as far as he was concerned, Mary could be put in the Tower and her servants hanged; 'The only thing he craves is her life.'[13] This, he soon learned, was an offer that was not on the table.

To have his mother beheaded would be a dreadful humiliation for James and for Scotland. But James knew the English Parliament had debarred all those who were privy to plots against Elizabeth from the throne. If he defended Mary too vigorously he risked losing any chance he would ever be King of England. He convinced himself, however, that he could persuade Elizabeth it would not be in her interest to execute a fellow monarch.

The trial of Mary, Queen of Scots took place in October. She defended herself with skill and dignity, but the outcome was never in doubt. Parliament delivered the death sentence in December. On the 19th Mary wrote to Elizabeth only to beg 'for the sake of Henry VII, your grandfather and mine, and by the honour and dignity we have both held, and of our sex in common', that her servants witness her end (so it would be known she died well), and that she be buried in France.[14] James did now plead for her life, reminding Elizabeth pointedly how Mary was 'alike in estate and sex to her', but he never threatened to break Scotland's treaties with England.

As James suspected, Elizabeth was indeed reluctant to bear the charge of regicide. In Europe, she feared, 'it shall be spread that for the safety of her life, a maiden queen could be content to spill the blood even of her own kinswoman'. Worse, cutting off a monarch's head would sever the notion of a monarch as a sacred being forever. But with Philip preparing the great fleet of warships, which in Spanish was called an 'Armada', for his invasion, and with English subjects prepared to murder her, Elizabeth judged that in preserving Mary, she would, as she told James, 'cherish a sword to cut my own throat'. To avoid a judicial execution Elizabeth therefore tried to persuade Mary's jailors to murder their prisoner under the Bond of Association.

Mary's last prison at Fotheringhay Castle in Northamptonshire was the ancestral seat of the House of York, the murderers of the mad Henry VI, but also victims of regicide in the disappearance of Edward V, elder of the princes in the Tower. Elizabeth's servants proved less willing, however, than those of her ancestors to carry out a murder on royal orders, leaving her obliged to pick up her pen and sign her cousin's death warrant. Still, she gave no orders for it to be sent. William Cecil did that on his own authority, as she must have trusted he would.

Elizabeth had instructed that Mary die in the privacy of the hall, rather than the cold and wet of Fotheringhay's courtyard. But Elizabeth ordered that the Queen of Scots be denied her request for her servants to accompany her. Elizabeth did not wish to risk the servants publicising Mary's death in a manner that would inspire pity for Mary and, by implication, condemnation of Elizabeth's actions. Mary got her way nonetheless, for when she insisted at the eleventh hour that 'far meaner persons than myself have not been denied so small a favour', the men on the spot shamefacedly gave way.[15]

Mary entered the room where she was to die on 8 February 1587, with a smile, her servants walking behind her in a royal procession. The murdered Kings of England had been disposed of quietly. This, by contrast, was theatre, and Mary, who had been the star of so many spectacles as a queen, knew how to make the best of the stage she had been given. She had dressed herself as a religious martyr for the Catholic cause. She had a crucifix in her hand, a pair of rosaries hung from her girdle, and when her clothes were stripped she stood before the witnesses dressed in a petticoat, bodice and sleeves of tawny red: the liturgical colour of martyrdom.

Once Mary was blindfolded and her prayers said, she remained kneeling, erect. Never having attended an English execution she assumed she was to be beheaded with a sword, as was the tradition for the nobility in France. But Mary was to be butchered with an axe, 'like those with which they cut wood', her doctor noted with disgust. The executioners, too crude to ask Mary to prostrate herself, roughly pushed her head down towards the hewn wooden block. Mary then lay flat, placing her hands under her chin on the wood as she began to pray: '*In te Domine confido, non confundar in aeternum*' (In you Lord is my trust, let me never be confounded). Mary's old jailor, George

Talbot, Earl of Shrewsbury, present as Earl Marshall, raised the baton of his office to signal the execution, but dreading what was coming he looked away. He did not notice, therefore, as the headsman now did, that Mary's hands would be cut off with her head. His attendant grabbed her hands and wrenched them behind her back so her face pressed on the wood.

'In the midst of the deathly silence of the room we heard her reciting "*In manus tuas, Domine, confido spiritum meum*" (Into your hands, O Lord, I commend my spirit)', the doctor recalled. As the executioner hesitated to strike, she repeated the words again, and again. The tension in the room had reached breaking point when at last he swung his axe. It smashed into Mary's head. Some thought they heard a cry. A second stroke almost severed the neck. The axe was then used like a cleaver on a chicken wing to cut it free. As the head fell the executioner raised it up, with the shout 'God save the queen', only to have it drop out of his hand leaving him clutching her chestnut wig. It had been severed from its moorings by the botched strike of the axe. As Shrewsbury wept, the executioners began to tear the dead queen's stockings from her corpse. In was a perk of the job to be allowed to keep or sell their victim's clothes. Their action disturbed her little dog, hidden under her skirts. Covered with blood, it rushed up and down the body, howling plaintively.[16]

As the news of Mary's death reached court, fires were lit across London in jubilation. In Paris, where she was mourned as a former Queen of France, it was said with disgust that the London mobs had demanded more fuel from the house of the French ambassador to celebrate the execution.[17] But Elizabeth put on mourning clothes and promised the French ambassador that Mary's death would 'wring her heart as long as she lives'. In a manner it did. It gave Elizabeth no pleasure to have been obliged to take the life of her fellow queen. But now she had to focus on the immediate crisis. Elizabeth sent a letter to James swearing her innocence of Mary's death and laying the blame with those who had delivered the warrant. James refused the messenger his presence for several days. Eventually, however, he accepted Elizabeth's version of events.

Mary's last request, to be buried alongside her mother in France, was denied her. This was not out of spite or cruelty, but again was a consequence of political anxieties: a burial in France would have risked prolonging the outrage there over what had occurred. Instead, after six months of Mary's corpse rotting at Fotheringhay, Elizabeth decided she should be buried at Peterborough Cathedral, the resting place of that other Catholic queen, Anne Boleyn's rival, Katherine of Aragon. Elizabeth now had to face in war Katherine's great-nephew, Philip II, and the full might of the world's greatest power.

40

THE ARMADA

'THE KING AND HIS ARMADA ARE BECOMING RIDICULOUS', POPE Sixtus observed to the Venetian ambassador in Rome. Five months after the execution of Mary, Queen of Scots, the Pope had given Philip's invasion of England his financial as well as moral support, but by the new year of 1588 he judged that Philip's plan to conquer Elizabeth's small island kingdom had little chance of success. There were interminable delays, and he found he rather admired Elizabeth's courage in confronting Philip's global empire. 'If that woman were only a Catholic, she would be loved by us more than any other sovereign for she has great qualities', he sighed.[1] With Mary, Queen of Scots dead, Philip could claim England in his own right, as a descendant of John of Gaunt. That the son of the man who had sacked Rome in 1527 should become still more powerful was not a prospect that gladdened the Pope's heart.

Come the spring of 1588 Sixtus refused a request to pay out any more money to Philip. He would give more only when the invasion had achieved its objective to overthrow Elizabeth and announced he had 'strong presentments' that it would not.[2] Nevertheless, on 30 May the 130 ships of the Armada, carrying over 18,000 men, set sail from Lisbon for the invasion of England. The intention was that the Armada join the Duke of Parma's army in the Netherlands, where Parma would provide the main invasion force. The fleet reached Calais on 7 August, sailing in a perfect crescent formation, flags flying from ships that resembled castles of oak. Impressive though the sight was, however, their wooden hulls made them vulnerable to fire, and when the English fleet sent eight blazing fireships in amongst these timber fortresses, the Spanish formation began to break up. Cannon then thundered into the ships.

The English began firing at 8 a.m. on 8 August and were still firing at 7 p.m. when the Armada was already 'in the Act of retiring', a Spanish captain called Cuellar recorded. His ship, the galleon *San Pedro*, was filling with water through huge holes made by cannonballs and – less easy to spot – also from shot. The wind blew them north and 'I don't know how I can say it – the fleet of our enemy followed behind us to drive us from their country', he wrote.[3]

As the Spanish fleet continued northwards Elizabeth set off in her barge from St James's Palace for Gravesend. She knew the Armada was badly damaged and the enemy had suffered mass casualties from England's cannonade. But the battle was not over yet and as she disembarked at West Tilbury 'in princely robes and rich array' to inspect the army, she faced a defining moment in her reign.

Elizabeth had to be careful how she approached the coming spectacle. To the English of this period the notion of a female warrior was a perversion of nature, akin to a talking dog, or a baby born with a cow's head.[4] Her sister Mary I had, however, already negotiated an inspection of her troops highly successfully. On 20 July 1553, when Mary I was poised to take her crown from the usurper Jane Grey, she had ridden 'out from Framlingham Castle to muster and inspect the most splendid and loyal army'. A contemporary described Mary's troops drawn up in battle line, 'the banners unfurled and the military colours set up'. She was mounted on a white horse and the men fell on their knees as she approached. Mary's animal had shied as she reached the line, so she had dismounted and walked, talking to each in turn. Elizabeth now rode by her troops and 'Her faithfull soldiers, great and small, upon their knees began to fall.' Her horse was better behaved than her sister's. Elizabeth was able to stay mounted, and when she spotted more troops further up the hill, 'on her feet upright she stepped, tossing up her plume of feathers . . . waving her royal hand'.[5]

The next day Elizabeth returned to Tilbury for a march past and a further inspection. Robert Dudley, who had been in charge of establishing the camp, was there to greet her. The former lovers had grown old. Robert Dudley was florid and sickly while Elizabeth, at fifty-four, was a generation older than Mary had been at the inspection of her army in 1553. Elizabeth was, however, once more 'bravely mounted on a stately steed', and this time she rode in a grand procession behind Robert Dudley and the Lord Marshal who carried their plumed hats in their hands.[6] Eight footmen walked at her stirrups and her ladies-in-waiting followed her in diamonds and cloth of gold, while she shone 'attired like an angel bright', carrying a staff as a symbol of her authority.[7] One description refers to her 'as armed Pallas'.[8] This has been misunderstood to mean Elizabeth was wearing armour. In fact Elizabeth was being compared to the classical figure of Pallas Athene, as Mary I had been in a Florentine pageant at her accession. In both cases it was done to project a positive image of a woman in a military context. Elizabeth probably wore white and gold, certainly not the breastplate of modern film fiction as she watched the march past of the men.

When Elizabeth's army came to a halt she rode alone with Robert Dudley to inspect the companies. She had not liked to see the men kneel in the mud the previous day, and as she passed the troops the men dipped their pikes, colours and lances in salute instead. Elizabeth now rode to a high spot to give her address. In 1554, when Mary I had given a speech that had mobilised London against the Wyatt rebellion, it was rumoured she had 'even asked to go and fight herself'.[9] According to a contemporary ballad account Elizabeth too now promised that 'in the midst of all your troop, we ourselves will be in place/to be your joy, your guide, your comfort, even before your enemies face'.

Decades later a chaplain who had been at Tilbury recalled Elizabeth's speech in full.[10] There had been fears that coming to Tilbury would put Elizabeth at risk of assassination. Robert Dudley had countered this, telling Elizabeth her visit would 'comfort not only these thousands but many more will get to hear of it.'[11] Elizabeth's famous address achieved far more than that and remains one of the most stirring speeches in the English language:

My loving people, we have been persuaded by some, that are careful of our safety, to take heed how we commit ourself to armed multitudes for fear of treachery, but I assure you, I do not desire to live to distrust my faithful, and loving people. Let tyrants fear, I have always so behaved myself, that under God I have placed my chief strength, and safeguard in the loyal hearts and goodwill of my subjects. And therefore I am come amongst you as you see, at this time, not for my recreation and disport; but being resolved in the midst, and heat of the battle to live, or die amongst you all, to lay down for my God, and for my kingdom, and for my people, my Honour, and my blood even in the dust. I know I have the body, but of a weak and feeble woman, but I have the heart and stomach of a king, and of a King of England too, and think foul scorn that Parma or Spain, or any prince of Europe should dare to invade the borders of my Realm, to which rather than any dishonour should grow by me, I myself will take up arms, I myself will be your General, Judge, and Rewarder of every one of your virtues in the field.[12]

Happily, there was to be no battle on English soil and the Spanish ships continued sailing north, up the east coast of England and around Scotland. Short of water, they were forced to throw their horses overboard and the animals were seen swimming desperately for a shore they would never reach. In time their masters would also be swimming in a series of shipwrecks as they continued on the long route home.

Cuellar recalled how, clinging to the top of the poop of his sinking ship in Sligo Bay, 'I gazed at the terrible spectacle' of other Spanish ships also breaking up in a storm: 'Many were drowning within the ships: others, casting themselves into the water, sank to the bottom without returning to the surface; others on rafts and barrels, and gentlemen on pieces of timber.' The Spaniard reached shore, and with difficulty made his way to what he hoped would be the sanctuary of a monastery. 'I found it deserted, and the church and images of the saints burned and ruined, and twelve Spaniards hanging within the church by order of the Lutheran English, who went about searching to make an end of all of us.'[13]

At least 9,000 men from the Armada perished, either drowned, murdered for their gold, or summarily executed in Ireland after being handed over to the English authorities. Elizabeth wrote to King James in Scotland that Philip's plans to destroy her had instead 'procured my greatest glory'.[14] She was right. But the war was not over, and Elizabeth's most difficult years were yet to come.[15]

41

SETTING SUN

Journeying home to Kenilworth in Warwickshire, just a few weeks after the defeat of the Armada, Robert Dudley wrote to ask Elizabeth 'how my gracious lady doth, and what ease of her late pains she finds?' He was also ill, but he assured her that he had been taking the medicine she had sent him for his fever and said it made him feel 'much better than any other thing given me'. It did not prove enough. He died six days later, at Cornbury in Oxfordshire. 'His last letter', Elizabeth wrote on it sorrowfully, and put it in a cabinet by her bed, where she kept her most precious and personal possessions.[1]

Dudley's death signalled the passing of the old order, but Elizabeth still hoped she could continue ruling according to her motto, '*Semper eadem*' (Always the same). As the years began to pass and her servants died she either did not replace them or found a near equivalent to the servant she had lost. Dudley's replacement was to be his stepson, the tall, handsome, soldier-scholar Robert Devereux, 2nd Earl of Essex. A man who longed for military glory and fame, he represented the aspirations of a young and frustrated generation of courtiers. When Essex joined Elizabeth's Privy Council in 1593 he was twenty-seven, while the average age of his fellow councillors was almost sixty and the seventy-three-year-old William Cecil, Lord Burghley had a secured position of unrivalled authority. The only other young member was

Burghley's son, Robert Cecil, appointed to the council in 1591 when he was twenty-eight, and he was being groomed to replace his father, just as Essex had replaced Dudley.

Robert Cecil was short, no more than five feet two, and hunch-backed. Elizabeth would refer to Cecil affectionately as her 'pygmy'; his many enemies preferred to call him 'Robert the Devil'. He was notoriously corrupt, even at a time when corruption had grown commonplace. Theft by royal official was adding to the burden of the vast cost of the continuing war with Spain and further impoverishing the queen. She did what she could to economise, and in consequence was accused of growing 'very covetous in her old days'. It was said Elizabeth neglected the court and 'people were weary of an old woman's government'.[2] Essex's followers, who fought in the war with Spain and gained little profit from their loyalty, resented the fact those 'goose-quilled gents', the pen-pusher Cecils, were so successful at lining their pockets and, increasingly, their hopes seemed to lie in the passing of the Virgin Queen.

Debate on the succession was now forbidden as treason, but the rival Essex and Cecilian factions made frantic – if secret – efforts to secure the throne for the heir who they believed would best represent their future interests.[3] William Cecil's association with the execution of King James' mother, Mary, Queen of Scots, saw him remain allied to the cause of Katherine Grey through his continued friendship with her widower, the Earl of Hertford. Unfortunately for the Cecils, Katherine Grey's eldest son had married the daughter of a mere gentleman, which did nothing to boost his royal status.

Essex was allied to by far the stronger candidate, King James. He was indisputably royal, and his wife, Anne of Denmark, delivered their first son, Henry, in 1594. James' candidature also had the advantage of attracting followers from across the religious spectrum. The so-called Puritans backed James because the Scottish church was far more Protestant than the one Elizabeth allowed. Catholics, on the other hand, saw James as the son of Mary, Queen of Scots, whom they regarded as virtually a martyr, and many believed he would allow Catholics the freedom to practise their faith.

There was, however, to be one last attempt to move the succession out of the Tudor bloodline. This came from another group of Catholics: those who suspected that James would never grant religious toleration, and who sought a Catholic successor to Elizabeth. In November 1595 a book written by English members of the Jesuit order was published under the name R. Doleman. Entitled *A Conference About the Next Succession to the Crowne of Ingland* it was to have a huge impact on the succession debate.

'Doleman' claimed that England had long been what was, to all intents and purposes, an elective monarchy. Henry VII had no blood claim to the English throne, yet his crown was endorsed by Parliament. Clearly 'ancestry of blood alone' was not of primary importance. It was, however, accepted as vital that a monarch have all the attributes of honour necessary to majesty and, Doleman argued, there was no such candidate within the Tudor family. All were tarred by illegitimacy or poor marriages, save James, who was disqualified under English law because his mother had plotted against Elizabeth.

Having dismissed the Tudor candidates, the Doleman book announced that in seeking a successor to Elizabeth, 'the first respect of all others ought to be God and religion.'[4] It was an argument that Protestants had made in the 1550s, and in the next century the exclusion of Catholics from the throne would become incorporated into English law. On this basis England would accept Dutch and German Protestants as their reigning kings. Doleman's argument was a precursor to this with Catholics told they could look to Europe for a monarch of their own faith, and that they were blessed with an excellent candidate: Philip II's favourite daughter, the twenty-nine-year-old infanta, Isabella Clara Eugenia.

Like her father, Isabella was a descendant in a legitimate bloodline from John of Gaunt. 'A princess of rare parts both for beauty, wisdom and piety', she also came from a rich kingdom, and was less likely to 'pill and poll' her English subjects than James, the king of poverty-stricken Scotland.[5] The Doleman arguments severely damaged the cause of Katherine Grey's eldest son, while also tapping into nationalist sentiment against 'the old beggarly enemy', the Scots. Everything was thus left to play for when André Hurault Sieur de Maisse, the ambassador of the French king Henri IV, arrived in England in 1597.

Elizabeth's kingdom had sunk into the kind of malaise it had known at the close of Mary I's reign. The people were bowed by successive harvest failures, disease, and the costs of war. The national mood was cynical and Elizabeth often ill, as de Maisse soon found. His first audience was put off because the queen had toothache, but on 8 December he was at last invited to the court at Whitehall. The Frenchman's barge pulled up near the entrance, a dark, covered alley from where he stepped into a low hall. A flight of steps took de Maisse to a series of small and gloomy rooms above. From there he was escorted to the Privy Chamber, with its giant Holbein mural of Henry VIII, codpiece thrust forward, and the fragile, receding figures of Henry VII and Elizabeth of York. On the far side of the room were the queen's ladies and several councillors. Amongst them William Cecil, so 'very old' he had to be 'carried in a chair'. Also sitting, but under a cloth of estate, and on a raised platform, was the shrivelled figure of Elizabeth I.

As the queen rose to greet the ambassador, de Maisse saw she was decked out in an extravagant dress of silver gauze and white satin, the sleeves slashed with scarlet and sown with false sleeves that hung to the ground. Her red wig was spangled with gold and silver, and two girlish curls fell almost to her shoulders. Her face, however, was 'very aged', 'long and thin, her teeth . . . very yellow and unequal'. Indeed she had lost so many teeth that he found 'one cannot understand her easily when she speaks quickly'. Elizabeth seemed fretful, twisting and untwisting her false sleeves, and she complained the winter room was too warm. This sensitivity to heat and anxious fiddling may be symptoms of the thyroid disease that her sister Mary I also suffered from. Despite the bitter December cold she kept pulling open her silver dress, exposing her wrinkled breasts, and eventually demanded the fire be doused with water.[6]

De Maisse came to notice that Elizabeth often wore low-cut dresses, after the fashion for unmarried girls. She feared that the older and nearer to death she was assumed to be, the bolder her enemies would become, so she dressed youthfully, wore thick make-up, and she would skip off to her rooms after their meetings, almost coquettishly. When she joked that she was 'foolish and old', de Maisse recognised that he was expected to demure. He often heard Elizabeth talk proudly 'of the friendship her people bore her, and how she loved them no less than they her, and she would rather die than see any diminution of the one part or the other'.[7] But it was also clear to him that the ordinary people hated her favoured servant William Cecil 'strangely', and some courtiers seemed to view her almost with contempt.

In the previous century it had been noted a king had 'a prerogative in his array above all others, whereby his dignity is worshipped'. The same held true for a reigning queen, yet there were times when Elizabeth had to remind her attendants of this. A famous story told by Elizabeth's godson, Sir John Harington, described how once she was so irritated by the envious attention being attracted by a maid of honour's wonderful gold and pearl trimmed velvet gown, that she decided to dress in it herself. It was far too short for her and, as she showed it off, she asked the owner if she agreed it was 'ill-becoming'. The girl nervously admitted it was; 'Why then if it become not me, as being too short, I am minded it shall never become thee, as being too fine, so it fits neither [of us] well', Elizabeth snorted. The girl never wore it again at Elizabeth's court, but she did put it aside, hoping to wear it when the queen died.[8]

More dangerous than the impertinence of Elizabeth's maids were the views of senior figures expressed to de Maisse by the royal favourite, the Earl of Essex ('a man of great designs', the ambassador judged). The earl complained bitterly to the Frenchman of Elizabeth's habit of stalling decisions, saying 'they laboured under two things at this court, delay and inconstancy', and these he judged 'proceeded from the sex of the queen'.[9] Essex was keen to pursue the war with Spain vigorously, but was being frustrated at every turn. William Cecil feared the military costs were driving social unrest. The queen shared his concern, although, being a woman, her wish for peace was ascribed merely to a lack of martial qualities. De Maisse reported a strong feeling at court that England would never again submit to female rule.

That new year of 1598, there was, one courtier recalled, 'a kind of weariness of the time, *mundus senescit*, that the world waxed old'.[10] William Cecil died on 4 August 1598, aged seventy-seven, leaving the queen bereft. The tenth anniversary of the Armada was approaching, there was no end in sight to that war, and only twelve days later she was faced also with a war of liberation that exploded in Ireland. It was to be there that Essex's contempt for the queen as a military leader emerged most strongly. Sent by Elizabeth to crush the rebel leader Hugh O'Neill, Earl of Tyrone, Essex ignored her orders and made a truce, before returning to court in September 1599, hoping to justify his actions. Elizabeth had, however, lost all trust in her former favourite. She froze him out and denied him income, leaving him facing financial and political ruin. 'The queen knows well how to humble the haughty spirit', her godson Harington observed, but he also predicted 'the haughty spirit knows not how to yield'.[11]

On the evening of 7 February 1601, a group of Essex's inner circle of friends paid the Lord Chamberlain's players forty shillings to perform William Shakespeare's play 'of the deposing and killing of that king, Richard II'. The players warned the men that the play was so old and out of use they would have little company for it. But their clients insisted, and if the stands were largely empty in the Globe for the play, the clients, at least, were there: Sir Charles and Sir Jocelyn Percy, Lord Monteagle, and many other court gallants. As the play unfolded the character of John of Gaunt bemoaned an England that has been allowed to go to rack and ruin: 'this scepter'd isle . . . This precious stone set in the silver sea ... This earth, this realm, this England' was 'leased out' and 'bound in with shame'. The audience of swordsmen in silk and lace were now ready to right such wrongs, with the play signalling the launch of a coup.[12]

The following day Essex marched from Ludgate to St Paul's with 300 of his young followers. They included the most glamorous of the new generation of noblemen: the Lords Monteagle and Lumley, the Earls of Southampton and Rutland. All Essex needed was the people to rally to his call and the last of the Tudors would be overthrown. But Londoners, whom Elizabeth had wooed since her smiling appearance following her coronation in January 1559, remained loyal to their queen. As Essex had marched down the narrow streets with his friends they merely gaped at his swordsmen, and 'marvelled that they could come out in that sort in a civil government and on a Sunday'.

Within a fortnight of Essex's surrender Elizabeth had signed his death warrant – but in death he became the hero he had never quite managed to be in life. Shakespeare's Gaunt had died with the hope that 'Though Richard my life's counsel would not hear/My death's sad tale may yet undeaf his ear'. The anger that had fuelled Essex's popularity still burned: the 'scandal' of the condition of England had not changed, and if William Cecil was dead, his son Robert 'the devil' had taken his place. People hoped Elizabeth would now remember Essex's complaints, and ballads romanticising him were soon heard being sung even at court and despite his traitor's death.[13]

Elizabeth's health and spirits deteriorated over the following months and by October she had reached a state of physical and mental collapse. At the opening of her last parliament in November 1601, she almost fell under the weight of her ceremonial robes. Many of the subsequent parliamentary debates saw furious attacks on the monopolies Elizabeth had granted to favoured servants. Robert Cecil had tripled the price of starch since he had been granted the monopoly on it. But, while he and other monopoly holders argued fiercely in their defence,

Elizabeth was sufficiently concerned by the expressions of public anger to promise to abolish or amend them by royal proclamation.

A few days later Elizabeth received a parliamentary deputation in the Council Chamber at Whitehall, where they delivered their fulsome thanks. The men then listened in silence as the queen spoke. 'Although God hath raised me high, yet this I account the glory of my crown, that I have reigned with your loves', she told them; 'Of myself I must say this . . . my heart was never set upon worldly goods, but only for my subjects' good. What you do bestow on me, I will not store up, but receive it to bestow on you again.' Her speech was described as one of 'golden words'. But when Parliament was dissolved in December 1601, Elizabeth recalled in her closing statement those who had sought to kill her by 'many and divers stratagems'.[14]

Elizabeth feared the bond with her people was breaking. In June 1602 she was overheard complaining desperately to Robert Cecil about 'the poverty of the state, the continuance of charge, the discontentment of all sorts of people'. She admitted to the French ambassador that she was weary of life, and wept over Essex's death.[15] He had been all she had had left of the man she had loved as a young queen, yet he had betrayed her, and now he was being idolised, even despite the threat he had posed to her life. The last pageants held in Elizabeth's honour that year venerated her as the 'queen of love and beauty', timeless and unchanging; but as Elizabeth's depression deepened, whispers about the succession became urgent once more.

King James' agents were working hard to gather support from powerful families offering 'liberty of conscience, confirmation of privileges and liberties, restitution of wrongs, honours, titles and dignities'. Many responded positively, but this was only because there was no outstanding English candidate. People did not wish to be ruled by either the Spanish Isabella or the Scottish James. There were rumours that, in order to create a viable English successor, a group of courtiers were planning to marry Margaret Douglas' granddaughter, the twenty-seven-year-old Arbella Stuart, to Katherine Grey's grandson, the sixteen-year-old Edward Seymour, 'and carry the succession that way'.[16] Such a marriage would recall that between Henry VII and Elizabeth of York, in that it would unite the lines of Henry VIII's sisters in a new union dynasty. But did it also offer the promise of peace to a nation on the brink of an uncertain future? That seemed less likely.

42

THE HOLLOW CROWN

ELIZABETH'S GODSON, SIR JOHN HARINGTON, WAS SHOCKED WHEN he saw the queen at Whitehall for Christmas 1602. She was sipping from a golden cup to soothe her sore throat and could only whisper. She confessed she was eating little, and when the subject of the rebellion in Ireland came up, and with it Essex's name, she wept and struck her breast repeatedly.

Over the next few days it became apparent that Elizabeth was also growing forgetful. A number of men arrived at her request only to be dismissed in anger for appearing without an appointment. No one dared voice the seriousness of her condition, but Harington was convinced she only had months to live and, he noted, already courtiers were looking to the future, 'some less mindful of what they are soon to lose, than of what they may perchance hereafter get'.[1]

A day or two later, on 30 December, Katherine Grey's widower, the sixty-three-year-old Earl of Hertford, received a visitor at his house in Tottenham. The man was a messenger from Arbella Stuart. It had been ten years since the twenty-seven-year old princess had last appeared at Elizabeth's court. Blonde and blue-eyed, she had been admired for her elegance of dress, 'her choice education, her rare skill in languages, her good judgement and sight in music'.[2] Elizabeth had become anxious that a party might build behind her claim, and had kept her ever since in rural exile, living at her grandmother Bess's new Hardwick

Hall. Arbella was lonely and desperate to marry, which she knew the queen would never permit. Arbella had heard often, however, about the secret marriage of her father, Charles Stuart, the brother of Lord Darnley, to Bess's daughter, and also of Hertford's secret marriage to Katherine Grey (her mother's godmother). She hoped Hertford would now not only sympathise with her plight, but help her do something about it.

One of Arbella's pages had suggested to her that Hertford's grandson Edward Seymour was the perfect groom for her. The child of Arbella's kinsman, David Owen Tudor, this page was a descendant of her ancestor Owen Tudor, through his illegitimate son, Sir David Owen. Before sinking into obscurity Owen's 'other' family were now poised to play a small but significant role in the last chapter of the Tudors' royal story. According to the page, Hertford had once approached his father as a possible intermediary with Bess, to test the water for the arrangement of a marriage between Arbella and his grandson. Although she realised this had been some years in the past, Arbella was desperate for Hertford to know that she now wanted such a marriage to go ahead immediately. Her messenger relayed to Hertford her suggestion that Edward Seymour come to Hardwick Hall in disguise. If her grandmother, Bess, realised who he was, he would be shut out, Arbella warned. She suggested that by way of identification Seymour bring 'some picture or handwriting of the Lady Jane Grey'.[3] 'The best thing', Arbella proposed, would be the farewell letter Jane wrote to her sister Katherine on the eve of her execution.

Hertford listened to Arbella's messenger with mounting fear and anger. Essex's death had enabled Robert Cecil to come to a secret accommodation with King James. Robert was not associated with the death of Mary, Queen of Scots, as William Cecil had been. Hertford accepted that without Robert Cecil's support, he could not hope to win the crown for his heirs. He was certain James VI of Scots would soon be James I of England, and intended to make the best of it. He certainly did not want any attention drawn to his former plans and hopes. Hertford sent the messenger under guard to Robert Cecil the following day.

The queen took the news of Arbella's actions badly. It reminded her of the dark time when she had learned of Katherine Grey's marriage to Hertford over forty years earlier, and which had left her 'the colour of a corpse'. When Arbella and her servants were interrogated at Hardwick, however, only a few servants and close family were found to have known anything about her plans. Robert Cecil judged it safe to leave Arbella in the care of her grandmother – safer, certainly, than placing her in the Tower where her presence might attract a little too much interest. Elizabeth was relieved and her health even seemed to rally. By mid-February she was well enough to grant an audience to a visiting Venetian ambassador at her grandfather's favourite palace, Richmond, with its towers and fourteen 'cloud capped' cupolas.[4]

The Venetian's first sight of Elizabeth was of her seated on her throne, dressed in a low-cut dress of silver and white taffeta trimmed with gold, and wearing a dramatic wig 'of a colour never made by nature'. Elizabeth's powerful personal image would prove as durable as any of the palaces the Tudor kings had built, and the Venetian was fascinated by Elizabeth's crumbling magnificence: her bony forehead wrapped in vast pearls 'like pears', her head bearing an imperial crown, her stomacher jewelled, and her wrists wrapped in ropes of yet more pearls. Alongside Elizabeth were her councillors, while the remainder of the Presence Chamber was 'full of ladies and gentlemen and the musicians who had been playing dance music up to that moment'. Elizabeth had enjoyed dancing in her youth, and in her old age she had continued to take pleasure in watching others do so. As she rose to greet the ambassador, they had a tart exchange, with the ambasador complaining about English piracy, and she observing 'the Republic of Venice . . . has never made herself heard by me except to ask for something', and wondering if 'my sex has brought me this demerit'.[5]

The Venetian spotted no signs of ill health in the queen, but her long hands were now swollen and, later that week, her coronation ring had to be cut off. Since Mary I had instituted the tradition that the coronation ring symbolised a queen's 'marriage' to her kingdom, its removal triggered new fears that Elizabeth's reign was soon to end, leaving a vacant throne and a battle for power.[6] Arbella's attempts to contact Hertford had convinced many at court that she was part of a plot to stop King James inheriting the throne. The two grandchildren of Margaret Douglas were, it seemed, being pitted against each other for the crown and the Venetian ambassador dispatched to the senate how their relative chances were being judged.

James believed he was the new 'Arthur . . . Come by good right to claim my seat and throne', and it was said he bore the birthmark of a lion, which proved it was his destiny.[7] His most significant support came from the Privy Council, but there was much talk about the legal objections to his candidature: 'first that he was not born in the kingdom and is therefore ineligible for the crown; and the second, that his mother, after her execution was declared a rebel by Parliament, and incapable of succession, and this incapacitates her son'. This put Arbella in the frame. She was English-born, 'of great beauty and remarkable qualities, being gifted with many accomplishments, among them the knowledge of Latin, French, Spanish and Italian, besides her native English'.[8] Elizabeth had forced her to live far from court in the hopes she would be forgotten, but Arbella's attempted marriage project had ensured she was now very much remembered. It had emerged that the infanta Isabella was uninterested in the English crown, yet there were also reports of a build-up of Spanish naval forces. Some conjectured that Spain hoped now to back Arbella's candidature against James, and perhaps later marry her to a Spanish ally.

Elizabeth remained concerned not only about Arbella's actions, however, but also the news from Ireland. There had been times – before Essex's attempted coup – when Elizabeth had been able to joke with her current Lord Deputy there. After he had moaned once that his task was as disagreeable as that of a kitchen wench, she had written addressing him as 'Mistress Kitchenmaid', and praising him for doing more harm to the rebels with his 'frying pan and other kitchen stuff . . . than those that promised more and did less'.[9] The rebel Earl of Tyrone's war of national liberation was now drawing towards Tyrone's defeat. Her Lord Deputy was pressing her hard to grant Tyrone a pardon so that a final peace could be agreed. Robert Cecil supported him, arguing that if they were to defend themselves from the Spanish, they had to secure Ireland. Elizabeth refused, concerned about 'how to terrify future traitors' if this one was allowed to go free.[10] Eventually Cecil persuaded her to change her mind, but her pardoning the enemy Tyrone – where she had been obliged to behead the English hero Essex – triggered another bout of deep depression.

On 25 February, the second anniversary of Essex's execution, Elizabeth disappeared to her chambers. One of her Boleyn ladies-in-waiting had died the previous day, and this only added to her misery.[11] Showing affection to the descendants of her aunt Mary Boleyn had been the only way she had been able to honour the memory of her mother, whose image she wore secretly in a closed ring. It was days before she appeared in public again and when she did she was described as in such 'a deep melancholy that she must die herself'. Her misery was made worse by letters that had arrived from Arbella, reminding the queen about Essex's fate and claiming she had a secret admirer at court. Rambling and accusatory, they were full of the self-obsessed paranoia of a woman who had spent too much time on her own, and Cecil marked one of Arbella's letters with the comment, 'I think she has some strange vapours to her brain.'[12]

Elizabeth remained extremely anxious. She voiced her suspicions that the men around her were 'ill affected', and complained frequently about Arbella and whoever might be supporting her.[13] On 9 March Cecil wrote to the English ambassador in Edinburgh, George Nicholson, describing the queen as eating little, her mouth and tongue dry and her chest hot; she couldn't sleep and wouldn't stay in bed or take physic. Instead, to everyone's dismay she had spent the previous three days walking restlessly in the garden in summer clothes. The mood at court was gloomy, with everyone 'in a damp'. Senior figures were stockpiling arms and buying up war horses, while James' supporters were doing their best to damage Arbella's reputation, spreading the rumour that she was mad.[14]

James remained in the strongest position to succeed, but was a far from popular choice, and the Venetian ambassador observed that agents of the Kings of Spain and France had now made it known that their masters both backed Arbella's cause, rather than accept James. Henri IV of France was horrified at the idea of a united Britain, and the end of the old alliance with Scotland. At the same time, Philip II's son, the current King Philip III of Spain, was prepared to back anyone – even a Protestant like Arbella – if they could stop James becoming King of England. James was judged a liar, who encouraged Catholics to believe he would allow them to practise their faith while having no intention of doing so, and beyond the pale for his complicity in his mother's death.

Many courtiers feared they faced the imminent prospect of either a Spanish invasion in favour of Arbella, or one by Scotland in favour of James. But the Spanish council was not yet ready for an invasion, and James was willing to wait for Robert Cecil and the Privy Council to deliver him the crown. What concerned these councillors most was the possibility of a revolution by the long-suffering poor. To pre-empt any social unrest on Elizabeth's death, the council was convened in perpetual session at Richmond on 15 March, and the guards were doubled at the royal palace. Peers were summoned to court, and potential troublemakers were impressed into the army or locked up.

Elizabeth was still not sleeping. It was reported she was weak, but otherwise she had no obvious symptoms 'except that a slight swelling of the glands under the jaw burst of itself, with a discharge of a small amount of matter'.[15] Two days later she was described as sitting on her cushions, staring at the ground, her finger in her mouth. She remained sitting on them on Saturday 19 March, when she gave an audience to Sir Robert Carey, the youngest grandson of her late aunt,

Mary Boleyn. Elizabeth wrung Carey's hand hard and told him sadly, 'Robin I am not well.' He tried to raise her spirits but found her 'melancholy humour . . . was too deep rooted in her heart'. The French had informed Elizabeth that several members of her court were in secret contact with James. Happily she did not know that Carey was amongst them, but he wrote to King James that night telling him Elizabeth was dying and promising to deliver the news of her death in person. His sister, Lady Scrope, who served in Elizabeth's bedchamber, had a blue ring James wanted as confirmation.

The next day Elizabeth did not appear in the royal chapel for the Sunday morning service. Instead she remained on her cushions in the Privy Chamber, and there she stayed, refusing to move, for a further two nights and two days, while frightened Londoners shut themselves in their houses. On the Tuesday, Elizabeth was, at last, lifted up from her cushions and walked to her bed. She had not written a will and the council were aware that her father's will therefore remained extant. Under its terms the crown passed from Elizabeth to the descendants of Frances Brandon (Katherine Grey's children and grandchildren) and in default of them, to the descendants of Eleanor Brandon; James was only to be king if these were excluded. A decision was therefore made to ask the dying queen to name her heir one last time. On the Wednesday afternoon Elizabeth responded and called for them.

Lying in her bed Elizabeth asked for liquid to ease her sore throat so that she could speak. The councillors suggested that instead she raise a finger when they named the successor 'whom she liked'.[16] Reports differ on what occurred next. Some claimed that when James was named Elizabeth raised her hand to her head, others that she never moved. But as one court servant noted, it made no difference which reports were true. The Privy Council was set on James and the alternative candidates lacked the power to oppose their decision. At six o'clock that evening the Archbishop of Canterbury and Elizabeth's other chaplains went to pray with her. Hours later, Elizabeth was left alone with her ladies, and it was with them that she died, sometime before two o'clock the following morning of 24 March 1603, 'easily like a ripe apple from the tree'. By 10 a.m Carey was galloping north to Scotland carrying the blue ring his sister had given him, as confirmation of the queen's death.

The iconic image of Elizabeth as Gloriana was, a contemporary noted, 'a painted face without a shadow to give it life'. The real, flesh-and-blood Elizabeth had been a more vulnerable figure. On her accession the Spanish ambassador Feria had noted that Elizabeth was determined to be governed by no one, and that she issued orders as commandingly as her father had. But Elizabeth's Protestant supporters – men like William Cecil – believed that a 'rightful' queen only ruled in accordance with the counsel of godly (that is Protestant) men. The truth was, Elizabeth could not impose her will as her father Henry VIII had done. What she could do was stall, not agree. She did not trust the elite, best represented in the nobility, any more than her grandfather had. There were fifty-seven peers at her accession and fifty-five at her death – as with Henry VII she had reduced their numbers. Where he had looked to professional servants who owed him everything, Elizabeth had also relied on the ordinary people who had flocked to support Mary in 1553. She owed her crown to them, she had told Feria, and nobody else.

Elizabeth found, however, that it was not only she who could appeal to public opinion. Essex had noticed that Elizabeth 'could be brought to nothing except by a kind of necessity', and there had been an increasing propensity to force her hand by seeking the support of a wide constituency. Such had been the motivation of the pamphlet campaigns promoted by Elizabeth's own councillors in favour of the succession candidates they had backed in the 1560s, and the campaigns waged to bounce her into killing Norfolk and Mary, Queen of Scots. This conspiracy-centred public posturing and spin, to convince the queen and others of a Catholic threat, had been taken up subsequently by those outside the council and shut out from power – Catholics and Puritans – and it left a dangerous legacy for Elizabeth's successor.

'A hapless kind of life is this I wear', Elizabeth had once observed; 'I serve the rout [rabble], and all their follies bear/To others' will my life is all addressed/and no way so as might content me best.'[17] Elizabeth's survival had, however, blessed England with a long period of stability. It was uncertain that this would now continue.

As Sir Robert Carey galloped north to Scotland, Elizabeth's councillors emerged nervously from Whitehall on to the green, and the diminutive figure of Robert Cecil read the proclamation that named James VI of Scots, King of England. The proclamation ignored the terms of Henry VIII's will, and other legal objections to James' claim; instead it listed his private virtues, claiming he had the 'rarest gifts of mind and body' and recorded his blood descent 'from the body of Margaret, daughter to the High and Renowned Prince, Henry the seventh . . . and of Elizabeth of York'. As the witnesses to the proclamation ran off to spread news of what they had heard, the Garter and heralds led the procession to Ludgate and then to the High Cross at Cheapside. By eleven o'clock a large crowd was gathered, 'of gallant knights and brave gentlemen of note well mounted, besides the huge number of common persons'.[18]

Cecil reread the proclamation loudly and clearly. When he had finished they all cried 'God save the king'. But one witness described the mood as 'flat' and the Venetian ambassador deduced 'that there was evidently neither sorrow for the death of the queen, nor joy for the succession of the king'. Fear was the dominant emotion and the price of basic foodstuffs rose sharply all day. Yet when night fell, a Londoner noted in his diary that there was 'no tumult, no contradiction, no disorder in the city; every man went about his business as readily, as peaceably, as securely as if there had been no change, nor any news ever heard of competitors'.[19]

Relief and joy were unbounded. As bonfires were lit from hill to hill, a courtier recorded in his journal 'the people both in City and

Country finding the just fear of forty years, for want of a known successor, dissolved in a minute did so rejoice, as few wished the queen alive again'.[20] One after another, England's towns and cities filled with the sound of bells. After a mere three generations, the Renaissance romance and gothic horror of the age of Tudor kings and queens was over. The new age of the Stuarts, of gunpowder plots, of civil war and of revolution, had begun. 'How daintily it did so e'er compose, the beauty of the white and scarlet rose/The Flower is parched, the silken leaf is blasted', a poet wrote. 'The rose decay'd, and all the glory wasted.'[21]

EPILOGUE

Take but degree away, untune that string,
And, hark, what discord follows! each thing meets
In mere oppugnancy . . .
Power into will, will into appetite;
And appetite, an universal wolf,
So doubly seconded with will and power,
Must make perforce an universal prey,
And last eat up himself.

WILLIAM SHAKESPEARE, TROILUS AND CRESSIDA,
ACT 1, SCENE 3

IN SEPTEMBER 2012, RICHARD III'S REMAINS WERE FOUND UNDER A Leicester car park. The monastery where he was buried had occupied that spot, and had been destroyed during the Reformation period, along with medieval libraries, art and music. One consequence of this cultural terrorism is that our sympathy with this past is cauterised: because it was destroyed it is unfamiliar, and so we try to make it fit what is familiar, viewing it through our own lenses. To understand the Tudors we must remember their context, which was shaped by their fifteenth-century past, not the post-Reformation, post-Enlightenment era which informs our view.

The fact that Richard's world could be brutal is evident in the broken bones that were dug out of the ground where his body lay.

They bring a sense of immediacy, even to us, of the very real violence of the late fifteenth century: Richard's skull was smashed and his brain exposed by a soldier of the Tudor army, a blade thrust into his buttocks. Here are echoes of the desecration of the corpse of that 'noble knight' Warwick the Kingmaker in 1471, and of the shattered bones of the thousands killed at Towton in 1461. They are also evidence of Richard's failure as a king, for ensuring peace and harmony was a vital duty of kingship. It would become the very *raison d'être* of his Tudor successors, symbolised in the striking image of the union rose, a visual representation of national reconciliation and redemption.

Today we aim to establish peace and harmony by other means, through the workings of democracy. We have learned to trust that elected governments will rule for all – not just the majority – and in accordance with established law. This is not true in other areas of the world, and was not true for our ancestors. For people of the Tudor age the king was seen as a protector, a bulwark against anarchy. We are fortunate that nowadays we are given only rare insights into the horrors of disorder. As Baghdad was looted in 2003, Donald Rumsfeld commented breezily that 'freedom's untidy ... and free people are free to make mistakes and commit crimes and do bad things'. Fifteenth-century Englishmen would have recognised immediately the seriousness of what was happening in Baghdad: it was not freedom but licence, the strong taking what they want from the weak according to their appetite – Shakespeare's 'universal wolf'. And for them, law and order went well beyond modern associations with courtrooms and policemen.

The law was revered, for its origins were divine. They lay in an ordered, rational and interconnected universe in which God had ranked everything from grasses to trees, from peasants to princes. This great chain of being did not fix a person's status at birth, however. It was part of the duty of care of higher ranks to advance chosen men through patronage. God's intervention on earth – divine providence

– might also raise a man up. At the apex of the earthly hierarchy, the king stood over everyone, divinely ordained down the ages to rule above personal interest or tribal quarrels, and above those with the sharpest elbows or most grasping hands. What we might call human rights – justice – lay in each man being given his due, while the sin of ambition lay in taking what was not due to you. For the ambitious to take a crown, or for the disgruntled to rebel against a rightful king, was akin to the revolt of Lucifer. It risked opening the gates of hell, and releasing chaos into the world. That was why the enemies of Henry VI and Edward V described them as 'false kings'. To do so justified their overthrow. It is also why subsequent monarchs had to demonstrate to the people that they were 'true' kings. In this respect the most obvious quality was royal blood, but true kingship was also reflected in a king's abilities as a ruler. To ensure peace and harmony a king ruled justly, fought his kingdom's battles, and also founded future stability on a secure succession. Instead of men vying for the chance to rule, kingship was settled in advance, so that when a king died, power passed to his heir. These issues – 'true' kingship, the securing of national stability and the need for a clear succession – were to be played out repeatedly during the Tudor period. Indeed the era began with them. This is why it is so important to look at the Tudor family story.

When Richard was crowned in the summer of 1483, not everyone accepted his contention that the overthrown twelve-year-old Edward V was a false king. In their eyes, while Edward V and his younger brother were alive, Richard was a usurper. This gives Richard a strong motive for removing the princes as a focus of opposition. Unfortunately for Richard, when their rumoured deaths were followed by rebellion that October it signalled continued national disharmony. The death of Richard's son and heir the following year appeared to offer further evidence that Richard was a usurper, cursed by God, a verdict confirmed by his death at Bosworth in 1485. Henry VII's victory allowed him to argue his reign was the result of divine intervention.

His Lancastrian blood claim, drawn through his mother, was extremely weak and so he had taken on the mantle of the 'fair unknown', the 'true' prince who emerges from obscurity to claim his rightful throne, just as the mythical King Arthur had once done. In support of this he had offered the story that the 'saint' Henry VI had prophesied his reign.

While his victory at Bosworth offered the crucial evidence that he was indeed blessed by God, a fact then accepted by Parliament, he still had to rule as a 'true' king, establishing national unity and a secure succession. His marriage to Elizabeth of York in 1486 was meant to reconcile Yorkists to his rule and within nine months they had a son: a living embodiment of the union rose and peace between the houses of Lancaster and York. Despite this union, it was crucial for Henry to claim his right independent of his marriage, otherwise his right was dependent on his wife's life, the claims of his children by her would be stronger than his own, and any children by subsequent wives would not be accepted as 'true' heirs. He therefore continued to project his kingship as providential, a new beginning that drew on a royal past, while promising something better, a hope expressed by naming his son Arthur.

Nevertheless, his disgruntled subjects never forgot the princes who had vanished in the Tower and whose royal blood was so much more impressive than Henry's. The modern debate over whether Richard III or Henry VII was responsible for the deaths of the princes has obscured how much the two kings had in common on this issue. Neither was wholly accepted as the princes' replacement. Neither gave the princes a public burial or requiem – and this is key to shedding light on this perennially fascinating mystery.

After 500 years, modern detective work is not going to prove that the butler murdered the princes with the candlestick in the Tower. Nor does it tell us anything when modern forensic psychologists assure us that Richard III was not a psychopath. You did not need to be a psychopath to do away with competing claimants to your throne, especially when maintaining stability was a king's duty.[1] The mystery of the princes comes down to the absolute importance of remembering the context of the lost world that lies beneath the Leicester car park.

In England we have no equivalent today to the shrine at Lourdes in France, visited every year by thousands of pilgrims looking for healing or spiritual renewal, but we can remember the vast crowds outside Buckingham Palace after the death of Diana, Princess of Wales. Imagine that feeling and enthusiasm in pilgrims visiting the relics and the tomb of two innocent child princes, greatly magnified by the closeness people then felt with the dead. A cult of the princes would have been immensely damaging for Richard III, who had taken their throne, and for Henry VII, who was fearful of being regarded as a mere king consort to his wife, the sister and heir to the princes. This is why the princes were simply 'disappeared', why they were given no tomb, and why they were nowhere officially remembered. Yet the ghosts of the princes – whom Henry VII never laid to rest – haunted the rest of his reign, and when his son Arthur Tudor died it seemed that, like Richard III, Henry too was cursed. But he survived, ruling with an iron hand and helped, crucially, by the fact he had a family, including a surviving son.

On Henry VIII's accession in 1509 it seemed England had a 'true' king again: he was the the senior male relative of the lost princes, and it was his resemblance to his glorious grandfather, Edward IV – not his father Henry VII – that made Henry VIII 'the more acclaimed and approved of'. For twenty years thereafter Henry VIII represented an ideal of chivalric kingship that his father had never achieved. Henry VIII's royal blood, his glamour, his martial qualities, charm and piety, together carried the most tremendous force. In Flanders it was said that the young Henry VIII's 'great nobleness and fame' was 'greater than any prince since King Arthur'.

The myth of the convivial 'bluff King Hal' lived on in national memory into the next century. Samuel Rowley's Jacobean play, *When You See Me You Know Me*, which helped inspire Shakespeare's *Henry*

VIII, depicted a king going out in disguise to mingle with his subjects, getting into brawls and even being arrested. It is impossible to imagine such a play being written about Henry VII. Even today, we still prefer to remember the young and virile Henry VIII to the old, impotent tyrant. The trigger for Henry's tyranny was – naturally – his anxieties concerning his inability to have a son with Katherine of Aragon. 'We think all our doings in our lifetime are clearly defaced and worthy of no memory, if we leave you in trouble at the time of our death', Henry once commented. Certain he was a 'true' king, he believed that his marriage must be false, and therefore cursed. After all, having no son was not only a personal blow, it also meant a possible future struggle for the crown, with his sisters and their heirs gaining a new importance in the future of the succession. These were the defining issues of Henry's reign and the key influences on his rule: the nature of a true king, the importance of securing national concord and a stable future in blood heirs. Of course, sons required not only a king to sire them but also a queen to bear them – and Henry VIII is remembered today, perhaps most of all, for his queens.

It was not just his wives who were important, however, in the matter of the succession. The second part of this book opens with the battle of Flodden, as seen through the eyes of two queens: Henry's sister Margaret Tudor, Queen of Scots, whose husband James IV was killed, as well as Katherine of Aragon, Captain General of the English army that killed him. It was a shattering defeat for Scotland, but having children was more important for the succession than winning battles. It was the losing side, in the shape of Queen Margaret, who was destined to carry the Tudor bloodline forward through her son, James V of Scots, and her daughter Lady Margaret Douglas – a long-overlooked figure, and highly significant as the grandmother of the future heir to the Tudors, James VI and I. Seventeen years after Flodden, the teenage Margaret Douglas arrived at her uncle Henry VIII's court. It was the eve of the break with Rome, the annulment of Henry's marriage to the aging Katherine and the coronation of his new queen, Anne

Boleyn, from whom Henry hoped to a have son. Margaret Douglas witnessed these events, as well as Anne's fall, and the unravelling of the Tudor Camelot, with Anne, beheaded with a sword, the symbol of King Arthur, betrayed by his Queen Guinevere. Henry VIII still did not have a son and Margaret Douglas was to experience at first hand that summer of 1536 Henry's attacks on the rights of his sisters' heirs as he sought to establish the succession via the potential rights of his now illegitimised daughters.

Beyond the walls of the Tower, peace and harmony were also breaking down in spectacular style with Henry VIII facing the greatest rebellion England had seen for 150 years. The old divisions of the Wars of the Roses had come to be replaced by religious strife. The rebellion failed, but the shock to Henry's ego was tremendous. His subsequent dissolution of the monasteries, and the execution of religious conservatives and reformers alike, were an attempt to forge a new religious unity and national harmony that he intended would lie within a nationalist, Henrician, Catholic Church.

In this he failed – but what he did succeed in doing in 1537 was to give England a prince in his son, tellingly named Edward. When Henry VIII died Edward VI was, however, younger even than the princes in the Tower had been when they disappeared. The Tudors always looked back for examples and warnings. Determined there would be no new Richard III, Henry VIII's will had placed his trust in former servants, while at the same time ensuring that Edward's heirs in the wider Tudor family were too weak to be a threat. What happened next – a coup led by Edward VI's senior maternal uncle, who became the Protector Somerset – acts as a valuable reminder of a past that might have been. Edward VI ended up living out the exact fate that Richard III had feared for his nephew Edward V: that of being dominated by non-royal relations, with dangerous consequences for any members of the royal family who threatened their power. In the end Edward VI's maternal family, the Seymours, did not benefit from his rule. But when Edward died he ignored his Tudor sisters and bequeathed the throne to his

Protestant cousin, Lady Jane Grey, a descendant of Elizabeth Woodville's marriage to her first husband. Richard III's fear of the upstart Woodvilles had become a reality for a Tudor.

Mary I's subsequent victory over Jane in 1553 was the victory of the once-scorned Tudor name, and the reaction of a deeply hierarchical society to the offence of having, in Guildford Dudley, a man of no royal blood as king. Mary had also proved herself personally well qualified to become England's first ruling queen. The popular image of Mary I has been greatly influenced by later sexual and religious prejudice. She is often depicted as weak and with little political skill, yet she had raised military and popular support and divided her enemies with stunning success. Advertising her intention to scapegoat Jane Grey's father-in-law, John Dudley, Duke of Northumberland, and offering mercy to almost everyone else, Mary promised to deliver the peace and harmony Jane's regime had failed to do. Mary hoped that by encouraging leading Protestants to go into exile she would be able to go on to restore a united Catholic country, in communion once again with Rome, but with a humanist-reformed vision.

It was a devastating blow when, only six months later, Mary was confronted by the Protestant-led rebellion that became known as the Wyatt revolt. As she faced these rebels, she gave a speech on the nature of her 'true' kingship. If she had been crowned 'by the Grace of God only', so they would owe her, she said, 'respect and due obedience solely on account of the holy unction' of the ceremony. Yet she had also won the crown on the battlefield, and was in addition queen 'by rightful law of succession, confirmed by your unanimous acclimations and votes' in Parliament. Yet after she defeated the rebels she knew she had to prove her right further, by gaining the peace that still eluded her.

If it is difficult to believe that Richard III might have been a good king and a religious man, and nevertheless ordered the deaths of two children in pursuit of national unity, it is worth considering what followed: Mary executed the sixteen-year-old Jane and the youthful

Guildford, simply because they remained a potential inspiration for further Protestant opposition, which would of course threaten stability. As Mary continued to face Protestant treason she became even more ruthless, with the infamous burnings intended to eliminate what she perceived as a stubborn and destabilising minority. In our context we see Mary's actions as those of a fanatic. In her context she was eliminating fanatics, and of the most dangerous kind, incorrigible rebels against God and queen. But Mary also had to work positively, to build a future, and this unravelled in the face of her infertility and declining health. She failed in her ultimate duty to produce a child and this meant, once again, that the wider family was key to the future. Mary's preferred choice as her heir, Margaret Douglas, could not compete with the claims of Henry VIII's second daughter and, as Elizabeth took note, it was the knowledge that she would succeed her sister that fuelled the disorder and rebellion against Mary.

With the loss of Calais in the last year of Mary's life it would be easy for her enemies to paint the young, Protestant Elizabeth's accession as a brilliant new dawn. It is as such that it is still projected. Mary remains associated with her late seventeenth-century sobriquet 'Bloody Mary', and an infamous recent advertisement for the London Dungeon depicted her face transforming into a demon-zombie. Elizabeth, by contrast, has been played in films by a series of beautiful actresses: Elizabeth is ever Cate Blanchett, fairy queen, to Mary's bitter, grey-faced Kathy Burke. Yet these sisters were neither simple heroines nor villains. Both were rulers of their time and we can only understand Elizabeth if we see, as she did, what the Tudor sisters had in common and how she could learn from Mary's example.[2] Most significant for Elizabeth was the fact that Mary's Protestant enemies had sought to redefine the nature of a 'true' king. They argued that religion was more important than blood, or victory in battles – a true king was Protestant – and that all women were by nature unsuited to rule over men. Elizabeth's response was to offer to her ordinary subjects a theatrical representation of herself as a 'true' ruler: the seeds of which had been sown by Mary herself in her speech during the Wyatt revolt, in which she is a mother who loves her subjects as if they were her children. Here was a female authority figure accepted as part of the divine order.

Elizabeth also sought to establish tranquility. Her conservatism and pragmatism have seen her described as a religious moderate, in contrast to the 'fanatical' Mary; but as the new Protestant queen of a largely conservative country Elizabeth was necessarily moderate, and as her reign grew longer, she proved that, like Mary, she could be utterly ruthless when faced by a threat. The executions of hundreds of villagers following the Northern rebellion far exceeded anything her predecessors had done in similar circumstances, while her later persecution of Catholics was relentless and cruel.

Where Elizabeth was strikingly original was on the matter of the succession. For her subjects the provision of heirs remained central to the monarch's duty to provide future security. But Elizabeth took her own path, having learned from the experiences of Mary I and Jane Grey. Elizabeth explained in 1561 that it was from fear of provoking unrest that she had thus far 'forborne to match with any husband'. That held true thereafter, with Elizabeth further bolstering her position by ensuring that she had 'no certain successor'. The royal family was, for Elizabeth, not a source of future stability, but of immediate threat.

Elizabeth imprisoned her cousins, Protestant and Catholic, from Katherine and Mary Grey, to Margaret Douglas and Mary, Queen of Scots, from Margaret Clifford to Arbella Stuart. She bastardised their children, or sought their murder, she drove them to despair and even madness, so she could die a natural death, as queen, in her bed. And unlike the childless Richard II, to whom she was compared by her enemies, Elizabeth achieved that aim. The last of the Tudors was buried in the same vault as her grandparents Henry VII and Elizabeth of York in Westminster Abbey. Three years later, however, she was reburied in her sister's vault in the north aisle of the Lady Chapel. She was granted an effigy, but King James built his mother, Mary, Queen of Scots, a far more magnificent tomb in the south aisle, flanked by the tombs of those other mothers of kings, Margaret Beaufort and Margaret Douglas.[3] Elizabeth had had Mary, Queen of Scots executed, but together the Tudor sisters represented only a dynastic dead end, and for England the future lay with the new royal family. James intended to be buried in the vault Elizabeth had chosen for herself, positioning himself as the true heir to Henry VII and Elizabeth of York.[4]

After a few years of King James' extravagance, however, and when his passion for male favourites became a matter of political significance, people began to look back wistfully to the reign of their parsimonious, spinster Tudor queen. Above all they missed the Elizabethan theatre of reciprocal love. In 1607 a Venetian reported people complaining bitterly that King James did 'not caress the people'. Rather, 'this king manifests no taste for them but rather contempt and dislike. The result is he is despised and almost hated.' The glorification of Elizabeth's memory soon became a popular means of criticising her successor. Indeed, the birth of the reputation of the Tudors as our great national dynasty would owe much to further Stuart failings. For hundreds of years English kings had had to earn obedience freely given and, as we have seen, this was at the heart of much that the Tudors did. James' son Charles I would discover he could not rule without it. But despite a civil war, the beheading of King Charles, and the overthrow of the last Stuart king, James II, a monarchy part elective and part hereditary has endured, passing through junior descendants of Henry VII, and of his grandparents, Owen Tudor and Catherine of Valois.

Tudor history is more popular than ever and, as always, contentious. We see echoes of the Reformation struggle in the polarised writing and thinking about the new global resurgence of religion, with the demonised Catholic Church used as a surrogate for expressing fears of Islamism. This is bounced back again into depictions of the Tudor period, notably in Shekhar Kapur's film *Elizabeth*, which depicts Philip II as a Catholic-Islamist. So fixed is this construction of an irreconcilable and dangerous religious 'other' that while the inferior place of women in the royal succession is set to be changed by the current coalition government, Catholics are to remain excluded by law.

The effigy that lay on Catherine of Valois' coffin at her funeral can still be seen in Westminster Abbey, dressed in her red painted shift, while her body lies under the altar in Henry V's chantry.[5] Sadly, however, Owen Tudor, with whom this story also began, is nowhere remembered. After the monastery of the Hereford Greyfriars was dissolved in 1538, his tomb vanished. The ancestor of all the Tudor monarchs, and every British monarch since, now lies in a grave beneath a 1970s housing estate. Perhaps, like Richard III, he will find someone willing to find him a more dignified place.[6] For those who lived under the Tudor kings and queens, what mattered was not the Welsh origins of the Tudors, but the royal marriage of the union rose to which James was proclaimed heir in 1603: the symbol of peace, harmony and stability. For us, however, the name of the rose is Tudor, and the family story that began with Owen ends with a salute to the memory of the clumsy servant who, with a pirouette and a trip, fell into the lap of English royal history.

APPENDIX 1

WHAT HAPPENED TO THE BODY OF JAMES IV?

ACCORDING TO A PROSE AND VERSE TRACT OF 1575, JAMES IV'S BODY
was brought through the streets of London after the Battle of Flodden
slung over a horse, just as Richard III's had been brought to Leicester
after Bosworth.[1] Katherine of Aragon received it at the Carthusian
monastery at Sheen, but it could not be buried until the Pope granted
his permission to lay the excommunicant in sacred ground. Henry
duly asked the Pope, stating his intention to bury the king eventually
at St Paul's, and it is often assumed that is where he was buried. In
fact, although Pope Leo gave Henry his permission, the body was left
at Sheen, unburied.[2]

The Elizabethan antiquarian Stow later saw James' body, where
it lay cast 'into an old waste room, amongst old timber, stone, lead,
and other rubble', as it had since the monastery at Sheen was
dissolved. After that, some Elizabethan workmen cut off James' head
'for their foolish pleasure'. It still had James' red hair and beard.
Another Londoner later rescued it, keeping it for a while in his
house, saying it smelled nice, until eventually he paid for it to be
buried at St Michael's Church, Wood Street, in the City of London.[3]
The church burned down in the Great Fire of London. There is a
pub on the site today.

James' English wife did not fare much better. The remains of

Margaret Tudor disappeared after her tomb was destroyed by a Protestant mob in May 1559. They had attacked the Carthusian priory in Perth where she was buried, killing one of the monks before desecrating her remains.

APPENDIX 2

THE MYSTERIOUS QUARREL BETWEEN HENRY VIII AND MARGARET DOUGLAS

HITHERTO HISTORIANS HAVE CLAIMED THAT HENRY VIII's DECISION to exclude Margaret Douglas from the succession in his will followed a quarrel she had with him in the autumn of 1546, and have suggested it was over religion.[1] This is false.

We know Margaret was at court at least until August 1546 when she was buying powder from the king's apothecary. Historians suggest the argument with Henry took place at around this time, or later. They base this on a memorandum written in 1562 by her husband's former secretary, Thomas Bishop.[2] At this time (during the reign of Queen Elizabeth) he had been digging for dirt on Margaret and her husband Lennox, who had been scheming to marry their son Darnley to Mary, Queen of Scots. They in turn tried to discredit Bishop. According to the Lennox account, 'after the death of King James [V] in Scotland the said Bishop returned into his country [i.e. Scotland] and was retained in service by the Earl of Lennox, and, for the faithful service which King Henry VIII supposed he had done to the said earl, he gave him the living which he now has, which thing the king did afterwards repent, understanding that he [Bishop] went about to set dissension between the said earl and his lady'.[3] The Lennoxes complained that Bishop was a frequent troublemaker, not only coming between married couples, but also in setting the Lennoxes' servants against each other, and that he was a coward and a thief to boot.

In the Bishop memorandum quoted by historians, Bishop defends himself by surveying all the work he has done for Elizabeth I's predecessors, despite the difficulties Margaret has put in his way and how he has been rewarded for it. In 1546, 'His majesty [Henry VIII], not repenting his former gifts of lands, pension and money, a little afore his death and after the breach with my lady Lennox, gave to me and my heirs . . .', etc. This refers to land grants Bishop received from Henry that October and dates Margaret's supposed argument with Henry to shortly before that time. He does not say what her argument with Henry was about, but he complains about her continued anger towards him ever since. He worked for Edward VI's councillors, Somerset and Northumberland, and then 'Queen Mary, though my lady Lennox told her I was a heretic, her majesty gave me, unknown to her . . . my pension anew'. He even claims that Queen Mary trusted him over her Catholic cousin and old friend. The memorandum concludes: 'I trust . . . the queen's majesty will be as good sovereign to me as her gracious father my master [Henry VIII] was in the like and as her highness predecessors, my masters, have been, whom without fear of my lady Lennox or any others truly and without malice I shall serve . . .', etc.[4]

It has been assumed that religion was at the cause of Margaret's supposed argument with Henry. But another previously overlooked manuscript remains extant in which Bishop clarifies the matter. His claim is that Henry VIII was so angry about false accusations the Lennoxes had made against him in the 1540s that '[Margaret] ever after lost a part of [the king's] heart, as appeared at his death'.[5] In other words, Henry VIII demoted Margaret in line of succession because she was rude about Thomas Bishop! Now, Henry VIII evidently did value Bishop's services, but Henry's efforts to describe Margaret as illegitimate in 1536 suggest that he had wished to demote her in line of succession long before Bishop came to England. Despite Bishop's memorandum in February 1562, the imprisonment of the Earl of Lennox in March and Margaret Douglas in April, the many accusations made against them, and specific efforts made to dismiss Lennox's claims of the positive achievements of his work for Henry VIII, it was nowhere else suggested in 1562 (or by anyone who had been alive in 1546, other then Bishop) that Margaret had ever quarrelled with Henry.

Bishop's subsequent career proved him a rather less reliable Tudor servant than he had claimed. In 1569 he was found to be in contact with adherents of the captive Mary, Queen of Scots. He ended up in the Tower where he remained until 1576, and was granted permission to return to Scotland by James VI after Mary's execution.[6] Margaret died in 1578, when she still owned a treasured tablet picture of the king. In her will it was bequeathed to Robert Dudley, Earl of Leicester.[7] This may be the tablet book with a picture of Henry VIII that survives in the British Library. A gold enamelled Tudor girdle prayer book with open leaf tracery covers dating from around 1540, the tiny book still contains its original manuscript with an illuminated miniature bust of Henry VIII.[8] It came to the British Library from a library that belonged to the heirs of William Seymour, Duke of Somerset, the widower of Margaret's granddaughter Arbella Stuart. Arbella had as a child been betrothed to Robert Dudley's short-lived legitimate son, and it could have passed to her then, if it had not always stayed in her care.

APPENDIX 3

GUILDFORD AND JANE DUDLEY

GUILDFORD DUDLEY'S PLACE IN THE MYTHS CONCERNING HIS WIFE Lady Jane Grey is a dark one. In some of the stories Guildford emerges as little better than a whining, spoilt, rapist. To clear his name it is worth recording the few facts we have concerning Guildford's relationship with his young wife, drawn from sources predating 19 July 1553.

The couple had an arranged marriage, as was the norm for children of the nobility, and at the usual age. There is no source written before Jane's overthrow to support the oft-repeated Italian story that Jane resisted the marriage.

It was expected that Guildford would be granted the title of king, most likely in the September parliament. The two subsequent consorts of reigning English queens were both given the title and Edward VI had already described Guildford as 'born to achieve celebrity' and a man from whom his subjects could expect 'great things'.[1] It seems doubtful Jane would have objected to this, later stories notwithstanding. Her European mentor and correspondent Heinrich Bullinger expressed the view that by the laws of nature and God a woman should not rule. Guildford was referred to sometimes as king while Jane was queen, but again there are no sources written before Jane's overthrow that suggest she was under any pressure to pre-empt Parliament's decision on the title. In the procession on the day Jane was proclaimed queen, Guildford was no more than her consort. His name was not mentioned in the proclamation that declared Jane the queen, and his signature does not appear alongside hers in the official documents she signed 'Jane the queen'.

Venetian reports, later written up by three different Italians, include what may be a garbled account of a petition Jane made in the Tower in the expectation of a pardon after 19 July.[2] These cast the blame for the attempt to keep Mary I from the throne in July 1553 on John Dudley's supposed ambition to make his son king. In these reports 'Jane' describes bitter arguments with Guildford and his mother over his expectation that he will be king. Despite this supposed ill feeling, the Italians also later relayed a story describing how Guildford asked to see Jane on the final night of their lives, and embrace her one last time. She was said to have rebuffed him, saying it would be too distressing for them both, and that it was better to prepare for what was to come with prayer. It paints a very Italian picture of a passionate young man thinking of fleshly matters, while the pious Jane focuses on God.

It is impossible to know what stories, from these reports, originated with Jane and what did not, but it is worth comparing what we know with what we are told. We know that on the last day of her reign Jane named her godson, Guildford. This suggests she respected him, at the very least. Such positive feelings are confirmed in later comments concerning Guildford, which are written and signed in her own hand, and therefore carry more weight that any reported speech. They describe him as a co-martyr. It is also notable that her last letters are signed using her married name, Lady Jane Dudley.[3]

English contemporaries described Guildford as a 'comely, virtuous and goodly gentleman' who 'most innocently was executed'.[4] On balance the evidence suggests his wife shared these views of him.

APPENDIX 4

THE MYTH OF FRANCES BRANDON THE CHILD ABUSER

I BELIEVED I HAD SUCCESSFULLY DEMOLISHED THE VARIOUS MYTHS concerning Frances in my triple biography of her daughters Jane, Katherine and Mary Grey, but one piece of 'evidence' is still used to support the old tropes.

The accusations of child abuse against Frances are built on a story, related about Jane almost a decade after she died, in a book called *The Schoolmaster*, written by Elizabeth Tudor's one-time tutor, Roger Ascham. It describes the thirteen-year-old Jane reading the *Phaedo* of Plato in Greek at her family home at Bradgate in Leicestershire while the rest of the household are out hunting. Interrupted briefly from her quiet study, Jane explains that she loves learning because her lessons with her kindly tutor are a respite from the abuse of her parents, who pinch and nip at her if she doesn't perform every task perfectly. 'One of the greatest benefits that God ever gave me, is that He sent me so sharp, severe parents and so gentle a schoolmaster', Ascham recalls her saying. Frances' modern-day detractors refer to these as 'Jane's own words'. They are, of course, no such things. They are reported speech, written by Roger Ascham.

As I described in *The Sisters Who Would be Queen*, while Roger Ascham really did meet Jane, when he wrote to her referring to their meeting a few months later he commented only on her parents' pride in her work.

Her 'gentle' tutor, John Aylmer, was meanwhile writing letters to a Swiss theologian complaining that the teenager 'was at that age [when] ... all people are inclined to follow their own ways', and asked how best to 'provide bridles for restive horses' such as this spirited girl.

So why did Ascham tell this story? His book, *The Schoolmaster*, was intended to promote a kindlier method of teaching than the beatings commonly delivered to recalcitrant pupils. But it is also notable that Ascham began writing *The Schoolmaster* in 1563, the year Katherine Grey had her second son, and while the MP John Hales was writing his book supporting Katherine's claim as Elizabeth's heir. It was obviously helpful that the passage about Jane chimed with elegies and ballads that were being published and republished that year, also praising her virtues and blaming her execution for treason either on the ambition of her father and father-in-law, or on Mary I's cruelty. Ascham recalled that it was William Cecil, that great protector of Katherine Grey's claim, who suggested, that summer, that he write his book.

The Schoolmaster was published (posthumously) in 1570, during the aftermath of the 1569 Catholic rising in favour of the rival claims to the throne of Mary, Queen of Scots. That same year a fraudulent letter appeared in a new edition of Foxe's *Martyrs*, from 'Jane' to her father, blaming her death on his actions. A final point to make about the Ascham story is that, in common with an Italian story describing Jane being bullied by her parents into marrying Guildford (for more on which see the Appendix on Guildford), Frances is only ever mentioned in conjunction with her husband, not as the dominating figure she has become in modern literature, in which she has been used very much as Mary I has been used with Elizabeth I, that is as the shadow that throws the heroine into a more brilliant light.

It is quite probable that Frances and her husband were strict – loving parents of this period were expected to be 'sharp, severe, parents'. But Jane's Italian tutor, Michel Angelo Florio, observed that Jane was particularly close to her mother and in 1559, when Frances died, both her remaining daughters were at her side.

APPENDIX 5

THE OBSCURE MARGARET CLIFFORD, HEIR TO THE THRONE 1578–96

MARGARET CLIFFORD WAS THE ONLY CHILD OF HENRY CLIFFORD, Earl of Cumberland, and Eleanor Brandon, the younger daughter of Henry VIII's sister, Mary, the French queen. Eleanor died young in 1547, leaving Cumberland so unhappy that his servants fed him on breast milk to keep him alive. Cumberland avoided court in King Edward's time, and in 1552 he refused to marry his daughter to Guildford Dudley, even when Edward VI had pressed him to do so. The following year, when Edward VI was dying, he agreed – under who knows what pressure – to betroth her instead to Guildford's aging uncle, Sir Andrew Dudley.

With the overthrow of Jane Grey the betrothal was broken, and Margaret Clifford was married to Lord Strange, later Earl of Derby – a descendant of Henry VII's stepfather. The wedding, which took place in 1555 and was attended by both Mary I and King Philip, provided some of the greatest court spectacles of the reign. Since it was evident Mary I did not want Elizabeth as her heir, Margaret Clifford hoped Mary I would name her, arguing that with the Grey sisters excluded by reason of their father's treason, she was next in line under the terms of Henry VIII's will.[1]

Margaret Clifford's sense of self-importance continued during the reign of Queen Elizabeth. Extravagant even by the standards of the higher nobility, Margaret Clifford fell out with her husband and they separated in 1567. Elizabeth was highly sensitive to scandal at court and tried to patch up the marriage, but without success. Following the death of Mary Grey in 1578 – and with Katherine's sons declared illegitimate – Margaret Clifford believed her place as Elizabeth's heir under Henry VIII's will was clear. Her position was strengthened by the fact she had at least two surviving sons of undoubted legitimacy.

At New Year 1579, the traditional time for the exchange of presents, Margaret received the most expensive of all the gifts the queen had made to her ladies. This recognised her as second only to Elizabeth at court in terms of royal blood. But she suffered a spectacular fall from grace that summer. In August Elizabeth's proposed groom the Duke of Anjou spent several days with the queen at Greenwich Palace in great secrecy, but the news was leaked. Those judged responsible were Margaret Clifford and 'a daughter of the Earl of Bedford'.[2] As the Spanish ambassador noted, it was Margaret Clifford, as a senior heir to the crown, whose name was the more significant; she was arrested and held at a gentleman's house in London.

Margaret Clifford was known to be close to Robert Dudley, and her partner in crime may have been his brother Ambrose's wife, Anne, whose father was the Earl of Bedford. But what were her motives? It is possible, given the religious conservatism with which the Cliffords were linked, that Margaret's actions represented an unholy alliance between Dudley's Puritan faction and Catholic opponents of the Anjou marriage, who feared it would weaken the Hapbsurgs in the Low Countries.[3] But her will indicates she later died a Protestant.[4] In any event, it seems her primary motives had little to do with religion at all, but rather with her hopes of one day being queen.

When Margaret Clifford's servants were questioned, one of them described how she had a horoscope cast to discover how long Elizabeth had to live.[5] Margaret insisted that the supposed 'magician' was merely her doctor, and that he had been employed since May to rub potions on her aching limbs. The doctor was executed for witchcraft and Margaret Clifford was never to return to royal favour.[6] Margaret Clifford's sons heeded the warning of their mother's fate and would never involve themselves in any plots concerning the succession. In this they had their mother's belated support. In 1593, when her eldest son was approached by a Catholic exile concerning the issue, she advised him to hand the man over to the authorities – which he did.[7] She died in 1596 the last surviving great-grandchild of Henry VII.

AUTHOR'S NOTE AND ACKNOWLEDGEMENTS

HIDDEN IN THE CLOSED ARCHIVES OF BELVOIR CASTLE IS A mysterious Tudor codex. This book bears no title. You open it to find sixty double pages of names and titles linked with inky black lines. In timescale these genealogies stretch back to the mythological last King of the Britons. In reach there are royal names, and those of mere gentry. Odd details stand out: a traitor highlighted, a monarch ignored. It reads like a puzzle waiting to be solved.

Why is Elizabeth Tudor's father unnamed? Her mother, Anne Boleyn, features, and under her name is written in Latin, 'Queen of England, wife of Henry VIII, decapitated'. Everyone of the period knew Anne's execution was followed with a parliamentary statue declaring Elizabeth illegitimate in law. Is this why she is not listed in the Tudor line, but only in her maternal grandmother's? Surely no one would have dared place her outside the royal family after she became Queen? Yet under Elizabeth's name it states she is 'regina angliae presens': 'The present Queen of England'.

The author may have copied information from earlier herald scrolls, updating details as he did so. This would explain why the bastardized Mary Tudor is not mentioned at all, although her husband, Philip of Spain, is listed as 'King of England'. But what was the purpose of this codex? The lines connecting different families read like a political map, navigating the bloodlines of those with power, status, land, and the precious royal blood of the family chosen by God to rule. It is likely that whoever commissioned this codex wanted to see how they fitted into it. Here was the basis of their self-esteem. Seeing themselves as part of a line with a past and a future they boosted their intense loyalty to family and to the land on which their wealth and power was based. The man (and in a patriarchal society it was almost always a man) at the head of a great family was steward of his estates, which it was his duty to pass on to his heirs. It was also for him to assert the family honour, and maintain the authority of his line.

In the fifteenth century the head of a family was owed not only the service and fidelity of his servants and tenants, but also his kin, who would follow him onto battle – as Owen Tudor's bastard son, Sir David Owen, did for his half nephew, Henry VII. A century later, kin were no longer bound to act in blood for the head of the family, especially against the crown. But family still represented an ideal of stability, which had a spiritual and well as a worldly dimension. In the early period knights were buried in tombs mounted with their effigy on armour, and where prayers were said regularly for their souls. And even after the Reformation, when the prayers had stopped, families still had heraldic symbols engraved where they were buried. These are masculine symbols, but for women family honour and authority was as important as it was for the men, and their role also significant, particularly in the protection and promotion of their sons.

With Elizabeth I time was running out for the Tudor line. This, my third book on the Tudor succession and the culmination of fifteen years of research, attempts to record their story, amongst the secrets and behind the riddles. My last two books cover later Tudor history and it was intimidating to consider how I might approach the earlier reigns. It was something David Starkey wrote in his biography of the young Henry VIII – *Virtuous Prince* – that encouraged me to begin before Bosworth: 'The story of how Henry Tudor [(i.e. Henry VII)] survived against the odds, and won his throne and his bride against even greater odds, is one of the world's great adventure stories.' It sounded irresistible, and indeed how could one understand the king, if you only began his life in 1485?

As I began my research in 2008 I came across another inspiring piece of writing: an article written in the *TLS* by the eminent historian Cliff Davies. It said, essentially, that there was no such thing as the Tudors, and the word was hardly used or known during the Tudor period. You might think that given I was writing a big, fat book on the Tudors I might not be too thrilled by that, but I read further articles he had written on this and found them all fascinating. I believe the Tudors did have a strong sense of family – even if they did not exactly boast about their humble Welsh origins – but Cliff Davies helped me shift perspective, to examine more closely not how we see the Tudors from our end of the telescope, but how they saw themselves. The Tudors constantly looked to the past as a guide to their actions. To understand what they did and why, we have to know that past. It helped me answer why the princes in the Tower were 'disappeared' in 1483, and why Henry VII didn't investigate their disappearance in 1485 – the source of so many conspiracy theories. It helped explain why Anne Boleyn was beheaded with a sword (clue: Henry VIII was not wondering how she would like to die); it also led me to discover what Henry is really supposed to have quarrelled about with his niece Margaret Douglas in 1547.

As with my last book I found that separating later comment on the lives of Tudor women from their actual lives was very revealing. Women of this period were often later depicted as either useless, or suspiciously successful, in which case somewhere along the line it is suggested they are 'unnatural' or a bit mad. Like Frances Brandon, Margaret Beaufort has been much maligned, as has Mary Tudor, and while I don't sugar-coat their actions I hope I have helped further erase their old caricatures. I was also very interested in the life of Margaret Douglas. The importance of her place in the succession issues and family politics of the 1560s helped add another dimension to what I already knew about that decade from the work I had done on Katherine Grey for my biography of the Grey sisters – but it is the whole sweep of Margaret's life that is so extraordinary, from the dramatic circumstances of her birth, to her years at Henry VIII's court, to her plotting her son Darnley's marriage to Mary, Queen of Scots, and, after her death, her grandson, James, becoming King of England. Where I cover the Greys again I have tried to add material to my earlier biography of the sisters; it was looking at Jane from Mary's perspective, for example, that led me to conclude that it is (ironically) with Mary that the legend of the Innocent Traitor originates.

This may seem difficult to believe, but I have endeavoured to keep names to a minimum. Many well-known figures don't get a mention. Those people who do get named are sometimes referred to by their title and sometimes not: the choice depends on what I think will be easier for the reader to remember. If, for example, they change title in the space of a few pages or chapters, or follow hard on the heels of someone else by the same title, or share the same title (like Jasper Tudor and William Herbert) I will stick to their name to avoid confusion. Stewarts and Stuarts are all spelled Stuart – although there was no 'Stuart' spelling before Mary, Queen of Scots, it is simply easier to grasp they are the same family when they are spelled the same way. Since I focus on family members, readers may also find the family trees helpful. I have not gone into detailed arguments over every contentious area in the text, but I hope that the Notes will answer most queries.

It can be a lonely old business writing books, but I am very lucky to have made many friends amongst Tudor historians. In particular I spoke regularly to Eric Ives. While I was doing my biography of the Grey sisters he was doing a biography of Jane and we were in occasional contact then. There was a lot we didn't agree on, but we became good friends, and with this book, if I had a flash of inspiration or was puzzled about something, I would immediately call him (we still didn't always agree). I have missed him very much since his death in 2012.

The knights in shining armour who very generously agreed to read drafts of this book in Eric's place were Peter Marshall and Tom

Freeman. Tom is one of the most brilliant people I know and has been extremely busy researching his own work as well as teaching some lucky students, so I am truly grateful that he found time to give me his advice on parts of an early draft and especially for sending me his as yet unpublished essay on Foxe and Katherine Parr. Peter read a later and full draft while working on his own forthcoming book on the Reformation. I really cannot properly express my appreciation of his incredible generosity with his time and his knowledge.

Many historians, archivists and librarians have been very helpful answering queries and helping in other ways. I would like to thank in particular, John Guy (who drew my attention to vital MSS concerning Thomas Bishop after I discussed my suspicions that there had never been a quarrel between Margaret and Henry VIII), Cliff Davies, Ralph Griffiths, Rosemary Horrox, Sean Cunningham, James Carley, Julia Fox, Susan Doran, Michael Questier, Stephan Edwards, Claire Ridgway, Andrea Clarke and Kathleen Doyle at the British Library, Mark Bateson at Canterbury Cathedral archives, Christine Reynolds at Westminster Abbey Muniments, Clare Rider and Eleanor Cracknell at St George's Chapel Archives and Chapter Library, Windsor, Anne Burge at Little Malvern Priory Archives, Carlotta Benedetti at the Vatican Archives, and Peter Foden at the Belvoir archives. I would also like to thank the staff at the wonderful London Library and especially Gosia Lawik in the Country Orders department.

I very much appreciate the guidance of my friends Henrietta Joy and Dominic Pierce, and I hope Henrietta notices I begin Chapter 1 as she instructed. Thank you also to Zia Soothill for patiently listening to my weekly rants and massaging my aching hands. I would like to thank my new editor at Chatto, Becky Hardie, whose razor-sharp efficiency I much appreciate, and also the contributions of Juliet Brooke. Finally I have the best agent in the world in Georgina Capel: it is worth becoming a writer just so you can have someone like Georgina in your life.

Abbreviations

ASV	Archivum Secretum Vaticanum
CSPD	Calendar of State Papers, Domestic
CSPF	Calendar of State Papers, Foreign
CSP, Milan	Calendar of State Papers relating to Milan
CSPS	Calendar of State Papers relating to Spain 1485–1558
CSP, Scotland	Calendar of State Papers relating to Scotland
CSPS Simancas	Calendar of State Papers relating to Spain (Simancas) 1558–1603
CSP, Venice	Calendar of State Papers relating to Venice
HMC	Historical Manuscripts Commission
L&P	Letters & Papers Foreign and Domestic, Henry VIII
PRO	Public Records Office

Introduction

1. P. S. Lewis, 'Two Pieces of Fifteenth-Century Political Iconography' in *Journal of the Warburg and Courtauld Institutes* 27 (1964), pp. 317–20.
2. Edward Hall, *Chronicle* (1809), p. 231.
3. In several inspiring essays by Cliff Davies.
4. As, indeed, Cliff Davies acknowledges – at least after Henry VIII!
5. For the latest research on this, see Jason Scott-Warren, 'Was

Elizabeth I Richard II?: The Authenticity of Lambarde's "Conversation"' in *Review of English Studies* (first published online 14 July 2012).

Part One
THE COMING OF THE TUDORS: A MOTHER'S LOVE

1   An Ordinary Man

1. Cloth of gold consists of gold either beaten or worked into long strips and wound around a core (such as silk). This thread is used in weaving a very rich fabric, which is relatively stiff, heavy, and expensive. The gold thread would be woven with a different colour in order to give it a red or gold tinge (in much the same way that one can blend pure gold, e.g. with copper to give it a red sheen). Thanks to Richard Walker from Watts and Co., London, for his advice.

2. Westminster Abbey Muniments MS 19678; Philip Lindley, 'The Funeral and Tomb Effigies of Queen Catherine of Valois and Henry V' in *Journal of the British Archaeological Association* 160 (2007), pp. 165–77.

3. Henry V's tomb had a wooden effigy with a head and regalia all of silver, and plates of silver covering the trunk. Little care, however, seems to have been taken of it by the later Yorkist king Edward IV. By 1479 the angels at his head, lions at his feet, a silver gilt antelope and two sceptres had vanished. The rest of the silver was stolen in January 1546 when thieves broke into the abbey during the night. Since Henry VIII's agents were stripping churches up and down the country of their goods, the thieves seemed to have joined in the free-for-all. Henry V was left headless, prompting questions from tourists in centuries to come. In 1971 a new head, hands and a crown for the effigy were modelled in polyester resin by Louisa Bolt, the features following

a contemporary description of the king and the earliest portrait of him.

4. The earliest known reference to Owen as a servant in Queen Katherine's chamber is in John Rylands Library, Latin MS 113 (a chronicle roll of *c*.1484).

5. The statute is printed in R. A. Griffiths, 'Queen Katherine of Valois and a Missing Statute of the Realm' in *Law Quarterly Review* 93 (1977), pp. 248–58; Elis Gruffudd and the Giles Chronicle, *Incerti Scriptoris Chronicon Angliae, etc.* (ed J. A. Giles) (1848), Pt IV, p. 17; Hall, *Chronicle*, p. 185).

6. *Incerti Scriptoris Chronicon Angliae*, Pt IV, p. 17.

7. Polydore Vergil, *Three Books of Polydore Vergil's English History* (ed. H. Ellis), Camden Society Old Series, Vol. 29 (1844), p. 62.

8. A story favoured by the Welshman Elis Gruffudd.

9. The story seems to be recalled in Owen Tudor's last words. See Chapter 3, p. 25.

10. Michael Drayton, 'England's Heroicall Epistles' (1597).

11. His name suggests his godfather may have been the king's cousin, Edmund Beaufort, who had been close to Catherine before she married Owen. Children were then named by their godparents, and often given the name of the godparent. There is no evidence that Edmund was Beaufort's child, as is sometimes claimed.

12. The early seventeenth-century historian referred to here was Giovanni Francesco Biondi. R. S. Thomas, 'The political career, estates and "connection" of Jasper Tudor, earl of Pembroke and duke of Bedford (d.1495)', PhD diss., Swansea (1971), p. 22.

13. The theory, inherited from the ancient Greeks, was that wombs were cold and needed to be filled constantly with hot sperm if women were to be happy and healthy. The Greek word '*hyster*' refers to the womb, and the term 'hysteria' is born from the assumption that women's wombs cause them to have uncontrollable emotions.

14. Croyland Chronicle, Cliff Davies, 'Information, disinformation and political knowledge under Henry VII and early Henry VIII' in *Historical Research* 85, issue 228 (May 2012), pp. 228–53.

15. Sir John Wynn of Gwydir, *The History of the Gwydir Family* (ed John Ballinger) (1927), p. 26.

16. In romantic tales of the period a nobleman raised as a peasant would reveal his hidden ancestry by his prowess at the joust, and a fake prince expose his humble origins by seducing a princess and making love to her on the floor.

17. Sir John Wynn of Gwydir, *The History of the Gwydir Family*, p. 26.

18. As she said in her will.

19. Sir Francis Palgrave, *The Ancient Kalendars and Inventories of His Majesty's Exchequer*, Vol. 2 (1836), pp. 172–5.

20. Maurice Keen, *English Society in the Later Middle Ages* (1990), pp. 109, 110.

21. *Proceedings and Ordinances of the Privy Council of England* (ed Sir Harris Nicolas) (7 vols, 1834–7), Vol. 5, p. 48; Thomas, PhD diss., op. cit., p. 25.

22. No comparable wooden female saint effigy survived the Reformation. Anthony Harvey and Richard Mortimer, *The Funeral Effigies of Westminster Abbey* (1994), p. 42; Westminster Abbey Muniments MS 19678.

23. *Rotuli Parliamentorum*, Vol. 3 (1783), p. 423.

24. *Proceedings and Ordinances of the Privy Council*, Vol. 5, p. 48; Chancery Warrants for the Great Seal, 708/3839 (15 July 1437).

25. In 1436 Thomas Knolles, a grocer, charitably provided the cost of laying leaden pipes to the prison from the cistern which served St Bartholomew's Hospital.

26. Margery Bassett, 'Newgate Prison in the Middle Ages' in *Speculum* 18, No. 2 (April 1943), pp. 239, 240.

27. The monk Owen Tudor is said to have died between 1498 and 1501. Catherine died earlier, when 'young': Hall, *Chronicle*, p. 185. At Barking the Tudors were placed in the care of Katherine

de la Pole, the sister of the Duke of Suffolk and Abbess of Barking. It is possible that another daughter existed called Tacina (d. 1469), who was married to Reginald de Grey, 7th Baron Grey of Wilton, but Tacina, or Thomasine, is also sometimes described as an illegitimate daughter of John Beaufort, Duke of Somerset.

28. His skeleton measured five feet ten inches. R. A. Griffiths, *The Reign of Henry VI* (1981), p. 241.

29. John Blakman, *Henry the Sixth* (ed M. R. James) (1919), pp. 8, 9.

30. Thomas, PhD diss., op. cit., p. 34. The final ceremony took place at the Tower of London on the feast of the Epiphany, 6 January. Edmund Tudor was resident at the magnificent Baynard's Castle on the Thames in March 1453. Griffiths, *The Reign of Henry VI*, p. 299.

31. Margaret was the niece of Catherine of Valois' old friend Edmund Beaufort, who had since inherited his brother's title, Duke of Somerset.

2 A Child Bride

1. Margaret Beaufort was born on 31 May 1443, and her father died in May 1444, a probable suicide. He had been unlucky since youth. Captured on campaign in France aged sixteen, he was held captive for seventeen years – longer than any other nobleman during the Hundred Years War. When he was eventually released he had a huge ransom to pay and no chance of making a lucrative marriage. Instead of a prized virgin from a noble family he had made do with the daughter of a gentleman, Margaret Beauchamp of Bletsoe, who was also the widow of one Oliver St John. Somerset had hoped to restore his tarnished honour by returning to France, but the money he made there was outweighed in the eyes of Henry VI by the costs incurred to the English crown. It led to him being banished from court. The chronicler of Crowland Abbey recorded the rumour that he killed himself shortly afterwards. His daughter later joined the confraternity of the abbey

with her mother, and so she knew the place well. Her mother's third marriage was to Lionel, Lord Welles.

2. She was living at this time at Maxey Castle in Northamptonshire.

3. Anthony Emery, *Greater Medieval Houses of England and Wales, 1300–1500: Volume 3, Southern England* (2006) p. 242.

4. Richard, Duke of York, was descended from Edward III's fifth son, Edmund of Langley.

5. They had later been legitimised in royal letters patent (1397 and this was confirmed in 1407). Crucially, however, the letters specifically excluded the Beauforts from any claim to the throne.

6. HMC Third Report, Appendix p. 280. Thomas, PhD diss., op. cit., p. 36.

7. John de la Pole, son of William, Duke of Suffolk. Suffolk, who was Steward of the King's Household, and was assassinated in 1450, was blamed for the government's failures at home and abroad. Suffolk's sister had raised Edmund and Jasper Tudor from 1437–42.

8. Michael K. Jones and Malcolm G. Underwood, *The King's Mother: Lady Margaret Beaufort, Countess of Richmond and Derby* (1992), p. 38. There is a small mistake here. Margaret's arrival at court during Shrovetide must have been before 14 February, as this was Ash Wednesday that year. Thanks to Eric Ives for this detail.

9. Bishop Russell in 1483.

10. Prayer at coronation of James I; Leanda de Lisle, *After Elizabeth* (2005), p. 311 and note.

11. Calendar of State Papers and Manuscripts, existing in the Archives and Collections of Milan, 1385–1618, London HMSO (1912), pp. 18–19. The queen would be twenty-three in March.

12. PRO E404/69/145.

13. According to legend, the fourth-century saint had provided a poor father with dowries for his daughters by secretly throwing bags of gold into his house, where they landed in stockings hanging by the fire (and, of course, he became, in modern times, Father Christmas, a name from old English folk stories).

14. *English Works of John Fisher, Bishop of Rochester (1469–1535): Sermons and Other Writings, 1520–1535* (ed Cecilia A. Hatt), p. 9; Caroline Halsted, *Life of Margaret Beaufort* (1839), p. 11.
15. Jones and Underwood, *The King's Mother*, p. 38.
16. Isabella, the daughter of Philip IV of France.
17. From whom George III was descended. Lindsay C. Hurst, 'Porphyria Revisited' in *Medical History* 26 (1982), pp. 179–82.
18. The queen named him after the saint and king, Edward the Confessor. This information is later mentioned in the main text. I have not done so here in an effort to reduce the blinding effect of a storm of names.
19. The abbot was called John Whethamstede. Peter Burley, Michael Elliott and Harvey Watson, *The Battles of St Albans* (2007), p. 35.
20. Probably inspired by Shakespeare's *Henry VI Part I*. In the relevant scene Richard, Duke of York, quarrels with Margaret Beaufort's uncle, Edmund Beaufort, 2nd Duke of Somerset. The two men ask others to show their respective positions by picking a rose – red for Somerset and white for York. The 'quarrel of the two roses' was first mentioned in 1646; see Michael Hicks, *The Wars of the Roses* (2010), p. 13. Walter Scott coined the term 'Wars of the Roses' in his 1829 novel *Anne of Geierstein*.
21. The earliest association with the House of Lancaster that I have found is the painting of the pavilion of Henry Bolingbroke, for the (cancelled) trial by combat he was to have with Thomas Mowbray, Duke of Norfolk, in 1398. According to the French chronicle *Traison et Mort* it was covered with '*rouge fleurs*'; Dan Jones, *Plantagenets* (2012), p. 573. It was thanks to the Tudors that by the time Shakespeare wrote *Henry VI Part I*, the red rose was as indelibly associated with Lancaster as the white rose was with York.
22. The white rose associated with York was not used, as far as is known, as a badge by Richard, Duke of York. It has been suggested, however, that his ancestors the Earls of March may have done so.

This seems very possible given the family's importance in subsequent Yorkist claims to the throne. His son Edward IV, his daughter Margaret of Burgundy, and his other son Richard III all used the white-rose badge.

23. Sir William Cary of Cookington, who fought at the battle of Tewkesbury on the Lancastrian side in 1471, had white roses on his coat of arms. See Davies, 'Information, disinformation . . .', op. cit., n. 75.

24. *Galar y Beirdd: Marwnadau Plant / Poets' Grief: Medieval Welsh Elegies for Children* (ed and tr. Dafydd Johnston) (1993), pp. 53–5.

25. Plague was recorded in England and Wales in eleven of the eighteen years between 1442 and 1459.

26. Henry VII built his father a modest Purbeck-marble tomb in the Franciscan monastery church and invested a few pounds for prayers and Masses to be said for his soul. It was erected in 1503, when Henry VII had been king for eighteen years, and he invested £8 a year towards a chantry for his father. See Cliff Davies, 'Representation, Repute, Reality' in *English Historical Review* 124, issue 511 (December 2009), pp. 1,432–47. The tomb was destroyed during the dissolution of the monasteries in the reign of Edmund's grandson Henry VIII, and Edmund's body was moved to St David's Cathedral. Today the site of the ancient monastery is a shopping precinct. Although it was originally named Greyfriars after the monastery, the precinct was rebranded in 2010 as Merlin's Walk. Local councillors argue that legend sells better than the town's actual history.

27. As she recorded later to John Fisher; Jones and Underwood, *The King's Mother*, p. 40.

28. Eighty years later a visitor to the castle was to be shown a new chimney piece being built in the same room overlooking the river. It was carved with the heraldic badges and arms of the first Tudor monarch and was built to commemorate his birth. *The Itinerary in Wales of John Leland* (ed Lucy Toulmin Smith) (1906), p. 116.

29. Henry Stafford's elder brother (who died later that year) was already married to a Beaufort cousin, who had borne a son. Also called Margaret, she was the daughter of the 2nd Duke of Somerset killed at St Albans.

30. This is taken from John Fisher's obituary sermon for Margaret; see *English Works of John Fisher*, op. cit.

31. Margaret's mealtime routine was very similar to that of Cecily, Duchess of York.

32. No one was certain what triggered the rebellion, but it was said to have occurred when God revealed to the angels that His son was to be born a man, in Christ, and that the angels would worship him.

33. Brut Chronicle, quoted in Keen, *English Society*, p. 194.

34. Dominic Mancini, *The Usurpation of Richard the Third* (ed C. A. J. Armstrong) (1969), pp. 100, 101.

3 A Prisoner, Honourably Brought up

1. The duke looked back to the time of Henry VI's grandfather. Henry Bolingbroke (later Henry IV) had overthrown the failing king, Richard II, and taken the throne as Richard's heir. York claimed that his ancestor, Roger Mortimer, Earl of March, had been the rightful claimant. He was the senior heir in the female line of Edward III's granddaughter, Philippa. But Edward III had entailed the crown through the male line and Henry VI was descended from his fourth son, John of Gaunt, founder of the House of Lancaster (and father of Henry IV); Richard, Duke of York from the fifth son, Edmund of Langley. York soon found he had little support for his claims. It was an argument that would nevertheless persist long after his death.

2. *Three Fifteenth-Century Chronicles* (ed James Gairdner), Camden Society New Series XXVIII (1880), p. 77.

3. On 20 February 1460. W. H. Blaauw, 'On the Effigy of Sir David Owen' etc., in *Sussex Archaeological Collection* 7, 845, p. 24.

4. Ralph A. Griffiths and Roger S. Thomas, *The Making of the Tudor Dynasty* (2011), pp. 52, 53, 192.

5. David Owen was born in Pembrokeshire. See Davies, 'Representation, Repute, Reality' in op. cit. Also Blaauw, 'On the Effigy . . .' in op. cit., p. 25. Jasper also would not forget his father. In his will he paid for prayers to be said for the souls of both his parents and bequeathed the Greyfriars one of his best gowns of cloth of gold for a priest's vestments. *Testamenta vetusta: being illustrations from wills, of manners, customs, &c. as well as of the descents and possessions of many distinguished families. From the reign of Henry the Second to the accession of Queen Elizabeth, Volume 1* (ed Sir Harris Nicolas) (1826), p. 430.

6. 30,000 out of a population of three million seems probable. See Michael D. Miller, at http://www.warsoftheroses.co.uk/chapter_56.htm. Other estimates are, however, much higher. The usually cautious Charles Ross estimates 50,000. See Charles Ross, *Edward IV* (1974), p. 36.

7. In 1996 a mass grave of the dead was excavated. The corpses showed multiple injuries to their skulls and the forearms they had raised to defend themselves.

8. D. H. Thomas, *The Herberts of Raglan* (1994), p. 26.

9. Blaauw, 'On the Effigy . . .' in op. cit., p. 25.

10. Herbert, whom Henry VI had knighted with Jasper and Edmund Tudor, had been raised to the peerage that July.

11. The governor was Sir John Skidmore.

12. Especially her property at Bourne in Lincolnshire, and Stafford's father's castle, Maxstoke in Warwickshire.

13. Jones and Underwood, *The King's Mother*, p. 42.

14. Kate Mertes, 'Aristocracy' in *Fifteenth-Century Attitudes* (ed Rosemary Horrox) (1994), pp. 55, 56.

15. Mancini, *Usurpation of Richard the Third*, p. 65.

16. This was not a new idea. Long royal pedigrees had been popular in the past – Henry VI had one that traced his lineage back to

Adam (Henry VII later used it as the basis of his own which still hung at Richmond Palace when Elizabeth I died). They were handwritten because William Caxton did not set up the first mechanical printing press in England until 1476.

17. The rose symbol also represented Edward in a more personal way. Yorkist poets referred to Edward as the 'rose of Rouen': the word 'rose' denoting a person of exceptional quality, and Rouen being his birthplace.

18. Livia Visser-Fuchs, 'English Events in Caspar Weinreich's Danzig Chronicle of 1461–1495' in *Ricardian* 7, No. 95 (December 1986), p. 313.

19. Ibid.

20. Sir John Grey of Groby died of battle wounds in 1461.

21. Earlier marks of favour included Margaret being granted the confiscated Beaufort manor of Woking in Surrey in 1466.

22. For a fifteenth-century lamprey recipe, see http://www.gode cookery.com/nboke/nboke68.html.

4 The Wheel of Fortune

1. Thomas, *The Herberts of Raglan*, p. 61.

2. The co-commander was the Earl of Devon.

3. The ragged staff on its own was simpler than the full bear and ragged staff used on his seals. The staff represented the branch of a tree, which an ancestor had, in legend, used to kill a giant. The bear was also sometimes used as a separate badge.

4. This brother-in-law was Walter Devereux, Lord Ferrers, who would be killed fighting for Richard III at Bosworth. One of his daughters was later married to a son of Owen Tudor's illegitimate son, David. Herbert had been made Earl of Pembroke by Edward IV, i.e. he was given Jasper's title.

5. Jones and Underwood, *The King's Mother*, p. 49.

6. As yet, neither Warwick nor Edward had sons, and Warwick hoped his daughter's marriage to Edward's heir would mean he would see

a future grandson one day become king. Clarence agreed to depose his brother and become king in his place, with Warwick's daughter as queen. The two children of this marriage were to be significant figures in the reigns of Henry VII and Henry VIII. But the Battle of Edgecote Moor did not end in Edward IV's deposition. It was far from evident that Clarence would make a better king than Edward and as a younger brother he had less right, so his candidature attracted little support. Warwick and Edward were thus obliged to come to terms – although they did not do so for long.

7. Lord Ferrers had been present at the fall of Harlech.

8. The arrival of Herbert's forces in Harlech is recalled today in the marching song 'Men of Harlech':

> Men of Harlech in the hollow,
> Do ye hear like rushing billow,
> Wave on wave that surging follow,
> Battle's distant sound?
> 'Tis the tramp of Saxon foemen,
> Saxon spearmen, Saxon bowmen,
> Be they knight, or hinds or yeomen
> They shall bite the ground!

9. Eric Ives, *The Reformation Experience* (2012), p. 38.

10. Pamela Nightingale, *A Medieval Mercantile Community: The Grocers Company* (1995), pp. 519, 535.

11. Vergil, *Three Books*, p. 135.

12. Ibid., p. 143.

13. Jones and Underwood, *The King's Mother*, pp. 54–5.

14. Vergil, *Three Books*, p. 146.

15. The account is that of John Warkworth, the Master of Peterhouse, Cambridge.

16. David Clark, *Barnet – 1471: Death of a Kingmaker* (2006), p. 56.

17. Cora L. Scofield, *The Life and Reign of Edward the Fourth: King*

of England and of France and Lord of Ireland (1923), Vol. 1, p. 587; HMC Report 12, Appendix 4, p. 4; Clarence witnessed Prince Edward's death and made comments in a letter written only two days later; the Lancastrian commander, Margaret's cousin Edmund Beaufort, Duke of Somerset – the last legitimate male of the Beaufort line – managed to escape to the local abbey and claimed sanctuary, but he was taken and executed. King Edward's contemporary apologists claimed the abbey had no franchise for protecting traitors. Mancini, *Usurpation of Richard the Third*, n. 54, p. 177.

18. John Warkworth's account, Scofield, *The Life and Reign of Edward the Fourth*, Vol. 1, p. 594. King Edward's youngest brother, Richard, Duke of Gloucester, was reportedly amongst those present.

19. J. L. Laynesmith, *The Last Medieval Queens: English Queenship 1445–1503* (2004), p. 175.

20. Griffiths, *The Reign of Henry VI*, p. 892; Henry Holland, Duke of Exeter, who would be drowned in 1475, was seen by the French chronicler Philippe de Commynes as 'next in line of succession to the Lancastrian family', but he was not a descendant of John of Gaunt. Henry Tudor was the last man standing in the House of Lancaster.

21. Sir Roger Vaughan.

22. John Leland, quoted in Thomas, PhD diss., op. cit., p. 224.

23. Philippe de Commynes, *Memoirs, The Reign of Louis XI* (ed and tr. M. Jones) (1972), p. 353.

24. Griffiths and Thomas, *The Making of the Tudor Dynasty*, pp. 76, 77; Jones and Underwood, *The King's Mother*, p. 58; *Memorials of King Henry VII* (ed James Gairdner) Rolls Series (1858), pp. 15, 16; Vergil, *Three Books*, p. 155.

25. Lord Stanley was appointed steward late in 1471 so this was a recent appointment at the time of her marriage, and took place exactly when she would have been considering her options.

26. He had inherited the title from his father thirteen years earlier.

5 Enter Richard III

1. Jones and Underwood, *The King's Mother*, p. 146; J Hoult, *The Village, Manor and Township of Knowsley* (1930), p. 32. Margaret was also close to her stepdaughter, for whom she would order clothes.

2. *The Travels of Leo of Rozmital* (ed and tr. M. Letts), Hakluyt Society, additional series cviii (1957), pp. 46, 47.

3. Mancini, *Usurpation of Richard the Third*, p. 67; Rosemary Horrox, 'Edward IV', *Oxford Dictionary of National Biography*.

4. The French chronicler Philippe de Commynes had seen him as 'next in line of succession to the Lancastrian family' after the death of Henry VI.

5. Writing only five years later, the Roman scholar and visitor to England Dominic Mancini described it as 'sweet wine', while Philippe de Commynes describes it unequivocally as Malmsey, which was a type of sweet wine imported from Greece. Today his name adorns Blandy's Duke of Clarence Madeira.

6. The pardon survives on the back of the patent that made his father Earl of Richmond.

7. Mancini, *Usurpation of Richard the Third*, p. 59; other sources mention his death as being caused by a surfeit of wine or vegetables.

8. Richard had travelled from Northampton to Stony Stratford 'at full gallop'. Mancini, *Usurpation of Richard the Third*, p. 77.

9. Ibid., p. 137, Appendix. Description by Nicolas von Poppeleau, who met him.

10. The type of scoliosis was idiopathic adolescent onset scoliosis. It would have developed after the age of ten and got worse as he got older. He may have stood as short as four foot eight inches tall. The body also had gracile radius bones, which would fit with descriptions of his slender limbs. John Rous' *Historia Regum Angliae*, completed after Richard's death, offered the earliest aspersions on his appearance. Richard was 'retained within his mother's

womb for two years, emerging with teeth and hair to his shoulders' and 'small of stature with a short face and unequal shoulders, the right higher than the left'. Scoliosis is often hereditary, so it may be relevant that not only was Richard's great-great-nephew Edward VI described as having one shoulder higher than another, but his great-great-great-niece Lady Mary Grey was described as extremely short, 'crook backed and very ugly'. On the other claims concerning Richard: babies are often born with full heads of hair and also long fingernails – although the story of Richard's teeth seems far-fetched. Alison Hanham, *Richard III and His Early Historians 1483–1535* (1975), pp. 120, 121.

11. A descendant in the male line of John of Gaunt's youngest brother, Thomas of Woodstock, he also had a Beaufort mother, the daughter of Edmund Beaufort, 2nd Duke of Somerset. Buckingham was the nephew of Margaret Beaufort's late husband Henry Stafford.

12. Mancini, *Usurpation of Richard the Third*, pp. 78, 79.

13. DeLloyd J. Guth, 'Richard III, Henry VII and the City' in *Kings and Nobles in the Later Middle Ages: A Tribute to Charles Derek Ross* (ed Ralph A. Griffiths and James Sherborne) (1987), p. 187.

14. Laynesmith, *The Last Medieval Queens*, p. 177.

15. Thomas More recorded how the night before the council meeting Margaret Beaufort's husband Thomas, Lord Stanley, had this nightmare. Awaking shortly before midnight Stanley sent a message to Hastings suggesting they flee the city. Hastings advised him to ignore the dream as insignificant, with fatal consequences.

16. In a public sermon that day it was alleged that Edward IV was not the son of Richard, Duke of York. According to rumours circulating in France later in the century, Cecily, Duchess of York had admitted to an affair in Rouen with a tall, blond archer called Blaybourne. The London sermon did not reveal who Edward IV's 'real' father was – it merely focused on Edward IV's lack of resemblance to the Duke of York in contrast to Richard, his 'real' heir.

But whoever Edward IV's father was, the fact remained that the Duke of York had recognised him as his son. Edward IV was therefore legitimate in law. Edward IV was to be characterised by Richard as a true, but failed king – and his children as illegitimate. Mancini, *Usurpation of Richard the Third*, pp. 94, 97.

17. The bishop was Robert Stillington; the woman was Eleanor Butler, who had in fact died before the princes were born.

18. *Rotuli Parliamentorum*, Vol. 3, p. 419.

19. His earldom had come through his mother, Isabella, the eldest daughter of Warwick the Kingmaker.

20. Mancini, *Usurpation of Richard the Third*, p. 105. £1,000 that the City had voted as Edward V's coronation gift was passed to his uncle as the elders bowed to what they now saw as inevitable.

21. The doctor was John Argentine. Mancini, *Usurpation of Richard the Third*, p. 93.

22. Ann Wroe, *Perkin* (2004), p. 68, quoting the Burgundian chronicler Jean Molinet.

23. Mancini, *Usurpation of Richard the Third*, p. 93. He suggests they vanished before the coronation.

24. From 3 July.

25. The younger daughter of Warwick the Kingmaker, and the widow of Edward of Lancaster (the son Henry VI lost at Tewkesbury).

6 The Princes in the Tower

1. So said Jean Molinet. Griffiths and Thomas, *The Making of the Tudor Dynasty*, p. 86.

2. Christopher Wilkins, *The Last Knight Errant: Sir Edward Woodville and the Age of Chivalry* (2010), p. 109.

3. Surviving correspondence reveals Richard III was in touch with Duke Francis in July concerning Sir Edward specifically, but later correspondence suggests Henry was also being discussed. Charles Ross, *Richard III* (2011), p. 195.

4. *Rotuli Parliamentorum*, Vol. 3, p. 419.

5. York Civic Records: John Kendall from Nottingham to the City of York, 23 August 1483.

6. One such, a copper alloy mount of a boar, crowned, was found by the Thames near the Tower in October 2012. 'Bore' may have been an anagram of *'ebor'*, the Latin for York – the 'white' boar reflecting the 'white rose' tradition.

7. John Ashdown-Hill, *Richard III's Beloved Cousin, John Howard and the House of York* (2009), pp. 99, 100, 107. Also Michael Hicks, 'Unweaving the Web' in *Ricardian* 9, No. 114 (September 1991), pp. 106–9.

8. By the middle of August Margaret Beaufort's half-brother John Welles was also in rebellion against Richard and had fled to Brittany.

9. Thomas More, *The History of Richard III*, at http://www.r3.org/bookcase/more/moretext.

10. The princes were last seen playing in the gardens of the Tower during a mayoralty that ended on 28 October. The mayor was Sir Edmund Shaa, and the timing given is in the *Great Chronicle of London*. The Croyland Chronicle indicates the princes were alive until at least the second week of September (when Thomas More claims they were killed). After then hope seems to have faded. One exactly contemporary record, the Colchester Oathbook, written on or about 29 September, described Edward V as the 'late son' of Edward IV (although this could have referred simply to his being declared illegitimate); on this and the July plot, see Ashdown-Hill, *Richard III's Beloved Cousin*, pp. 99, 100, 107. Also Hicks, 'Unweaving the Web' in op. cit., pp. 106–9. Intriguingly a requiem Mass was held at the Sistine Chapel in Rome on 23 September for 'Edward, king of England'. This may refer to Edward IV, yet it was usual for such Masses to be held soon after news reached the Vatican of a monarch's death. See Cliff Davies, 'A Requiem for King Edward' in *Ricardian* 9, No. 114 (September 1991), pp. 102–5.

11. In the absence of any hard facts, fiction has provided the popular answers as to who did it, and when. On the one hand we have Shakespeare's Richard III: a biblical Herod, killer of innocents, whose hunchback is an outward sign of a disfigured soul. This built on a tradition that already existed. After the Tudor period, however, Shakespeare's demonising of Richard provoked a reaction and Henry Tudor was put in the frame. One of the most influential works in this regard is Josephine Tey's detective story, *Daughter of Time*. Written not long after Stalin's show trials, which strongly influenced Tey's viewpoint, the novel 'proves' that the princes were killed because they had a better claim to the throne than Henry Tudor.

12. Davies, 'Information, disinformation . . .' in op. cit., p. 24.

13. Commynes, *Memoirs, The Reign of Louis XI*, Introduction and pp. 354, 397.

14. This is drawn from Polydore Vergil. Thomas More, writing later during the reign of Henry VIII, claimed it was the other way round and that Morton had 'turned' the duke to support Henry Tudor's distant Lancastrian claims.

15. Mancini, *Usurpation of Richard the Third*, pp. 90–1.

16. The physician was Lewis Caerleon.

17. Elizabeth Woodville had never shown any enthusiasm for such a match, and dropped it in the spring of 1485 when she considered Henry a busted flush.

18. That he took it seriously is also evident in the fact he would have Henry VI's body transferred the following year from its resting place at Chertsey Abbey in Surrey to St George's Chapel, Windsor. This was both a gesture of reconciliation, such as Henry V had made when he had Richard II's body translated to Westminster Abbey in 1413, but also an attempt to co-opt and take control of the cult.

19. Indeed it is exactly this role that he would come to play after 1485. Richard would first be accused by the Welsh poet Daffyd ap

Llywelyn ap Gruffydd of Mathafarn in 1485/6 of being 'the sad lipped Saracen' (note the anti-Semitic description) 'cruel Herod' who 'slew Christ's Angels'. Jonathan Hughes, *The Religious Life of Richard III* (2000), p. 8.

20. Barbara Harris, *Edward Stafford 3rd Duke of Buckingham* (1986), pp. 29, 30.

21. On the deaths of the princes see the *Great Chronicle of London* (ed A. H. Thomas and I. D. Thornley) (1938), pp. 234–7. This was written by someone in London at the time. Also see Mancini, *Usurpation of Richard the Third*, pp. 92–3; then we have the later elaborations – or inventions – of Thomas More's *The History of Richard III* (ed R. S. Sylvester) (1963), pp. 88, 89, and his brother-in-law, John Rastell, quoted in Desmond Seward, *The Wars of the Roses* (1995), p. 364. For the story that their murder had been disguised as blood-letting, see I. Arthurson, 'Perkin Warbeck and the Princes in the Tower' in *Much Heaving and Shaving: Essays for Colin Richmond* (eds M. Aston and R. Horrox) (2005), pp. 158–217. Polydore Vergil's *Anglica Historia* (ed and tr. D. Hay), Camden Third Series, Vol. 74 (1950) suggests the death of the princes was a punishment for Edward IV's killing of Clarence.

22. Griffiths and Thomas, *The Making of the Tudor Dynasty*, pp. 93, 94.

23. Croyland Chronicle at http://www.r3.org/bookcase/croyland/croy8.html.

24. *Great Chronicle of London* (ed Thomas and Thornley), pp. 236–7.

7 The Exile

1. Henry was based at the Chateaux de l'Hermine.

2. Brother of the executed Richard Grey, and half-brother to the princes in the tower.

3. Described as a wart: 'The Song of the Lady Bessy', Griffiths and Thomas p. 168. Popular around 1500 it survives only in versions that date from a century later. For full text see http://www.archive.

org/stream/mostpleasantsong00londrich/mostpleasantsong00 londrich_djvu.txt.

4. Henry may also have believed that Richard was involved in the death of Henry VI. 'Of the death of [Henry VI] diverse tales were told, but the most common fame went, that he was sticked with a dagger, by the hands of the duke of Gloucester' (Robert Gaugin's *Compendium* (1497). See Davies, 'Information, disinformation . . .', op.cit., p. 22).

5. Henry was still sending gifts to the cathedral in 1502, and St Vincent's intercession is sought in Henry's will. Margaret Condon, 'The Last Will of Henry VII' in *Westminster Abbey: The Lady Chapel of Henry VII* (ed T. Tatton-Brown and R. Mortimer) (2003), p. 133.

6. Virginia K. Henderson, 'Rethinking Henry VII: The Man and His Piety in the Context of the Observant Franciscans' in *Reputation and Representation in Fifteenth-Century Europe* (ed D. Biggs, S. D. Michalove and A. C. Reeves) (2004), n. 111 p. 344.

7. Buckingham's former prisoner turned ally, the Bishop of Ely, John Morton, had escaped England and had a spy at Richard's court. In August or September 1484 Morton contacted Henry from his place of exile in Burgundy and warned him that plans were laid in Brittany for his arrest. Pierre Landais was the same man the duke had sent at the last minute to prevent Henry's repatriation in 1476. On Duke Francis' senility, see Robert J. Knecht, *The Valois* (2004), pp. 108, 109.

8. Vergil, *Three Books*, pp. 206, 307. To the relief of the remaining exiles in Britanny Duke Francis was so embarrassed to discover his Tudor guests had been obliged to flee that he paid their passage to follow Henry.

9. Anne disliked Richard's rapprochement with Brittany. But the situation in France was far from stable. Anne had a rival for the regency in the senior prince of the blood, Louis, Duke of Orléans.

10. There are those that argue that her subsequent return to court

proves she didn't believe Richard had killed the princes. But this document spells out pretty clearly what she feared for her daughters at his hands without a written agreement. And if the princes' fate was unknown, Richard's execution of her other son Richard Grey, and her brother, Lord Rivers, was acknowledged. She was simply doing the best she could for her daughters just as Frances, Duchess of Suffolk would do in the next century when she and her younger daughters served as ladies-in-waiting to Mary I, after the queen had executed her husband and elder daughter, Lady Jane Dudley in February 1554. British Library Harleian MSS 443, f. 308.

11. Davies, 'Information, disinformation . . .', op. cit., p. 47. Vergil was wrong to claim that Henry planned to marry Maude Herbert instead. She was already married to Henry Percy, Earl of Northumberland (see *Oxford Dictionary of National Biography* entry). Maude's brother, William Herbert 2nd Earl of Pembroke, had been married to Richard's bastard daughter, Katherine, in February 1484.

8 Bosworth

1. *Original letters illustrative of English history; including numerous royal letters: from autographs in the British Museum, and one or two other collections* (ed H. Ellis) (second series, 1827), Vol. 1, p. 163.
2. 'The Song of Lady Bessy': Helen Cooper, *The English Romance in Time: Transforming Motifs from Geoffrey of Monmouth to the Death of Shakespeare* (2004), p. 346.
3. The Mortimers were descended from Cadwaladr through the Welsh prince Llywelyn the Great. By contrast the Tudors' closest verifiable connection was an ancestor who had been an officer of Llywelyn's. Virginia K. Henderson, 'Retrieving the "Crown in the Hawthorn Bush": The Origins of the Badges of Henry VII' in *Traditions and Transformations in Late Medieval England* (ed D. Biggs, S. D. Michalove and A. C. Reeves) (2002), n. 41, p. 255.

4. The narratives were attached to painted genealogies circulated at court. Alison Allan, 'Yorkist Propaganda: Pedigree, Prophecy and the "British History" in the Reign of Edward IV' in *Patronage, Pedigree and Power in Later Medieval England* (ed Charles Ross) (1979), pp. 171–92. The prophecy begins as follows: Geoffrey of Monmouth, Book 7, Chapter 3: The Prophecy of Merlin: 'As Vortegirn, king of the Britons, was sitting upon the bank of the drained pond, the two dragons, one of which was white, the other red, came forth, and approaching one another, began a terrible fight, and cast forth fire with their breath. But the white dragon had the advantage, and made the other fly to the end of the lake. And he, for grief at his flight, renewed the assault upon his pursuer, and forced him to retire. After this battle of the dragons, the king commanded Ambrose Merlin to tell him what it portended. Upon which he, bursting into tears, delivered what his prophetical spirit suggested to him, as follows: "Woe to the red dragon, for his banishment hasteneth on. His lurking holes shall be seized by the white dragon, which signifies the Saxons whom you invited over; but the red denotes the British nation, which shall be oppressed by the white. Therefore shall its mountains be levelled as the valleys, and the rivers of the valleys shall run with blood. The exercise of religion shall be destroyed, and churches be laid open to ruin. At last the oppressed shall prevail, and oppose the cruelty of foreigners. For a boar of Cornwall shall give his assistance, and trample their necks under his feet."' http://www.caerleon.net/history/geoffrey/Prophecy1.htm.

5. Sydney Anglo, 'The British History in Early Tudor Propaganda' in *Bulletin of the John Rylands Library* 44 (1961–2), pp. 17–48, esp. pp. 23, 24, 37, 38. And these stories inspired other prophecies. A notable example describes the overthrow of Richard II by Henry Bolingbroke and prophesies how this act of injustice was to be avenged by a king who would come to the throne in 1460 – the year Edward was crowned (according to the contemporary

method of dating the year from the feast of the Annunciation, 25 March).

6. David Starkey, 'King Henry and King Arthur' in *Arthurian Literature* 16 (ed James P. Carley and Felicity Riddy) (1998), p. 181.

7. Philippe de Commynes, quoted in Griffiths and Thomas, *The Making of the Tudor Dynasty*, p. 129.

8. Blaauw, 'On the Effigy . . .' in op. cit., pp. 25, 38, 39.

9. R. A. Griffiths, 'Henry Tudor: The Training of a King' in *Huntington Library Quarterly* 49, No. 3 (summer 1986), pp. 208, 209.

10. It also helped that she was a woman: as Polydore Vergil observed, 'the working's of a woman's wit was thought of small account'. Vergil, *Three Books*, p. 204.

11. Sir William was chamberlain of Chester and chief justice of north Wales.

12. According to legend the Dun Cow was a 'monstrous beast four yards high and six yards long', providing an inexhaustible supply of milk to people in Shropshire. One day a woman decided to see if the cow would fill a sieve. This so enraged the cow that it broke loose and ran amok. It was slain on Dunsmore Heath near Rugby by the mythical Guy of Warwick from whom the Nevilles claimed descent. There is a theory that 'Dun Cow' is a corruption of 'Dena Gau', or Danish region, and that Guy of Warwick defeated the Danes there. Henry could recruit amongst the Neville affinity because Warwick the Kingmaker had died in the Lancastrian cause, and although Richard III had married his daughter, Anne Neville, when she died Henry's allies had spread rumours successfully that Richard had poisoned her. DeLloyd J. Guth 'Richard III, Henry VII and the City' in op. cit., pp. 192, 197, 198. In the seventeenth century the Cow's rib was at Warwick Castle.

13. *Great Chronicle of London* in *English Historical Documents Vol. 5 1485–1558* (ed David Douglas) (1967), p. 110.

14. Ibid.; Vergil, *Three Books*, p. 222.

15. *Great Chronicle of London* in op. cit., p. 110.

16. Mancini, *Usurpation of Richard the Third*, pp. 100, 101.
17. Vergil, *Three Books*, pp. 222, 223.
18. This man, named Bigod, later worked in the household of Margaret Beaufort. Quoted in Michael Bennett, *The Battle of Bosworth* (2000), p. 87.
19. Hall, *Chronicle*, p. 419. He refers to 'Jack of Norfolk', Shakespeare to 'Jockey', also a diminutive of John. Dickon is the equivalent of the modern 'Dicky' for Richard.
20. She was dead by 1485 but they had several children.
21. 'The Ballad of Bosworth Field' in Bennett, *The Battle of Bosworth*, pp. 152–7; springals fired stones using a compressed spring.
22. The chronicler Hall recalled Norfolk 'manfully died . . . to his great fame and laud'. Hall, *Chronicle*, p. 419. Other accounts suggest a different death. According to the Burgundian Jean Molinet writing in around 1490, Norfolk was captured and Henry Tudor sent him to the Earl of Oxford, who executed him. For yet more accounts of his death and descriptions of the hole in the skull of what may be Norfolk's body, dug up in the nineteenth century, see Ashdown-Hill, *Richard III's Beloved Cousin*, pp. 114, 115, 129. Several fifteenth-century sources including Molinet are also quoted at length at http://www.r3.org/bosworth/chron3.html. On Longe, see John Alban, 'The Will of a Norfolk Soldier at Bosworth' in *Richardian* 22 (2012).
23. http://www.r3.org/bosworth/chron3.html: early 1486, Diego de Valera, Castilian courtier, in E. M. Nokes and G. Wheeler, 'A Spanish account of the battle of Bosworth' in *Ricardian* 2, No. 36 (1972), p. 2. It is a sentiment repeated in 'The Song of Lady Bessy': 'For upon this field will I like a many die.' http://www.archive.org/stream/mostpleasantsong00londrich/mostpleasantsog00londrich_djvu.txt.
24. Hall, *Chronicle*, p. 418.
25. Recorded by John Rous of Warwick (d.1492).
26. Hall, *Chronicle*, p. 419.

27. http://www.r3.org/bosworth/chron3.html#molinet. The halberd is a long shaft with an axe blade mounted with a spike, and a hook or thorn behind. It remains the ceremonial weapon of the Swiss Guard to the Vatican.

28. According to the ballad tradition of 'The Song of Lady Bessy', the original of which was current in 1500, 'They beat his bassnet to his head/Untill the braine came out with bloode.' Several accounts describe the body being assaulted, although the helmet must have stayed in reasonable condition to be used later to crown Henry.

29. Contemporaries never mentioned any hawthorn bushes at Bosworth. The colour green, also used by the Tudors, is another symbol of renewal. Henderson, 'Retrieving the "Crown in the Hawthorn Bush"', in op. cit., pp. 170, 245.

30. *Great Chronicle of London*, in op. cit., p. 110.

31. Diego de Valera's account: see Bennett, *The Battle of Bosworth*, p. 138.

32. A. F. Sutton and L. Visser-Fuchs, *The Hours of Richard III* (1990), pp. 39–40.

33. York Memoranda, 23 August 1485: see Bennett, *The Battle of Bosworth*, p. 131. The Earl of Northumberland would never be forgiven for his failure to fight for his king. A few years later, when he was attacked by a Yorkshire mob angry over tax collection, his retainers stood by and allowed him to be lynched.

> Barons, knightis, squyers, one and alle,
> ... Turnd ther backis and let ther master fall,
> ... Alas his golde, his fee, his annuall rente,
> Upon suche a sort was ille bestowde and spent!

(John Skelton 1460?–1529, 'An Elegy on Henry 4th Earl of Northumberland').

34. DeLloyd J. Guth, 'Richard III, Henry VII and the City' in op. cit., pp. 194–5.

9 The Rose and the Passion

1. Mancini, *Usurpation of Richard the Third*, p. 103.
2. More, *The History of Richard III*.
3. Visser-Fuchs, 'English Events in Caspar Weinreich's Danzig Chronicle' in op. cit., pp. 316, 317.
4. Dates differ: *Great Chronicle of London* says 3 September in op. cit., p. 111; Vergil, *Anglica Historia*, pp. 2–5.
5. Griffiths and Thomas, *The Making of the Tudor Dynasty*, p. 167.
6. Sean Cunningham, *Henry VII* (2007), p. 117.
7. *Great Chronicle of London* in op. cit., p. 111.
8. *The Parliament Rolls of Medieval England 1275–1504* (ed Chris Given-Wilson) (16 vols., 2005), Vol. 15 (ed Rosemary Horrox), p. 107.
9. His mother's possessions illustrate the connection: amongst them she would later bequeath a jewelled ornament of a 'rose with an image of Our Lord and in every nail a pointed diamond, and four pearls, with tokens of the passion on the backside'. Henderson, 'Retrieving the "Crown in the Hawthorn Bush"' in op. cit., p. 245. The Passion was also associated with the fashionable cult of the Holy Name, of which Margaret Beaufort was an enthusiast, and would do much to promote. The symbol IHS (an abbreviation of Jesus) even became a badge of the Tudors, and the rose was often depicted with the monogram at its heart. Susan Wabuda, *Preaching During the English Reformation* (2002), pp. 147–63. See the image on p. 157 depicted in Margaret Beaufort's translation of 'The Mirror of Gold for the Sinful Soul', etc. Today the red rose is a symbol of love – as, in a religious sense, it always was.
10. Henderson, 'Rethinking Henry VII' in op. cit., p. 336.
11. *English Coronation Records* (ed Leopold George Wickham Legg) (1901), pp. 203–6.
12. Harris, *Edward Stafford*, pp. 29, 30.
13. As well as that of his younger brother, Henry.
14. They do not seem ever to have grown close – Jasper never mentioned her in his will.

15. His heirs would later come to be the last white-rose opponents of the Lancastrian house.

16. As John Fisher recalled.

17. Ross, *Richard III*, pp. 136, 138.

18. Just how important his wife's looks were to him is indicated by the detailed list of twenty-four questions he later posed concerning a possible future bride – the young Queen of Naples in 1505. He was very concerned to discover whether she had 'any hair on her lips' and asked open-ended questions about her breasts, hair and eye colour, complexion, fingers, arms, neck, and almost every other part of her body. *CSPS* 1 (436). For details of Elizabeth of York's effigy, see Harvey and Mortimer, *The Funeral Effigies of Westminister Abbey*, p. 45.

19. The heiress was Mary Bohun; also for reference to the position of carver see National Archives, Cowdray 4934, f. 67.

20. Blaauw, 'On the Effigy . . .', op. cit., p. 25, quoting British Library Cotton MSS Vitellius B XII, p. 124. Sir David would also attend the baptisms of Elizabeth and Henry's first son, Arthur, and the future Henry VIII, as well as attending Arthur's marriage to Katherine of Aragon.

21. Henry's great ally John Morton, Bishop of Ely, had spent several months in Rome early in 1485 promoting the advantages of Henry Tudor as King of England. The papal bull was issued with astonishing speed on 27 March 1486, confirming Henry's right to the throne as endorsed by victory in battle, 'and by the ordinance and authority of Parliament made by the three estates of this land'. *Tudor Royal Proclamations*, 3 vols. (eds P. L. Hughes and J. F. Larkin) (1964–9), Vol. 1, No. 5, pp. 6–7.

22. Henry also stopped using the heraldic device of the Dun Cow, with its Neville associations.

23. Anglo, 'Early Tudor Propaganda' in op. cit., p. 27.

24. Public vows of betrothal followed by consummation made a marriage legal before a wedding. It is therefore possible Elizabeth's

child was conceived before the ceremony. Roy Strong, *Coronation: A History of Kingship and the British Monarchy* (2005), p. 139.

25. Raluca Radulescu, 'Malory and Fifteenth-Century Political Ideas' in *Arthuriana* 13, No. 3 (2003), p. 39.

10 Securing the Succession

1. A Benedictine monastery.
2. Beaufort Hours in F. Madden, 'Genealogical and Historical notes in Ancient Calenders' in *Collectanea Topographia et Genealogica* I (1834), p. 279.
3. Sir Thomas Malory, *Le Morte d'Arthur* (1485): 'And many men say that there ys wrytten uppon the thumbe thys: HIC IACET ARTHURUS, REX QUONDAM, REXQUE FUTURUS'.
4. *A Collection of Letters and State Papers, from the Original Manuscripts of Several Princes and Great Personages in the Two Last Centuries, etc.* (comp. Leonard Howard) (2 vols., 1756), Vol. 1, pp. 228, 229.
5. E. M. G. Routh, *Lady Margaret: A Memoir of Lady Margaret Beaufort* (1924), pp. 64, 65.
6. Griffiths and Thomas, *The Making of the Tudor Dynasty*, p. 183; Jones and Underwood, *The King's Mother*, p. 69.
7. For the servant Henry Parker's account, see British Library Add MSS 12060.
8. The esquire was Thomas Kyme.
9. Arlene Naylor Okerlund, *Elizabeth of York* (2009) pp. 95–7; *Excerpta Historica* (ed Samuel Bentley) (1831), p. 285.
10. John Leland, *De Rebus Britannicis* (ed Thomas Hearne) (1774), Vol. 4, p. 254.
11. Ibid.
12. Davies, 'Information, disinformation . . .' in op. cit., p. 6; *Ricardian* 7, No. 95 (December 1986).
13. Leigh Ann Craig, 'Royalty, Virtue, and Adversity: The Cult of King Henry VI' in *Albion: A Quarterly Journal Concerned with British Studies* 35, No. 2 (summer 2003), p. 190.

14. Condon, 'The Last Will of Henry VII' in op. cit., p. 133.

15. On her subsequent treatment and funeral, see Chapter 11.

16. The Danzig merchant who knew Henry as 'King Richmond' referred to the pretender without quibble in his chronicle as 'the son of . . . the Duke of Clarence'. Visser-Fuchs, 'English Events in Caspar Weinreich's Danzig Chronicle' in op. cit., p. 317.

17. The fact that her only surviving son, Thomas Grey, Marquess of Dorset, was arrested during the crises is indicative of Henry's suspicion that even members of the extended family could not be entirely trusted not to betray him.

18. The duke had been killed fighting the Swiss at Nancy in January 1477, losing the French province of Burgundy back to the French crown.

19. The father is variously described as an organ maker, a tailor, a barber or a baker. It has also been suggested the name Simnel could have origins from within the Duchy of Burgundy. There is mention of a 'son of Clarence' in Mechelen in July 1486 (Hicks, *The Wars of the Roses*, p. 243). Simnel was a word often used to describe a sweet bread or cake in England. Lambert was an occupational name for a shepherd (lamb-herd) and also an old English name (from Landbeorht). Whether Lambert Simnel was his real name is another matter. People were overheard calling the boy 'John' in conversation.

20. Vergil, *Anglica Historia*, p. 25.

21. Beaufort Hours, f.240v: thanks to Eric Ives for help with the Latin translation.

22. David Starkey, 'London: Flower of Cities All' in *Royal River: Power, Pageantry and the Thames* (ed Sue Doran) (2012), p. 13.

23. John Leland, *Collectanea IV* (1774), p. 259. Interestingly the ray cloth at the coronation of Henry VIII and Katherine of Aragon was striped.

24. Vergil, *Anglica Historia*, p. 25.

25. Desmond Seward, *The Last White Rose* (2010), p. 40.

26. This includes the wills of their grandmother, mother, or aunts. I also looked at Little Malvern Priory and Canterbury Cathedral, both of which had stained glass depicting the princes commissioned in 1482, but found nothing. The nearest I found was associated with the chantry set up originally by William Hastings, Edward IV's best friend, at St George's Chapel, Windsor. Hastings made his will on 27 June 1481, when the children were still alive. He directed his body to be buried in the place assigned to him by the king, and for Mass and divine service 'at the awter next to the place where my body shall be buryed'. However, when the full chantry was established in 1504, the children were (probably) dead. The terms of the grant of the manors of Farmanby and East Hallgarth were that every 10 June Mass was to be said for the souls of William, late Lord Hastings, Katherine his wife, Edward, now Lord Hastings, Mary his wife, for their fathers and mothers, and for the souls of King Edward IV and Queen Elizabeth his wife and for their children (unnamed) and all Christian souls. An annual obituary was established in which the children, presumably also Edward V and Richard, were to be included. Then there was to be in addition daily Mass said at the altar at the chapel where Lord Hastings was buried, for the souls of the said Lord Hastings and for all souls abovesaid. It would seem that although not specifically mentioned, Edward V and Richard were to be included in the daily prayers and annual obituary said by the Hastings chantry priest. Thank you to Eleanor Cracknell, Windsor Archives, St George's Chapel, Windsor. MSS refs SGC IV 8.2; SGC XV 58 C 17.

27. Henderson, 'Rethinking Henry VII' in op. cit., p. 325.

28. Vergil, *Anglica Historia*, p. 56.

11 The Lost Prince

1. Laynesmith, *The Last Medieval Queens*, p. 217.

2. Ralph Griffiths, 'Succession and the Royal Dead in Later Medieval England' in *Making and Breaking the Rules: Succession in Medieval Europe c.1000–c.1600* (eds Michael Penman and Frederique Lachaud) (2008), p. 102.

3. We do not know how the duchess had viewed the disappearance of her nephews, the princes in the Tower, in 1483. But she accepted Richard III's rule and was in contact with him in 1484 without any signs of there being ill will between them.

4. As Maximilian told the Venetian ambassador in Worms in 1495; A. J. J. Schnitker, 'Margaret of York, Princess of England and Duchess of Burgundy, 1446–1503: female power, influence and authority in later fifteenth-century North-western Europe', PhD diss., Edinburgh (2007), p. 125.

5. It had the added advantage of highlighting that York came second to Lancaster, the dukedom he held, and which continues to be held by the monarch, while York remains that of a second son.

6. Okerlund, *Elizabeth of York*, p. 192. http://www.archive.org/details/privypurseexpens00nicouoft, pp. 74, 75.

7. The conspirator was Sir Robert Clifford.

8. During the later investigations into the 3rd Duke of Buckingham in 1521 it was recalled that Henry VII knew of Sir William's treason and that of his co-conspirators 'two or three years before he charged them with it'. *L&P* 3 (1283).

9. Okerlund, *Elizabeth of York*, pp. 120, 121; *Great Chronicle of London* (ed Thomas and Thornley), p. 151.

10. Elizabeth I behaved similarly. There were fifty-seven peers at her accession and fifty-five at her death. Like her grandfather Elizabeth also kept an eye on marriage alliances.

11. In return for his army Perkin had promised the Duchess of Burgundy the manors of Hunsden in Hertfordshire and Scarborough in Yorkshire, as well as the money he owed for her

financial support. Maximilian was offered a potentially still greater prize: if Perkin died without issue, Maximilian was to inherit England, France and Ireland.

12. James would have dropped Perkin in a moment if the Spanish had responded positively to his own request for an infanta as his bride – but none was available. Norman Macdougall, *James IV* (2006), pp. 124, 125.

13. Davies, 'Information, disinformation . . .' in op.cit., p. 3.

14. Vergil, *Three Books*, p. 89.

15. Raphael Holinshed, *Chronicle* (1587), Vol. 2, p. 782.

16. *CSPV* 1 (751) (754); *CSPM* (539) (540).

17. Ibid.

18. *CSPV* 1 (751).

19. *CSPM* (541). Another of Perkin's standards was of a boy escaping a wolf's mouth, as Richard had escaped his would-be murderer, Richard III.

20. Perkin's confession is in *English Historical Documents Vol. 5 1485–1558* (ed David Douglas) (1967), p. 118.

21. It was probably written by the blind poet Bernard André whose tedious Latin verses had greeted Henry on the outskirts of London in September 1485. The first three triumphs described Henry's escapes from the clutches of Edward IV and Richard III (who appears as the epitome of evil, not least for the 'affair of the nephews'). But the dominant narrative concerned Henry and the duchess.

22. In England the mud thrown at the duchess would stick. Francis Bacon, writing in the seventeenth century, echoed 'The Twelve Triumphs of Henry VII', observing that 'having the spirit of a man and the malice of a woman . . . [the duchess] was for the king what Juno was to Aeneas troubling heaven and hell to annoy him'. Christine Weightman, *Margaret of York, Duchess of Burgundy* (1989), p. 154.

23. *CSPS* 1 (221). Perkin was not seen in the dungeon as is often said.

24. Warrant dated 25 November, National Archives, E36/209 f. 10v.
25. Condon, 'The Last Will of Henry VII' in op. cit., p. 130.
26. *CSPS* 1 (239).
27. See consultant forensic psychologist Ian Stephen on Jon Venables, imprisoned aged eleven, *The Times*, Saturday 24 July 2010, p. 9, headline: 'He may be stuck in his own abusive and fearful childhood'.
28. *CSPS* 1 (249).
29. Or so Francis Bacon tells us.
30. The tombs were at Bisham Priory in Berkshire, and were destroyed in the Reformation. The heads of Henry Tudor's great-granddaughter, Mary, Queen of Scots, and great-grandson, Charles I, were also (later) buried with their bodies.
31. Vergil, *Anglica Historia*, p. 119.
32. Ibid.

12 Punishment

1. *Original letters* (ed Ellis), Vol. 1, pp. 43–6.
2. Francis Bacon; see http://www.philological.bham.ac.uk/henry/11eng.html.
3. David Starkey, *Henry: Virtuous Prince* (2008), pp. 195, 196.
4. The last Earl of Bohun had died in 1373. The three earldoms and the broad lands of the Bohuns had then been divided between two co-heiresses. Both married members of the then royal house. The elder, Eleanor, was given in 1374 to Thomas of Woodstock, seventh son of Edward III. The younger, Mary, in 1380 or 1381, to Henry, son of John of Gaunt and afterwards Henry IV. The swan and the antelope was their device.
5. Ian Arthurson, 'The King of Spain's daughter came to visit me: marriage, princes and politics' in *Arthur Tudor, Prince of Wales: Life, Death and Commemoration* (eds Steven Gunn and Linda Monckton) (2009), pp. 20–9.
6. Ives, *The Reformation Experience*, pp. 13, 14, 19, 20.

7. *CSPS* 1 (312).

8. 'Impression of England by an Italian Visitor, November 1497' in *English Historical Documents Vol. 5 1485–1558* (ed David Douglas) (1967), pp. 188, 189.

9. Many of the leading court women of the next century would similarly take control of their lives following child marriages, either by staying widows, or by marrying their servants. It may be there is no connection with Margaret Beaufort's actions, but her intellectual pursuits were much imitated, and her decision in this regard would have been carefully noted.

10. 'The Mirror of Gold for the Sinful Soul', and Thomas à Kempis' 'The Imitation of Christ'.

11. When Margaret Beaufort had wanted to promote a particular candidate to the bishopric of Worcester, a letter from Pope Alexander warned her that Henry had promised the queen to appoint her candidate, and so her choice had to be dropped. Okerlund, *Elizabeth of York*, p. 136.

12. Starkey, *Henry*, p. 158.

13. Routh, *Lady Margaret*, p. 92.

14. Thomas More, quoted in Starkey, *Henry*, p. 143.

15. *The Receyt of the Ladie Kateryne* (ed G. Kipling), Early English Text Society original series 296 (1990), p. 38.

16. Amongst whom remained Perkin Warbeck's widow, the former Lady Catherine Gordon.

17. Some reliquaries contained fakes: the equivalent today of 'healing crystals', they still offered hope of well-being, even if the artefacts had no intrinsic spiritual qualities. Many others, however, were the genuine remains or former possessions of men and women admired for the extraordinary qualities they had demonstrated in life. Just as people today visit the graves of relatives they have lost, so people then liked to have some physical connection to the saints who were so much part of their spiritual life – the English more than most.

18. *L&P* 4, Pt III, 2577; British Library Cotton MSS Vitellius B XII, f. 98.
19. Frederick Hepburn, 'The Portraiture of Arthur and Katherine', in *Arthur Tudor, Prince of Wales* (eds Steven Gunn and Linda Monkton) (2009), p. 38.
20. Simon Thurley, *The Royal Palaces of Tudor England* (1993), p. 31.
21. *CSPS* 1 (176).
22. Thurley, *Royal Palaces*, pp. 35, 36.
23. S. B. Chrimes, *Henry VII* (1999). This contemporary description is quoted in full on pp. 302, 303.
24. Okerlund, *Elizabeth of York*, pp. 185, 186, 204.
25. See http://www.historyextra.com/henrypicture.
26. It may be coincidence but it was in 1502, the year Arthur died, that Henry paid for a rich chasuble and two altar fronts for the cathedral at Vannes, which had the shrine to St Vincent Ferrer. Condon, 'The Last Will of Henry VII', in op. cit., n. 4, p. 113.

13 Death and Judgement

1. *CSPS* 1, 295. Henry, Duke of York was made Prince of Wales in 1503.
2. J. Scarisbrick, *Henry VIII* (1997), p. 7.
3. It is mentioned in the Scottish Treasury accounts of January 1507. *Accounts of the Lord High Treasurer of Scotland 1473–1513* (eds T. Dickson and J. B. Paul) (1877–1902), Vol. 3, p. 250, cols i–iv.
4. Fiona Kisby, 'A Mirror of Monarchy: Music and Musicians in the Household Chapel of the Lady Margaret Beaufort, Mother of Henry VII' in *Early Music History, Vol. 16* (ed Iain Fenlon) (1997), pp. 225, 227.
5. Spanish ambassador Don Pedro de Ayala, quoted in Macdougall, *James IV*, p. 283.
6. Maria Perry, *The Sisters of Henry VIII: The Tumultuous Lives of Margaret of Scotland and Mary of France* (1999), p. 44.
7. Condon, 'The Last Will of Henry VII' in op. cit., p. 133. Interestingly,

given what followed under Henry VIII, his will also invested in a silver gilt image of himself, to be placed in the shrine at Canterbury of Thomas Becket. On it were to be the words 'Saint Thomas Intercede for Me'. Another image of Henry, similar in scale, was to be placed at the famous shrine to the Virgin at Walsingham, where he had prayed for victory against the pretender Lambert Simnel.

8. Twenty-nine such copes were bequeathed to the abbey in 1509. A hundred years later only eleven were left, which the Puritans burned in 1643. The Jesuits had, however, removed some before 1608 and one set survives. It belongs to the Jesuit college at Stoneyhurst and celebrates the houses of Beaufort and Lancaster with its embroidered portcullis surmounted by a crown and the border representing the Lancaster SS collar worn by Margaret Beaufort's grandfather on his tomb.

9. *Testamenta vetusta* in op. cit., p. 430.

10. As the twentieth-century novelist T. H. White romantically translated Thomas Malory's 'REX QUONDAM, REXQUE FUTURUS'.

11. Thomas Penn, *Winter King: The Dawn of Tudor England* (2012), pp. 166, 167.

12. Vergil, *Anglica Historia*, p. 129.

13. It was to their father, the late John de la Pole, Duke of Suffolk, that Margaret Beaufort had been betrothed before she was married to Edmund Tudor. If he had married her instead of Edward IV's sister (another Elizabeth), the story of his children's lives might have been very different.

14. *CSPS* 1 (552).

15. Jones and Underwood, *The Making of the Tudor Dynasty*, p. 89.

16. Margaret Aston, 'Death' in *Fifteenth-Century Attitudes* (ed R. Horrox) (1994), p. 203.

17. Starkey, *Henry*, p. 264.

18. Sydney Anglo, *Images of Tudor Kingship* (1992) p. 100.

19. This comment of Fisher's is usually misunderstood and given a

political rather than the religious meaning intended. Henderson, 'Rethinking Henry VII', pp. 333, 334.

20. Ibid., p. 331. Henry had already paid for 10,000 or more Masses to be said during the previous three Lenten seasons, for his health, soul and family.

21. Hall, *Chronicle*, in *English Historical Documents Vol. 5 1485–1558* (ed David Douglas) (1967), p. 146.

22. I wonder if this influenced the Hastings chantry at Windsor instituting prayers for the souls of Edward IV's children in 1504.

23. More's *The History of Richard III* can be seen at http://www.r3.org/bookcase/more/moretext.html. It offers a detailed account (or 'story') of the murder of the princes.

14 Exit Margaret Beaufort

1. Tuberculosis is a slow killer that induces fatigue, and the genito-urinary tract is the most common site, after the lungs, for infection. This is turn can spread to the testes, as it may have done in Arthur's case.

2. Craig, 'Royalty, Virtue, and Adversity: The Cult of King Henry VI' in op. cit., p. 199.

3. Giles Tremlett, *Catherine of Aragon* (2010), p. 164.

4. Henry was dressed in a costume of red and gold, furred with ermine and studded with rubies, diamonds, pearls and emeralds.

5. John Fisher, *A Mourning Remembrance of Margaret, Countess of Richmond* (1509).

6. According to the later cardinal, Reginald Pole, whose parents' marriage Margaret had arranged, her last words were to commend Henry to Fisher's guidance (Margaret Beaufort arranged the marriage of Margaret Plantagenet, daughter of the Duke of Clarence, to her nephew of the half-blood Richard Pole).

7. It is now in the British Library.

15 The Elder Sister: Margaret, Queen of Scots

1. Margaret McIntyre, 'Tudor Family Politics in Early Sixteenth-Century Scotland' in *History, Literature and Music in Scotland 700–1560* (ed R. Andrew McDonald) (2002), p. 198.

2. *L&P* 1, Pt I (1775).

3. William Shakespeare, *Henry V*, Act 4, Scene 3.

4. Suzannah Lipscomb, *1536: The Year That Changed Henry VIII* (2009), p. 32; and the 'better things' were like what the English victory at Shakespeare's Agincourt would ensure: 'From this day until the ending of the world/But we in it shall be remember'd.' Shakespeare, *Henry V*, Act 4, Scene 3.

5. Tremlett, *Catherine of Aragon*, p. 194.

6. 'Such large...': *L&P* 1 (2283); 'with many muckle...': John Sadler and Stephen Walsh, *Flodden 1513: Scotland's Greatest Defeat* (2006), p. 76. Priests were not supposed to spill blood, but in the Middle Ages they had often argued to their own satisfaction that it was permissible to fight with a mace and bludgeon their enemy, rather than cut with a sword.

7. The words were written in the eighteenth century.

8. The Royal Arms of Scotland are 'a lion rampant gules, armed and langued azure, within a double tressure flory-counter-flory of the second'.

9. J. Leslie, *History of Scotland* (1895), p. 95. James IV's body was identified by Thomas, Lord Dacre who knew the king well. Henry VIII also reported the king was found dead on the battlefield. But an Italian heard that James had been captured only to die of his wounds within the hour: *CSPV* 2 (332). He was, perhaps, not quite dead when his body was found. In Scotland rumours would later circulate that he was still alive and in hiding.

10. *L&P* 1 (2246).
11. *L&P* 1, Pt II (2283–84); Macdougall, *James IV*, pp. 274, 275, 276. For King Henry reporting death of James IV, *CSPM* 1 (655).
12. *L&P* 1 (2460).
13. *L&P* 1 (4451).
14. *CSPV* 2 (316).
15. *CSPV* 2 (309), *CSPS* 2 (142). For the fate of James' body see Appendix 1.
16. *L&P* 2 (2440).
17. *L&P* 1, Pt II (2973). Reported by Lord Dacre to Henry VIII. I have modernised the English. James IV had done much to restore law and order to Scotland, but the violence had returned worse than ever.
18. His father had died at Flodden.
19. Bishop Leslie, quoted in Caroline Bingham, *James V King of Scots* (1971), p. 32 and William Kevin Emond, 'The Minority of James V 1513–1528', PhD diss., St Andrews (1988), p. 24.
20. Erin A. Sadlack, *The French Queen's Letters* (2011), p. 156.

16 The Younger Sister: Mary, The French Queen

1. 'Narrative of the visit of the duke de Najera' in *Archaeologia* 33 (1831), p. 350.
2. *CSPV* 2 (500); *L&P* 2 (395).
3. *L&P* 2 (227).
4. *L&P* 2 (327).
5. *L&P* 2 (228).
6. *CSPV* 2, pp. 211, 496; Perry, *Sisters*, pp. 141, 142.
7. Michael Sherman, 'Pomp and Circumstances: Pageantry, Politics, and Propaganda in France during the Reign of Louis XII, 1498–1515' in *The Sixteenth Century Journal* (winter 1978), p. 26.
8. *L&P* 1, Pt II (3416); Perry, *Sisters*, p. 144.
9. Walter C. Richardson, *Mary Tudor, The White Queen* (1970), p. 113.
10. Ibid., p. 126.

11. Henry's future daughter Elizabeth would similarly want to know about the appearance of Mary, Queen of Scots, and how they compared. She inherited her infamous vanity from her father. *L&P* 2 (411).

12. *L&P* 2 (222).

13. *L&P* 2 (224).

14. *L&P* 2 (226) (227); Richardson, *Mary Tudor*, pp. 174, 175.

15. Richardson, *Mary Tudor*, p. 173.

16. *L&P* 2 (327).

17. Richardson, *Mary Tudor*, p. 82.

18. *English Historical Documents* (ed Douglas), p. 388. Elizabeth I owned a Mirror of France, which may well be the Mirror of Naples. A jewel matching its description features in a portrait of Anne of Denmark (wife of James VI and I). James also refers to the Mirror of France in a letter to the future Charles I, suggesting he wear it in his hat with a little black feather. It appears to have been pawned in 1625, and vanished thereafter. Roy Strong, 'Three Royal Jewels: The Three Brothers, the Mirror of Great Britain and the Feather' in *Burlington Magazine* 108, No. 760 (July 1966), pp. 350–3.

19. *L&P* 2 (343).

20. The drawing is in the Bibliothèque Nationale, Paris.

21. Emond, PhD diss., op. cit., p. 52.

17 A Family Reunion and a Royal Rival

1. My research indicates it was not Edinburgh Castle as described by Maria Perry, Rosalind Marshall and others. See *L&P* 2 (779).

2. Ibid.

3. The cannon, which can be seen today at Edinburgh Castle, had been presented to King James II by his uncle by marriage, Philip the Good, Duke of Burgundy in 1457. The name comes from the town of Mons where it was made, in present-day Belgium.

4. *L&P* 2 (783).

5. *L&P* 2 (788).

6. By 16 September the party had reached Blackadder Castle, the stronghold of Angus' family, the Douglasses. They did not stay for long before departing for Coldstream Abbey in England, and then on. Emond, PhD diss., op. cit., p. 92.

7. *Original letters* (ed Ellis), Vol. 1, p. 266.

8. *L&P* 2 (1380).

9. Emond, PhD diss., op. cit., p. 112. Queen Margaret's letters to Albany during this period ask for the restoration of her husband's castles, as well as the release of his imprisoned uncle Gavin Douglas, and grandfather, Lord Drummond. Although Dacre talks of Angus' 'desertion', it was not unplanned or without Margaret's approval.

10. *L&P* 2 (1829).

11. Eric Ives, 'Henry VIII', *Oxford Dictionary of National Biography*.

12. Hall, *Chronicle*, p. 515. The virginals are a keyboard instrument of the harpsichord family.

13. *L&P* 2 (1562) (1845) (1861) (1863). Wolsey was godfather to Henry Brandon, and the godmother was Katherine, Countess of Devon. The cardinal was also godmother to Mary Tudor. The sources indicate variously Henry's aunt, Katherine, as godmother, and the Duchess of Norfolk. Mary Tudor, through her mother, Katherine of Aragon, claimed legitimate descent from John of Gaunt from whom Henry VII drew his right to the throne (albeit through an illegitimate line). No child by any of Henry VIII's future wives would be able to claim as much.

14. *L&P* 2 (1585).

15. *L&P* 2 (410).

16. Sebastian Giustinian, *CSPV* 2 (1287).

17. John Stow, *A Survey of London* (2005), p. 377.

18. It is now in the Austrian National Library in Vienna.

19. *CSPV* 2 (1287).

20. Hall, *Chronicle*, pp. 595, 703. The only surviving likeness of her is a brass memorial, which shows her kneeling in profile, and can be seen at the British Museum.

21. Ibid., p. 703.
22. Those who became heirs to their family estate as minors became wards of the Crown. The Crown could sell or gift the wardship, or arrange the marriage of their wards.
23. *CSPV* 2 (1287).
24. *L&P* 3, calendared early 1519, quoted in Scarisbrick, *Henry VIII*, p. 120.
25. Vergil, *Anglica Historia*, p. 263.
26. *L&P* 3 (1283). As his father had hoped to do to Richard III: Buckingham's temper was a character flaw he had shared with his two ducal predecessors. The first Duke of Buckingham had to be held back to prevent him stabbing the French rebel leader Joan of Arc during an interrogation in 1431. The second duke was so disliked that one of his servants sold his life to Richard III. Edward Buckingham was similarly given to 'fumes and displeasure'.
27. *L&P* 3 (1284).
28. Then called Henton.
29. *L&P* 3 (1284).
30. *CSPV* 3 (213).
31. Ibid.
32. My own rather rough translation: '*Dieu a sa ame graunte mercy car il fuit tresnoble prince & prudent & mirror de tout courtoise*' (Yearbook Pasch.13 Henry VIII, p.1 f. 11). Thanks to Eric Ives for drawing my attention to this reference. Much of the blame for Buckingham's death was laid not at the feet of Henry VIII, but rather his chief minister. Verses were written decrying the 'cruelty of the red man', Wolsey, dressed in the scarlet of his office, a 'vile Butcher's son' who 'hath devoured the beautiful swan [Buckingham]'. Buckingham's grandson, Thomas Stafford, would try and overthrow a later Tudor. He was executed after he led an invasion of England in 1557 against Mary I.

18 Enter Anne Boleyn

1. Pavia is thirty-five kilometres south of Milan. The date, 24 February, was Charles V's birthday.

2. His eldest brother was the Earl of Lincoln, who Richard III was said to have named as his heir. He was killed in 1487 at the Battle of Stoke Field, after his invasion from Ireland brought Lambert Simnel to England. The second brother, Edmund de la Pole, Duke of Suffolk, had been imprisoned by Henry VII and executed by Henry VIII before his war in France in 1513.

3. Scarisbrick, *Henry VIII*, p. 136.

4. Beverley Anne Murphy, 'The Life and Political Significance of Henry Fitzroy, Duke of Richmond 1525–1536', PhD diss., University of Wales (1997), pp. 80, 81.

5. Fitzroy was endowed with lands whose revenues amounted to £4,845 in the first year. He was appointed warden-general of the marches toward Scotland on 22 June and installed into the Order of the Garter on 25 June. On 16 July he became Lord Admiral of England.

6. *CSPV* 3 (902).

7. Henry, Lord Morley, The Prologue Royal MSS, British Library 17 C CVI f. 2v, quoted in A. Pollnitz, 'Humanism and Court Culture' in *Tudor Court Culture* (ed Thomas Betteridge and Anna Riehl) (2012), p. 53.

8. *CSPV* 4 (824); G. W. Bernard, *Anne Boleyn: Fatal Attractions* (2010), p. 19. Also see the medal of Anne for the shape of her face.

9. Retha Warnicke, *The Rise and Fall of Anne Boleyn* (1989), p. 56.

10. This follows private conversations with Eric Ives. Mary Boleyn's affair with Henry, and possible presence at the Field of Cloth of Gold, could explain King Francis' later reported comment that she was a notorious slut; *L&P* 10 (450). The Bishop of Faenza who reported this story talks about 'the queen's sister' – the queen at the time being Anne Boleyn. But it also strikes me that

people often got gossip about royals confused. Stories about Charles V were later applied to Edward VI, for example (the story of the skinned falcon, which was applied to Charles V after his betrothal to Henry's sister Mary was revoked, was also applied to Edward VI following the executions of his uncles, 'this falcon has been stripped . . . just as I . . . am skinned'). It has not been suggested before, but I believe it very possible Francis' comments referred instead to Anne's sister-in-law – the French queen. Her behaviour with Charles Brandon in France when recently widowed had been scandalous. *'Plus sale que royne'* (more dirty than queenly) Francis had written on her portrait, and his mother had made her own barbed comment about her marriage with a man of 'low estate'.

11. Thomas Skydmore of Syon, the religious conservative who claimed 'Master Carey' was Henry's son, also called Henry a robber, and accused him of sleeping with Anne's mother. He was addressing John Hale, vicar of Isleworth, who is celebrated as a Catholic martyr. *L&P* 8 (565) (567). There is no evidence that Henry fathered Carey's children.

12. James Butler. Thomas Boleyn had claims to the title himself, through the female line, and was eventually granted it.

13. George Cavendish, *The Life and Death of Cardinal Wolsey* (ed R. S. Sylvester) (1959), p. 30.

14. Baldassare Castiglione, *The Book of the Courtier* quoted in Elizabeth Heale, 'Women and the Courtly Love Lyric: The Devonshire MS (BL Additional 17492)' in *Modern Language Review* 90, No. 2 (April 1995), pp. 296–313.

15. Hall, *Chronicle*, p. 707. A letter Henry wrote in what appears to have been 1527 says he had been in love with her for about a year.

16. Eric Ives, *The Life and Death of Anne Boleyn: The Most Happy* (2004), p. 75.

17. It also argued that Communion in both kinds should be given to laity as well as clergy and rejected the hypothesis of

transubstantiation. The Mass was not a sacrifice, he claimed, and the special identity of the priesthood a delusion. All Christians were priests and anyone could preside at a Communion service.

18. Henry's views are expressed in the 1532 work, *A Glass of the Truth*.

19. Thomas P. Campbell, *Henry VIII and the Art of Majesty* (2007) pp. 180, 181, 183.

20. The previous October, she had also caught Angus taking advantage of her absence from Scotland to profit from her rents. Emond, PhD diss., op. cit., p. 121.

21. *L&P* 3 (166), misdated April 1519. She had asked for Henry's support, but Angus had been too useful to English interests for him to give it.

19 A Marriage on Trial

1. *CSPS* 3, Pt II (70).

2. Ibid.

3. *CSPS* 3, Pt II (113).

4. Ives, *The Reformation Experience*, p. 68.

5. Matthew 16:19. Maria Dowling, *Fisher of Men, A Life of John Fisher 1469–1535* (1999), p. 133.

6. *CSPS* 3, Pt II (224).

7. Cavendish, *Wolsey*, p. 249; Shakespeare, *Henry VI Part III*, Act 5, Scene 6. 'Aboding' is synonymous with foreboding. Edmund Spenser refers to 'night ravens', 'The hateful messengers of heavy things/Of death and dolor telling sad tidings.' *The Faerie Queen*, Book II, Canto VII, 23.

8. The thread was in varying heights and thickness, and the silk ground would be lampas – i.e. silk taffeta with gold thread, or brocatelle, which was similar to brocade but with designs in high relief, made on a jacquard loom. Edward Hall provides the detail that the canopy was of tissue.

9. David Starkey, *Six Wives: The Queens of Henry VIII* (2004), pp. 240, 241; Cavendish, *Wolsey*, p. 79.

10. Cavendish, *Wolsey*, pp. 80, 81, 82.
11. British Library Cotton MSS Vitellius B XII.
12. Clement was born Giulio di Giuliano de' Medici.
13. Hall, *Chronicle*, p. 758. Cavendish, *Wolsey*, p. 90, has him saying 'it was never merry in England while we had cardinals amongst us'.
14. *CSPS* 4, Pt I (373).
15. Cavendish, *Wolsey*, pp. 178, 179. Shakespeare later paraphrased this in *Henry VIII*, Act 3, Scene 2, with Wolsey warning Cromwell 'Had I but served my God with half the zeal/I served my king, he would not in mine age/Have left me naked to mine enemies.' I also enjoy Wolsey's soliloquy in the same scene:

> Farewell! a long farewell, to all my greatness!
> This is the state of man: to-day he puts forth
> The tender leaves of hopes; to-morrow blossoms,
> And bears his blushing honours thick upon him;
> The third day comes a frost, a killing frost,
> And, when he thinks, good easy man, full surely
> His greatness is a-ripening, nips his root,
> And then he falls, as I do. I have ventured,
> Like little wanton boys that swim on bladders,
> This many summers in a sea of glory,
> But far beyond my depth: my high-blown pride
> At length broke under me and now has left me,
> Weary and old with service, to the mercy
> Of a rude stream, that must for ever hide me.
> Vain pomp and glory of this world, I hate ye:
> I feel my heart new open'd. O, how wretched
> Is that poor man that hangs on princes' favours!
> There is, betwixt that smile we would aspire to,
> That sweet aspect of princes, and their ruin,

> More pangs and fears than wars or women have:
> And when he falls, he falls like Lucifer,
> Never to hope again.

The grandiose tomb he had commissioned was plundered by Henry and has largely disappeared, except for the sarcophagus and base. These were moved to St Paul's Cathedral in 1808 to house the body of Lord Nelson.

20 The Return of Margaret Douglas

1. *L&P* 4 (5794). Also in a letter dated 25 November 1528 Margaret Tudor states the Earl of Angus 'wald nocht suffere oure ane doghter to remane wicht ws for our comfort, quha wald nocht have been disherest, scho being wicht ws'; William Fraser, *The Douglas Book*, Vol. 2 (1885), p. 289.
2. Ibid.
3. *The Great Wardrobe Accounts of Henry VII and Henry VIII* (ed Maria Haywood) (2012), p. 197.
4. *CSPS* 4 (445).
5. Certainly there were areas of disagreement about the precise nature and scope of papal authority. The weakness of the papacy in the early fifteenth century had prompted the development of conciliarist theories that placed authority with councils rather than just popes. Indeed, the future Catholic martyr Thomas More had objected to Henry's earlier exultation of papal authority in his attack on Luther. But these subtle differences of interpretation were a very different thing from wholesale rejection of papal authority.
6. Eamon Duffy, 'Rome and Catholicity', in *Saints, Sacrilege, Sedition: Religion and Conflict in the Tudor Reformations* (ed E. Duffy) (2012), pp. 195–211.
7. Starkey, *Six Wives*, pp. 409, 410.
8. Henry showed the painted table to Charles V in 1522, when the

paintwork still looked new, but it may have been done as early as 1516 when repair work was done on the hall and 'le Round table'. See Jon Whitman, 'National Icon: The Winchester Round Table and the Revelation of Authority' in *Arthuriana* 18, No. 4 (winter 2008), p. 47.

9. Scarisbrick, *Henry VIII*, p. 272.

10. Richard Roose was described as the cook by the Imperial ambassador Eustace Chapuys and in the Act of Attainder. A subsequent description of Roose as a friend of the cook appears to be wrong. See William R. Stacey, 'Richard Roose and the Parliamentary Use of Attainder in the Reign of Henry VIII' in *Historical Journal* 29, 1 (1986), n. 13, p. 3.

11. Ibid., pp. 1–15.

12. 'The Chronicle of the Grey Friars: Henry VIII' in *Chronicle of the Grey Friars of London*', Camden Society old series, Vol. 53 (1852), pp. 29–53.

13. For other cases of men and women being boiled alive for poisoning see 'Additional notes' in ibid., pp. 99–104.

14. *CSPV* 4 (682).

15. Lacey Baldwin-Smith, *Treason in Tudor England* (2006), p. 21.

16. *CSPS* 5, Pt II (739). On the importance of the French queen, see *CSPV* 4 (694), *CSPS* 4, Pt II (765).

17. It was inspired by that of her former mistress Margaret of Austria, '*Groigne qui groigne: vive Bourgoine!*' (Complain who must: long live Burgundy!).

18. *L&P* 6 (1199). According to David Loades she had replaced Perkin Warbeck's widow, Lady Catherine Gordon; see *Mary Tudor: A Life* (1992), p. 71. Lady Catherine's third husband died that year.

19. *L&P* 5 (498).

20. Campbell, *Henry VIII*, p. 207.

21. They had made binding promises to each other, followed by intercourse, which under canon law was a valid marriage – for those not already married – on 14 November.

22. Ives, *Anne Boleyn*, p. 161; Bernard, *Anne Boleyn*, p. 66 (i.e. in front of a priest).
23. *L&P* 8 (1150).
24. *L&P* 6 (720).
25. *Chronicle of King Henry VIII of England: Being a Contemporary Record of Some of the Principal Events* (ed Martin Andrew Sharp Hume) (1889), p. 135. Mary Tudor, Duchess of Suffolk and Queen of France, was buried on 21 July 1533.
26. A couple of years earlier Fitzroy had passed on to one of his servants what he considered to be the second-rate Spanish saddle horse that Anne had given him. It was 'very ill to ride and of worse condition'. See Murphy, PhD diss., op. cit., p. 146; HMC Longleat Miscellaneous Manuscripts XVII, f. 98.
27. Charles Wriothesley, *Chronicle of England during the reign of the Tudors, 1485–1559* (ed William Douglas Hamilton), Vol. 1 (1875), p. 18.
28. *CSPV* 4 (694).
29. Society of Antiquaries, London, MSS 129, f. 8. It remained in royal inventories until 1547 when it was 'acquired' by the Protector of Somerset.
30. For a detailed description of the coronation, see *L&P* 6 (601).
31. *L&P* 6 (585).
32. Ibid.
33. *Two Chronicles of London* (ed C. L. Kingsford) (1910), p. 8.
34. Wriothesley, *Chronicle*, pp. 19, 20.

21 The Terror Begins

1. His mother was Elizabeth of York's sister, Katherine.
2. *L&P* 6 (1111) (1112) (1125).
3. Diane Watt, 'Elizabeth Barton', *Oxford Dictionary of National Biography*.
4. *L&P* 6 (1207).
5. Margaret Douglas' name appears in the New Year gift list so she was at court by 1 January.

6. *L&P* 7, Appendix 16 March.

7. *L&P* 6 (1528).

8. It later emerged that Lord Hussey (whose wife served in Mary's household) was one such.

9. Stanford Lehmberg, 'Parliamentary Attainder in the Reign of Henry VIII' in *Historical Journal* 18 (1975), pp. 681, 682. 'During the earlier part of Henry VIII's reign, then, attainder was used sparingly and traditionally. No one was sent to his death solely by an act of Parliament . . . The breach with Rome altered the situation dramatically.' 'The pivotal act was the famous measure directed against Elizabeth Barton and her confederates, brought before the Reformation Parliament in 1534.' 'The Act is clearly a political measure, not a financial one, for the offenders had little property; it is the first act to deal with religious dissent, the first act filled with propaganda, the first act to be proclaimed throughout the realm, the first act to specify the death penalty, the first act of the Tudors which in itself sent offenders to the scaffold [in fact Fisher's cook Richard Roose was the first], the first Tudor attainder for misprision, the first attainder commanding the surrender of treasonous printed matter.'

10. *CSPS* 5, Pt I, (90): 'Ever since the king began to entertain doubts as to his mistress' reported pregnancy, he has renewed and increased the love which he formerly bore to another very handsome young lady of this court; and whereas the royal mistress, hearing of it, attempted to dismiss the damsel from her service, the king has been very sad, and has sent her a message to this effect: that she ought to be satisfied with what he had done for her; for, were he to commence again, he would certainly not do as much; she ought to consider where she came from, and many other things of the same kind. Yet no great stress is to be laid on such words, considering the king's versatility, and the wiliness (*astuce*) of the said lady, who knows perfectly well how to deal with him.'

11. Dowling, *Fisher*, p. 161.

12. *CSPS* 4 (445).

13. *L&P* 8 (666).

14. John Guy, *A Daughter's Love: Thomas and Margaret More* (2008), p. 259.

15. There is a 1588 copy of this bull in the Vatican archives. *Copia bullae Pauli III contra Henricum regem Angliae, quem totumque regnum ecclesiastico interdicto supponti, mandando cunctis ut contra eum arma capiant.* The incipit is '*Eius qui immobilis permanes*'. The datation: '*Datum Rome apud Sanctum Marchum anno incarnatione dominice millesimo quingentesimo trigesimo quinto anno tertio calendas septembris*', i.e. 1 September 1535. (The signature is AA Arm. Arc. 1588).

16. *L&P* 11 (48). The daughter of Sir John and Lady Anne Shelton, and sister-in-law of Madge/Margaret Shelton née Parker; see Warnicke, *The Rise and Fall of Anne Boleyn*, p. 46. There is a view that she also had a sister called Margaret, but the evidence is pretty thin; see Paul G. Remley, 'Mary Shelton and her Tudor Literary Milieu', in *Rethinking the Henrician Era* (ed Peter C. Herman) (1994), pp. 40–77. For the further suggestion that Margaret Shelton was Mary's sister-in-law see Heale, 'Women and the Courtly Love Lyric', in op. cit., pp. 296–313.

17. Heale, 'Women and the Courtly Love Lyric' in op. cit., p. 301.

18. *CSPS* 5, Pt I (142).

19. *L&P* 10 (141).

20. Katherine was buried with the status of Prince Arthur's widow, not that of a queen consort, and a junior member of the royal family – the French queen's younger daughter, Eleanor – played the role of chief mourner. An annual service is still held for Katherine at what is now Peterborough Cathedral and the Spanish embassy continues to send a wreath in commemoration.

21. *CSPS* 5, Pt II (29).

22. George Wyatt, son of Sir Thomas Wyatt; *CSPS* 5, Pt II (29).

23. *L&P* 10 (199).
24. His later impotence in his marriage with Anne of Cleves may also to have reflected concern about the validity of that marriage; see Retha Warnicke, *The Marrying of Anne of Cleves* (2000), pp. 162, 167.
25. *CSPS* 5, Pt II (84).

22 The Fall of Anne Boleyn

1. Elizabeth Wood, wife of Sir James Boleyn.
2. *L&P* 11 (48).
3. Nicola Shulman, *Graven With Diamonds* (2011), p. 144.
4. *L&P* 10 (601).
5. *L&P* 10 (782).
6. Henry later told Jane Seymour that it was Anne's meddling in a political matter that was her undoing.
7. *L&P* 10 (699).
8. There were witnesses but Thomas Howard admitted only to Margaret telling William Howard's wife, Margaret Gamage, the next day. William and Margaret's eldest daughter was named Douglas after her godmother Lady Margaret Douglas. She later 'married' Robert Dudley, Earl of Leicester in a ceremony that was never recognised in law.
9. *L&P* 10 (908).
10. *L&P* 10 (798).
11. *L&P* 10 (793).
12. Ives, *Anne Boleyn*, p. 325.
13. *L&P* 10 (956); R. B. Merriman, *The Life and Letters of Thomas Cromwell Vol. 2* (1902), p. 12.
14. More than 200 people came forward in 1932 to confess they had kidnapped the baby of the famous aviator Charles Lindbergh.
15. Norris held the Garter office of Black Rod. *L&P* 10 (878).
16. *L&P* 10 (793).
17. Sir William Page (a friend of Cromwell) and Sir Francis Bryan

(who had powerful support amongst court conservatives who were needed to bring Anne down).

18. The judge was John Spelman. The lady-in-waiting was Lady Wingfield. It is possible that Lady Wingfield was aware of some minor indiscretion by Anne. A surviving letter from the queen to Lady Wingfield indicates she had been keen to keep on the right side of her.

19. The rumours about Lady Wingfield, who died in 1534, are the probable origin of a story later spun in verse by a Frenchman at court called Lancelot de Carles. It describes a woman whose brother accuses her of immorality. She insists she is no worse than others at court, and better than the queen, who has slept with Smeaton, Norris and George Boleyn. The brother tells two friends what he has heard, and they tell the king. These verses are clearly inspired by a combination of the accusations against Anne and dramatic licence – the author describes his view of how things 'must' have happened, while creating a living drama between a brother and sister that is more vivid than a deathbed confession. But some historians have accepted the de Carles story as literal truth. They suggest the woman in the poem is Lady Worcester.

20. John Hussey in a letter to Lord Lisle. He also mentions 'one maid more'. The unnamed maid was probably Margery Horsman; see Ives, *Anne Boleyn*, p. 332.

21. Anne Braye, wife of George Brooke, Lord Cobham.

22. The evidence that Jane, Lady Rochford was part of the women's protest again Anne Boleyn in the summer of 1535 is very weak; see it in *L&P* 9 (566) and n. It is also worth pointing out that although Lady Rochford was treated generously by Cromwell after her husband's death (something her detractors have made much of), it was not unusual to look after the interests of the wives of executed traitors. Examples are the widows of Perkin Warbeck under Henry VII, the widow of the Duke of Buckingham under Henry VIII, and of Harry Grey, Duke of Suffolk under

Mary I. On other 'evidence', see John Guy's review of Alison Weir's *The Lady in the Tower*, *Sunday Times*, 1 November 2009. Jane would become a tempting target for slander following a scandal that was still a few years away – and unfortunately many women of the Tudor period have been slandered.

23. Spelman.

23 Love and Death

1. Shulman, *Graven With Diamonds*, p. 196.
2. *L&P* 2, August 1536 (203).
3. Ibid.
4. *L&P* 11 (41).
5. At some point that year a set of new and magnificent tapestries were delivered to court depicting the seven deadly sins. That Henry chose this period to buy very expensive works of art illustrating the vices which dupe and mislead mankind is striking. Campbell, *Henry VIII*, p. 226.
6. *L&P* 10 (908).
7. A witness recalled seeing him from a window, but we do not know if he could see Anne; see Shulman, *Graven With Diamonds*, p. 202.
8. A manuscript in the Vatican archives reveals that in France the papal nuncio heard that they were married already: this may be why. ASV, *Serg. St Francia*, Vol. 1B, f. 40r: '*Al Signor Protonotaro Ambrogio: se non che hiersera venne un corriere d'Inghilterra, che porta per quel ch'io ne intendo come quel Re ha pigliato per moglie quella dama che vivendo anche l'altra, mostrava che più gli piacesse, ne per anchora ho saputo altro particolare. Da Lione alli X di giugno 1536.*'
9. Linda Porter, *Mary Tudor: The First Queen* (2007), p. 123.
10. Her status was helped further by the fact that Charles Brandon's last surviving son with Mary, the French queen, had died in 1534. Only their daughters Frances and Eleanor survived.
11. *CSPS* 5, Pt II (61).

12. *CSPS* 7, Pt II (71).
13. *L&P* 11 (40).
14. Helen Baron, 'Mary (Howard) Fitzroy's Hand in the Devonshire Manuscript' in *Review of English Studies* 45, No. 179 (August 1994), p. 327.
15. Remley, 'Mary Shelton' in op. cit., pp. 53, 54.
16. Lehmberg, 'Parliamentary Attainder in the Reign of Henry VIII' in op. cit., pp. 691, 692. Within four years the Howards had their revenge and Cromwell was attainted, as so many others had been after 1533.
17. *L&P* 11 (147).
18. Margaret Douglas was ignored in the Third Act of Succession, in which Henry said that he would later appoint Elizabeth's heirs.
19. *L&P* 11 (293).
20. *L&P* 11 (294).
21. *L&P* 11 (994).
22. *L&P* 11 (1373).
23. *L&P* 11 (202.37); Blaauw, 'On the Effigy . . .' in op. cit., pp. 30, 31, 32. Although there is a probate to his will dated 1542, Sir David had died in 1535.

24 Three Wives

1. *L&P* 12, Pt I, p. 81, Pt II, p. 280.
2. Leanda de Lisle, *The Sisters Who Would be Queen* (2009), pp. 11, 12. Frances' brothers had died before reaching adulthood. Frances' appearance can be judged from the effigy on her tomb at Westminster Abbey. Jane Grey was named after Jane Seymour.
3. Her biographer Kimberly Schutte claims she was there in the first carriage with Frances, but is mistaken. See *L&P* 12, Pt II (1060).
4. *L&P* 12 (1023); Wriothesley, *Chronicle*, p. 70. He died on 31 October.
5. The opening stanza, written in thick, smudged ink, calls together her family and friends to hear her plans:

> Now that ye be assembled here,
> All ye my friends and my request,
> 'specially you my father dear,
> that of my blood are the nearest,
> this unto you is my request,
> that ye will patiently hear,
> by these my last words expressed,
> my testament entire.

They cannot stop what she intends, for she has prepared a defence as strong as the high Tower, and the 'door fast barred'. What she intends amounts to suicide, and she asks her father's forgiveness:

> Wherefore sweet father I you pray,
> Bear this my death with patience,
> And torment not your hairs grey
> But freely pardon my offence.

Her reason, she explains, is the suffering she endures through her constant love for a man who has died because of her, and with whom she now wishes to be:

> Let me not from the sweet presence
> Of him that I have caused to die.

His epitaph was also written into the book she would one day pass on to her sons:

> But when you come by my sepulchre
> Remember that your fellow resteth here
> For I loved much, though I unworthy were.

(The original last line reads 'But I louyd eke'. Remley, 'Mary Shelton' in op. cit., p. 52.)

6. The abortive attempt to make a tomb for Henry VIII at Westminster Abbey began in 1518/19 with payments being made intermittently up to 1536 when payments ceased; various sculptors were involved. Henry had seen the completion of the magnificent high altar he had built in the Lady Chapel of Westminster Abbey in 1526: the year he fell in love with Anne Boleyn.

7. Kevin Sharpe, *Selling the Tudor Monarchy* (2009), p. 137.

8. Ibid., p. 136; Ives, *The Reformation Experience*, p. 199.

9. The image in Canterbury, commissioned in Henry VII's will, was to have the words 'Saint Thomas Intercede for Me' written in enamel letters on it.

10. The friar was John Forrest, the image was Derfel Gadran, said to have been one of King Arthur's warriors.

11. The reformer was John Lambert.

12. *CSPS* 6, Pt I (166).

13. This took place at the royal hunting lodge at Royston in Hertfordshire; see 'Edward VI', *Oxford Dictionary of National Biography*.

14. Margaret and James IV, Mary and Louis XII.

15. *L&P* 15 (22).

16. Warnicke, *The Marrying of Anne of Cleves*, p. 141.

17. High cholesterol levels can affect sexual performance as the tiny artilleries in the penis shut down. Obesity is also associated with hormonal changes and lowered testosterone levels. Although weight has not previously been linked with Henry's impotence, it may help explain his failure to father more children.

18. See the illuminations depicting Henry in his psalter, painted in 1540 by Jean Mallard. In the one I refer to here he is depicted as the biblical King David playing his harp. It was a comparison designed to delight the king who saw himself as David's heir: a warrior, musician and theocratic monarch. http://www.bl.uk/onlinegallery/sacredtexts/henrypsalter.html.

19. They married at Oatlands Palace, Surrey. *See Oxford Dictionary of National Biography.*

20. The former Margaret Tudor died at Methven Castle on 18 October. She had asked that her daughter might have her goods, but the day following her death James V had issued counter-orders 'to lock up her goods to his use'; *L&P* 16 (1307). She was buried in the Carthusian abbey at Perth. Unfortunately, like her husband James IV, her body would not rest in peace. The tomb was to be desecrated and her skeleton burned by Protestant reformers in 1559.

21. Charles de Marillac; Starkey, *Six Wives*, p. 651.

22. The music teacher, Henry Manox, had not, however, had her 'maidenhead' although she had promised it to him; Starkey, *Six Wives*, p. 669.

23. *L&P* 16 (1334).

24. The king's niece, Margaret Douglas, was to be sent to Kenninghall in Norfolk, the family seat of the duke. *L&P* 16 (1331).

25. *L&P* 16 (1332).

26. *L&P* 16 (1333); *State Papers During the Reign of Henry VIII*, 11 vols. (1830–2), Vol. 1, p. 694.

27. *State Papers During the Reign of Henry VIII*, Vol. 1, p. 694.

25 The Last Years of Henry VIII

1. *Hamilton Papers* (ed J. Bain), Vol. 1 (1890), pp. 337, 338. One, Oliver Sinclair, was carrying the banner.

2. George Douglas' report: *Hamilton Papers* (ed J. Bain), Vol. 1 (1890), pp. 339, 340.

3. Marjorie Bruce.

4. So claimed John Knox.

5. Sir John Haywood, *The Life and Reign of King Edward VI* (1630), p. 196.

6. *L&P* 18, Pt I (210), Pt II (202) (257) (275) (281). There were doubts about the legitimacy of the governor of Scotland and heir

presumptive, the Earl of Arran, who had also emerged as an enemy of Henry's plans.

7. *L&P* 19, Pt I (522): 'if Lenaxe perform the above covenants according to the king's expectation, and Lady Margaret and Lenaxe on seeing each other agree for that purpose, he will both agree to the marriage and further consider Lenaxe's good service'.

8. Matthew Stuart, Earl of Lennox, quoting Robert Lindsay of Pittscottie, *Oxford Dictionary of National Biography*.

9. *L&P* 19, Pt I (799).

10. *L&P* 19, Pt II (201). Her husband was already back in Scotland on the king's business. While she was named, her cousins Frances and Eleanor were not.

11. Henry, Lord Darnley was named after the king and was then six months old. Her first son had died.

12. *L&P* 21, Pt I (969).

13. William Thomas quoted in John Strype, *Ecclesiastical Memorials Relating Chiefly to Religion*, Vol. 2, Pt I (1822), p. 13.

14. British Library Harleian MSS 5087 f. 11; Chris Skidmore, *Edward VI: The Lost King of England* (2007), pp. 38, 39.

15. Anne of Beaujeu had played such a role for her brother Charles VIII of France when Henry VII was in exile there.

16. Starkey, *Six Wives*, pp. 752–64.

17. Thank you to Tom Freeman for allowing me to see a forthcoming and groundbreaking essay on the story recorded in Foxe on which my comments are based. It will appear under the title 'One survived' in a collection on Henry VIII and his court edited by Tom Betteridge and Suzannah Lipscomb, and is due to be published by Ashgate in the UK in 2013.

18. William Herbert was a distant kinsman of Henry VII's guardian.

19. Thanks to John Guy for drawing my attention to the fact the Stuarts were ignored in Henry's will, and not barred.

20. *L&P* 21, Pt II (181).

21. According to this story Henry was so protective of the reputation of this individual, who acted as an English spy in Scotland, that Margaret's accusations against him 'ever after lost a part of [the king's] heart, as appeared at his death'. British Library Cotton MS Caligula B VIII, ff. 165–8.

22. She would affectionately keep a tablet picture of the king until she died. See her will online, National Archives Prob 11/60; also see my Appendix on Margaret Douglas.

26 Elizabeth in Danger

1. Thurley, *Royal Palaces*, p. 236.
2. His eyes were described as grey by Girolamo Cardano, *Opera*, Vol. 5 (1663), pp. 503–8.
3. *L&P* 19, Pt II (201).
4. David Starkey, *Elizabeth: The Struggle for the Throne* (2000), p. 39.
5. 'Bede' is a prayer, from Old English 'bidden', to pray.
6. In Catholic legend it was at Syon that a prophecy given by the Observant Franciscan William Peto is said to have come to pass. Peto had given a sermon before Henry VIII at Greenwich in 1532, comparing Henry VIII to King Ahab – whose wife Jezebel had replaced the Lord's true prophets with the pagan priests of Baal, the obvious inference being that Boleyn was England's Jezebel. Peto went on to warn Henry that if he continued to behave like Ahab then his corpse would suffer the same indignity that had befallen the Israelite king (after his death wild dogs had licked Ahab's blood). It was later said that at Syon Henry's coffin burst as a result of gases leaking from the putrefying body and a dog licked the blood that dripped from it.
7. Jennifer Loach, 'The Function of Ceremonial in the Reign of Henry VIII' in *Past & Present* 142, I (1994), p. 63.
8. Francesco Cagliotti, 'Benedetto da Rovezzano in England: New Light on the Cardinal Wolsey-Henry VII Tomb' in *The Anglo-Florentine Art for the Early Tudors* (eds Cinzia Maria Sicca and

Louis A. Waldman) (2012), pp. 177–293. My thanks to Dr Clare Rider at St George's Chapel Archives and Chapter Library for further information.

9. Strype, *Memorials*, Vol. 2, Pt II (1822), pp. 292–311.
10. Nicander Nacius, quoted in Susan E. James, *Kateryn Parr: The Making of a Queen* (1999), p. 88.
11. The sculptor Nicholas Bellin de Modena, who would work on Henry's tomb in the Westminster Abbey workshop with his wages paid by Edward VI, was unable to finish his work because the new iconoclastic 'priests of Westminster' kept throwing him out as a papist (Judith M. Walker, *English Literary Renaissance 26*, issue 3 [September 1996], n. 17 p. 520). Edward VI asked in his will that money be put aside to finish the tomb, but although Elizabeth I would eventually move what was left at Westminster to Windsor, nothing further was done. Henry VIII's unfinished tomb was eventually demolished by order of the Long Parliament in 1646, the brass statues sold to pay for the garrison at Windsor, with the additional order 'that such images as may be used in any superstitious manner be defaced'. At least some parts of the monument were discovered during the reign of Charles II, but what happened then is unknown. (Windsor Chapter Acts, 31 May 1661.) Two nine-feet tall bronze candlesticks ended up in St Bavon's Cathedral in Ghent, replicas of which were later commissioned by Edward VII, and now stand by the high altar in St George's. There is also some debate over two large angels, which may be original or copies of those from Henry VIII's tomb, and which were sold by Sotheby's in 1994. It was also under Edward VI that the chapel's relics were removed to be sold or destroyed. These appear to have included Henry VI's hat and spurs (which were mentioned in an inventory of 1534) and a piece of his bedstead, which were revered by pilgrims to his shrine. *The Inventories of St George's Chapel, Windsor Castle, 1384–1667* (ed Maurice Bond) (1947), pp. 284–6. Nevertheless, Edward's will repeated Henry

VIII's instructions that the tomb be made more princely. *Literary Remains of King Edward the Sixth* (ed J. G. Nichols) (1857), p. 576. The tomb was described by Paul Hentzner in 1598, but John Speed recorded that it had disappeared by 1611. It appears to have fallen into decay and so been removed. Edward IV's tomb also suffered: his coat of mail and banner, which were hung over his grave, were plundered during the Civil War in 1642. Thanks to Dr Clare Rider for this information.

12. *CSPS* 9 pp. 46, 47.
13. Ives, *The Reformation Experience*, p. 181.
14. Stow, *Survey of London*, p. 54.
15. De Lisle, *Sisters*, p. 37.
16. *Chronicle of the Grey Friars*, p. 55.
17. J. L. McIntosh, *From Heads of Household to Heads of State* (2009), Appendix A. The following year, Henry VIII's widow Katherine Parr told her Master of the Horse that all the lands given to supporters of the Protectorate should be returned to the king when he reached his majority: a conversation that suggests there were concerns about the morality of their actions.
18. Janet Arnold, 'The Coronation Portrait of Queen Elizabeth' in *Burlington Magazine* 120 (1978), pp. 727–41.
19. John Astley joined Elizabeth's household before 1540. McIntosh, *From Heads of Household*, p. 89.
20. *Original letters* (ed Ellis), Vol. 2, p. 150.
21. Susan James, *Catherine Parr: Henry VIII's Last Love* (2008), p. 323.
22. Katherine Parr's chaplain, John Parkhurst, wrote her epitaph in Latin as if spoken by the little girl: 'With what great travail/And at her life's expense/My mother, the queen, gave birth/A wayfarer I, her infant child/lie beneath this marble stone/If cruel death had given me/A longer while to live/Those virtues of that best of mothers . . . Would have lived again as my own nature/Now whoever you are, farewell.'
23. *Elizabeth, Selected Works* (ed Steven May) (2004), p. 113.

24. Written by the seventeenth-century Italian writer Gregorio Leti.

25. *Katherine Parr: Complete Works and Correspondence* (ed Janel Mueller) (2011), pp. 623, 624, 625.

27 Mary in Danger

1. February 1550.

2. *Literary Remains of King Edward the Sixth* (ed Nichols), p. 227.

3. *CSPS* 9 , 7 November 1549.

4. The date of this visit is often given as 1550. This is a misreading of the source. The following February is described as being in the fourth year of Edward's reign – which began in January 1550, making the previous November, 1549. *HMC Report on the Manuscripts of Lord Middleton preserved at Wollaton Hall, Notts.* (London 1911), p. 520.

5. This description of Frances' appearance is based on her tomb effigy and not the double portrait of the overweight Lady Dacre and her son which is still sometimes mistakenly referred to as a portrait of Frances and Adrian Stokes.

6. Queen's College Oxford MSS 349.

7. Frances' close relationship with her daughter was recorded by Jane's Italian tutor, Michel Angelo Florio.

8. From the Latin '*monstrare*' meaning 'to show': the monstrance is a stand, often with an elaborate sunburst design, and with a crystal or glass circular panel in the centre to display the host.

9. hrionline/i563 edition, Bk 12, p. 1,746.

10. De Lisle, *Sisters*, pp. 26, 27.

11. Edward VI referred to Henry Grey as Harry in his diary. I have done so simply to avoid referring to yet another Henry in the text.

12. *CSPS* 10, 14 January (1550–2). Elizabeth also found herself in difficulties with the new regime. John Dudley attempted to grab Hatfield, given to her in 1547 and which had belonged to her great-grandmother, Margaret Beaufort. He failed largely because

at sixteen she had reached what was the age of majority for a woman, and had legal title to her estates.

13. Diarmaid MacCulloch, *The Boy King: Edward VI and the Protestant Reformation* (2002), p. 134. He bases this on 'the extraordinarily small survival rates of known books'. The medieval donational books in the royal library were also ruthlessly weeded out.

14. British Library Add MSS 10169, f. 56v.

15. Henry Machyn, *The Diary of Henry Machyn* (ed J. G. Nichols) (1848), pp. 4, 5.

16. 22 January 1552.

17. Lennox's relations with the royal guest Mary of Guise were, however, rather trickier. Mary of Guise had been in France planning her return to Scotland as regent, and visiting her daughter who was betrothed to the dauphin. While she was there one of Lennox's kinsmen was arrested for a plot to poison the little girl by lacing her favourite frittered pears. It was said that Lennox hoped killing Mary, Queen of Scots would clear the path for his becoming King of Scots. Lennox had been sufficiently embarrassed to offer to give up his claim to the Scottish throne altogether, and despite the tensions the dinner passed without incident. *CSPS* 10, June 1551, and *England's Boy King: The Diary of Edward VI, 1547–1553* (ed Jonathan North) (2005), n. 3 p. 82.

18. John Aylmer, *An harbrowe for faithful and trew subjects* (1559, reprinted 1972), margin ref: 'The pomp of English ladies abated by the queen's example.'

19. *CSPV* 1534–54, pp. 535–6.

20. *CSPD* 7 April 1552.

21. Girolamo Cardano, who was much admired by Edward's tutor, Sir John Cheke.

22. Diarmaid MacCulloch, *Thomas Cranmer: A Life* (1996), p. 509; Mark Nicholls, *A History of the Modern British Isles 1529–1603* (1999), p. 138.

28 The Last Tudor King

1. He stopped writing his diary at this time.
2. Barrett L. Beer, *Northumberland: Political Career of John Dudley, Earl of Warwick and Duke of Northumberland* (1974), p. 109; see also Gilbert Burnet, *The History of the Reformation* Vol. 1 (1841), p. 453.
3. *Original Letters* (ed Ellis), Vol. 2, pp. 145, 146n. The letter is undated. David Starkey argues it was written around Candlemas (February); Starkey, *Elizabeth*, p. 108. It may even have been marginally earlier: see *England under the reigns of Edward VI and Mary* (ed Patrick Fraser Tytler) (1839), Vol. 1, pp. 161, 162.
4. *Diary of Edward VI* (ed North), p. 128.
5. According to an anonymous French source, his evangelical tutor, Sir John Cheke, and his confessor, Thomas Goodrich, Bishop of Ely, urged him on in this.
6. 'The *Vita Mariae Angliae Reginae* of Robert Wingfield of Brantham' (tr. and ed D. MacCulloch) in *Camden Miscellany XXVIII*, Camden fourth series, Vol. 29 (1984), p. 247.
7. Her symptoms suggest renal tuberculosis.
8. Edward envisaged that the mother of the future king would act as governor until her son reached the age of eighteen. She could do nothing, however, without the sanction of an inner core of the council, men whom Edward would appoint. When the king reached fourteen, his agreement would also be required. The will included a proviso that if there were no male children at the time of Edward's death, Frances was to be appointed governor until such time as one was born. But he clearly did not think this a likely event, since he made no further mention of the council's sanction.
9. The wife was Elizabeth Brooke. Conyers Read, *Mr Secretary Cecil & Queen Elizabeth* (1955), pp. 94, 95. John Dudley claimed during his later confessions that it had been a joint decision promoted by Harry Grey, Duke of Suffolk, William Herbert, Earl of Pembroke and William Parr, Marquess of Northampton.

10. His godfather Diego Hurtado de Mendoza was in England June 1537 to the end of August 1538. Mary Tudor played godparent to a Dudley son (perhaps Guildford) March 1537. It is likely Henry Dudley was a younger brother as he was married to a less prestigious bride.

11. She was said to be acquainted with another four.

12. Commendone, in C. V. Malfatti, *The Accession, Coronation and Marriage of Mary Tudor as Related in Four Manuscripts of the Escorial* (1956), p. 5; de Lisle, *Sisters*, pp. 68–70. This is one area where Eric Ives and I agreed.

13. Richard Grafton, *Abridgement of the Chronicles of England* (1563) in *The Chronicle of Queen Jane, and of two years of Queen Mary* (ed J. G. Nichols) (1850), p. 55.

14. *CSPS* 11, p. 35.

15. John Dudley had expressed mild concern about the king's health that summer, and by the end of November he had stopped writing his diary.

16. *CSPS* 11, p. 35.

17. McIntosh, *From Heads of Household*, pp. 150, 151, 155. Strenuous efforts were also made to heal other quarrels. For example, the rift with Archbishop Cranmer that had opened at Somerset's execution was addressed with plans to release the Protector's widow from the Tower.

18. *The Discovery of Muscovy, from the Collections of Richard Hakluyt* (1889), openlibrary.org, pp. 17, 18.

19. The list is a long and complex one, but worth recording: Harry Grey agreed to marry his second daughter, Katherine, aged twelve, to William Parr's nephew, the fifteen-year-old Lord Henry Herbert, son of William Herbert, the Earl of Pembroke. The youngest, Mary Grey, a stunted child of nine, was betrothed to a middle-aged kinsman, Lord Grey of Wilton. A battle-scarred warrior, whose face had been disfigured by a Scottish pike thrust through the roof of his mouth in 1547, Grey of Wilton must have

looked terrifying to the little girl. He was regarded, however, as 'the best soldier in the kingdom'. John Dudley's youngest son, Henry Dudley, was to marry Harry Grey's only niece of marriageable age, the non-royal but very rich heiress, Margaret Audley. This would help further bind the two families. His daughter, Katherine Dudley – also aged twelve – was to marry Henry Hastings, the teenage son of the Greys' neighbour the evangelical Earl of Huntingdon. The boy's mother was descended from the daughter of Edward IV's brother, the Duke of Clarence – and although not a Tudor he had the advantage of being male. A few weeks later one more marriage would also be arranged. The Earl of Cumberland had rejected Guildford Dudley for his royal daughter, Margaret Clifford, the previous summer. But mysteriously he now agreed to marry her instead to John Dudley's aging older brother, Sir Henry Dudley.

20. *CSPS* 11, p. 55. How willingly the judges gave their agreement is a matter of debate. The judges in question later recalled that they agreed that, aged fifteen, he was still a minor and his father's will therefore remained valid. They insisted they gave way only after Edward promised pardons under the Great Seal for any treason they might commit in obeying his instructions. But after Mary became queen they had good reason to wish it to appear they had been pressurised.

21. Under English law half-siblings could not inherit off each other. See n. 23, http://www.somegreymatter.com/rossoenglish.htm. However, as Eric Ives informed me, this applies only for assets pertaining to the parent from which the half-sibling in question has no blood connection. This would not apply to Elizabeth and Mary as children of Henry VIII. Edward was on safer ground in excluding them as bastards.

22. www.tudorplace.com.ar/documents/EdwardWill.htm.

23. McIntosh, *From Heads of Household*, p. 162.

24. Ibid., p. 163.

25. *CSPS* 11, p. 70.
26. The aristocrat, Antoine de Noailles.
27. *The Discovery of Muscovy, from the Collections of Richard Hakluyt*, openlibrary.org, p. 23. I was inspired here by a passage in Edith Sitwell's *The Queens and the Hive*.

Part Three
SETTING SUN:
THE TUDOR QUEENS

29 Nine Days

1. No one has ever seen the manuscript he refers to, and I discovered he gives a different description of Jane in a book published a year later. See, for example, Leanda de Lisle, 'Faking Jane' in *New Criterion* (September 2009), the paperback UK edition and US hardback of de Lisle, *Sisters*.
2. There is no source dating from Jane's reign, or before it, that she had said, on hearing of Edward's decision, that she believed Mary was the rightful ruler, as her French allies later claimed she had.
3. Its chief 'captains' under Edward VI were the foreigners John Calvin, Peter Martyr, Heinrich Bullinger 'and such other rutterkyns [crafty creatures]', one pamphleteer noted, adding of these, 'I would to God thou hadst [stayed] drunk with Hans and Jacob in Strasbourg . . . I would to God thou hadst remained in Switzerland.' Duffy, *Saints, Sacrilege, Sedition*, p. 19.
4. *CSPS* 11, 7 and 10 July.
5. Tracy Borman, *Elizabeth's Women: The Hidden Story of the Virgin Queen* (2009), p. 133.
6. Elizabeth's tutor Roger Ascham would later claim that he had long prepared Elizabeth for rule, but Ascham played up the achievements of a number of evangelical women (Jane Grey is another) while ignoring the achievements of conservatives. One example is the young aristocrat Lady Jane Fitzalan. This relative unknown was

the first person to translate one of Euripides' plays into English and in doing so composed the earliest piece of extant English drama by a woman. On Elizabeth's and Mary's education, see Aysha Pollnitz, 'Christian Women or Sovereign Queens? The Schooling of Mary and Elizabeth' in *Tudor Queenship: The Reigns of Mary and Elizabeth* (ed Anna Whitelock and Alice Hunt) (2010), p. 136.

7. *CSPS* 11, 11 July.

8. *CSPS* 11, p. 83; the Lord Treasurer William Paulet, Marquess of Winchester, brought the jewels to her on 12 July (British Library Harleian MSS 611, f. 1a).

9. Wriothesley, *Chronicle*, Vol. 2, p. 87.

10. Alan Bryson, '"The speciall men in every shere": The Edwardian regime, 1547–1553', PhD diss., St Andrews (2001), p. 280.

11. The Protestant John de Vere, Earl of Oxford, was persuaded by his common servants to imprison his own pro-Grey gentlemen. Amongst them were several members of the Golding family, one of whom later witnessed Mary Grey's marriage to Thomas Keyes. See *Oxford Dictionary of National Biography* for the Earl of Oxford, and de Lisle, *Sisters*, for Mary Grey's marriage.

12. There are echoes here of Jane as the 'queen of a new and pretty invention'. Oxburgh Hall, Bedingfield MSS in Porter, *Mary Tudor*, pp. 208, 209.

13. De Lisle, *Sisters*, p. 121.

14. Lady Throckmorton. Her father, Sir Nicholas Carew, had been an ally to Charles Brandon, Duke of Suffolk, and as a widow she would later marry Frances' widower, Adrian Stokes.

15. Lady Throckmorton.

16. *Narratives of the days of the Reformation* (ed J. G. Nichols) (1859), pp. 151, 152, 153, 226; Estienne Perlin, *Description des Royaulmes D'Angleterre et D'Escosse 1558* (1775), pp. vi, vii; *CSPS* 11, p. 113; *CSPD, Edward VI and Mary I* (ed C. S. Knighton) (1998), p. 344.

17. Julius Ternetianius to Ab Ulmis; *Original Letters Relative to the English Reformation* (ed Hastings Robinson), Vol. 1 (1846), p. 367.

18. N. P. Sil, *Tudor Placemen and Statesmen: Select Case Histories* (2001), p. 86.
19. *CSPS* 11, 4 September.
20. Elizabeth would wear the same costume for the same procession – a strong indication that Mary wore what the contemporary recorders described. J. R. Planché, *Regal Records: or a Chronicle of the Coronations of the Queen Regnants of England* (1838), p. 6. The story of her wearing a huge heavy crown that she had to hold on her head is later anti-Marian propaganda.
21. Malfatti, *The Accession, Coronation and Marriage of Mary Tudor*, p. 67.

30 Revolt

1. *CSPS* 11, 19 October 1553.
2. Ibid.
3. On 10 October; see Porter, *Mary Tudor*, p. 276.
4. Anna Whitelock, *Mary Tudor: England's First Queen* (2010), p. 224.
5. *CSPS* 11, 28 November 1553.
6. The case for the Grey family's 'innocence' was made in Robert Wingfield's *Vita Mariae Angliae Reginae*. This ignored the religious basis of the attempt to exclude Mary from the throne. Instead Frances is said to have opposed Jane's marriage in May 1553, but John Dudley persuaded her husband, nevertheless, to agree to it by promising 'a scarcely imaginable haul of great wealth and honour to his house'. In other words he had been bought off, just as the regime had tried to buy Mary off. It was further claimed that after the wedding, John Dudley had tried to poison Harry Grey, just as he had supposedly poisoned Edward. Doing so would have cleared the way for Guildford to be crowned in a joint ceremony with Jane, thus achieving Dudley's supposed ambition to make his son king (De Lisle, *Sisters*, pp. 126, 127).
7. Prince Philip of Spain and William of Orange.
8. A girdle prayer book from this period, which by tradition belonged to Elizabeth, and was passed by descent through her Boleyn

relatives, contains a 'manuscript copy of the last prayer of Edward VI': the sort of thing Jane's might also have contained. The book had gold enamelled covers, with a classical head (not black velvet), and had belonged to the Carey family – Henry Carey, the elder son of Mary Boleyn was at this time a gentleman in Elizabeth's household. Hugh Tait, 'The Girdle Prayer Book or "Tablet"' in *Jewellery Studies* 2 (1985), p. 53.

9. It wasn't often carried out, but Henry VIII burned a gentlewoman for treason in 1537, and in 1538 James V burned an aunt of Margaret Douglas.

10. De Lisle, *Sisters*, p. 139. The Catholic convert in question was Thomas Harding.

11. The Lord Chamberlain was Sir John Gage.

12. A. F. Pollard, *Tudor Tracts* (1903), p. 190.

13. *The Chronicle of Queen Jane* (ed Nichols), p. 49.

14. John Foxe, *Acts and Monuments* (ed Stephen Reed) (1838), Vol. 6, Bk 10, pp. 1,418–9.

15. *Narratives of the days of the Reformation* (ed Nichols), p. 161.

16. Pollard, *Tudor Tracts*, p. 190.

17. *The Chronicle of Queen Jane* (ed Nichols), p. 49; John Ponet, *A Shorte Treatise of Politike Pouuer* (1556) in Winthrop Hudson, *John Ponet* (1942), p. 134.

18. Nor does she cast any blame on her father for her death. This contrasts with a fraudulent letter which appeared in 1570, published by John Foxe. In this Jane proclaims her innocence and implies her father is responsible for her fate. In the prayer book Guildford had also composed a farewell to Jane's father, although the optimism concerning his fate suggests it was written before the Wyatt revolt failed, and after Guildford's conviction for treason in November. It reads 'your loving and obedient son wisheth unto your grace long life in this world with as much joy and comfort as ever I wished to myself, and in the world to come joy everlasting, your most humble son to his death GDudley'. I am not convinced

by Janel Mueller's contention that the flourish that follows is an 'r' for 'rex' as a) Rex would have been done with a capital R, b) he would have signed it Guildford R, and c) he would surely not have signed it thus after 19 July. Thank you to Dr Andrea Clarke of the British Library for her advice and comments on the transcription. Mueller also points out the interesting detail that the prayer book contains prayers already written in the Tower by the Catholic martyrs Thomas More and John Fisher.

19. *The Chronicle of Queen Jane* (ed Nichols), p. 55.

20. Ibid., pp. 56, 57; *The Literary Remains of Lady Jane Grey* (ed N. H. Nicolas) (1825), pp. 58–9. The Lieutenant of the Tower was Sir John Bridges.

31 Marriage and Sons

1. Harry Grey also sent John Harington, whose son and namesake was Elizabeth's godson.

2. Frances' stepmother, Katherine Willoughby, Duchess of Suffolk, the widow of Charles Brandon, had married her gentleman usher Richard Bertie, sometime before 20 March the previous year. Frances was close to her, and may have married Stokes at her suggestion. Katherine Willoughby would flee to exile in Europe later that year. Stokes was approximately eighteen months younger than Frances. For the marriage date, see PRO C 142/128/91 for the inquisition post-mortem on Frances; I had previously assumed she had married in 1555, since no mention was made of her marriage in the royal gifts of land to her in 1554.

3. Frances' marriage would, unfortunately, later tap into the old prejudices about women being unable to control their lust. In 1727, a portrait by Hans Eworth of the hard-faced Lady Dacre and her beardless twenty-one-year-old son was mislabelled as being of Frances and Stokes (who was, in fact, close to her in age). Historians afterwards made much of the resemblance of the female sitter to Henry VIII in his later years, and a myth grew up

that Frances was not only lustful but matched her royal uncle in cruelty and ambition. Stokes was, in fact, only about eighteen months younger than Frances. See Appendix 4 on Frances.

4. english history.net/tudor/marydesc.html.

5. *The Chronicle of Queen Jane* (ed Nichols), p. 166; tudorhistory. org/primary/janemary/app10.html.

6. *CSPS* 13 (37).

7. *Narratives of the days of Reformation* (ed Nichols), p. 289.

8. Loades, *Mary Tudor*, p. 239.

9. *The Chronicle of Queen Jane* (ed Nichols), p. 163.

10. Ives, *The Reformation Experience*, p. 213.

11. Ibid., p. 205.

12. Her ladies included such Protestants as Lady Anne Bacon.

13. By 1559 fourteen per cent of Sussex wills and by 1560 ten per cent of Kent wills would use Protestant formulae, and behind these figures lay the zealous faithful. Sue Doran, *Elizabeth I & Religion* (1994), p. 48.

14. A total of 312 died, when those who died in prison are added to the number burned at the stake.

15. The friar was John Forrest. The mockery would not have troubled Latimer. 'If it be your pleasure that I shall play the fool after my customary manner when Forrest shall suffer,' he had written to Cromwell, 'I would wish that my stage stood near to Forrest.'

16. John Foxe wrote to the queen, Lord Burghley, the Privy Council and the Ecclesiastical Commissioners, urging that the sentences of two Flemish Anabapists be commuted. His efforts were to no avail and they were burned at Smithfield on 22 July 1575.

17. Henry VIII had burned a mere seventy-six; Thomas Freeman, 'Burning Zeal' in *Mary Tudor: Old & New Perspectives* (ed Susan Doran and Thomas Freeman) (2011), p. 180.

18. *CSPV* 13 (884).

19. PRO C 142/128/91. Frances had a baby that month, and named

her Elizabeth, a telling indication of where it was judged the future now lay. Frances's elder daughters all had names with royal connections: Jane Grey, after Queen Jane Seymour (1537), Katherine Grey after Queen Katherine Howard (1540), and Mary Grey after Mary Tudor was appointed Edward's heir in the Third Act of Succession. It therefore seems probable Elizabeth Stokes was named after Elizabeth Tudor. She died in infancy.

20. Doctors I have spoken to note that autoimmune hyperthyroid disease is quite a common condition, especially in women. It runs in families and I do wonder if Elizabeth also suffered from it, as I discuss later. 'Thyroid Dysfunction and False Pregnancy' in *Western Journal of Medicine* (January 1992), p. 89. A much more rare condition, with symptoms that mimic those associated with pregnancy, would be benign tumours on the pituitary gland. On the benign tumour theory, see M. Keynes, 'The Aching and increasing blindness of Queen Mary' in *Journal of Medical Biography* 8/2 (2000), pp. 102–9. Suggestions that she suffered from ovarian cancer seem less likely, as this would have killed her relatively quickly.

21. Charles' empire in the Netherlands included the inheritance of the former Dukes of Burgundy inherited through his paternal grandmother (Marie, the daughter of Charles the Bold), except for the province of Burgundy itself, which had passed to France. He had added to these, however, and united seventeen provinces in the region, a rich and densely populated area covering the modern Netherlands, Belgium, Luxembourg, much of northern France, and extending even into western Germany.

32 A Flickering Light

1. Starkey, *Elizabeth*, p. 78.
2. *Elizabeth I: Collected Works* (ed Leah S. Marcus, Janel Mueller and Mary Beth Rose) (2002), pp. 43–4.
3. On 1 December 1556.

4. When she described it to the Count of Feria at Brocket Hall in November 1559.

5. *CSPV* 6 (884).

6. Ibid.

7. *CSPS* 13 (339).

8. R. A. Houlbrooke, *Death, Religion and Family in England 1480–1750* (1998), p. 6.

9. See note 12.

10. *CSPV* 6 (884).

11. 'The Count of Feria's Dispatch to Philip II of 14 November 1558' (ed and tr. Simon Adams and M. Rodriguez-Salgado) in *Camden Miscellany XXVIII*, Camden Fourth Series, Vol. 29 (1984), p. 332.

12. Ibid., pp. 330–3.

13. *CSPV* 6 (884).

14. 'The Count of Feria's Dispatch to Philip II of 14 November 1558' (ed Adams and Rodriguez) in op. cit., p. 335.

15. *CSPV* 13 (884).

33 A Married Man

1. Glyn Parry, *The Arch-Conjurer of England, John Dee* (2011), pp. 48, 49.

2. *CSPV* 7 (10).

3. De Lisle, *Sisters*, p. 224.

4. Dale Hoak, 'The Coronations of Edward VI, Mary I, and Elizabeth I, and the Transformation of the Tudor monarchy' in *Westmintser Abbey Reformed* (ed C. S. Knighton and Richard Mortimer) (2003), pp. 139, 140, 141.

5. The treatise was written by Jane Grey's former tutor John Aylmer and published by John Day in April 1554.

6. *Elizabeth I: Collected Works*, p. 58.

7. *CSPS* Simancas 1 (29).

8. *CSPS* Simancas 1 (27).

9. Philip's empire in the Netherlands had been increased and unified by his father Charles V. See Chapter 31, Note 21.

10. *CSPS* Simancas 1, p. 45; de Lisle, *Sisters*, p. 187.

11. Richard Rex, *Elizabeth I* (2003), p. 55.

12. His opponent's lance had pierced his headgear and shattered into fragments, penetrating his right orbit and temple.

13. British Library Harleian MSS 4712.

14. Richard Rex, *The Tudors* (2011), p. 165 for comparisons with similarly staged scenes.

15. *CSPF* 1559–60, p. 370.

16. Ives, *The Reformation Experience*, pp. 143, 46.

17. *CSPS* Simancas 1, 11 September 1560 (119).

34 Dangerous Cousins

1. *CSPS* Simancas 1, 11 September 1560 (119).

2. Ibid.

3. Ibid.

4. A fact that attracted support from the Earl of Huntingdon, a Protestant descendant of Edward IV's brother, the Duke of Clarence.

5. *CSPS* Simancas 1 (120).

6. In a response to a parliamentary delegation on her marriage, 1566.

7. Named after the new King of France, Charles IX.

8. Darnley was the senior male heir to the kingdoms of England (through his mother) and Scotland (through his father).

9. *CSPF* 5 (412). She was in direct contact with Lennox's brother in France, and in Spain with Jane Dormer, the English wife of Philip II's confidant, the Count of Feria.

10. The messenger was John Gordon, Earl of Sutherland.

11. *CSPF* 5 (26).

12. Ibid.

13. *CSPF* 5 (26) (332).

14. Cecil's immediate reasons had concerned Robert Dudley, who had promised the Spanish he would ensure Elizabeth sent a representative to the Council of Trent on church reform if Philip supported

his marriage to Elizabeth. The publicity surrounding the Catholic witchcraft trials had helped confound Dudley, by discrediting the Spanish ambassador and smearing Catholics in general.

15. *CSPS* Simancas 1 (144) (153) (154) (155) (156).
16. British Library Add MSS 37749, ff. 41, 50, 58.
17. *Miscellaneous State Papers from 1501 to 1726* (ed Philip Yorke, Earl of Hardwicke) (1778), Vol. 1, p. 172; British Library Add MSS 37740, f. 63.
18. British Library Add MSS 37749, ff. 43, 59.
19. De Lisle, *Sisters*, p. 206.
20. British Library Add MSS 37749, ff. 41, 50, 58. For more details see de Lisle, *Sisters*.
21. For more on this and who else was linked to the marriage, see de Lisle, *Sisters*, Chapters 17, 18 and 19.
22. *CSPS* Simancas 1, p. 214.
23. *CSPF* 5 (26).

35 Royal Prisoners

1. *CSPS* Simancas 1 (144).
2. *A Collection of State Papers relating to Affairs in the Reigns of King Henry VIII, King Edward VI, Queen Mary and Queen Elizabeth from the year 1542–1570, Left by William Cecil Lord Burghley* (ed Samuel Haynes), Vol. 1 (1740), p. 378.
3. British Library Cotton MS Caligula B VIII, ff. 165–8, 184–5. Thanks to John Guy for drawing my attention to this MSS. See the Appendix on Margaret Douglas.
4. *CSPF* 5 (26); *CSPD* 1547–89, March 1562 (48).
5. *CSPF* 4 (980); *CSPF* 5 (168).
6. *CSPF* 5 (59) (168); *CSPD* 1547–80, 14 May, 12 and 19 June, 1562; *CSPD* 1547–80, 20 September 1560.
7. *CSPF* 5 (181).
8. *CSPF* 5 (168).
9. *CSPF* 5 (34).

10. Glyn Parry, *Arch-Conjurer*, p. 61.

11. *CSPF* 5 (26) (34) (412).

12. Norman Jones, *Birth of the Elizabethan Age: England in the 1560s* (1995), p. 38. Thomas Bishop had noted Margaret quoting the prophecy concerning Darnley becoming King of England and Scotland. *CSPF* 5 (26).

13. *CSPF* 5 (26).

14. *CSPF* 5 (121) (223).

15. Bishop concluded his long list of Margaret's supposed crimes by denying her English birth, on the grounds that her mother, Margaret Tudor, had been a refugee from Scotland when she was born. He claimed she was also excluded from the throne under the terms of the marriage contract between Margaret Tudor and James IV, which was also nonsense. For the marriage contract, see PRO E39/92/18 E 30/81; for Bishop's claims, see *CSPF* 5 (26).

16. *CSPF* 5 (912).

17. They were arrested on 14 October. Parry, p. 61 Huntingdon was a great-great-grandson of the Duke of Clarence twice in the female line. Arthur was the great-grandson once in the female line.

18. *CSPS* Simancas 1, p. 296.

19. *Reports From the Lost Notebooks of Sir James Dyer, Vol. 1* (ed J. H. Baker) (1994) p. 82; Longleat PO/I/93.

20. Longleat PO/I/93.

21. Mortimer Levine, *The Early Elizabethan Succession Question, 1558–1568* (1966), p. 28; HMC Salisbury Vol. 1 (1883), p. 396.

22. Longleat PO Vol. 1, ff. 92, 93.

23. De Lisle, *Sisters*, p. 245.

24. *CSPV* 5 (934).

25. The title was usually reserved for royal children in right of the Duchy of Lancaster.

26. John Guy, *My Heart is My Own: The Life of Mary Queen of Scots* (2004), p. 198.

27. Or so the emissary Sir James Melville later recalled.

28. The baby was born in July 1564 and christened at Cecil House. See John Nichols, *The Progresses and Public Processions of Queen Elizabeth, Vol. 1* (1823), p. 149.
29. Guy, *My Heart is My Own*, pp. 205, 206.

36 Murder in the Family

1. *CSPS* Simancas 1 (286).
2. *CSPS* Simancas 1 (290). I have modernised some of the English and punctuation in this translation.
3. Ibid., and ditto.
4. *CSPS* Simancas 1 (144). The arrival in Scotland of Margaret Douglas' husband, the Earl of Lennox, had also triggered a realignment of the noble factions, with his allies lined up against those of Mary's illegitimate half-brother, the Protestant and pro-English Earl of Moray.
5. *CSPS* Simancas 1 (296).
6. *CSPS* Simancas 1 (314); Charlotte Isabelle Merton, 'The Women who Served Queen Mary and Queen Elizabeth', PhD diss., Trinity College, Cambridge (1992), pp. 64, 66.
7. Kristen Walton, 'The Queen's Aunt; The King's Mother: Margaret Douglas, Countess of Lennox, religion and politics in the Scottish Court, 1565–72' (unpublished), p. 3.
8. *CSPS* Simancas 1 (357).
9. Arthur and Edmund Pole. The Poles would remain in the Tower until their deaths.
10. *CSPS* Simancas 1 (365).
11. *CSPS* Simancas 1 (405).
12. *CSPS* 1 (409).
13. *CSP* Scotland 2 (477).
14. The Duke of Savoy's ambassador Signor di Moretta, *CSPV* 7, 1558–80, 20 March 1567 (384).
15. See Linda Porter, *Crown of Thistles: The Fatal Interitance of Mary, Queen of Scots* (2013).

16. De Lisle, *Sisters*, pp. 264, 265.

17. Sir David's daughter Ann married Sir Arthur Hopton; Blaauw, 'On the Effigy . . .' in op. cit., p. 26.

18. *Notes and Queries*, Eleventh Series, Vol. 5 (January-June 1912), p. 82, Eighth Series, Vol. 8 (February–August 1895), p. 233.

19. British Library Cotton Titus MS No. 107, ff. 124, 131.

20. Ibid.

21. Katherine's clothes and a prayer book survived into the twentieth century, along with a chest. The clothes and prayer book vanished, however, after the house was bombed during World War II. If these items really did belong to Katherine it suggests the Hoptons kept them almost as relics. It is also worth noting that Sir Owen attended Mary Grey's funeral ten years later. Thanks to Caroline Blois for information on the Katherine Grey prayer book and clothing. For Mary Grey's funeral, see de Lisle, *Sisters*, p. 290 and notes.

22. *The Literary Remains of Lady Jane Grey* (ed Nicolas).

23. Andy Wood, *Riot, Rebellion and Popular Politics in Early Modern England* (2002), p. 73.

24. Speech to parliamentary deputation with a petition requesting she marry and name an heir, 1566 Levine EESQ pp. 184, 185. Susan Doran, *Monarchy and Matrimony: The courtships of Elizabeth I* (1996), p. 87.

37 Exit Margaret Douglas

1. These are only some of twenty-eight emblems and six verses.

2. *CSP* Scotland 3 (110).

3. Charles had spent time imprisoned with her at Sheen in 1562, and in 1565 when she was in the Tower he had been placed in the care of a servant of the state, a man called John Vaughan. *CSPD* 1 (25).

4. *CSP* Scotland 5 (21).

5. *A Collection of Letters and State Papers*, (comp. Howard), p. 237.

6. *CSP* Scotland 5 (21). Those she was in touch with included John Lesley, Bishop of Ross and the Laird of Kilsyth.

7. Letter dated 3 December quoted in Kimberly Schutte, 'A Biography of Margaret Douglas, Countess of Lennox (1515–1578): Niece of Henry VIII and Mother-in-law of Mary Queen of Scots' in *Studies in British History* (31 January 2002), pp. 229–30.

8. HMC Salisbury Vol. 13, Addenda, p. 123.

9. Bothwell was, in fact, still alive in Denmark.

10. *CSP* Scotland 5 (210).

11. Robert Dudley had for several years had an affair with Margaret Douglas' god-daughter, who was named after her, 'Douglas' Sheffield (the parents were Margaret's old confidants, the former Lord William Howard and his wife, now Earl and Countess of Effingham). But fearful of the queen's reaction if she found out, he had refused to marry her even after they had a son. The relationship was now over.

12. I have seen various dates given for her death. 10 March is the date given on her tomb, and fits with her will which was sealed on 11 March.

13. The will is available for download from the National Archives, Prob. 11/60.

38 The Virgin Queen

1. *Queen Elizabeth I: Selected Works* (ed Steven W. May) (2004), p. 12.

2. Henry's views are expressed in the 1532 work, *A Glass of the Truth*.

3. Later in 1566; Jones, *Birth of the Elizabethan Age*, p. 119.

4. Ives, *The Reformation Experience*, p. 235.

5. *CSPS* Simancas 1 (286).

6. Duffy, *Saints, Sacrilege, Sedition*, p. 240.

7. Ives, *The Reformation Experience*, p. 250; Doran, *Elizabeth I and Religion*, p. 65.

8. Doran, *Elizabeth I and Religion*, p. 53.

9. Merton, PhD diss., op. cit., p. 119.

10. Patrick Collinson, 'Religion and Politics in the Progress of 1578'

in *The Progresses, Pageants and Entertainments of Queen Elizabeth I* (ed Jayne Elizabeth Archer, Elizabeth Goldring and Sarah Knight) (2007), p. 138.

11. Ibid.

12. *Queen Elizabeth I: Selected Works* (ed May), p. 12.

13. It appears Elizabeth tried to destroy Robert Dudley's marriage by persuading Douglas Sheffield to claim he had already married her, but this failed. For the timing of Dudley's disgrace, see Simon Adams on Robert Dudley, etc. in the *Oxford Dictionary of National Biography*.

14. See Appendix 5.

39 The Daughter of Debate

1. A young English captain, one of a number of English volunteers supporting the Protestant rebels, was at the prince's Delft residence, the Prinsenhof, when the assassination took place. The captain dropped to his knee as William of Orange emerged from lunch with his family. Orange rested his hand briefly on the captain's head, before turning to mount the stairs to his chamber. As he did so another man stepped forward, and pointing a pistol point blank at the prince fired three shots into his body. Two passed straight through him, lodging in the stairway wall. The third remained under his breastbone. William of Orange was carried to an adjoining room and died as his weeping wife tried desperately to staunch his wounds. His murderer was tortured to death in public: his hand was burned off with an iron, and flesh torn from his body in six places with pincers before he was drawn and quartered. Lisa Jardine, *The Awful End of William the Silent* (2005), p. 50.

2. Something he had been trying to achieve since 1563.

3. *CSP Scotland* 15 August 1584.

4. Ibid.

5. Ibid.

6. Ibid.

7. *Lettres, Instructions & Memoires de Marie Stuart, Reine D'Ecosse* (ed Alexandre Labanoff) (1844), Vol. 6, p. 125.

8. J. Lynch, 'Philip II and the Papacy' in *Transactions of the Royal Historical Society*, Fifth Series, Vol. 11 (1961), pp. 23, 24.

9. Anne Somerset, *Elizabeth I* (1991), p. 518.

10. See Penry Williams, 'Anthony Babington' in *Oxford Dictionary of National Biography*.

11. Stephen Alford, *The Watchers* (2012), p. 213.

12. Ibid., p. 235.

13. Harris D. Willson, *King James VI and I* (1956), p. 73.

14. *Lettres, Instructions & Memoires de Marie Stuart, Reine D'Ecosse,* (ed Labanoff), Vol. 6, pp. 474–80.

15. Guy, *My Heart is My Own*, p. 4.

16. The Hon. Mrs Maxwell Scott, *The Tragedy of Fotheringay* (1895), pp. 417–23.

17. *CSPS* Simancas 4 (35).

40 The Armada

1. Lynch, 'Philip II and the Papacy' in op. cit., pp. 37, 38.

2. Ibid.

3. *Captain Cuellar's Adventures in Connacht & Ulster, 1588* (ed Hugh Allington), p. 49.

4. That brave Lancastrian queen, Margaret of Anjou, was to be damned by Shakespeare as a 'she-wolf', and 'a tiger's heart wrapped in a woman's hide' for having taken political leadership of her mad husband's armies.

5. http://www.lukehistory.com/ballads/tilsbury.html, Thomas Deloney; Elizabeth is often depicted on a white horse, although no written record describes her mount in this detail.

6. The Lord Marshal was Sir John Norris; http://www.lukehistory.com/ballads/tilsbury.html, Thomas Deloney.

7. James Aske, 'Elizabetha Triumphans' in Nichols, *Progresses and Processions of Queen Elizabeth*, Vol. 2, p. 570.

8. Dr Leonel Sharp, who recorded the best-known version of the Tilbury speech.

9. Anna Whitelock, 'Woman, Warrior Queen' in *Tudor Queenship* (ed Hunt and Whitelock), pp. 173–91.

10. The words are not exactly Elizabeth's, but the evidence suggests it is an accurate representation of them. Deloney's contemporary verse records: 'And then bespake our noble Queene, my louing friends and countriemen:/I hope this day the worst is seen, that in our wars ye shall sustain./But if our enimies do assaile you, neuer let your stomackes falle you./For in the midst of all your troupe, we our selues will be in place:/To be you ioy, your guide and comfort, euen before your enimies face'.

11. R. Leicester and Miller Christy, 'Queen Elizabeth's Visit to Tilbury in 1588' in *English Historical Review* 34 (1919), p. 47.

12. Susan Frye, 'The Myth of Elizabeth at Tilbury' in *Sixteenth-Century Journal* 23, No. 1 (spring 1992), p. 98.

13. *Captain Cuellar's Adventures* (ed Allington), pp. 49, 52.

14. *Queen Elizabeth I: Selected Works* (ed May), p. 181.

15. John Clapham, *Elizabeth of England* (ed E. Plummer Read and C. Read) (1951), p. 97.

41 Setting Sun

1. Simon Adams, *Leicester and the Court* (1988), p. 149; Frederic Gerschow, 'Diary of the Duke of Stettin's Journey through England in 1602' in *Transactions of the Royal Historical Society* 6 (1892), p. 25.

2. Godfrey Goodman, *The Court of James the First* (from the original manuscript), 2 vols. (1839), Vol. 1, pp. 96–7.

3. Under the 1571 Treasons Act.

4. R. Doleman, *A Conference About the Next Succession to the Crowne of Ingland* (1594), Pt II, p. 183.

5. Ibid., Pt II, p. 196.

6. André de Maisse, *A Journal of all that was Accomplished by Monsieur de Maisse, Ambassador in England from King Henri IV to Queen*

Elizabeth, *Anno Domini 1597* (ed and tr. G. B. Harrison) (1931), pp. 25, 26, 29.

7. Ibid., p. 82.

8. Merton, PhD diss., op. cit., p. 127.

9. De Maisse, *Journal*, p. 115.

10. Sir John Harington, *A Tract on the Succession to the Crown, AD 1602* (1880), p. 106.

11. Sir John Harington, *Nugae Antiquae, being a miscellaneous collection of original papers*, with notes by Thomas Park FSA, 2 vols. (1804), Vol. 1, pp. 179, 180.

12. There has been debate over whether this was Shakespeare's play (as I believe) or some other one, and also whether it was intended to overthrow Elizabeth or merely her councillors (on which I take the view that monarchs realised that one easily led to the other). See Jason Scott-Warren, 'Was Elizabeth I Richard II?: The Authenticity of Lambarde's "Conversation"' in *Review of English Studies* (first published online 14 July 2012).

13. Gerschow, 'Diary of the Duke of Stettin's Journey through England' in op. cit., p. 15.

14. De Lisle, *After Elizabeth*, p. 42 and notes.

15. Henry Howard to Edward Bruce, in Goodman, *The Court of James the First*, Vol. 1, p. 97n.

16. De Lisle, *After Elizabeth*, p. 43.

42 The Hollow Crown

1. Harington: *Nugae Antiquae*, pp. 321, 33.

2. Harington, *A Tract on the Succession to the Crown, AD 1602*, p. 45.

3. HMC, *Calendar of the Manuscripts of the Most Honourable the Marquess of Salisbury . . . Preserved at Hatfield House, Hertfordshire*, Vol. 12, pp. 583–7; *The Letters of Arbella Stuart* (ed Sara Jayne Steen) (1994), p. 121.

4. The ambassador's name was Giovanni Carlo Scaramelli.

5. *CSPV* 9 (1135).

6. William Camden, *The History of Elizabeth, Late Queen of England*, 3rd edition (1675), Bk IV, p. 659.

7. De Lisle, *After Elizabeth*, p. 160.

8. *CSPV* 9 (1143).

9. *Queen Elizabeth I: Selected Works* (ed May), p. 235.

10. De Lisle, *After Elizabeth*, p. 105.

11. Katherine Howard, Countess of Nottingham.

12. De Lisle, *After Elizabeth*, pp. 106, 107.

13. *Records of the English Province of the Society of Jesus* (ed Henry Foley) (1877), pp. 54, 57.

14. De Lisle, *After Elizabeth*, pp. 114, 144.

15. *CSPV* 9, p. 558.

16. Catherine Loomis, 'Elizabeth Southwell's Manuscript Account of the Death of Queen Elizabeth (with text)' in *English Literary Renaissance* (autumn 1996), p. 486; E. Arbert, *English Stuart Tracts 1603–1693* (1903), p. 4.

17. *Queen Elizabeth I: Selected Works* (ed May), p. 10.

18. John Manningham, *The Diary of John Manningham of the Middle Temple 1602–1603* (ed Robert Parker) (1976), pp. 208, 209.

19. Hall, *Chronicle* Vol. 2, p. 145; *CSPS* Simancas 1 (144); Manningham, *Diary*, p. 209.

20. Sir Roger Wilbraham, *The Journal of Sir Roger Wilbraham for the years 1593–1616* (ed Harold Spencer Scott) in *Camden Miscellany* 10 (1902), p. 55; de Lisle, *After Elizabeth*, p. 140.

21. John Lane, *An Elegy Upon the Death of Our Most High and Renowned Princess, Our Late Sovereign Elizabeth* (1603).

Epilogue

1. Mark Lansdale and Julian Boon, a forensic psychologist, spent eighteen months analysing records from the period spanning the king's life. Their research, commissioned by the Richard III Society, concludes he showed few signs of the traits psychologists would use to identify psychopaths today – including narcissism,

deviousness and lack of empathy in close relationships. Instead, it argues, Richard III exhibited signs of suffering from a common psychological syndrome known as 'intolerance to uncertainty' which 'is associated with a number of positive aspects of personality, including a strong sense of right and wrong, piety, loyalty to trusted colleagues and a belief in legal processes – all exhibited by Richard'. They say their analysis indicates Richard III was unlikely to have murdered his two nephews, one of whom was to have taken the throne, in the Tower. They argue he would have been 'more likely to have removed them to a secret place of safety'.

2   Much of what I have said on what Elizabeth learned from Mary is inspired by Judith M. Richards. See 'The Two Tudor Queens Regnant', *History Today*, Issue 53 (December 2005), p.7–12.

3. Anne McLaren, 'Memorialising Mary and Elizabeth' in *Tudor Queenship* (ed Hunt and Whitelock), pp. 11–27.

4. The Renaissance altar erected by Pietro Torrigiano, under which Edward was buried and which was to be Henry VII's monument as well as Elizabeth's, was removed during the Civil War, the steps levelled and the 'stately screen of copper richly gilt' sold to tinkers. Elaborate stained glass put in by Henry VII, which he requested be decorated with 'stories, images, arms and badges', was similarly broken and replaced with white glass. New stained glass was put in during the late twentieth and early twenty-first centuries. One – the central east window celebrating the Virgin Mary – is a nod to the original name of what is now called the Henry VII Chapel.

5. Henry VII had disinterred Katherine of Valois from the Lady Chapel while it was being re-built. He was proud of his Valois blood and had given his grandmother's presence in Westminster Abbey as a major reason for choosing to be buried there. Her body, loosely wrapped in lead from the chapel roof, had been placed by Henry V's tomb monument and was still awaiting reburial when he died. Shockingly, however, for the next two hundred years she had remained abandoned in a coffin above

ground, covered by lose boards that exposed her skeleton from the waist up. In 1669 the diarist Samuel Pepys celebrated his birthday by playing a small fee to give her a kiss, and during the eighteenth century, her body, still exposed, was described as only, 'thinly clothed, with flesh like scrapings of tanned leather'(John Dart, *West-monasterium*, (1723) Vol II p.38). It was Queen Victoria who eventually buried Katherine where she lies today.

6. As well as Owen Tudor, a number of other notable people were buried at Greyfriars including members of the Chaundos, Cornewall and Pembridge families (who were probably all bene- factors of the friary). After the Dissolution, the tomb of Sir Richard Pembridge (a renowned knight) was moved to the nave of Hereford Cathedral where it can still be seen. There appears to be no information on what happened to the other bodies buried at Greyfriars. Owen Tudor's grave is said to have been in a chapel or chantry on the northern side of the friary church. Dr Nigel Baker, who has carried out an in-depth study of Hereford, thinks it is likely that Owen Tudor's body is still at the Greyfriars site, along with others. Unfortunately, all remains of the friary have been removed, and it is uncertain where the church was actually situated. There has been little archaeological work done there, although when part of the site was dug over for allotments in 1918 'rough stone foundations' were found along with fragments of monastic tiles. In 1933, during digging for drainage trenches, three skeletons were discovered, although their precise location was not recorded. None of them had been decapitated. The Greyfriars site is now mostly covered by housing built in 1971. Thanks to Melissa Seddon of Herefordshire Archeology, Herefordshire Council.

APPENDICES

1 What Happened to the body of James IV

1. Ulpian Falwell, *The Flower of Fame*.

2. *L&P* 1 (2469).
3. Stow, *Survey of London*, pp. 258, 259. (Also note that James V asked for his father's body to be returned in 1532. Hester Chapman, *The Sisters of Henry VIII* (1969), p. 146.)

2 The Mysterious Quarrel between Henry VIII and Margaret Douglas

1. The numerous payments Margaret Douglas and her husband made that year to chantry priests, who prayed for souls in purgatory, indicate they were conservative, but Henry VIII's will also paid priests to pray for his soul. *L&P* 21, Pt II (181).
2. British Library Harleian MS 289, ff. 73–5.
3. For the Lennoxes' full version, see British Library Cotton MS Caligula B VIII, ff. 184–5.
4. British Library Harleian MS 289, ff. 73–5.
5. British Library Cotton MS Caligula B VIII, f. 165. 'The Political Life of Margaret Douglas, Countess of Lennox, c. 1530-1578', by Morgan Ring, Gonville and Caius College (2012).
6. From John Gough Nichols, *The Herald & Genealogist* 8 (1874), accessed online at archive.org.
7. See her will online at National Archives Prob. 11/60.
8. Stow MSS 956. The picture of Henry VIII is based on the Holbein portrait of 1536 which alone disproves the romantic claim that it was once owned by Anne Boleyn. The words are Richard Croke's collection of twelve psalm paraphrases in octosyllabic quatrains (the Penitential Psalms, plus Pss. 18/19, 12/13, 42/43, 105/106 and 138/139). It also includes a 'Veni Creator' in the same metre. Although the psalms are in English, nothing about Croke's paraphrases – which are translated directly and literally from the Vulgate – points to a particularly reformed sensibility. They look very much like an outgrowth and adaptation of the rhymed hymns in English Books of Hours. Also see Tait, 'The Girdle Prayer Book or "Tablett"' p. 30 (*Jewellery Studies*, Vol. 2 (1985), pp. 29–57).

3 Guildford and Jane Dudley

1. Prince Philip of Spain and William of Orange.
2. The first reports were those of Giulio Raviglio Rosso and Giovanni Commendone; Girolamo Pollini came much later.
3. See her comments concerning Guildford written in her own hand in her prayer book, Chapter 30.
4. *The Chronicle of Queen Jane* (ed Nichols), p. 55.

5 The Obscure Margaret Clifford, Heir to the Throne 1578–96

1. *CSPV* 6, p. 107.
2. This was either Margaret Russell, daughter of the Puritan the Earl of Bedford, who was married to the Earl of Cumberland, or her sister Anne, who was married to Ambrose Dudley, Earl of Warwick, i.e. it was either Margaret Clifford's stepsister-in-law, or Robert Dudley's sister-in-law. *CSPS* 2 (592).
3. This was a view represented by William Allen, the later cardinal. The seminary he had founded at Douai had been closed in March 1578 by Calvinist advances in the region.
4. PRO Prob 11/88, ff. 217–8. She died in 1596.
5. *CSPS* Simancas 2 (593). The Venetians heard that Margaret was accused of wishing to poison Elizabeth. *CSPV* (774).
6. Margaret Clifford to Francis Walsingham, undated: Sir Nicholas Harris Nicolas, *Memoirs of the Life and Times of Sir Christoper Hatton* (1847), pp. 146–7. Stow refers to the execution taking place in November 1580, but it had taken place by the time this letter was written in May 1580 (I suspect in November 1579).
7. Some said of her eldest son Ferdinando, Earl of Derby, that he was 'of all three religions [i.e. Protestant, Puritan and Catholic] and others of none'. Doleman, *Conference About the Next Succession*, p. 253. The Catholic exile in question, Richard Hesketh, was examined and executed.

INDEX

Albany, John Stuart, Duke of: struggles with Margaret, Queen of Scots, for regency, 138–9; at French court, 142; takes over regency of Scotland and Margaret's children, 148, 149–50; begs Margaret to stay in Scotland, 151–2; to be recalled to France, 154; gives Angus permission to visit Margaret, 167

Alexandra, Queen of Great Britain and Ireland, 119

Anabaptists, 293

Angus, Archibald Douglas, Earl of: marriage to Margaret, Queen of Scots, 138–9; asks Henry VIII's agents for help against Albany, 149–50; goes to Linlithgow, 151; comes to accommodation with Albany and returns to Scotland, 152; marriage annulled, 167; seizes power in Scotland, 177; seeks refuge in England, 177, 178; unable to help imprisoned daughter, 211

Anjou, Duke of, 355, 357, 359, 361, 420

Anne of Beaujeu, 61

Anne of Cleves, 220–2

Anne of Denmark, 380

Aquinas, St Thomas, 161

Armada, 368, 374–8

Armel, St, 57

armour, 68

Arran, Earl of, 138

Arthur, King, 64, 65, 81–2, 179–80, 207

Arthur, Prince of Wales: appearance and character, 103, 106; birth, 83–4; created Prince of Wales, 86; marriage planned, 99, 101, 102; household at Ludlow, 103; marriage, 105–9, 125–6, 174; death, 110–11

Arundel, Henry Fitzalan, Earl of, 310, 321

Ascham, Roger: *The Schoolmaster*, 417–18

Astley, John, 246

Astley, Kat, 245–6, 247–8, 296, 310–11

Audley, Lord, 98

Aylmer, John, 418

Babington, Anthony, 368–9

Barnet, Battle of (1471), 37–8

Barton, Elizabeth ('Holy Maid of Kent'), 188, 190

Bath, Knights of the, 127

Leanda de Lisle is the highly acclaimed author of *The Sisters Who Would Be Queen: The Tragedy of Mary, Katherine and Lady Jane Grey* and *After Elizabeth: How James King of Scots Won the Crown of England in 1603.* She has been a columnist on the *Spectator, Country Life, the Guardian, the Sunday Telegraph,* and the *Daily Express,* and writes for the *Daily Mail,* the *New Statesman,* and the *Sunday Telegraph.* She lives in Leicestershire, England.